MANIPULATION AND BODY LANGUAGE

Oliver Bennet

Table of Contents – Nlp Dark Psychology

Table of Contents – Master your emotions

Table of Contents – How to analyze people

Table of Contents – Body language of people

NLP DARK PSYCHOLOGY

Introduction

The NLP, which stands for Neuro-Linguistic Programming, indicates a methodology for changing the thoughts and behaviors of one or more people, to help them achieve the desired results.

Born in the 1970's in California in the middle of the New Age era, NLP owes its success with the promise (often kept) to improve work performance and achieve happiness through personal development. The founders of NLP, the psychologist Richard Bandler and the linguist John Grinder, started from the belief that they could identify successful individuals' thought patterns and behaviors and then teach them to others.

One of NLP's core techniques is constituted by imitation or, as adepts define it, modeling: by imitating the language and behaviors of successful people, it would be possible to make our skills our own and achieve their results.

NLP is mainly based on language processing and uses other communication techniques to make people change their thoughts and behaviors.

How Does It Work?

NLP is based on the idea that people operate through internal "maps" to represent the world.

Thus, NLP tries to identify these maps (which are nothing more than subjective experiences of what surrounds us) to change their orientations. It is a methodology that aims at a change of thought and behavior.

It should be specified that NLP has nothing to do with hypnosis. On the contrary, it works through the conscious use of language to modify a person's mental and behavioral patterns.

What Is It For?

NLP finds a wide field of intervention, using various techniques according to the desired purposes.

Starting from the idea that thought and behavior can be modelled, NLP is used for:

- treat anxiety, phobias and stress, thus improving emotional responses to certain situations;
- achieve successful professional goals, such as increased productivity at work and motivation;
- remove negative thoughts and feelings associated with a past event;
- improve their communication skills.

In general, NLP is used as a personal development method through the "enhancement" of one's skills, which aims to have greater self- confidence and to communicate better with others.

But What Exactly Is NLP?

NLP is a psychological method that studies people's behavior, analyses models. It thus extracts the practical techniques to teach to potentially overcome any situation (work, success, relationships).

NLP teaches that each of us can, with willpower, change and revolutionize one's life in an instant, abandoning limits through the help of concrete techniques. Each person is the architect of her destiny, determined exclusively by her decisions and not by the living conditions as many believe and which are already "prescribed" and not changeable.

NLP's message to us is the secret of living well, which is "living life trying to make the most of it". It is we, and only us, who can make everything we want possible, starting from the constancy and determination, which from the beginning must not be missing, together with the desire to fight for a purpose, therefore the energy that goes put into practice, up to the exercise, application, construction and achievement of our goal.

In a nutshell, this method would help us become the people we always wanted to be; an opportunity to learn how to use our mind and body in the most functional way possible.

Talking about NLP is equivalent to dealing with themes based on creativity, freedom, self-esteem, choices, and courage. The founders of NLP coined this term (Neuro Linguistic Programming) precisely to highlight a link between neurological processes (neuro), language (linguistics) and the various behavioral screens that have been learned only through experience (programming).

According to Bandler and Grinden, it is indeed impossible to find a field where this model cannot be applied: from self-esteem problems to sports or school skills, from courtship to success, and some even claim that this discipline somehow manages to fight depression and other psychological disorders.

Summing up, NLP has among its main purposes, the goal of developing successful habits / reactions, amplifying effective behaviors to make what we want for us to happen and decreasing unwanted ones, which limit the occurrence of our design drawings.

With Neuro Linguistic Programming, you learn to model the quality of the internal images lived and the sensations perceived to act for our benefit in the future. NLP makes us aware of our unconscious behaviors and programs that we can modify as we wish.

There are NLP academies where you can learn and put into practice all the possible techniques to achieve what you want a purpose: motivation, the basis for all our desire, is the ingredient fundamental that pushes us to fight to get it. Without it, none would be able to reach the end to which it aspires.

Optimism, joy of life and cooperation are the three secrets of living in harmony. Everyone needs a paladin.

Have you ever wished for some things for yourself and done nothing to get what you want? Have you ever wanted to let go yourself from the slavery of some addiction such as alcohol or smoking, to lose weight, to learn a language or play an instrument?

Certainly yes, but how many of you have put your goals into practice and how many people have been stuck? This is how it happens, for all those belonging to the second sphere, we finds us doing only one action: complaining. The coach then takes over and helps us take stock, find our orientation, define ourselves as people. It spurs us to find a motivation so sour "journey" becomes tortuous.

There are four types of coaches:

- Life coach: the one who helps us achieve personal goals;
- Company coach: the one who helps companies and professionals in the sector to act more effectively and with determination in professional life;
- Career coach: one who helps people in the phases of professional change, therefore a career jump or even a professional regression;
- Sport coach: helps students raise the level of performance and thus triggers mental and physical training.

Therefore, the main objective of NLP is to explain to us how everything we are is the simple result of what we have thought. Our life is in our hands.

Don't believe it? Try it for yourself!

NLP is an attitude ...

An attitude described by a sense of curiosity, adventure, and desire to learn the necessary skills to understand what communication types affect others. It is the desire to know things that are worth knowing. It is looking at life as a rare opportunity to learn.

NLP is a methodology ...

A methodology based on the principle that every behavior has a structure ... and that this structure can be extrapolated, learned, taught and even changed. The guiding criterion of this method is to know what will be useful and effective.

NLP is a technology ...

A technology that allows a person to organize information and perceptions to achieve results deemed impossible in the past.

Neuro-Linguistic Programming therefore, deals with studying the structure of subjective experience and what can be calculated from it.

The fundamental belief and promise are that effective thinking strategies can be identified, assumed and used by anyone.

NLP was born from the fruitful years of research, carried out by Richard Bandler and John Grinder, to find out what the behavioral and linguistic elements allowed successful people to have such a significant constancy of positive results.

The results were the identification of a series of specific and reproducible behavioral strategies and linguistic models.

The Hoaxes of Neuro Linguistic Programming

From psychotherapy to coaching, NLP is still lacking of substantial experimental evidence, and has many characteristics of pseudo sciences.

Neuro-Linguistic Programming (NLP) has been rejected by science in every possible and imaginable way, yet it continues to be discussed.

We can notice that in the film Kingsman - Secret service (2014), neuro linguistic programming is passed off as a seduction weapon.

It is almost impossible to find a field where the NLP, according to its supporters, cannot be applied: from courtship to leadership, from self-esteem problems to sports skills, success is at hand, and there are even those who come to propose discipline, to combat depression and other psychological disorders.

The Origins

The NLP was born in the first half of the 70s, the golden age of the New-Age, and perhaps it is no coincidence that the crib was the California lysergic. The dads in the new discipline were Richard Bandler, a psychology student at the time, and linguist John Grinder, both from the University of California, Santa Cruz, who had begun to work out a "theory of everything" of psychotherapy from their respective fields of study.

One of the foundations of the new, revolutionary branch of psychology would be imitation or, as the adepts define it, modelling: by imitating successful people's language and behavior, it would be possible to make our skills our own and achieve their results.

It is thus in fact, according to the Gospel of Neuro-Linguistic Programming, that Grinder and Bandler arrived at another fundamental intuition called Meta-model: studying the work of three famous psychotherapists and integrating it with theories by famous linguists such as Gregory Bateson and Noam

Chomsky, they convinced themselves that the key to therapy was not so much what the patient said, but how he said it.

According to the NLP, three processes exist in language (generalization, cancellation and distortion) through which we unconsciously eliminate part of the information. According to the NLP, the psychotherapist's task would be to ask the patient for the words he chooses to use to understand the underlying structure. Simplifying, if the patient says, "Everyone is treating me badly" (generalization) the therapist could reply "Is there nobody who treats her well?" and so on.

Grinder and Bandler also distilled the concept of the representational system. In our mind, we create subjective representations of the reality that surrounds us based on what our senses perceive, from which derives one of the evocative mottos made by the NLP followers: "The map is not the territory". But from this reasonable (and certainly not original) premise, the fathers of the NLP arbitrarily deduced that it is possible to understand how each of us thinks, based on a series of clues from language and eye movements.

If we frequently use expressions like "I see you like cinema" we will reveal that our preferred representational system is visual. The auditory symbolic system will instead be indicated by words such as "I have heard too many speeches on this issue". Simultaneously, the kinesthetics, that is, the people who relate to reality above all in terms of touch, taste and smell, will tell us "his handshake I didn't like it." You could then use this information to experiment, experiment, other ways of processing information, or get in tune quickly.

Chapter 1:   What Is Manipulation?

 Manipulation is a social influence that works to change the habits or understanding of others, or the subject, through violent, misleading, or questionable methods. The manipulator will use to advance their interests, generally, at the expense of others, so many of their techniques would be considered deceptive, devious, violent, and exploitative.

Social influence, such as when it comes to a medical professional working to persuade their patients to start adopting healthy routines, is usually perceived to be something safe. This is true of any social impact capable of appreciating the right of those included to choose and is not unduly coercive. On the other hand, if somebody is trying to get their way and is using people against their will, the social impact can be damaging and is generally towered above.

Emotional or mental manipulation is seen as a kind of persuasion and coercion. Some parts are in this type of mind control, such as bullying and brainwashing. For such many components, individuals will see this as misleading or abusive.

Those who decide to use control will do so to manage the habits of those around them. The manipulator will have some objective in mind and will work through various abuse kinds to coerce those around them into helping the manipulator get to the last goal. Frequently, emotional blackmail will be involved.

Those who practice control will use mind control, brainwashing, or bullying techniques to get others to complete the jobs for them. The manipulator's subject may not wish to carry out the task; however, they feel that they have no other option because of the blackmail or different technique used. The majority of manipulative people has no proper caring and sensitivity towards others, so they might not see an issue with their actions.

Other manipulators just want to get to their final goal and are not concerned with who has been bothered or hurt along the way.

Also, manipulative people are typically scared to enter into a healthy relationship because they think others will decline them. Somebody who has a manipulative personality will frequently have the inability to take responsibility for their behaviors, problems, and life. Considering that they are unable to take the blame for these concerns, the manipulator will use the methods of adjustment to get another person to take control of the responsibility.

Manipulators are frequently able to use the same strategies discovered in other forms of mind control to get the impact they want over others. Among the most commonly used methods is known as emotional blackmail. This is where the manipulator will effort to inspire compassion or guilt in the subject they are manipulating. These two emotions are chosen because they are considered the two highest of all human feelings and are the most likely to stimulate others into the manipulator's action. The manipulator will then have the ability to take full benefit of the subject, using the sympathy or regret that they have developed to persuade others to comply or help them reach their final goal.

Frequently, the manipulator will not just be able to create these feelings; they will have the ability to motivate degrees of sympathy or guilt that can be an escape for the situation that is going on. This means that they can take a case such as missing out on a party, like the subject is losing out on a funeral or something more important.

Emotional blackmail is just one of the strategies that are used by manipulators. Another way that have been successful for many manipulators is to use an abuse that is called crazy-making. This technique is typically aimed at the hope of producing insecurity in the subject being manipulated; frequently, this self-doubt will.

At times, the manipulator will use types of passive-aggressive habits to bring about crazy-making. If the manipulator is trapped in the act, they will use rejection, reason, rationalization, and deceptiveness of ill intent to get out of the difficulty.

One of the most significant concerns with psychological manipulators is that they are not always able to recognize what others around them might need, and they will lose the ability to fulfill or perhaps think about these needs. This does not justify the behavior that they are doing. Still, frequently, others' requirements are not considered or are not a top priority to the manipulator, so they can perform manipulative jobs without feeling guilt or pity. This can make it hard to discuss and stop the habits in a rational way why the manipulator should stop.

Besides, the manipulator might find that it is challenging for them to form long and significant relationships and friendships because the people they are with, will always feel used and will have trouble trusting the manipulator. The problem goes both ways in the development of relationships; the manipulator will not have the ability to recognize the other individual's needs while the other person will not have the ability to form the needed emotional connections or trust with the manipulator.

Needs to Manipulate Successfully

An active manipulator should have strategies at hand that will make them effective at using people to get to their final objective. While there are different theories on what makes an active manipulator, we will look at the three needs set out by George K. Simon, a capable psychology author. According to Simon, the manipulator will need to:

1. Have the ability to conceal their aggressive behaviors and objectives from the subject.

2. Have the ability to figure out the vulnerabilities of their designated topic.

3. Have some level of ruthlessness readily available so that they will not require to deal with any doubts that may develop due to hurting the issues if it comes to that. This harm can be either psychological or physical.

The first requirement that the manipulator has to achieve:

If the manipulator goes around informing everyone their strategies or always acts mean to others, no one will stay long enough to be manipulated. Instead, the manipulator needs to have the ability to conceal their thoughts from others and act like everything is normal. By the time the subject is conscious of the concern, the manipulator has enough details to persuade the issue to continue.

Next, the manipulator will need to have the ability to determine what the vulnerabilities of their intended victim or victims are. This can help them to figure out which tactics need to be used to reach the overall goal. In some cases, the manipulator might be able to do this action through a little bit of observation while other times, they will need to have some kind of interaction with the subject before coming up with the full strategy.

The third requirement is that the manipulator needs to be ruthless.

It will not work out if the manipulator puts in all their work and then frets on how the subject will be fair at the end. It is not most likely that they would be going with this plan at all if they did care about the subject. The manipulator will not care about the subject at all and does not manage if any damage, either psychological or physical, befalls the issue as long as the general goal is fulfilled.

One reason why manipulator is so capable is that the subject often does not know they are being manipulated until later. They may believe that whatever is going on is fine; possibly, they think they have made a brand-new friend in the manipulator. By the time the subject knows they are being used or no longer wishes to be a part of the process, they are stuck. The manipulator will have the ability to use strategies, including emotional blackmail, to achieve their goal.

Chapter 2: The Manipulation Ethics: Can Be Good and Bad

Is It Possible Manipulation Could Be Good and Bad?

Mention the term 'manipulation,' and that which springs to mind is the negative connotations linked with this expression. Manipulation means deceit. Manipulation means utilizing unscrupulous and underhanded strategies to make the most of somebody else. Manipulation signifies fraud and lying. Manipulation is untrue.

The expression has got a lousy reputation through time and the words used to describe manipulation in drama paint an image that's somewhat ugly or disagreeable. "She has him enclosed around her little finger," "I advised my boss just what he wished to listen to," "He has got a reputation for being a heartbreaker," "I talked to my friend to do exactly what I desired." These typical examples of exploitation surely do not place a favorable spin on the two parties involved with the procedure. It gets the manipulator outside to be somebody who's egotistical, self-serving, misleading, and worry about having somebody else to their benefit. It earns the person who has been manipulated look absurd, clueless and perhaps even feeble of character to "allowing" themselves to be duped so easily.

Manipulation has ever been seen as an act that's callous, smart yet adorable, and consistently where one ends up being manipulated or taken advantage of. Psychotherapy is seen more negatively as it will become evident the person has heartlessly disregarded another's feelings, setting their selfish desires over everybody else. Worse is that, the manipulator has manipulated another by pretending to become their pal and then utilizing data shared in confidence.

Whether personal or professional lives, there's one fact which stays. Nobody enjoys knowing they've been manipulated. Nobody. With this kind of negativity connected with this challenging, it gets nearly impossible to feel there is a chance manipulation might be used to get an excellent, or perhaps cause change for the better.

As unexpected as it might sound, manipulation isn't all evil. Manipulation is all around us, and you often don't need to look very far to find proof of it. Take advertisers and entrepreneurs, for example, using their continuous messages telling people to purchase this, buy this, stop doing so, and quit doing this. They are all attempting to control our choices in one manner or another. Which kinds of exploitation, however, are in reality seeking to make us change for the better?

Ads that let to stop smoking and eat healthily are attempting to control our choices, and however, in this circumstance, they are trying to elicit favorable change. Stopping smoking is to your benefit. Therefore, it is eating wholesome. When it's to your good, does not that make it a right type of exploitation? Governments across the globe manipulate their people. So does faith. However, we sometimes decide to ignore it since it comes in a more "authoritative" source to speak. Businesses control their clients by producing products to improve their revenue figures and telling customers, "they can't survive without it."

Whether used for "good" or "poor," manipulation remains, after the afternoon, manipulation. Do any of us have any right to order a person's choices or activities, even when we think it's advantageous? What makes the concept of exploitation this kind of embarrassing notion to bargain with is possibly the simple fact that we do not enjoy the notion of somebody else attempting to dictate what we need to do, or even forcing us into doing anything we would not otherwise be more inclined to perform ourselves.

Managers in work attempt to control their employees all of the time, even though the fantastic leaders take action to attempt to keep their employees motivated or function at their finest. Successful supervisors have mastered the craft of favorable manipulation and flipped it into a powerful instrument used to handle their workers' performance, forcing them to achieve their objectives.

This identifying detail will be the defining distinction between what is categorized as misuse, and what is known as persuasion. Persuasion remains a kind of exploitation, but what distinguishes it in the negative standing related to exploitation boils down to 3 things:

- Your goal.
- Your honesty.
- Precisely what the advantage or positive effect will be to the person that you're attempting to convince.

These three critical points are the determining factor to know if you are trying to control or persuade. Whenever you're taking advantage of your goal, you are selfish. When you convince, it is generally well-meaning for the benefit of another individual. When you control, you lie, fool and attempt to hide what is happening. When you convince, you are competent, upfront, and honest about what you are trying to do, since you've got no reason to conceal if it is not done for personal profit. When you control, there's not any positive effect or benefit on the other party, just yourself. When you convince, another party you are attempting to influence will be the person who reaps the maximum benefit from this circumstance. Non-profit organizations hotels of persuasion attempt to get other people to behave and transform for the best way to make a positive effect on the entire world. They convince donors, increase the essential financing, and promote awareness among others concerning significant matters that have to be dealt with or altered.

Chapter 3:   Manipulation Techniques

Lying is one of the very first techniques that manipulators use. It is a technique that pathological liars or psychopaths use when they want to confuse their victims. If they are continually lying to them, their victims will often be unaware of the truth. Those who use this tactic have no moral or ethical apprehension about it.

Telling half-truths or only telling part of a story is another tactic that can be used to manipulate someone. People like this will often keep things to themselves because it puts the victim at a disadvantage. They can get what they desire by waiting to tell them the rest of the story until their needs are met.

Being around someone who has frequent mood swings can often make a person vulnerable to their manipulations. Not knowing what mood, they will be in, whether they will be happy, sad, or angry can be a beneficial tactic for the manipulator. It keeps the victim off balance and easy to manipulate because they will often do what the manipulator wants to keep them in a good mood.

Another tactic that is often used by narcissists is known as love bombing. This doesn't automatically mean that you have to be in a relationship but it can be used in a friendship. Those that use this tactic will charm the victim to death and have them believe that this is the best relationship or company

that has ever happened to them. They will use the victim for what they want, and then when they are done, they drop them and the victim has no idea of what happened.

A tactic that can be used in extreme cases by the manipulator is that of punishment. This makes the victim feel guilty for something they did wrong, even if they didn't do anything at all. Some of the disciplines that they can inflict on their victims are consistent nagging, shouting, mental abuse, giving them the silent treatment, and even as bad as physical violence.

Denial is often a tactic used when a manipulator feels pushed in a corner, and they feel like they will be exposed for the fake that they are. In this instance, they will manipulate the victim into believing that they are doing the very thing the manipulator is accused of.

Spinning the truth is a tactic often used by politicians. It is used to twist the facts to suit their needs or wants. Sociopaths use this technique to disguise their bad behavior and justify it to their victims.

Minimizing is when a manipulator will play down their behavior and actions. They move the blame onto the victim for overreacting when their actions are harmful, and the person has a valid reason for feeling the way they do.

It is often enjoyable when the manipulator pretends to become the victim. They do this to gain sympathy or compassion from their real victims. They do this so that their victims feel a sense of responsibility to help and end their suffering, especially if they feel that they are the cause of that person's suffering.

Another way that the manipulator can move the blame onto the victim is by targeting the victim and accusing them of wrongdoing. The victim will then start to defend themselves, while the manipulator hides their manipulation away from the victim. This can be dangerous because the victim is so focused on defending themselves that they forget to see what is right in front of them.

Using the positive reinforcement tactic tricks the victim into thinking that they are getting something for helping the manipulator get what they want. This can be through purchasing them expensive presents, praising them, giving them money, constantly apologizing for their behavior, giving them lots of attention and all-around buttering them up.

There are times when a person knows where they stand with someone. However, in any type of relationship, the manipulator might keep moving the goal to confuse their victim because they thought everyone was still on the same page.

Another manipulation tactic that manipulators like to use is known as diversion. This tactic is commonly used to divert a certain conversation away from what the manipulator is doing. The new topic is created to get the victim to lose focus on what the manipulator is doing or trying to do.

Sarcasm is a tactic that can lower the self-esteem and confidence of a victim through embarrassment. The manipulator will use sarcasm – usually saying something about the victim- in front of other people. This gives the manipulator power over the victim because they just made them feel very small.

Guilt trips are another tactic that a manipulator will use against their victim. In this instance, they will often tell their victims that they don't care about them or love them; they will indicate that they are selfish and that their life is easy. It keeps the victim confused and anxious because they want to please the manipulator by letting them know that they care about them and do anything for them.

Using flattery is the exact opposite of guilt-tripping. In this instance, the manipulator will use charm, praise, or other flattery types to gain the victim's trust. They victim enjoys the compliments and lets their guard down.

Another way that a manipulator will move the blame is to play the innocent card when the victim accuses them of their tactics. They will act shocked or show confusion at the accusation. The act of being surprised is convincing to the victim, and it makes them question their judgment and if what they are feeling is wrong.

A dangerous tactic that a manipulator can use is that of extreme aggression. Rage and aggression are used to force the victim to submit. The anger and rage are a tactic that scares the victim to stop talking about the conversation. They pretty much want to help keep the manipulator's anger in check.

Isolation is another dangerous tactic used by manipulators. It is a control mechanism used by manipulators to keep their victims from their family, friends, and loved ones who can expose the manipulator for who they are. The manipulator might know that their victim can be manipulated, but their friends and family can perceive right through them, and they are not done using their victim yet.

One of the last tactics that manipulators, such as psychopaths and sociopaths use, is fake love and empathy. These people do not know how to love others besides themselves and have a hard time loving others and showing empathy towards others. They use this tactic to entangle themselves into their victims' lives to extract what they want (Learning Mind, 2012).

Remember that Dark Manipulation is a very dangerous thing and not something that anyone would want to be caught up in if they can help it. Therefore, it is important to protect yourself against anyone who would try to take advantage of you and manipulate you to get what they want. The more knowledge you have about these devious acts, the easier it is to protect yourself from it.

Chapter 4: Recognize When Someone Manipulate You

Now that we have learn about manipulation and what it is all about, it is time to take a look at how to tell when manipulation is being used against you. Many people who would love to use the power of persuasion, mind control, and more against you. This is not a bad thing all of the time. But when the manipulation is done at the expense of you and your wants, it can derail your life.

We have already consumed some time talking about how manipulation will benefit the manipulator while harming one or more victims at the same time. This is pretty scary stuff, and it is crucial we learn how to detect this manipulation to protect ourselves as much as possible. Some of the things you can do to ensure you detect manipulation when used against you include:

Watching the Behavior of the Other Person

The first thing that we like to look for is some of the behaviors that come with the manipulative person. We want to look at whether the other person talks first, if they want you to talk first, or a good combination of both.  Manipulative people will like to listen to what you want to say, and they always want you to put out the information first. This is because they want to hear from you and learn what your weaknesses and strengths are over the long term. They like to ask many questions, especially ones that are about their personal life without having to answer any from you. They will seem to know a ton of information, especially personal information about you while not giving up any of their own.

Then when the manipulator does respond to you, the actions and responses will be based on any of the information they have been given. Some of the things that you should look for here include

Always wanting you to speak first is not a sign of manipulation all on its own. You should pay attention and see if there are a few other symptoms of manipulation that come into play.

The person who is doing the manipulation will not reveal a ton of personal information when they go through this conversation, but they will make sure that the focus is more on you as possible.

If you find that this behavior doesn't happen just once, but it happens regularly, it is a manipulation sign.

Although it can sometimes, come off as the person showing a genuine interest in you, remember that there will be a hidden agenda behind this questioning. If you stop for a moment and no longer answer the manipulator's questions, but instead try to ask them things, they will refuse to answer or try to change the subject if they are manipulative.

Another thing to consider here is how the person accomplishes things. If they tend to use charm, then this could be a problem. While some people will be charming, the manipulator will use this to give them something they want. This person may use charm to compliment someone before making a request. They could cook a nice dinner, ask someone for money, or help them with a project. This behavior will seem pretty harmless, but it pries you to be more willing to agree to whatever the manipulator wants.

Next, you need to look at some coercive behavior. This means that manipulators will use it to persuade someone else to do what they want, and it is often going to work with threats and some force along the way. They could threaten, criticize, and yell at the other person to get what they want.

You can also notice how the other person will handle any facts that they have. If you see that the other person likes to overwhelm you with facts or mess around with facts, this could be a sign that they are working to manipulate you a bit. Facts may be manipulated using excuses, exaggerating, withholding information, and lying. The reason why manipulator is going to do this is that it helps them to feel like they have more power in the situation than you do.

Look at the Communication

 The next thing that you need to take a look at here is whether you are feeling judged or you are not good enough to the other person. This is a common technique that a manipulator is going to use. They will make sure that you can find something that you did wrong no matter how hard you try. This gives them the power, and hopefully keep you working harder to appease them. This is done by picking on them, doing sarcasm, jokes, and more.

Another tactic that the person could use is the silent treatment. This is a good one for them to gain some control. They may choose to ignore your calls, emails, text messages, and more for an unreasonable amount of time. This is done to ensure you feel some uncertainty or make you know you are punished because of something that you did. Your actions will sometimes provoke this, but often because the manipulator wants to gain some more control. And when you try to oppose them about it, they are just going to deny it, or shift the blame back on to you.

You may also notice that the manipulator uses some form of guilt trip to get what they want. This guilt trip will make you feel like you are the one responsible for the manipulator's behavior. It is also going to make it so that the victim is responsible for the happiness, success, anger, failure, and more of the manipulator. You are going to notice some things when dealing with this guilt trip from the other person, and would include:

You may see that before the guilt trip starts, there will be some phrases like "If you were more considerate, you'd" or "If you loved me, you'd."

If you find that this is causing you to agree to some things that would have never registered before, then this is a good sign that you are a victim of manipulation tactic.

And you should also take notice of whether you are regularly apologizing with the other person. This can be done when you are blamed for something that had nothing to do with you, or they make you feel responsible for the situation that you are in. For example, if you said that you would meet with the manipulator at 1, but they show up two hours late. You say that it is fine that they were late, but then they go on a guilt trip and act like the martyr saying that they never seem to do anything right ever. You end up being the wrong one and you apologize, even though they were the ones who were late in this whole case.

Chapter 5:   Dark Psychology

Dark psychology has many different elements and aspects that encompass it. While it is real that we all have these fundamentals within us to some extent, we are not all inclined to using them all the time. Most of us will use them when we feel there is no other course to take, so we get manipulative.

Ordinary people prefer not to deceive or manipulate. They will usually lean towards doing things more honestly and try their best not to hurt those around them. They will eventually go dark if they feel they were pushed into using these techniques. However, not everyone operates like this.

For various reasons that aren't always obvious, some people will dive straight into these tactics as their go-to. They can be for our good at times, but they often aren't. They will use these tricks on unsuspecting people regardless of the effects they might have on them.

You will often find that the kinds of people who actively use dark psychology techniques will usually have morals that don't match those most people might follow. These are usually people who are damaged and live their lives expressing their inner demons in toxic ways. However, some will use dark psychology because they are what can be considered cold-hearted or even evil. They usually have no regard for the wellbeing of other people whatsoever.

This will give you some insight into how these people may behave. What are few of the most common strategies you will find people using on you in situations that may have nothing to do with your work? Some of them might be used on you in your social life.

The hope is that deeper insight into these tools that have probably been used against most people, will allow them to know what to look out for and perhaps react accordingly. The other hope is that it may help people use them to change their lives for the better in various aspects of their lives, be it in their careers, education, social lives, or even their love lives.

Benign/Covert

Reverse Psychology

This is possibly one of the most popular and possibly clichéd forms of dark psychology. The main reason it can be considered benign, or non-threatening is that so many people know this method is not that difficult to spot.

However, it can be a powerful tool when used right. It is most likely to work against very stubborn people who are always likely to do the exact opposite of what they are told. With this in mind, one begins to understand why telling them to do the opposite of what you desire them to do will most likely move in the direction you want them to.

This method is also a great way to disguise your intentions and make it seem as if the target acted of their own free will.

Love Flooding

This insidious method is one of the most difficult methods to detect, especially when used subtly enough and in conjunction with reinforcement and withdrawal/denial.

Love flooding (sometimes known as love bombing) is when a predator suddenly showers a potential victim with gifts, praise and positivity. Love flooding can be dangerous because it can be used to disguise sadistic motivations behind positive actions sustained for a calculated amount of time.

How it works is that one would use this technique to have their intended victim subconsciously associate them with positive feelings. Once a dependency has been established and the wanted rapport is created, it becomes easier to get the target to do as the persuader wants them to.

This method works best at the beginning of the relationship when trust is still being built.

Reinforcement

Used correctly (usually as a follow up from love flooding/bombing) this very covert tool can create an almost Pavlovian behavior in a target.

It is easy to think that the work ends when the love flooding has done its job. However there needs to be another rung on the ladder that leads to getting what one wants or interest may wane before the original desire of the persuader is met.

Restricting one's affection, attention, and praise for when someone does as the manipulator pleases creates a deep desire in the victim to do whatever it is that will make them feel good again. The target will soon behave in the required manner in order to get the positive reinforcement they believe they can get only from you.

Love Withdrawal/Denial

This step may seem a little counter-intuitive, but there is a lot of good reasoning behind using a tactic like this. It is a great follow up after love flooding/bombing and then reinforcement.

Once a person, say a potential love interest, for example, has already started associating the persuader with feelings of positivity and little reward has to be given to elicit that response, then occasionally withdrawing or denying love can be a powerful closer.

It simply creates an air of unpredictability around the manipulator while giving them complete control of their victim's mind and emotions.

This is achieved by 'randomly' giving rewards for required behavior where the reward was given every time the desired behavior was shown. It keeps the victim guessing about the manipulator's state of mind while increasingly making them crave the old attention they came to expect from them.

Passive Aggressiveness:

Guilt tripping: it is a very common way for people to avoid a confrontation to get what they want without risking an undesirable outcome.

It heavily relies on making a person feel bad by bringing up something they did, said, or even implied. It doesn't even matter if it happened. What's important is that they feel swayed by their guilt to lowering their guard enough to be nudged in the right direction.

Sarcasm: this is another tactic for getting the desired response without risking a confrontation because sarcasm is often used humorously.

Sarcasm can be used to deliver biting words funnily without giving the victim reasonable cause to flare up and get confrontational without looking like the wrong ones.

This works especially well in public areas where the one who seems to be in the wrong might call on the judgement and wrath of an on-looking crowd.

Bribery

This can take several forms and will not be as lustful as one would imagine if done right.

The trick to this is never being seen to be the one offering the bribe, but rather getting the other party to ask or even expect the bribe.

This works best if it started as simply rewarding/reinforcing good behavior so that one is never suspected of bribing, but simply cashing in on the favor they have built up over time.

It can come in the form of small gifts, money, favors, etc. It doesn't matter. What does matter is that they align with the needs of the person who is to be bribed.

This can be tricky to accomplish in the heat of the moment if favor hasn't been garnered over time, but can slowly be built up to if one is patient, compliant, and is willing to ask questions that seem innocuous while looking for the weak spot where a need can be met.

Deception:

Lying: while most people are not as good as lying as they think they are, it is not uncommon for people we meet every day to try anyway, just to be given away by their body language, if one knows where to look.

Half-truths: while these are easier to pull off, they can be trickier to remember as they can weave a story that's too difficult to navigate under pressure.

Exaggeration: blowing the truth out of proportion to some degree can be a good way to get what you desire or get out of trouble, but is difficult to get out of it if caught red-handed.

Diminishing: downplaying the truth can be just as difficult as exaggerating, but can be a good way to delay trouble while looking for an escape route.

Omission: leaving out facts in a story is easily a favorite of many persuaders as the blame can be placed on the victim if anything goes wrong.

Fraud: this is the drawn-up act of creating an elaborate scheme to get one's way, but the consequences of it can far outweigh the good, in most cases.

Implication: this entails using certain words just to claim one may have a different understanding of those words if questioned later. It offers plausible deniability.

Yes-stacking

'Yes-stacking' is simply asking someone a series of questions they are most likely to answer yes to. Once they have done this more than three times in a row, it becomes easier to ask them for what you like as most humans feel a strong need to seem

 congruent with themselves. So if someone suddenly answers 'no' after having answered in the affirmative so many times they can end up answering yes just to avoid the discomfort of feeling, or even seeming incongruent with themselves.

Slightly harder cases can often be leaned on with a bit of guilt by reminding them of their own words and this will further trigger their innate need to seem congruent to themselves and others. Yes-stacking is often used by many people in the sales industry to 'close' the sale with a customer.

Subliminal Influence:

Visual: this is the method of using images, often subtly, to get certain ideas into someone's mind without them suspecting that they are being manipulated.

Carefully placing an object, color, or image that triggers certain feelings where they'll be visible without being obvious will ingrain those feelings in a deeply subconscious way. This can be seen anywhere from presidents (and presidential candidates) wearing specifically colored neckties, to an everyday person placing an object with a certain picture in the background of a video chat because one knows that it will subconsciously bring those feelings to the surface.

Audio: using this can be trickier to use on an individual, but can be very powerful to get them to do what one wants without their knowledge. Examples of this can be in Hollywood horror movies where the sound is used to set up a 'jump-scare'. The sounds themselves can create such an intense atmosphere that nothing scary has to happen on the screen for people to jump out of their seats. Marketers with memorable jingles in their adverts can use this to get people to think about their products long after the ad is over.

Chapter 6:   What is NLP?

NLP is short for neuro-linguistic programming. The term neuro refers to one's nervous system, while linguistic refers to language control. Neuro-linguistic programming is a form of conscious programming used to control neural languages or, in layman's terms, a translator and controller into how your brain thinks.

Why is NLP a thing? Well, it's pretty hard to communicate when you don't speak the language. Now imagine you want to go to a K-pop concert in South Korea. To go, you will have to get the ticket and find the venue and then stand in line and get in. Now imagine any of those three things get lost in translation, either you end up at the wrong ticket site because you don't understand the language or have the tickets. Still, you end up at the wrong venue because you went to the Hong riverfront instead of the Hang riverfront. How about you did all that but got thrown out of the concert venue because you tried to rush through the doors when it clearly said that particular entrance wasn't for fans?

One tiny mess up and your entire experience is ruined. Even just thinking about it makes you want to scream, doesn't it?

Now, imagine how that relationship works in terms of your mind.

Your conscious mind and subconscious mind are like two identical twin brothers separated at birth and raised in two different countries. They may have the identical genetic makeup, but it makes next to no sense when they talk to each other because they don't speak each other's language.

Why Is This A Problem?

Because the two brothers have to work together!

Now imagine your conscious mind plans to get fit and healthy. You have decided that as of today, you will be eating well, cut out sugars and all those processed trans fats, and top it all off you are also going to hit the gym and start working on your body. You've made up your mind, gone out and bought everything you need, written everything down, told everyone not to call you and randomly order pizza—you've done everything you need to do, except let your subconscious brain know.

Now, this is a problem, because while your conscious brain is your goal setter and the main decision maker when it comes to what you are going to do and what you aren't going to do, your subconscious brain plays an equally important role, as a goal getter. Your subconscious brain is the facilitator, it's the engineer that made the Apple products so good that Steve Jobs could go out and be Steve Jobs.

Your subconscious brain is like the procurement officer of a major supermarket. While your consciousness is out there being the salesman convincing everyone to shop here, your subconscious is getting you all the products and produce you need to ensure that your consciousness has something to sell.

NLP is your bridge. It not only makes sure your conscious brain receives clear instructions, but it also has those instructions translated so that your subconscious brain can implement it! How great is that!

How Common is NLP?

But hold up! What if NLP is so easy to use, is everyone using it?

Well, to be honest, there is no way to tell.

They could be, although it's unlikely that every single person around you is employing NLP on you, that doesn't mean it can't happen!

What you're trying to ask here, though, doesn't have a lot to do with NLP being all the rave or being the social outcast. You're trying to figure out how likely you are to be exposed to NLP and if you will be controlled by it.

No, we're not using NLP on you right now, we're not reading your mind either—it's just simple deduction.

What you should do, though, is get rid of this unnecessary fear. If you are scared of something, and it is weighing on your mind to the extent where you are forcing yourself to ask indirect questions to sum it out, you need to face it head-on.

Does being manipulated scare you?

Do you think the form of mind control you are most likely to face is NLP? Don't cower and pretend it's not a problem when you think it is, if it's NLP you are scared of, deal with it.

Learn it, and arm yourself against its application.

Remember, your fears and problems are only as big as you make them out to be. Meaning if you think NLP is a treat, all you have to do is neutralize it.

Chapter 7: NLP Techniques

NLP techniques have proved useful in many situations. It is also a fascinating subject from a psychological perspective.

One of its main aims is to link our neurological functions and language with how we behave through experience. In other words, we can gradually begin to develop more flexible behaviors by correcting our cognitive representations and reducing the importance we attach to fixed mental maps.

NLP is an interesting and useful way of changing our reality and shaping our minds to see the world more freely, more positively, and happily.

1- Separation Technique

Neuro-linguistic programming, anxiety, and stress, such as lack of confidence, are some activities and processes, not permanent situations. So, it is necessary to control these processes and change them to work for us, not against us.

One way to accomplish this is by the separation technique. The steps of this technique are as follows:

Identify the feeling you no longer want to feel and remove it from your mind. This can be many things from nervous, sadness, fear, and frustration.

Focus on the particular feeling or situation that usually makes you feel that way. For example, I get angry every time I find out my colleague is talking behind my back.

Activate that scene as if you were in a movie. Then put a fun soundtrack in the background that will make it less of a drama. Then, play this scene several times to reduce the negative feeling. This way, you will feel that things are under your control and this is not important. It may even seem funny to you now. Your anger must have disappeared like this.

2- Redirection

The second thing about the neuro-linguistic programming techniques is that we don't use or don't use it correctly, no matter how obvious. If you think obsessively those bad things will happen and the worst possibility of everything, you can cause something bad to happen to you.

For example, some people can't stop thinking about what will happen if their spouse leaves them. So much so they develop obsessive behaviors that include jealousy, insecurity, and many destructive emotions. Then their biggest fears come true: they leave their wives because they can't stand them.

One of the NLP techniques is changing its meaning. It is a cognitive technique that takes our attention from fear and redirects it towards more constructive things.

For example, you should stop focusing on the fear of losing your partner and spend quality time with him.

You can turn your fear of being alone into accepting your responsibilities. So you learn to love yourself enough and learn to be strong rather than stuck with fears.

3- Neuro-Linguistic Programming: Hoeing Technique

Hoeing technique is a classic NLP technique for personal growth. What about the anchor? The anchor is the link between stimulus and emotion. The aim is to achieve more appropriate, but powerful thinking. This will make you more successful in what you need to do later.

Think about situations that make you worry or feel insecure: exams, public speaking, approaching someone you like, etc. If you succeed in being in the right mood, you get the motivation and self-esteem to get rid of worrying about these situations as if you were pulling the butter out. Here are a few steps to apply the hoeing technique by NLP principles:

First, decide how you want to feel: confident, happy, calm...

Then try to remember a time when you had these intense feelings.

Focus on this moment and take a picture of it in your mind.

Now, to apply the hoeing technique, choose a sentence of your own: "I am peaceful" or "Everything will be fine."

You must repeat this sentence until it is integrated with your mind (a desired emotion, memory, visual, anchor word). This will automatically happen whenever you need it.

Manipulate the Mind through NLP

How does the mind of a successful and happy person work? What is the key to your triumphs? What is it that makes you so productive? Could their patterns be copied so anyone could also succeed in everything that was proposed? These are queries that were asked, in the mid-70s, by the mathematician, computer expert and Gestalt therapy student, Richard Bandler, and the linguist John Grinder at the University of California (Santa Cruz, USA).

To find answers, they spent several years filming, observing, analyzing and modeling great communicators of the time, extraordinary people who excelled in their profession, in the sciences, in the arts, and business. At the beginning of this study, they focused their research on understanding how, through communication and language, changes in people's behavior occurred. To do this, they took as models three famous psychotherapists, Fritz Perls, creator of Gestalt therapy,

49

Virginia Satir, family therapist, and Milton Erickson, a hypnosis specialist and one of the most recognized psychiatrists of our time. Through this search, they identified and codified the verbal and behavioral patterns these privileged heads used systematically and spontaneously in communicating with their patients. That was the basis of the effectiveness and success of their work.

NLP has continued to evolve. Today, it is used with great success in psychotherapy, health, sales, business, leadership, public speaking, negotiation, education, sports training, and assertive communication, among other fields. Indeed, as the psychologist, Frank Pucelik, a collaborator who worked with Bandler and Grinder in the early years of the study says, "NLP can be applied to everything in the head to do something used. Anything that being human builds, learns, or creates is a mirror of how the mind works. If your mind works better, the things you do will be better."

NLP has revolutionized the world of personal development, and not only gives us the keys to deciphering how our mind works, but with the practice of its simple and powerful tools everyone "can generate new behaviors in any area of their lives and modify unwanted behaviors (habits, fears, phobias, traumas...) Solve self-esteem problems, and communication such as difficulties to speak in public, shyness, better understand or understand what they say. The attainment of its objectives and purposes in any other field," says Gustavo Bertoloto, who introduced NLP's teaching in Spain, and author of Activate your potential with NLP in 1989.

How can a person be good at something? Judith Delozier, a participant in the original group of students of John Grinder and Richard Bandler, gives us the answer: "With practice, practice and more practice, and is that the continued practice develops an understanding and mastery of the structure that allows us to do. We become familiar with the underlying strategy, that is, with the series of events (attitudes and actions) that sustain our success, if we become aware of what the beliefs, values , and actions that form the basis of our success are, we can reproduce it and perhaps apply it in other contexts in which we want equally successful results.

For example, the most efficient people have a map of the world that allows them to perceive as many options and perspectives as possible. They have a road map, an open mind."

Techu Arranz adds: "The most effective people are those who have beliefs, internal dialogue and imagination that work in their favor, enhancing their resources and generating a state of happiness and confidence." Throughout our lives, we have all been programming vital strategies that were useful at a given moment, but after their positive intention has expired, they may be limiting us. NLP techniques make it possible to deactivate many of these limiting programs simply and enjoyably, in a curious journey that offers you a possibility of redecorating your life and re-map your map.

Chapter 8:   Using NLP To Manage People: Verbal and Nonverbal

When it comes to managing people effectively, it's important that you first understand the non-verbal cues they provide, to be able to apply your skills toward influencing them. This is an important principle in applying the NLP technique. Following are a few NLP techniques that can allow you to influence people's perception and thinking:

Deciphering Eye Movements

It is essential to understand the meaning of eye movements because each eye movement tells its tale. For instance, when searching for the right word, or trying to remember a name, you automatically move your eyes in a certain way (most likely, squinting). Rolling the eyes signals contempt, or exasperation.

Winking indicates flirtation, or a joke.

Widening the eyes signals surprise, or shock; even extreme excitement. Eye movements are also implicated in other facial expressions.

The eyes can reveal much more about people's mental and emotional status, all on their own.

Once you understand what other people's thought processes are, you can accurately follow a course of action or dialogue which acknowledges the unspoken response, as signaled by the eyes. And as you may know, eye movements complement other communication forms such as hand movements, speech, and facial expressions.

Dilation of the pupils, breathing, angle of the body, and the hands' position – all these are complementary to the spoken message. Still, eye movement is very important in communication, because every movement is influenced by particular senses and the different parts of the brain.

Here is how you can generally interpret eye movement:

Visual Responsiveness

- Eyes upward, then towards the right:

Whenever a person tilts eyes upward and then to the right, it means that the person is formulating a mental picture.

- Eyes upward, then towards the left:

Whenever a person tilts eyes upward, followed by an eye movement to the left, it means the person is recalling a certain image.

- Eyes looking straight ahead:

Whenever someone focuses directly in front of them, as though looking at a point in the distance, this indicates that they are not focused on anything in particular. That is the look often referred to as 'glazed'.

Auditory Responsiveness

- Eyes looking towards the right:

When a person's eyes shift straight towards the right, it means the person is constructing a sound.

- Eyes looking towards the left:

When a person's eyes shift straight towards the left, it indicates that the person is recalling a sound.

Audio-digital responsiveness

- Eyes looking downward, then switching to the left:

When someone drops their eyes and then proceeds to turn their eyes to the left, this signals that the person is engaged in internal dialogue.

- Eyes looking right down then left to right:

When a person looks downward and then proceeds to turn their eyes to the left and then, to the right in consecutive movements, it means the person is engaged in negative self-talk.

Kinesthetic Responsiveness

Here, the person looks directly down, only to turn the eyes to the right. That is an indication that the person is evaluating emotional status. This further indicates that the person is not at ease.

Verbal Responses

Rhythmic Speech

The idea here is not to be poetic as you speak, but to speak regularly. The recommended pace of speaking is equated to the heartbeat, say, between 45 and 72 beats per minute. At that pace, you are likely to sustain the listener's attention and establish greater receptivity to what you're saying. While normal conversational speed averages about 140 words per minute, slowing down a little and taking time to pause is highly effective to sustain people's attention. Your regular cadence should be punctuated by fluctuations in tone and emphasis not to sound monotonous.

Repeating Key Words

When you are trying to influence someone, there are key words or phrases that carry additional weight as far as your message is concerned. This speaking method is a way of embedding the message in the listener and subtly suggesting that your message is valid and worthy of reception. Repeating key words also suggests commitment, conviction and mastery of the subject matter.

Using Strongly Suggestive Language

Use a supportive and positive language of what you are saying, using a selection set of strong, descriptive words or phrases. As you do this, you should observe the person you are speaking to closely, in a manner that makes them feel as though you are seeing right through them and aware of what they are thinking. Don't be invasive about this, or aggressive.

Merely suggest that you have a keen appreciation of what makes people tick by way of your gaze. This places you in a dominant position, especially when accompanied by dominant body language, like "steepling". It helps to use suitable, complementary body language as you speak, to underscore the message subtly.

Touching The Person Lightly, As You Speak

Touching the person as you speak to them draws their attention to you in a relaxed and familiar way. By employing this technique, you're preparing the listener to absorb what you are saying to them and programming attentiveness. Those engaging in inter-gender conversations in the workplace should take great care with this technique, as it can lead to misunderstandings.

Using A Mixture Of "Hot" And "Vague" Words

"Hot" words are those that tend to provoke specific sensations in the listener. When you use them to influence someone's thinking, it is advisable to use them in a suitable pattern. Examples of phrases containing hot words are: feel free; see this; because; hear this. The effect of employing these words and phrases is that you're directing influencing the listener's state of mind, including how they feel, imagine, and perceive. You're also appealing to the sense most prevalent in the listener's conscious style (as observed through the movement of their eyes).

For example, the phrase "hear this" will appeal to those who indicate a tendency to respond most actively to auditory stimuli.

Using The Interspersal Technique

The interspersal technique is the practice of stating one thing while hoping to impress something entirely different on the listener. For example, you could make a positive statement like:

John is very generous, but some people take advantage of him and treat him as gullible.

When someone hears this statement, the likely assumption is that you want people to appreciate John's generosity. That is likely to be the message heard and yet, the subtext is that while John is generous, he is also considered gullible and thus, at a disadvantage in life, when it comes to other people. Your hidden agenda may be to influence the listener to think of John as gullible, which calls into question his judgment. So, emphasize the words "but" and "gullible". The word "but" serves to transition the perceived compliment to John to an implicit slight.

The techniques just described form strategies in the service of influencing people. They're not intended to force a viewpoint, or to control people's behavior for nefarious ends. These techniques are intended to modify undesirable behaviors, resulting in workplace difficulties, including the failure of staff to work well together, or to complete team projects. They're also extremely helpful in the context of relationships with young people and children, whether at home, or in a learning environment.

Techniques of subtle manipulative effect like those described, though capable of influencing people and their behavior, don't amount to anything even approaching coercion. The person being spoken to chooses all responses and is merely influenced, or steered toward those responses.

Chapter 9:   Persuasion

What Is Persuasion?

What comes to your mind when you think about this question? Some think it is creating a desperate message to buy a product, while others think it tries to influence voters. The problem is a powerful force in everyday life, which has a major impact on security. Policies, legal decisions, media, news, and insights are all influenced by decisions' power and influence us. At times, we want to believe that we are not affected by persuasion. We have the natural ability to look at this sale, recognize the situation's truth, and make our own decisions. This may be true in some scenarios, but it is not necessarily the seller trying to convince you, or a TV commercial asking you to buy the latest and greatest item. Persuasion can be subtle, and there can be many factors in how we try to gain influence.

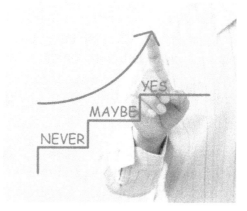

According to Perloff (2003), influence can be defined as a symbolic process in which communicators try to persuade other people to change their perspectives or behaviors regarding an issue through the transmission of a message in an atmosphere of free choice.

The Main Reasons for this Definition are:

- It is recommended to use words, photos, sounds, etc.
- This is an explanation to influence others.
- Persuasion is useful. No one found the choice is yours.
- How to provide a particular action in different cases, including verbal, unnecessary, dissemination, and information.

How Is It Different Today?

Art and the method we chose accurately determined the ancient Grecques' times, but there are significant differences shown in the past. In his book "The Dynamics of Belief: Communication and Attitudes in the 21st Century, Richard M. Perlov describes the five most important questions that new questions are different from others.

The number of persuasive measures has increased significantly. For a moment, think about how many you can find each day. To ensure the number of times the US results are reached, it ranges from about 300 to over 3,000. Make sure the communication is quick. This is the reason, and the intent to spread it very quick. Persuasion is a business that is followed by companies (distributors, companies, public companies, etc.) that only operate for a specific purpose.

Persuasion is not trivial. Of course, few ads use very compelling strategies, but many messages are much more subtle. For example, a particular schedule may be set very precisely to plan for product purchase or life extension. The question is more complicated. As customers are more identifiable and make more decisions, they need to determine when they can persuade compelling media and messages.

Modern Persuasion:

Pratkans & Aron (1991) states that some companies make better decision than others. In contrast to the means of communication that control transactions, the right decisions are left to the advertisers. Discussions are raised in response to the authority, not by or in the power of the administration. Rules are chosen based on their ability, not the royal family, but one of the biggest reasons. Good looking and behaving candidates almost always win.

The old Greeks had a better approach to making decisions. The Greeks, who are stationed, can hire an employee to protect him. The hiking teachers and writers probably decided to know-you can say they were the best students in the world. Sophists argued that a persuasion is a tool that helps find the truth. They thought that the discussion and the reason for the debate would generate good ideas and allow good ideas to come back. It did not matter what problem he was working on. Sophists would have been in the middle of discussions for some time. The stated goals of them have been confirmed that the truth has been resolved. They believed in the free practice of good ideas.

Does it sound like our world? No, we are leveraging success, and we can state that this is more than an opportunity did. But what is the modern approach to answering the question of whether it is right or wrong? Of course. It is important to reach the masses "through the manipulation of symbols and most of us human emotions." to achieve their goals, I think that subject is taught at school because the ability to ask and examine questions is directly related to someone's success in life. I think they know the right tactics as much as they know the letters of the alphabet and the right way, or how to improve CPR.

But how can we reflect the ten principles of belief? How many of us can find the situation and the right tool for the job? How many people know the times when someone is influenced by someone every day? Do this: Take a look at your decision, or your pantry, or your organization. Everyone you see is a trophy that represents some of the companies that exceed their goals. For some reason, or perhaps no reason at all, they may allow you to make your money on your products. Many influencing factors play a role in our security. They are at the top of your business and thrive by letting you think, do what you want, and get it done.

Most people are unaware of these effects or, if they are, overestimate the amount of freedom needed to realize their thoughts. But we know that a strong influence is a question that will help your decision to determine his approach if he can handle the situation and choose the right approach.

Methods of Persuasion:

The ultimate goal of persuasion is to persuade one to internalize the right argument and adopt that new attitude as part of the decision. Below are just a few of the most effective ways to persuade. Other methods include rewards, positive or negative experiences, and many other uses.

Create your Needs:

One way of identifying is to create the needs you really need. This kind of exam is a fundamental pre-requisite for whether it is a matter of self-determination and self-realization. Manufacturers often use this method to solve problems. For example, think about how many suggestions you need to find a particular product and make sure it is good.

Addressing Social Needs:

It is another very effective method that appeals to the need to be popular, and renowned. Television ads provide many examples of these types of questions. It is essential to buy these questions to look like a known or familiar person. Television is a big challenge to convince people.

Use Old Words and Photos:

It is also widely used for using loaded words and images. Advocates will notice the power of positive words that frequently use phrases such as "new and improved" or "all-natural."

Put Your Foot in the Door:

Another reason why it is ineffective to get people to meet their requirements is known as the "get it started" technique. This means that it is important to ask a question to answer a small question, such as asking a small question to be answered by creating the query. By having a person accept the first favor, the applicant is more likely to "feel," and that person is more likely to agree with the more extensive requirements. For example, a neighbor has asked you to babysit two children for one or two. If you agree, ask if you can ask your child for the rest of the time.

You have always chosen smaller requirements, so you might feel the obligation to face larger ones. This is an excellent example of what applies to approval rules, and we recommend that you use this method to encourage consumers to buy your product.

Increase and then Decrease:

This approach is different from the foot-in-the-door approach. Specific questions often start with making unnecessary requests. A person responds by rejecting the door for sale and figuratively blaming it. The answer to this question is to create a much smaller requirement that is often considered invalid. Feel the obligation to meet these offers. Since they rejected this initial request, they often help answer small requests.

Harness the Power of Security:

When you have someone in you, it can be overwhelming to bring your family back kindly. It is known as a kind of correctness. Someone did something for you, so a particular obligation to do something for someone. Manufacturers can use this method as if they were giving kindness, including "extras" and making decisions to force offers or purchases of offers.

Create another Point for Innovation:

Decisions are subtle cognitive biases that can impact diet and decisions. If you try to reach a decision, the first offer tends to decide for all future decisions. Therefore, if you try to propose a number first and try to negotiate for a particular question, it can affect future negotiations in your life, especially if the number is a little higher. This first number is the correct point. You may not get it, but a high start can lead to higher offers from your employer.

Limit Availability:

Robert Cardin's decision is known for six principles that influence the fact that it is best explained in his strongest influence in 1984 on influence. One of the keys he identified is known to be secure or to limit the availability of something.

He suggested that situations improve when things are scared or limited. We would buy something if they believed it was the last one or it would be there soon. For example, the answer could only be a limited run of a particular print. Only some printouts are available, so you may decide before you leave.

Spend Time Realizing that you have a Question:

Examples are just a few of the main persuasion techniques described by certain psychologists. Look for persuasive examples in your daily life. An interesting experiment is to revisit the 30 minutes of a particular schedule and write down a compelling assessment of all kinds. With a certain number of techniques used in a short time, you may be surprised.

Chapter 10: Principles of Persuasion

In general, persuasion can be understood as a form of strategic communication that has the purpose of convincing others. Through persuasion, it is possible to cause someone to assume a particular position, perform a specific task or accept an idea.

This communication incorporates an adequate posture, emotional appeals and, mainly, a strong and logical argumentation. In this manner, you will see that the psychology of persuasion is associated with some basic topics such as knowledge, rhetoric, and image.

This competence is important for everyone, regardless of profession or branch of activity. Still, it becomes even more indispensable for leadership positions, sales professionals, and those who work on projects, among others. And, like most behavioral skills, it can be assimilated and perfected.

The Psychology of Persuasion

In the book The Psychology of Persuasion, author Robert Cialdini states that the individual can develop this ability to communicate to persuade others' actions and decisions. Based on his studies, Robert Cialdini created the persuasive communication theory, which is based on the concept of taking advantage of some collectively internalized patterns of behavior to suggest behaviors. As stated above, this theory lists the 6 principles of the psychology of persuasion, which can be taught, learned, and applied. They are:

Reciprocity

This principle of persuasion defines that people are more willing to agree to a request when they have received something in return. Social norms urge us to respond positively to those who have done us a favor or helped us at some other time.

Consistency

The individual is also more likely to follow a pattern if he finds that this model is consistent with his ideals and values.

Authority

According to this principle, the seniority and authority transmitted by the communicator are determining aspects for others to feel liable to approve or validate something. At this point, the argument and posture of the communicator have special emphasis.

Social Validation

According to Cialdini, the greater the common sense about a behavior, the greater the probability of adopting attitudes that fit this standard.

Shortage

In this principle, the author reiterates that the charm generated by a product, service or situation is inversely proportional to its availability. That is, the more scarce, the more relevant.

Friendship / Sympathy

Finally, the sixth principle indicates that people are more inclined to collaborate or form an agreement with others when they identify with them, have a friendly relationship or some kind of attraction.

It is worth remembering that the principles of Robert Cialdini's influence should not be used in an autonomous manner but in a combined way as part of more efficient and provocative communication.

The Importance of Empathy

It is worth emphasizing that the power of persuasion can only be perfected through an additional ability: to listen with the sincere intention of understanding the other. Thus, the issuer's speech deserves full attention. It is necessary to understand the message and the lines between and everything behind each comment, such as concerns, expectations, and feelings.

For this, it is essential to be prepared to listen and at the same time collect information, emotions, and impressions. It is important to emphasize that knowing how to listen encompasses rational and emotional aspects, but does not imply an agreement with the other. Disagreements can remain, but with effective communication, they become better understood.

The Strength of Argumentation

The argumentation, in turn, is based on coherence and uses real facts to consolidate a thesis. A good argument is filled with examples, data, technical studies, research, and comparisons, to prove the integrity of an affirmation or the feasibility of a proposal. Thus, the communicator manages to involve others, causing everyone to follow the same reasoning line until they are persuaded.

This power of persuasion is appreciably amplified when argumentation joins empathy. In this case, you will be able to create a communication that mixes reason and emotion, reaching the main centers of the conviction.

Persuasion in The Corporate Universe

It is now easy to see that relationships have become increasingly virtual and often less productive. This movement is caused not only by the advancement of technology but also by the underutilization of important skills.

Among these skills are empathy and the ability to argue, which can ensure healthier and more collaborative relationships, especially in the corporate environment - where peaceful coexistence between professionals with the most diverse profiles is a basic need.

Individualism has become a major problem, hampering teamwork and collectivity. That's why you need to be careful about the virtualization of communication and the almost exclusive use of e-mail, messaging applications, and social networks.

It is also important to consider that dialogue is one of the most efficient ways to perceive fears, motives, and needs, normally hidden in fully digital communication. Personal contact creates ideal conditions for feedback, negotiation, guidance, counseling, and persuasion.

Besides, the correct application of the psychology of persuasion is one of the main characteristics of true leaders who can inspire and engage their teams. Therefore, this subject must be present in the leadership development program. With powerful argumentation, it is possible to induce critical thinking - a key ingredient in forming high-performance teams. The results will be even better if the communicator is recognized as a positive reference that inspires others.

Aspects That Impact The Power Of Persuasion

Some simple aspects can impact the persuasive power of the individual. Therefore, attention should be paid to the following tips:

Posture, Gesture, and Tone of Voice

Posture, gestures, and tone of voice are points that generate trust and credibility. Thus, it is necessary to perceive these characteristics and to conform to the model imposed by its interlocutor. Eye contact is part of this same tactic because it ensures greater proximity. With a few attempts, a connection arises.

Language

The language should also be appropriate to the model of the interlocutor so that the conversation flows naturally. It is also important to reach the emotions of the people through stimuli aligned with personal yearnings and goals. These are excellent ways to persuade.

Interruptions

To be persuasive, avoiding interruptions is essential. Cuts and hasty conclusions are signs of anxiety and unpreparedness. A productive dialogue demands time, tranquility, and attention.

Convergent Questions

Questions help the communicator keep the conversation focused on his or her primary goal. This attitude contributes to a more dynamic conversation because, through structured questions, the interlocutor is also invited to rethink his opinions and evaluate new alternatives.

Knowledge

A sound argument depends on knowledge. Therefore, it is essential to be updated, have clear answers, understand the events, interpret data, and establish communication strategies.

The psychology of persuasion principles are important skills that can be gained through specific training, discipline, and focus. Adjustments in one's behavior are fundamental in this process of improvement, which will reward one to achieve more productive interpersonal relationships - indispensable for a successful career.

Chapter 11:   NLP Techniques for Persuasion

Here's a couple of useful techniques that can help persuade someone.

1. Start a Conversation

Firstly, initiate your conversation on the correct path. This technique requires that the persuader make sure that the individual is familiar with the topic. Next is to be very clear and straightforward in what you say. Saying that "Anna failed" is a very unclear statement. Did you mean to indicate that Anna failed in her exams, an interview, or a quest? When you put forward a statement that can be misinterpreted, you need to use the correct vocabulary to explain it.

2. Pulsate the Person

The next thing is to know what pulsates the individual. Trying to get permission from your principal to organize a night party, you need to know what pulsates your principal. If your principal is someone who feels good when he is appreciated and praised, you can praise him as much as possible to get the permission. Give the individual a brief idea about the bigger picture in your words.

3. Build Rapport

Next is to build rapport while staying humble. If you are skilled enough to build rapport, then you are entitled to a pass to their trust. A successful persuasion starts with a good rapport based on the trust the individual harbors towards the persuader.

4. Remain Calm, Composed and Humble

Staying humble, without seeming to compete with the individual and not making them feel that you think you are better than them, is critical during the persuasion process. Sending that sort of message will usually only cause the individual to stick strongly to his point, making it hard for you to persuade.

5. Absorb and Concentrate

Instead of figuring out what should be said next, absorb and concentrate on the individual's being said. Now, this is a pretty hard task; this develops gradually as you go along the way. When you pay enough attention to what the individual says, you will be able to reply to him properly. Still, if you were only thinking of what to say next, you might go off topic, indicating your inattention and leading to a poor discussion. When the person is talking, make sure that you don't interrupt their statement just because you got the point; if that happens, the person might forget his point and get stressed about it.

6. Keep Track and Target a Suitable Time

One of the most important factors to consider when staring the persuasion process is time. If the person does not have adequate time to discuss with you, then whatever you have to say might be not considered due to the lack of time they possess. Therefore, before initiating the conversation, you need to ask if the individual has enough time for a talk.

7. Be Respectful and Do Not Judge

Don't judge or disrespect anything that the individual says; you need to empathize with what that individual says without giving him direct opposing comments or replies. You need to be well aware of the language that you use so that the other person does not get offended. Sometimes during the discussion, you might get emotional, which can make the process like an argument, indicating an unhealthy persuasion process.

Advantages of NLP

These NLP techniques can increase the level of influence that you exert on others. Companies that engage in marketing and sales completely depend on persuading their customers or clients to buy their products; the strategies presented in NLP guide these sellers and dealers to increase the chance of influencing their customers in making decisions. NLP also increases the person's performances; NLP helps you modify and replace your negative behaviors with more positive ones. These strategies also help you to improve your leadership style. Being humble and non-judgmental allows you to have a better communication style, even outside the persuasion process.

Essentials for Persuasion

1. Empathy – this is an essential quality that a persuader requires. You should not only be thinking about yourself, but you also should try to put yourself in the other person's shoes and think about how they might be feeling. Empathy also helps deter you from being judgmental.

2. Listening Skills – only a good listener will persuade another person; a person who is always ready for an argument will never be a good listener. If you want to be a positive and good persuader, you need to listen to what the other individual says and pay attention to their body language.

3. Indirect and Clever Commands – people tend to be more responsive to suggestions than questions. For example, instead of using the words "Would you like to go to the concert?", you can say "Come, let's go to the concert"; this motivates a more positive response.

4. Restrict The Choices That You Provide – try not to allow the individual to say "No" or make it as hard as possible for the individual to say "No." Taking the same example, instead of asking, "Will you be able to stay long at the concert?", ask them, "Would you like to stay here for three hours or four?". The latter question makes it hard for the individual to say a "No."

5. Allow the Person to Visualize – successful persuaders always help the client or the individual visualize so that they can convince them. An example would be, "this concert will make us scream the lyrics of our favorite songs."

6. Always Make It Simple as Possible – trying to convince the other person by bragging will only be a failure; keep it as simple as possible and remember you should never put their views down.

Chapter 12: Gaslighting

We would like to go over several reality denial techniques that have been grouped under the term 'Gas lighting.' This particular form of manipulation can be quite insidious and difficult to protect yourself from. We can still introduce you to some common methods and suggest to you some possible means of defense to combat this dark art.

Gas lighting is popularly used by the Dark Triad, most commonly in the following ways:

· Machiavellians - Machiavellians will typically employ Gas lighting to protect a particular self-image that they would like to portray. On Internet forums or social media such as Facebook, this most commonly includes taking arguments out of context or looking for an argument's weakest aspect to attack the other person's credibility. They often spend a lot of time in political forums as this is an emotional subject for many and therefore an easy place to get themselves the attention they crave. Typically, they offer a broad subject, a vague solution (or no solution), and then let people start arguing. It's trolling, but trolling in the sense that the Machiavellian is doing it to forward a self-image of appearing calm and rational to cultivate their self-image at the expense of the unsuspecting.

· Psychotics - Psychotic motives are much harder to place, but typically they involve self-advancement. A psychotic might seem cheerful and kind at work, for instance, and yet if they are competing with another for a promotion, they will spend a lot of their free time deciding how they can discredit the other. They will not hesitate to magnify the details of a situation to get a co-worker fired if they are in their way. This lack of remorse and empathy is what makes this member of the Dark Triad so deadly. They are easily the worst of the group.

· Narcissists - Narcissists will typically employ Gas lighting to attack anyone they feel is arguing with them. The goal is to debilitate the individual in the eyes of others; thus, elevating the Narcissist status. It may also be used as simple punishment for someone who has dared to challenge their precious self-image.

So, how do you recognize when someone is attempting to use Gas lighting techniques to disorient you or to undermine your confidence? We've compiled some techniques here to give you an idea of some of the more common methods. Reality denial manipulation can be quite nasty, so you will want to study these techniques so that you can recognize when dark manipulation is afoot and is pointed at YOU.

Here are some common methods employed in Gas lighting:

1. Lying about friends to isolate you - Dark manipulators want you isolated and, to do that, they need to erode your base of support. They begin dropping hints about your friends, accusing them of belittling you behind your back, not respecting you, or having a romantic interest in the manipulator. They know which buttons to push so this can be very effective, especially if they have been using the next item on our list.

2. They often take their time to become your best friend - Master dark manipulators will take their time to begin tampering with your mental stability. It will likely begin with small examples from this list and then proceed to a full-on assault. Over time, it gets worse and worse and there is added confusion from the 'nice period' that came before. Watch for small examples from this list and, if you see them, take it as a warning sign.

3. Project their feelings on to you - Dark manipulators will often project their feelings and insecurities to you. A very common example in a relationship with one of these individuals is constant accusations that you might be cheating on them. You'll

notice that they seem to know a lot about the subject, and this is a warning sign that can help you see what is going on more quickly. If you are getting accusations of this sort for no reason, then be on the alert and ask yourself why they seem to know so much about how a cheating person is likely to act.

4. Tell you that you are imagining things - This generally goes with the previous relationship tactic and can be indicative that they are doing something or many things behind your back. In relationships, we tend to notice when our partners experience a change in behavior. If it is easier to accuse you of having an overactive imagination than it is to explain themselves so that you don't worry, this can be a very big warning sign to watch.

5. Lie to discredit your memory - This is a favorite Gas lighting tactic and very easy to do. If someone sets up a day to meet, for instance, and then later tells you that they never set that up time to meet with you, then you will find it curious at first, but likely never suspect it to be deliberate. They can also express interest in going to a concert or a movie with you and then, when the time comes, act bored or irritated at the event, later claiming that they told you that they didn't want to go to that but that you insisted. It is a tried and true technique and you should watch out for it. A good way to combat this is simply write things down or put them in your calendar immediately and discretely, so that you will know if it occurs more than once. If so, either their memory is quite poor or they may be attempting to Gas light you.

6. Get you angry and accuse you of being crazy - When a dark manipulator knows how to push your buttons, they will often take advantage of this to make you doubt your very sanity by using your temper. It will seem as if every quarrel consists of you yelling and frustrated, while they calmly suggest you have a drink, relax, or perhaps that you both meet another time 'when you are less irrational' or 'less crazy.' Of course, this will make

you angrier, giving them an excuse to leave, and later to question whether or not your response was appropriate (especially if followed by the silent treatment, forcing you to communicate first). If you DO have a temper, that doesn't necessarily mean that someone is taking advantage of it, but a constructive way to help determine what occurred is to write down your version of events when you get home and wait to read it until the next day. That way, you can view it when you are less upset and if it is occurring regularly, you will be better equipped to determine if it is an actual problem with anger, or if this person might be manipulating you towards their ends.

7. Mix abuse with praise or gifts - Dark manipulators like to keep you off-balance by mixing abuse with praise. For instance, you may find yourself being complimented for something innocuous after a brutal argument, or treated to a nice dinner or event after days of silence, with the abusive behavior which was recently experienced never spoke of... as if it never happened. These mixed messages allow the manipulator to prolong their control. If someone is being abusive in the first place, it is best to disassociate with them as soon as possible but, barring this, analyze their behavior and look for patterns from this list.

8. They will use your children - If you have children, dark manipulators will not hesitate to use them against you – raising the volume of their speech so that you will capitulate with their wishes, rather than let your children hear you arguing. They will also bribe children with treats and push your buttons so children will always associate the manipulator with ice cream and toys and anger and yelling. If you notice this behavior, take it for exactly what it is, blatant manipulation, and get as far away as you can from this individual. This is not the sort of thing that gets better over time.

9. Accuse you of wasting efforts in the wrong place – This one can occur in the home or the workplace. You will find your Manager asking, "Why are you wasting time doing this particular assignment when I needed you to do this other one?" after asking you to focus on the first. This is an attempt to bully you, an act of dominance. The only way to combat this is to mark items on your calendar 'Priority per Boss' as they come in or, otherwise, create a paper trail for yourself. While taxing and monotonous, this method is an effective way to defend yourself from manipulation.

10. Turn others against you - Gas lighters know the people who dislike you already and will resort to name dropping to this effect. "Joe knows you are lazy at work" or "Jill says you cheated on a boyfriend once." This works well with the isolation technique as suddenly not only do you not have your friends, but everyone around is an enemy. Watch out for name-dropping of this sort, as dark manipulators love to use this technique.

We hope that this list of techniques employed by dark manipulators has been of use to you. Use this information well and you'll certainly have the basics of defense at hand should you need it!

Chapter 13: How to Avoid Being Gaslighted

Education. The first step to avoiding being gaslighted is education. Being able to spot the tell-tale signs of gaslighting can be a deciding factor in whether you'll become a victim. Many people become victims of gaslighting because they do not know how gaslighters operate. They spend most of their time thinking that they are the problem, so the gaslighter just continues abusing them. It is a good thing that you are educating yourself on gaslighting by reading this book. And by now, I believe you know the modus operandi of gaslighters. So, when next you encounter a narcissist or a gaslighter, and they try to pull a fast one on you, quickly remind yourself that you are not the problem—they are the problem.

One trick you can use to remind yourself that the gaslighter is the problem is to understand that they are probably doing it because they are trying to remedy their low self-esteem, or perhaps it is because they're trying to regain control of their own lives. Once you convince yourself that they are acting the way they do because of their battles, you will learn to consider their treatments lightly, which means more control. Now that you are not taking them seriously, you are regaining the power you were being denied in the relationship.

The ability to understand that they are the problem and not you will help you regain control of your life and position. It will also be easier not to take what they say personally, thus thwarting their plans and goals to manipulate you.

Get outside advice. Gaslighters aim to have you not trust your mind. If you cannot judge your position, feelings, or reasoning, get someone you trust to help you assess the situation. This step is important early on, as a gaslighter might try to make you distrust those people. But you must learn to get outside advice because if you only listen to your gaslighter, they will confuse you even further. The way out is meant to help you keep your external relationships as strong as possible. It is even possible for your friends and families to notice something off and help you so that you don't get swallowed up by the abuse.

In terms of your external relationships, if you break off from a gaslighter in the process of avoiding gaslighting, you may need a sturdy support system (outside relationships); this is especially crucial if the gaslighter is your partner. If you do not have this support system in place, the gaslighter might maneuver their way back into your life.

Remove yourself from the situation. At work, if you are unable to change positions or companies, you can have HR assess the situation and help you work out a way in which you will not have to work with the gaslighter. This may lead to the abuser switching to another target if they find a suitable one. Spreading information on gaslighting around can be helpful to others as well.

In the family, it may be more difficult. You can move (even to a different city) if you can do so. Try to cut off all contact with the gaslighter. In relationships, it's vital to recognize the symptoms early on. Otherwise, you may get pulled into the abuser's scheme. End a relationship with a gaslighter as soon as possible.

Sometimes, it might not be easy for you to just walk out on the abuser like when they are a co-worker, and you cannot easily change jobs.

Change Your Perspective

Shift your perspective from being a victim to being a winner, warrior, or whatever word feels the most empowering to you. You don't have to keep on being a victim for the rest of your life, and by retrieving your power, you'll also be able to help others in similar circumstances.

Ignore Motives

Most gaslighters have a motive for their gaslighting, and more often than not, it is to control you. There could be other reasons we saw in the film Gaslight where Gregory's motive was to steal Paula's inheritance. But you must ignore the motives. If you don't, you will be further trapping yourself because it will never be apparent, and it will increase your confusion and self-doubt.

Using Cognitive Behavioral Therapy To Avoid Gaslighting

As you already know, gaslighting thrives on your perception of yourself. While the methods and steps can help you avoid gaslighting, it may be difficult for you alone to handle, especially if the gaslighter has firmly wrapped their hands around your mind. Cognitive-behavioral therapy (CBT) is a type of therapy that is concerned with your perception of yourself. It looks at the impact of your thoughts on your behavior. It is also effective for other mental health issues such as anxiety and depression.

For us to see just how CBT can help you avoid gaslighting, let's look at the ABC's of gaslighting. The ABC's stand for Activating, Belief, and Consequences. Activating is the issue that triggers the belief that brings about the consequences. In the case of gaslighting, the gaslighter's attitude towards you is the activating. This activating is not the cause of your trauma; it is the thought or interpretation you give to it that brings about the consequences, which is the trauma. So, if you interpret the gaslighter's actions to mean that your instincts are not correct and you are insane, then the trauma sets in. But if you refuse to interpret it that way, then you will save yourself from the impending trauma. CBT says that if you allow yourself to accommodate negative thoughts always, then it will weigh you down. That is why you can use CBT not to feel what the gaslighter wants you to feel.

Another reason why CBT can help you avoid gaslighting is that a therapist uses structured sessions to become aware of the lies and deceit around you. If you become more aware of the situation around you, then it is very unlikely that you will allow it to get to you.

CBT is a therapy that will require a therapist to carry out effectively. So, you might need to contact a therapist to help you avoid becoming a gaslighting victim or falling back into old habits.

Chapter 14: Laws of Manipulation

Manipulators respond to one, two, or more tactics to reach their aims, always at someone else's expense. While the strategies may vary from manipulator to manipulator, there are 13 manipulative laws each manipulator uses at one time or another:

Law #1 - Hide Your Intentions. Lying may be the oldest and most effective manipulative form around. Manipulators often respond to this strategy when trying to avoid responsibility or twist the truth. Some manipulators also admit to lies where there is no particular justification to do so, only living on the joy of causing confusion or knowing that they play with someone else's emotions. A talented manipulator knows how to operate so subtly on this angle that you don't even realize the lie they are spinning until it's too late. There may be various reasons why a manipulator needs to resort to telling lies. It could be another to take advantage of. To hide their true intentions, so that you do not know what they are up to. Or maybe even to level out the playing field so they can stay a point ahead of you.

Law #2 - Attention Seeking. A little excitement in existence makes things exciting but chaos occurs all too much for a manipulator. Why? For what? And they set it up intentionally. Manipulators want to be the center of focus for validating themselves and offering their egos the boost of trust they feel they deserve. A friend at work may have recourse to generating friction among colleague A and colleague B by sharing tales about each other. This guarantees that while colleagues A or B are at odds with one another, they transform to a manipulator for "comfort," making the manipulator look special afterward. One person may continuously pick a conflict in a partnership to ensure that the other's energy is consistently centered on them and attempting to fix an issue that does not exist.

Law #3 - Behaving Emotionally. Manipulators may be individuals who are extremely emotional, prone to sensational, and even hysterical rantings whenever they want stuff accomplished their way. Overly dramatic, rude, offensive, over-the-top, a manipulator can revert to irrational actions even at the smallest provocation, which is unacceptable in a social environment. A pair fighting aggressively in the cafeteria when one spouse is acting unreasonably because things are not handled their way resort to this action, thinking that their spouse will feel humiliated sufficiently to cede to their requests allows this an incredibly successful coercion tactic when employed correctly.

Law #4 - Playing Victim. Everybody always feels bad. They appear to have the world's toughest luck. Any issue you might have, they search a way of making you feel bad for even thinking about that by finding out how "10 times worse" their issue is than yours. Now and again we all profit from a bit of bad luck; however, the manipulator has learned to use that unfortunate streak skillfully to raise their own "victim" status and to place themselves above all others. A buddy who is continually bringing up all the bad elements of his life when ignoring the problems will resort to this cynical technique to get the publicity they seek. Tell them you've got a rough day since you've had a flat tire on the drive to work the next morning and they'll remind you how fortunate you could still have a vehicle to worry about because they're trying to suffer the public transit difficulties. This emotionally exhausting technique is used by manipulators to receive support from people, that is another means of getting publicity and ensuring that all is centered on them.

Law #5 - Taking Credit Where It's Not Due. Manipulators don't hesitate to get you to do all of the legwork, and afterward, swoop in at the last moment to take credit as they did the lion's job. A common tactic that is often used in a skilled setting, normally in group or team-work projects. Such crafty manipulators are fluttering around delegating tasks, apparently "busy" when they don't do much at all, however, when it comes to claiming credit, they have no problem brushing you back and demanding credit for the innovations and the effort you've put into it.

Law #6 - Depend on Me. Manipulators want you, in your life, to feel like you need them. That you just can't live without them. They are the "popular" ones in a social setting to which everybody seems to flock, making you anxious to want to become a part of that community. They might be the partner in a relationship that keeps reminding you "what you would do without me" or "how you would survive without me." They do you favor and assist you out at a moment when you need it the most, going to make you feel deeply in debt to them so that at a later date they can come as well as cash in on those favors.

Law #7 - Selective Honesty. Have you ever felt so enchanted by how a generous person you know could unexpectedly turn around and stab you back? Or felt so wrong-footed when you recognized you only knew half of what was going on? That's because the person who was feeding you with data was a manipulator, and the reason you feel stabbed in the back or wrong-footed is that they only fed you information that they wanted you to know while intentionally withholding the rest. Selective honesty, a controlling manipulative tactic that can be used to charm an unsuspecting "victim".

Law #8 - Pretending to Be A "Friend". Don't be deceived by the exceedingly pleasant person you merely met at the office on your first day. They might claim to be your buddy while collecting information regarding you to use to everyone's advantage later on. While some individuals may be genuinely friendly, if this individual is a little too pleasant, start raising the red flag by posing very specific or inquiring questions, especially if you've just met them. Inside a professional environment, this technique is popular and if your gut tells you something wrong, it's off.

Law #9 - Non-Committal. Do you know whoever has a hard time willing to commit to anything in your life? Even after you told them how essential it is and just now you could use their support? The non-committal person is not your mate, they are a manipulator. They find delight in withholding their authorization or support if it means they have a chance to give themselves the advantage to control the situation to their advantage. They just look out for themselves and especially deter from contributing to something if it involves taking liability. Being non-committal is a tactic of manipulation which is often used in romantic relations. When a romantic partner is non-committal, it helps keep the other on their feet and keeps them coming back for even more, thus giving the upper hand to the manipulator. The longer they withhold their dedication, the more you will be willing to bend backward, just to get their approval.

Law #10 - Playing Dumb. Is that friend you do not know what's going on? Or will they feign ignorance to prevent shouldering additional workload? Playing stupid is a deceitful tactic that is often neglected, but if people pay attention, you will find that obvious in a lot of talented settings. If you were a community project leader at work, should you delegate the extra duty to the one member of the team who "wasn't as confident about anything?" Or assign that additional responsibility to someone else? The worker who was "playing stupid" tries to get away with just doing far less but receiving the same quantity of recognition in the group as everyone else. When a community of friends is in disagreement, could one person who "doesn't realize what's going on" say the truth? Or may they be feigning ignorance, realizing full well that they were solely liable for causing the conflict? In a loving relationship, can your spouse, who "doesn't know what you're talking about," tell the truth about a problem when you interrogate them? Or could they be "acting foolish" to stop getting swept up in a lie? The "innocent party" may not have been so innocent at times, after all.

Law #11 - Pointing the Finger at Others. In the first place, a manipulator would always strive to maintain their hands clean, never take accountability, and in the second place by always attempting to point a finger at somebody else because they get off brit-free when a problem arises. Particularly when that issue might endanger their credibility and reveal them besides who they are. You could be trying to deal with a manipulator if you know someone in your relatives, mates, or even with other coworkers who always criticize everything and anyone other than themselves. Keep an eye out for anyone who's behavior pattern always involves making someone the scapegoat.

Law #12 - Telling You What You Want to Hear. When you're flattered, it's impossible not to think good and you're more willing to like the person who does all the fashionable more than the others. If one person constantly asks you all the stuff you want to learn in your life, wouldn't you be more likely to pursue them or invest more time around them? It's impossible not to think good about such people but tell you all the stuff you would like to listen to is not certainly a better friend's sign. They might be buttering you so that at a later date they can money in on a big favor that you will be "guilty" to help them with "because they were so nice to you."

Law #13 - Controlling Your Decisions. A classic setting is within a loving relationship when there is manipulation in regulating another's decision. While it is completely normal for your partner to base or start changing your decisions, is it because there is a genuine desire within you to make them happy? Or do you do it because you don't want them to risk getting angry? There is a very fine line in one relationship between what constitutes deception. If you find yourself with friends canceling schemes far too often because your partner conveys their disappointment or makes you feel bad, manipulation in the play. It's a subtle type of coercion if you keep from wearing clothing that your partner criticizes or having a haircut after your partner said "they don't like short hair" They are manipulating the choices without actually making it clear they are. It could start casually enough with a comment or two, with something so negligible like conveying how the clothes you wear don't look better on you. The kind of dress you wear should be something else especially if you find that their things have turned into nothing more than decisions that don't make you happy because they are dictated by somebody who claims to love you.

Chapter 15: Tips to Protect Yourself from Manipulation

Here are the practical tips to protect yourself from manipulation you could use to keep your mind and emotions safe every day.

- Keeping Close Connections, You Can Trust-Keeping close contact with family and friends you can trust will keep the manipulator's mind-control efforts on you to a minimum. The family and friends you can trust can give you the support you need and strengthen your self-confidence, so the manipulator has no room to plant their seeds of doubt or shake your faith.

- Speak to Your Friends and Family-Another reason the manipulator never allows you to detach from those you love and trust because you can still trust them to have your best heart interest. Those who love you (in a non-manipulative fashion) will always look to your safety. If you're ever unsure if you're subjected to manipulation (though you may have your suspicions), talk to them about what's going on and see how they react. Their immediate response-if it is shock and anger-should serve the wake-up call you need something that may not be entirely correct.

- Choosing Not to Tolerate Your Moods — Relationship manipulators sometimes sulk or resort to temperatures to get things done. If you allow them, the only one that takes an emotional toll on this kind of conduct is you. Choose not to tolerate it by walking away from the situation every time they resort to such behavior. Explain why you should not put up with this, and if they fail to change their ways, it might be time to doubt whether there is any need to hold on to this relationship for a long time.

- Ignore them-It is the best practical advice that you can find on your own. Ignore them because your time, effort, and emotions are not worth wasting on. Ignore them when they are trying to give you "advice." Ignore them as they try and tell you what to do, just go ahead and do what you wanted to do anyway. Manipulators can never be trusted, and they are always going to try to get you to do their dirty work. When you seek to hold them to account, they are going to refuse all accountability. They flip flop, go back and forth, and change their minds as often as they change clothes. Ignore them and forget everything they say; this is the only thing you can do.

- Don't try to correct them when you do, you just sink deeper into their trap. Remember, they're trying to confuse you enough so you can't see what they're up to when you're an emotional wreck and whenever you're trying to "fix" the situation, it's too easy for them to twist you around their little finger. These little traps are often set to see how you respond so they can figure out your triggers and use them to their advantage. Do not communicate, do not answer, and do not seek to correct them. It is a never-winning game.

- Don't doubt yourself-the the manipulator needs you to do just that. Why is that exactly what you shouldn't be doing? You know yourself better than anyone else might ever have, and you shouldn't have to depend on affirmation from someone to let you know you're good enough just the way you're. What separates the successful individuals from all the others is that they don't base their self-worth on someone else's opinions. We depend on their judgment, and that's perfect if we make mistakes along the way. They are learning from it and coming back up again. Believing in yourself can be among your most potent defenses against an attack by a manipulator.

- Quit Trying So Hard to Fit in The Wrong Crowd-If you've got to work too hard to fit in with a group of people, they're not the right group for you. Manipulators are charming and popular enough to make you feel like you're part of their crowd, and they love feeling in control by making you work hard to earn their approval. They know that keeping you in this state enables them to get away with more "favor" because you will be more than willing to do what they just want to feel accepted. Don't let yourself be subjected to their manipulative ways any longer unless they can accept you for who you are; don't worry, there are plenty of other people who will. Each time you've had to work so hard to feel welcomed, that means you're working hard for the wrong people.

- Don't compromise-Undermining your own beliefs and principles is one of the many significant mistakes you might make when dealing with a manipulator. When you go against everything you believe in just to do what they want, you play right into their hands. It's all right if they make you feel bad or guilty (just another one of their tricks), let them do whatever they want. What's important is that you don't compromise your happiness, emotions, time, and energy in circles that try to accommodate them anymore. Ask yourself this: If the roles were reversed, would they be willing to do the same for you? Go back to basic rules once again, where you have the right to put your happiness and your needs first.

- Don't ask for permission-It's a hard habit to ask for permission to break. Ever since we were children, we have been taught to do that, asking our parents for permission whenever we wanted to do something. We had to ask the teachers in school for permission for the things we needed. As adults, we ask our supervisors or managers for permission before taking action. We ask permission from our partners in a relationship to get their approval before we make a move. Asking for permission can be a tough habit to break because of this. When you allow the manipulator to be in charge, you are continually seeking consent and demanding permission, rather than taking control and making your own decisions. Isn't it time to end this? This is your life, after all, and not theirs. Why are you waiting around to get their permission to tell you what to do?

- Choose Your Own Intent-You certainly don't want to do what the manipulator wants you to do. Those operating without a sense of purpose make it easier for those with a stronger will and agenda to control themselves. That is why manipulators continue to be influential today because so many people go around without a sense of purpose, leaving themselves open to being exploited. If you don't have a good sense of your own identity, you're more likely to believe what you're told and do what you're ordered to do. Because you don't have that bigger purpose of focusing on, of basing your choices on. The bigger purpose that dictates what you are ready to do and what you are not. It is easy to spot other people around you who may not even have a strong sense of purpose. They're the ones who often flit without any real rhyme or reason throughout their lives. They are the ones who work useless jobs that either inspire or fill them with happiness, yet they do not have any real desire to change the situation. They are the ones who spend far too much time concentrating on negative gossip and other meaningless information that does not serve any real purpose. This lack of focus is what manipulators are just waiting to pounce on, so it's time to start thinking long and hard about what your goal will be if you haven't found your sense of purpose yet. Give yourself something specific to concentrate on, and you're less likely to fall victim to temptation and deceit.

- Take on New Challenges-there are new possibilities all around you; all you need to do is be bold enough to take a risk and a leap of faith. Manipulators tend to stop you from taking on new opportunities, and in the same process, they want to tie you down. They want you to live in the same loop that you are because this makes it much easier for them to retain control. That's why they are sowing seeds of self-doubt in your mind, and why they're working hard to discourage you from improving yourself or seizing new chances. Every time you grow more durable and more comfortable, you lose their grip over you, which they work hard to prevent. They're going to try too hard to keep you in your place; they're going to even resort to making you feel ashamed even to entertain the thought of taking on new opportunities to improve yourself. Don't let them stop you, and don't let go of self-doubt. Even successful people made many mistakes along the way to get to where they are right now; all they did was have the courage to take the leap and make a change for the better.

- Stop Being a Punching Bag-Manipulators will only continue to treat you as a punching bag if you allow them to do so. Respect yourself enough to stand up and say you're not worthy of this type of treatment. Because, you are not. Stop being a punching bag, start taking responsibility for your decisions, and remember that there's no reason to feel guilty about standing up to someone who doesn't treat you fairly.

Manipulators will always seek to do whatever they can to undermine your faith and weaken you enough to take control of you. They will claim to be concerned about you, or that they just have the best interest in mind. They will convince you they want to "help," when the truth is, they will be the only person they want to help, and if they have to step on their toes to do so, they will. They can be hard to get rid of once you bring them into your life, but your know-how can be done now. The final key is never to stop working to build your self-confidence, the healthier you are, the less control they have over you.

Chapter 16: Reasons of Manipulation and How to Overcome It

The only time when manipulation is considered successful is the time when you allow it to control your emotions and thoughts. Thus, you must start to distinguish what is going on in you that allows you to be easily manipulated by other people. The three most basic reasons we let ourselves to be manipulated are as follows:

• Fear

This emotion comes in numerous structures. As human beings, we tend to fear losing a relationship; we may fear the disapprobation of other people; we dread to make somebody discontent with our actions. We additionally dread the dangers and outcomes of the manipulator's actions. Imagine a scenario in which they prevail at doing what they threaten.

• Guilt

Today, we are clouded by the idea and responsibility that we should dependably prioritize other people's needs and wants rather than our own. At times when people would talk about the right to fulfill their own needs and wants, manipulators frequently abuse us and endeavor to allow us to feel like we are accomplishing something immoral if we do not generally put their needs and wants in front of our own. Those individuals who are skilled at these manipulative tactics would tend to define love as the act of fulfilling their needs and wants as part of your obligation. Hence, if we have an opinion that goes against their beliefs, we are manipulated into thinking that we are heartless; at this point, they would make us feel very regretful of our existence and would use guilt to manipulate us.

• Being too nice

We appreciate being a provider, fulfilling individuals, and dealing with the needs of other people. We discover fulfillment. Moreover, our confidence would regularly originate from doing what we can for other people. In any case, at times when there is a lack of an unmistakable feeling of these and fair limitations, skilled manipulators can detect this in people who are easy targets of this phenomenon, and will use certain tactics to further their selfish gains.

What You Need To Do To Overcome Manipulation

We have come to a point where we are here to talk about the basic skills to overcome manipulation. Moreover, manipulation would only work if you allow them to control you. Much like hypnosis, any hypnosis is self-hypnosis. We are trying to state here that knowledge that you are being manipulated defeats its entire purpose.

• Establish a clear sense of self

There is a need to know your identity, your needs and wants, what your emotions are, and what you are fond of and not fond of. You must learn to accept these and not become apologetic, as these are the things that make you. At times, we dread that we are viewed by others as egotistical and called out for being selfish in the event of speaking up. Nevertheless, knowing your identity or what you need in life is not at all an act of selfishness. Self-centeredness demands that you always get what you want or that other has always put your needs and wants first. Similarly, when another person calls you out for not following their orders or fulfilling their needs and wants, they are the ones being selfish, not you.

• Say "no" despite the other person's disapproval

The ability to say "no" despite somebody's objection is a solid demonstration. Individuals who can do this are present in

97

reality. Because in reality, there is no way that we can accommodate all of their needs and wants. When this happens, they will become baffled, even disappointed. However, keep in mind that what they are feeling is part of human nature. Most of these individuals would then forgive and forget. Sound individuals realize that getting what you want all the time is not possible, even when the desires are genuine. In any case, when we cannot endure another person's mistake or objection, it ends up hard stating "no." It winds up more diligently for us to state it or have limits. Manipulators exploit this shortcoming and use dissatisfaction and objection in extraordinary structures to get us to do what they need.

• Tolerate the other person's negative affect

We can demonstrate compassion for people's pity, hurt, or even annoyance when accommodating them without needing to back down and reverse our decision. Keep in mind, a solid relationship is described by common minding, shared genuineness, and shared regard. If you are involved with somebody who uses manipulation and unhealthy control consistently, begin to see little propensities that may not be clear to you at first. As you are more grounded, you are better ready to endure how the other individual's negative impact on you is only bringing you down. Thus, this turns into a positive development that liberates you from their manipulative grasps. This will engender a complexity of sorts with the people in your life. The manipulator may start to withdraw and consider your time, emotions, wants, and needs, or they will proceed onward to someone else who is an easy target of manipulation practices.

Chapter 17: Character Traits of a Manipulator

Is language the primary tool of deviously manipulative people? How can words have such a powerful effect on us?

How a manipulative person's mind works, is most likely only something a manipulative person could comprehend. The rest of us think about in confusion, wondering why or how someone could behave this way. Though, in some small way, we can all be a little manipulative at times. For example, most people will be willing to bend the truth, or omit information, on the odd occasion. For much the same reasons, such as trying to get others to do something for them or even to get permission for something. Trying to convince someone of your argument or get them to come around to your way of thinking, is a natural and evolutionary process. Pinker and Bloom (1990) claimed that we evolved to use language because it helped us adapt to our environments. Surviving hostile elements is easier if we can persuade others to help us persevere.

The use of language to manipulate others to help us is the evolutionary adaptation, appears to be a natural process. Why then, do some individuals manipulate others for more pervasive means? Not for survival or evolutionary means, but purely for their own selfish needs. If they cannot achieve this control, they feel helpless and lack any agency in their lives. Why? Are they evil, are they unkind, are they born that way? Some might say it is a personality disorder that is bordering on a narcissistic level.

We will all try to persuade someone at some point in our lives, but we are not all narcissists. Whatever the reason for our attempts at persuasion, we usually want to remain on good terms with the person we are trying to manipulate. Not so for those who manipulate to control.

Kier Harding, a lead Mental Health practitioner, wrote a relevant article in The Diagnosis of Exclusion. He argued that those diagnosed with a personality disorder are people who are not very good at manipulating. Their attempts tend to be forceful and over exaggerated. Whereas a skillful manipulator will aim to persuade someone less overtly. It is because they are not very good at it, that makes them unlikable characters with poor interpersonal skills. Usually also with a low self-esteem because of their background in life. This could be an argument indicating that controlling manipulators are from dysfunctional backgrounds.

How Then Can We Recognize Such A Deviant Person?

Common Traits

Use of Language

We have shown how powerful language can be, as a prime tool of persuasion. There is more to the manipulative controller though than mere words. They will use tactics that mislead and unbalance their target's inner thoughts. We now understand that through language, they will:

- Use mistruths to mislead and confuse their target's normal thinking pattern.
- Force their target to decide speed, so they don't have time to analyze and think.
- Overwhelmingly talk to their target, making them feel small.
- Criticize their target's judgment so they begin to lose their self-esteem.
- Raise the tone of their voice and not be afraid to use aggressive body language.
- Ignore their target's needs, they are only interested in getting what they want and at any cost.

Invasion of Personal Space

Most of us set boundaries around ourselves without realizing we are doing so. It is a kind of unspoken rule to protect our private space, such as not sitting so close that you are touching another person, especially a stranger. A manipulative character cares nothing about overstepping such boundaries. Whether this is because they do not understand, or they do not care is unclear. Initially, they are unlikely to invade their target's personal space. They will seek to build up a good rapport first. This shows that they understand boundaries because once they gain the confidence of their target, they will then ignore them.

Fodder For Thought

Manipulators tend to be very ego-centric, with limited social skills. Their only concern is for themselves. Everything they do in life will be about how it affects them, not how their actions affect others. Does this mean that they have a psychopathic disorder?

Take empathy for instance. Controlling manipulators are unlikely ever to show empathy. Empathy is a natural human emotion that aids in our survival techniques. A study by Meffert et al. indicates that those with a psychopathic disorder can control empathetic emotions. They lack sympathy of any kind because another weakness is simply another tool for them. When they detect any weakness in their target's resolve or personality, they will exploit it. The consequences to their victim are of little importance. The targets weakness's feed the manipulator's strength, making them bolder and often crueler in their actions.

Creating Rivalry

Another tactic of the controlling manipulator is backstabbing. They may tell you how great a person you are to your face, making themselves look good. Behind your back, they are busy spreading malicious gossip and untruths about you. This is a classic trait of a controlling manipulator as it creates a rivalry between people. Then, they can pick sides that will make them look favorable, particularly to their target. It can act as the first stage to getting close to their target. Once bonded, they can build up trust, making it easier to manipulate the target in the future. If you recognize a backstabber, keep them at a distance. Their plan is selfish so it is better not let them into your personal life. There is no point treating them as they treat you, in revenge. It will turn out to be exhausting playing them at their own game. If they know that you are on to them, they may attempt to lure you back with praise, remember that it is false.

Domineering Personality

It is unlikely that a manipulative person will outwardly show any form of weakness. An important part of their facade is to show conviction about their views. They seek to impress,

believing they are right about everything. Almost to the point that if they realize they are wrong, they will still argue that they are right. On a one-to-one level, that invariably means that your position is always wrong. As they will chip away at your beliefs, they seek to undermine your sense of self-esteem. Once they have achieved this, then there is no holding them back. They seek to domineer others, often speaking with a condescending tone to belittle their victims. Using ridicule is yet another tool against their target, merely because it will make themselves look better. If you ridicule them back, they will seek to turn the tables, accusing you of being oversensitive to their "joke." The kind of joke that only the teller sees the funny side.

Passive Aggressive Behavior

A common trait of many hard-core manipulators is passive aggressive behavior. Because they prefer to be popular, they do not wish to be seen as doing anything wrong. Not that a manipulator would ever admit to doing anything wrong. They are experts with facial expressions that are meant to dominate and intimidate. This may include; knitting eyebrows, grinding teeth and rolling eyes. It may also include noises such as tutting and grunting sounds. It is a very common behavior for such a character, as little anyone else has to say that they will agree upon. For most manipulators, it is their life's ambition to show people up by proving them wrong.

This can range from the confrontational look, where they seek to stare their target down. Or, It could be in response to their disagreement on something their target said. They may smirk and shake their head, turn their back, anything to show their strong disapproval. It is all a ploy to make themselves look superior and put others down.

Moody Blues

What of emotional stability of the manipulator? Is it that which makes them behave the way they do? Do they even know what happiness is? The answer to that is a most definite yes, at least to the latter.

Happiness is a tool used initially to help them manipulate, a happy target is more likely to comply. In itself, this makes the manipulator happy, or at least in a sense of what they consider happiness. But their joyfulness is a perverted model of what most others consider happiness to be. Their happiness is often built on the foundations of another's misery. A misery that they have caused with their cruel manipulations. Equally though, a manipulator is prone to mood swings. Most likely to happen when things are not going to plan. One minute they are euphoric at their latest conquest. Then next they could be completely deflated at their failure to succeed. One thing is certain for those who live with or become a target of this type of domineering character, they will be unhappy all the time.

Intimidation

One aspect of manipulation, often used as a last resort, is intimidation and bullying. When everything else has failed, they begin to use threats to get their way. Some though may use intimidation from the onset. It may in a source of authority. For example, let's take the role of a manipulative boss. You have requested a day off. They don't want to allow you your request but have no choice, it is your right. This type of person would want their pound of flesh first. They will set goals for you to reach so it will delay or cancel your request, such as moving project deadlines forward. This way they have their little victory over you.

Alternatively, such a manipulator may use the tactic of the silent treatment. Ignoring someone to the point that it becomes obvious you have displeased them. They seek to make you feel the guilty party.

Other more direct intimidating actions may include stance. Using their height or build to tower over you, or standing uncomfortably close.

Be careful as they will seek revenge for wrongdoings they perceive done to them. Nothing will go unnoticed under their watchful eye. Everyone is a potential target. But, the weak are more likely to walk into their traps, because they are the ones who are easier to dominate. The vulnerable will have little resistance and are easier to bully and coerce. Many of these traits seem more fitting to men, but women can be cruelly manipulative too.

This is a person who will never back down in an argument. Never admit they are wrong. Never apologize for anything. A manipulator will never show respect but will expect everyone else to show them respect.

They love nothing more than to embarrass others. Playing the dumb one is common practice, just to force another person to explain themselves further. At every opportunity, the manipulator will jump in with some sarcastic remark, "hurry up, we're all waiting for your intellectual explanation," or "why has no one else ever heard of this?" Their sole aim is to make the other person look a fool, but without seeming to be the one who made it happen. Oh no, the victim did that to themselves because they are stupid.

Chapter 18: Behavioral Traits of Favorite Victims of Manipulators

Certain characteristics and behavioral traits make people more vulnerable to manipulation, and people with dark psychology traits know this full well. They tend to seek out victims who have those specific behavioral traits because they are essentially easy targets. Let's discuss 6 of the traits of the favorite victims of manipulators.

Emotional Insecurity and Fragility

Manipulators like to target victims who are emotionally insecure or emotionally fragile. Unfortunately for these victims, such traits are very easy to identify even in total strangers, so it's easy for experienced manipulators to find them.

Emotionally insecure people tend to be very defensive when they are attacked or under pressure, making them easy to spot in social situations. Even after just a few interactions, a manipulator can gauge how insecure a person is with a certain degree of accuracy. They'll try to provoke their potential targets subtly, and then wait to see how they react. If they are overly defensive, manipulators will take it as a sign of insecurity, and they will intensify their manipulative attacks.

Manipulators can also tell if a target is emotionally insecure if he/she redirects accusations or negative comments. They will find a way to put you on the spot, and if you try to throw it back at them or make excuses instead of confronting the situation head-on, the manipulator could conclude that you are insecure and therefore an easy target.

People who have social anxiety also tend to have emotional insecurity, and manipulators are aware of it. In social gatherings, they can easily spot individuals who have social anxiety, then target them for manipulation. "Pickup artists" can

106

identify the girls who seem uneasy in social situations by conducting themselves. Social anxiety is difficult to conceal, especially to manipulators who are experienced at preying on emotional vulnerability.

Emotional fragility is different from emotional insecurity. Emotionally insecure people tend to show it all the time, while emotionally fragile people appear to be normal, but they break down emotionally at the slightest provocation. Manipulators like targeting emotionally fragile people because it's very easy to elicit a reaction from them. Once a manipulator finds out that you are emotionally fragile, he will jump at the change to manipulate you because he knows it would be fairly easy.

Sensitive People

Highly sensitive people are those individuals who process information at a deeper level and are more aware of the subtleties in social dynamics. They have lots of positive attributes because they tend to be very considerate of others, and they watch their step to avoid causing people any harm, whether directly or indirectly. Such people tend to dislike any form of violence or cruelty, and they are easily upset by news reports about disastrous occurrences, or even depictions of gory scenes in movies.

Sensitive people also tend to get emotionally exhausted from taking in other people's feelings. When they walk into a room, they have the immediate ability to detect other people's moods, because they are naturally skilled at identifying and interpreting other people's body language cues, facial expressions, and tonal variations.

Manipulators like to target sensitive people because they are easy to manipulate. If you are sensitive to certain things, manipulators can use them against you. They will feign certain emotions to draw sensitive people in so that they can exploit them.

Sensitive people also tend to scare easily. They have a heightened "startle reflex," which means that they are more likely to show clear signs of fear or nervousness in potentially threatening situations. For example, sensitive people are more likely to jump up when someone sneaks up on them, even before determining whether they are in any real danger. If you are a sensitive person, this trait can be very difficult to hide, and malicious people will see it from a mile away.

Manipulators can also identify sensitive people by listening to how they talk. Sensitive people tend to be very proper; they never use vulgar language, and they tend to be very politically correct because they are trying to avoid offending anyone. They also tend to be polite, and they say please and thank you more often than others. Manipulators go after such people because they know that they are too polite to dismiss them right away; sensitive people will indulge anyone because they don't want to be rude. That gives maliciously people a way in.

Emphatic People

Emphatic people are generally similar to highly sensitive people, except that they are more attuned to others' feelings and the energy of the world around them. They tend to internalize other people's suffering to the point that it becomes their own. In fact, for some of them, it can be difficult to distinguish someone's discomfort from their own. Emphatic people make the best partners because they feel everything you feel. However, this makes them particularly easy to manipulate, so malicious people like to target them.

Malicious people can feign certain emotions, and convey those emotions to emphatic people, who will feel them as real. That opens them up for exploitation. Emphatic people are the favorite targets of psychopathic conmen because they feel so deeply for others. A conman can make up stories about financial difficulties and swindle lots of money from emphatic people.

The problem with being emphatic is that because you have such strong emotions, you easily dismiss your doubts about people because you would much rather offer help to a person who turns out to be a lair than deny help to a person who turns out to be telling the truth.

Malicious people like to get into relationships with emphatic people because they are easy to take advantage of. Emphatic people try to avoid getting into intimate relationships in the first place because they know that it's easy for them to get engulfed in such relationships and to lose their identities in the process. However, manipulators will doggedly pursue them because they know that they can guilt the emphatic person into doing anything they want once they get it.

Fear of Loneliness

Many people are afraid of being alone, but this fear is heightened in a small percentage of the population. This kind of fear can be truly paralyzing for those who experience it, and it can open them up to exploitation by malicious people. For example, many people stay in dysfunctional relationships because they are afraid, they will never find someone else to love them if they break up with an abusive partner. Manipulators can identify this fear in a victim, and they'll often do everything they can to fuel it further to make sure that the person is crippled by it. People who are afraid of being alone can tolerate or even rationalize any kind of abuse.

The fear of being alone can be easy to spot in a potential victim. People with this kind of fear tend to exude some desperation level at the beginning of relationships, and they can sometimes come across as clingy. While ordinary people may think of being clingy as a red flag, manipulative people will see it as an opportunity to exploit somebody. If you are attached to them, they'll use manipulative techniques to become even more dependent on them. They can withhold love and affection (e.g., by using the silent treatment) to make the victim fear that he/she is about to get dumped so that they act out of desperation and cede more control to the manipulator.

The fear of being alone is, for the most part, a social construct, and it disproportionately affects women more than men. For generations, our society has taught women that their goal in life is to get married and have children. Even the more progressive women who reject this social construct are still plagued by social pressures to adhere to those old standards. That being said, the fact is that men also tend to be afraid of being alone.

People with abandonment issues stemming from childhood tend to experience the fear of loneliness to a higher degree. Some may not necessarily fear loneliness in general, but they are afraid of being separated from important people. For example, many people end up staying in abusive or dysfunctional relationships because they are afraid of being separated from their children.

Fear of Disappointing Others

We all feel a certain sense of obligation towards the people in our lives, but some are extremely afraid of disappointing others. This kind of fear is similar to the fear of embarrassment and the fear of rejection because it means that the person puts a lot of stock into how others perceive them. The fear of disappointing others can occur naturally. It can be useful in some situations; parents who are afraid of disappointing their families will work harder to provide for them, and children who are afraid of disappointing their parents will study harder at school. In this case, the fear is constructive. However, it becomes unhealthy when directed at the wrong people, or when it forces you to compromise your comfort and happiness.

When manipulators find out that you have a fear of disappointing others, they'll try to put you in a position where you feel like you owe them something. They'll do certain favors for you, and then they'll manipulate you into believing that you have a sense of obligation towards them. They will then guilt you into complying with any request whenever they want something from you.

Personality Dependent Disorders and Emotional Dependency

Dependent personality disorder refers to a real disorder characterized by a person having an excessive and even pervasive need to be taken care of. This need often leads the person to be submissive towards the people in their lives and be clingy and afraid of separation. People with this disorder act in ways that are meant to elicit caregiving. They tend to practice what's called "learned helplessness." This is where they act out of a conviction that they cannot do certain things for themselves, and they need the help of others.

Manipulators like to target people with dependent personality disorders because they are very easy to control and dominate.

These people willingly cede control over their lives to others, so when manipulators come knocking, they don't face much resistance. Manipulators start by giving them a false sense of security, but once they have won their trust, they switch gears and start imposing their will on them.

Emotional dependency is somewhat similar to dependent personality disorder, but it doesn't rise to clinical significance. It stems from having low self-esteem, and it's often a result of childhood abandonment issues. People with an emotional dependency will play the submissive role in relationships for fear of losing their partners. They tend to be very agreeable because they want to please the people in their lives. Such people are easy to manipulate, and malicious people can easily dominate them.

Chapter 19: Manipulators Are Everywhere

It is worth noting that manipulative people don't always come out of nowhere. Often, we find individuals with this behavior in the workplace, at school, and in the family. The characteristics presented above are shaped according to the mode of conviviality. Here's how to deal with manipulative people in these environments:

At Work

In a professional environment, the manipulator is the employee always ready to help. But remember, it's a compulsive help. He stays at the heels of colleagues, reinforcing at all times how much he loves helping colleagues who have difficulties in their tasks. The manipulator on the desktop can stay up later, and even take a break in the office, all for the "pleasure of helping others". The targets of "goodwill" are charmed with such dedication.

The manipulator is seen as the company's legal person, employee and fellow in charge in most of the work. However, this establishes a relationship of dependence. Whoever is the target of "goodwill" is being placed in a web. The one who receives the "help" loses his autonomy since he cannot act without asking for the manipulator's opinion. Consequently, he loses confidence and does everything not to lose this "friendship". When the victim begins to perceive himself as such and tries to escape, the manipulator reverses the roles and convinces his prey that he is bad. The prey, in turn, accepts such a condition and follows the will of his tormentor.

- How to get rid of the manipulator at work?

Be firm and kindly dispense unsolicited favors. When the manipulator takes the day off to flatter you, return the compliments, but make it clear that you are just doing your duty, and anyone else would do the same. The manipulator will be amazed at your steadiness.

In School

At school, the manipulator is the perfect colleague. The manipulator targets unpopular students who are constantly ridiculed.

The manipulator praises the high notes, you are sure that the "new friend" is the best student. When his grades are low, he places the teacher's blame because the teacher certainly did it to harm him. He does not hesitate to defend injustice. There is no bad time that prevents you from helping with the activities and the manipulator makes a point of doing the work with you. The target of such unknowing friendship reveals what time he leaves home, what time it takes to drive there, reveals possible enmities with other students, tells of his fears and anguish. The manipulator reveals nothing about his life.

When the victim begins to realize that something is strange and tries to disengage, the manipulator feels extremely offended. He

114

places the "friend" as an unjust person, unable to recognize true friendship. The manipulator depreciates the "friend", listing his defects, and claims that he will return to being a solitary person and be ridiculed if the friendship ends. The prey, who already had low self-esteem, is even more vulnerable. Thus, the victim believes the manipulator, apologizes, and no longer measures their efforts to do all the manipulator's will, so afraid of losing the "friendship".

- How to get rid of the manipulator in school?

If you feel that you are being cheated again, move away slowly. Speak only as necessary and ask other people's opinions on how to deal with the situation.

In The Family

In the family, the manipulator sticks close to that shy relative and is considered good by everyone. It may be that cousin who always compliments, even when the victim has done something that isn't so great. The manipulator justifies his "object of affection" blockades and believes that his target is wronged. He insists on telling us how much he loves us and is happy to be with such special people.

The manipulator is always ready to go to the mall, help with school activities, go to the doctor's office and do some repairs. However, when the target begins to be bothered by the excessive clinginess and flattery, the manipulator turns the tables and lowers his victim. The manipulator underscores his lack of social skills and how he is seen as lonely, poor, and unable to have friends. The sentences that the victim says will continue to be seen as unimportant. The already emotionally unstable target agrees with everything, apologizes, and resumes "friendship", doing everything according to his tormentor's will, afraid of not being able to count on such a valuable person.

- How to get rid of the manipulator in the family?

Family ties make things harder. But we must put an end to this vicious circle. Ask the opinion of people outside the family spectrum. Even if it is not possible to cut the manipulator out of the conversation, talk only when necessary.

Differences Between Male And Female Manipulators

The behavior between men and women is different in several respects. In the question of manipulation, there are also singularities.

Men

Male manipulators have the following characteristics:

Shy: The manipulator observes the behavior of everyone around him. He transmits fragility and submission to convince himself that he is a needy person;

Handsome: Manipulators are always friendly, extroverted and know how to live life. They show extremely worried and attentive with their "friends", but they make a point of showing who is in charge. The victims do not feel the courage to disagree with such a nice man. But when he goes to a boring event, he does not bother to disguise his boredom;

Altruist: He gives many gifts, does numerous favors, always intending to receive something in return. When it is not "retributed" it gives people a sense of guilt;

Seductive: Vain and attractive. He looks into others' eyes, asks embarrassing questions and loves to make a mystery of himself;

Worship: Has excessive admiration for diplomas, pompous professional curricula, and social projection. He subtly shows contempt for those who do not have the same knowledge. He loves to embarrass people, monopolizes conversations, and gets annoyed when someone interrupts his speech.

Women

Manipulative women behave in the following ways:

In front of everyone, they are true porcelain dolls. But when the target moves away, she's stupid with people. When the victim returns she will be candid with him/her;

Use beauty as a weapon to get what she wants. It seems absurd to someone not to praise it.

She uses a sensual tone of voice and promises a thousand wonders to those who satisfy her requests; she wants the target to guess her wishes and surprise her with trips, restaurants, and luxury gifts. She becomes angry if her requests are not answered.

Her emotions can be radical. When you are right, she wants to prove that it's better that you are wrong. When she is wrong, she does not admit it and insists until someone believes in her.

They cry too much. If the victim wants to go out with other people, she cries because she was "betrayed." If she is asked how the car got scratched, she cries because she was accused of being a bad driver. She is "fragile" to the point of not carrying a suitcase or not being able to open the car door.

Manipulative people enter our lives because they see that we are going through a moment of vulnerability. We feed these people by providing intimate information. But if we allow them to enter our lives, it is up to us to remove them from the scene. The task is difficult, but these tips can be useful:

Do not feel guilty for not satisfying the wishes of the manipulator. Often they are irrational and seem like things a child who wants attention at any cost may request. Ask probing questions, question what will change if you attend to the manipulator's wishes. Ask yourself how your feelings were before and how they are now. Learn not to speak to those who do not do you good; this means you must avoid saying yes to the manipulator.

If none of this works out, move away. If it is not possible to physically get the person out of your life, move away emotionally and speak only about the basics. Remember that manipulative people are "toxic people", non-evolved beings who want to suck energy and steal others' autonomy. No one deserves to live in the shadow of others, no one deserves to live having to consult someone at every step. Emotional independence is the key to a happy existence.

Chapter 20: Understanding the Dark Triad and What It Means

Now, we need to take a look at the dark triad. This is a very important concept because it will help tie together some of the other aspects that we have in Dark Psychology. The name "dark triad" may sound like something that comes from a horror movie, but it is a legitimate psychological concept that is well recognized.

The dark triad is nothing more than an identification system for the three most destructive and harmful psychological personality traits a person can have. This will take some time to detail each of the traits, including narcissism, psychopathy, and Machiavellianism. Let's take a look at each part and see what it means when it comes to dark psychology.

What Is Machiavellianism?

The first aspect of the Dark Triad that we will discuss is known as Machiavellianism. This aspect gets its name from the political philosopher known as Machiavelli. In his classical work, "The Prince," the ideas, principles, and tactics used by those who seek to influence others are outlined. But how exactly does a Machiavellian person come across?

The hallmarks of this trait include a willingness to focus on your self-interest all the time, an understanding of the importance of your image, the perception of appearance, and even the ruthless exercise of power and cruelty rather than using mercy or compassion.

To keep it simple, people who have this trait always have a strategy when approaching life. The consequences and any ramifications about any action will be thought out and then assessed in terms of how they will impact the one who is carrying them out. The Machiavellian approach to the world is summed up with a simple question: "How will this action benefit me, and how will my public perception be impacted as a result?"

Machiavellian people will be masters of doing what is going to personally serve them well, while still being able to maintain the good public image that they want. This allows the manipulator to do what they want, while getting people around them to like them still.

What Is Psychopathy?

The next aspect that we will discuss is psychopathy. This will refer to a psychological condition that involves a superficial charm, impulsivity, and a lack of commonly held human emotions, such as remorse and empathy. Someone who exhibits enough of these traits can be known as a psychopath. These individuals are seen as some of the most dangerous people because they can hide their true intentions while still causing a lot of trouble.

People often associate the word "psychopath" with an image of madness and wields a machete. The reality is different, and this can make it more deadly. A true psychopath is more likely to be that charming and handsome stranger who can win over their victim before they ruin their lives.

Interestingly, some of the top people in business score high on psychopathy personality tests. But as time goes on, it is becoming more common to see psychopathy as more of a problem to the victim and society rather than an issue in the psychopath's own life. Psychopaths can get to the top of anything they choose because they don't have to worry about some of the compassionate indecision that other humans will experience.

What Is Narcissism?

The third aspect of the Dark Triad that we need to explore is narcissism. This is often thought of like the idea that a person loves themselves too much. This is close but quite the right definition for someone who is a narcissist. You can have self-love without being considered a narcissist.

Someone who is considered a narcissist is likely to have a range of traits that are there. They will have an overly inflated self-worth, such as seeing that their lives are extra special and one of the most important lives in history. If this has been inflated enough, they may see that they are the most important in the world.

In the mind of a narcissist, they are not only special, but they are superior to everyone else. They consider themselves to be a better species of person, higher than what normal people would be. And because a narcissist believes this way, their behaviors are going to change. The behavior that you see in a narcissist is going to reflect the self-worth that the person has.

Some of the outward signs or manifestations of this aspect would include the person's inability to accept any dissent or criticism of any kind. Even if they feel that someone is trying to criticize them, they will have a hard time dealing with this. This kind of person also feels the need to have others agree with them all the time, and they like to be flattered. If you are around someone who seems always to need constant praise, recognition, and approval, and if they seem to organize their lives to give them constant access to those who will fill this need, then it is likely that you are dealing with someone who is a narcissist.

These three aspects are going to come together to form the Dark Triad. When one person has all of these three traits in them, it can be a hard task to stay away and not get pulled into whatever plan they have. Being on the lookout for these can make a big difference in how much control you have in your personal life.

Chapter 21: Mind Games

 When a person plays "mind games" on us, it is attributed to being innocent. Many people have come across this at some point in their life. Take an example when someone is planning a surprise party and doesn't want the other person to know and he does this by playing mind tricks not to give away what the surprise is. This is merely considered innocent and silly. Dark psychology mind games are not in any way innocent. Mind games in dark psychology are attributed to the hypnotist toying with his victim's will power and sanity. This differs from other dark psychological manipulation in the sense that the manipulator is playing with his victim for his pleasure and enjoyment and is not invested in what the outcome will be. His interest in the victim would be to test the victim so to speak. Mind games are used by a hypnotist when other forms of suggestions to the victim are not effective and may decide to use mind games which are rather less obvious to the audience. The manipulator may decide to use mind games to his pleasure and amusement. Mind games are very effective in reducing the assuredness and psychological strength of the victim. The victim is eluded into thinking that he still has control. Manipulators can satisfy their twisted amusement when playing mind games. Such dark psychological manipulators do not see their victims as equal human beings. Instead, they choose to see the victim as a 'toy' and, therefore, watch with amusement when victims do what they tell them to. Sometimes, a dark manipulator will have known mind games all his life and knows no other forms of dark psychology manipulation. These manipulators can be dangerous because they know not of any other option and therefore no need to

change and be more humane. Let us dive into the specific types of mind games used by dark manipulators.

Ultimatum

An ultimatum can be defined as a final proposition or condition. One, therefore, is presented with a severe choice. They are viewed more as demands other than a request. An example is, "Be more outgoing...or I will see other people". Certain factors will decide whether an ultimatum will be considered as a mind game. The three factors are one, the type of person giving the ultimatum, second the intention for giving the ultimatum and lastly the nature of the ultimatum.

Persons who give ultimatums and genuinely care about the persons and have a valid reason for doing so, and then it will fall under the non-dark manipulation. These persons will generally include spouses, parents, siblings or close relatives. However, if they fall into any of the categories mentioned, it does not necessarily rid them of dark intentions from the ultimatum.

What was the intention of the person giving the ultimatum? People with good intentions are often driven by the desire to help or assist in bettering a person's life. A person gives an ultimatum to stop smoking or drinking too much, then this seen as good intentions. Being able to tell the intention of an ultimatum is difficult, so looking at the nature of the ultimatum itself is the surest way to tell whether it is dark.

Dark manipulative ultimatums will involve the person doing something that goes against what they stand for and goes against their self-interest. The victim ends up comprising their moral standards in the process. Manipulators test their victims to see how far they go in compromising what they believe in. As we have seen, non-dark ultimatums are usually to benefit another person and the does not have to go against what they know is wrong.

What is a dark psychological ultimatum? The person giving the ultimatum will be a friend, a boss or a person who the victim is in a toxic relationship with. It could also the form of a spouse, a parent or a sibling. The manipulator will often give ultimatums that go against the victim's moral conviction or possibly be dangerous to the victim. Here, the dark manipulator will notice a disinclination towards something and take advantage of this to make their victim do their bidding.

An example will be a girl who is not comfortable in wearing costumes or revealing clothes. Some of the ultimatums will be, "It's an only costume party, it is either you wear one or you are not invited". Some ultimatums lead to harm to others such as assault and even murder. At very extreme cases, the victim ends up taking his own life in completing a suicide pact in which the manipulator does not honor his end.

The External Break Up

Everybody likes to be in a relationship where there is that sense of security and knowing that your partner is content. A manipulator will know this but will use these for their dark intentions. A manipulator will ensure that their partner will be powerless by instigating feelings of instability, and negativity. This technique of 'The External Break up' is often deployed in a romantic relationship. It manifests itself when a partner continuously to scares the other that he or she will leave them. This is aimed at creating feelings of anxiety and instability within the relationship. This mind game takes the form of promised breakups, implied breakups and actual breakups that do not happen.

Implied breakups are those that are not expressly stating the words 'break up'. Instead, the manipulator throws hints there and then to create some doubt in the partner's mind. They can do this by making statements that exclude their partner from plans together. Promised breakups happen where the dark manipulator scares their partner instead of breaking up with them somewhere soon. Words like, "Don't worry I won't have to deal with this anymore because I'll be leaving soon" show the intention of a breakup in the future. Promise breakups fall in between the implied breakups and the actual breakups. Where the dark manipulator mentions the idea of cutting ties with their partner, either by divorcing, separating or breaking up, but does not follow through then it calls under the promised breakup.

The actual break is the most severe compared to the implied and promised breakups. It happens when the manipulator decides to leave their victim without actually leaving in the end. They may pack up their clothes and belongings in the attempt to leave but once they see the sadness all over their victim's face, they decide otherwise.

After understanding the tactic of the "external break up" we ask ourselves what therefore is the end game for manipulator when they use this tactic? The manipulator aims to have the upper hand in the relationship by creating feelings of uncertainty and lack of security from the victim's life and therefore reducing their power in the hands of the manipulator. By repeatedly simulating a breakup with the victim, the manipulator tries to test the waters of how far one will go in putting up with being treated like a toy. In the end, when the manipulator gives in to the victims' begging for the relationship to continue, they make themselves look like the generous ones. This works so well for the manipulator because his or her victim is not thinking rationally to figure out why they relationship should end. They are therefore willing to continue with the relationship. Many people do not understand this concept of dark psychology and why a person would want to continue to be in a relationship with a dark manipulator in the first place. The impact of this on the victim includes the likelihood of developing serious trust issues where they will have a hard time trusting another person. This could take a toll on the victim's professional relationships and family relationships as well. After a long period of constant threats, the victims become almost like a slave to the manipulator. The manipulator eventually grows tired and moves on to their next prey.

Hard To Get

And just like ultimatums, the hard to get tactic can easily pass off as being normal. Hard to get can be dark as it can be also harmless and normal. Hard to get when it is harmless it occurs when a person will want to make them seem trying to be with them is not as easy. They will do this by making themselves less available by not making to every date and leaving the phone to ring a couple of time before finally picking up. The 'hard to get' dark psychology is much riskier. The manipulator will use this tactic during the relationship rather than at the beginning of the relationship. Unlike the innocent hard to get where the intention is to be in a happy relationship eventually, dark psychology hard is far from taking into account the victim's wellbeing. When used at the beginning of the relationship it is innocent because no expectations are infringed. No one is dependent or reliant on either of the person, so no harm comes from playing hard to get. Further along in a relationship when things are going on well, suddenly, a person is unreliable and often tries to make themselves busy. This kind of behaviour is not normal because relationships are about making and spending time with each other as this will firm up the relationship. A manipulator will be very cunning and start pulling away when their partner us already reliant on them. The victim will therefore put an extra effort to reconnect with their partner. In the end, the manipulator has the upper hand and will use this power to his or her purpose while the victim is left in deep confusion and instability.

Chapter 22: Mind Control Technique

Having control over everyday situations is something all human beings wish for. The ability to command what will happen is the dream of most people. Although it is impossible to accomplish 100% of the time, some techniques allow you to achieve the desired results more often. If you did not know, it is possible to influence someone's actions with simple behaviors and signals sent directly to the person you would like to impact. You can apply the following tips in meetings with your boss, at a job interview, or even with that platonic passion!

1. Honest Smile

You should know that a smile is one of the most important and significant aspects of body language, yet do you know how to give a perfect smile? Some smiles are visibly forceful and hostile, so you should seek to convey truth. But how can we maximize this action? Simply, you should keep your normal countenance and, after only a few seconds, greet the person and give him a sincere smile. Whoever smiles the most can gain greater emotional control of the other person, who will feel more comfortable with his presence.

2. Look

When you are in a group of friends and the person of your interest is there, do not hesitate to direct your attention to him/her. The tendency is to pay attention to what is being deliberated at the wheel of the conversation, but what will attract your interest's attention is the look. When you focus your eyes on the other person, you will automatically catch their attention eventually. If you know how to gauge your looks, it will soon be within your power to get their attention. If you're at a job interview or speaking to the boss, keep your eye on the eyes of the person you're talking to because this increases the chances of that person feeling greater empathy and confidence in you!

3. Be Insistent

You will be impressed by how you can persuade your friends. We already heard the famous phrase that says "A lie repeated a thousand times becomes true", right? But although we are not dealing with lies, you can apply this phrase in the present technique. If you want someone to believe and give credence to what you say, just insist on their perspective. For example, imagine that you want to sell some product and need to show that it is worth buying it. To persuade your buyer, it is no use to be insistent by repeating the same arguments because you will become inconvenient. Instead, try to increase the list of good points to gain credibility, and you will be successful.

4. Justifications

You may not trust it, but you increase your ability to convince the other person to do the desired favor when you justify your requests. Researchers conducted a test in which a woman went to five locations and asked, "Could you pick up the five pages of Xerox for me?" In 60% of the situations, people did not respond to her request. Subsequently, the same test was carried out only with the justification "because I have so much work here that I will not be able to arrive on time" About 94% of the people responded promptly to the request! The next time you have to make a request, be sure to justify the reason!

5. Narrow Ties

Studies have proven that tightening bonds is one of the best techniques for gaining control over another person. The quickest way to have power over someone is to make them feel good in your presence, involving them emotionally. Researchers have discovered that engaging in some kind of activity with the other person generates an emotional connection. While you might find it complicated at first, it's quite simple. For example, you can share your songs as well as find which songs you like together. This will make them feel attached to you!

6. Listen More

If you are a very shy and introspective person, you will probably do this technique successfully. But if you are a more communicative person, do not worry. Studies have shown that people who listen more in the workplace or social gatherings assume a position of power over the others. If you are faced with a hard situation, try to control yourself and listen to everything others have to say. Expect them to ask you for your opinion. At times like this, all the caller's attention will come to you and it will be easier to have a pleasant conversation. This technique will increase your credibility and make your opinion the most considerable in any dialogue.

7. Tell the Truth

Did you know that little lies can end up hurting more than helping? Show the people around you that your life is not based on telling lies to please someone, but that you have a personality strong enough to speak the truth, even if it hurts. Be honest and you will have control of the situation much more easily than telling a lie and slipping afterward.

Use The Past to Influence a Person's Future

Do you realize how much the things you learned in childhood influence your present? Have you noticed that the way parents and educators created an individual's childhood affects their current talents and their fears and limitations? It is almost mathematical the result obtained nowadays. We can even use the equation: parents + education that we had = influence.

Want some practical examples to verify this reality? There is nothing better than the Numerological Challenges to show us the influence - positive or negative - of the way we were educated. The numbers in this position represent those fears that needed to be faced and overcome with our parents' help. It represents the kinds of attitudes and activities we fear most to develop and engage. Hence, the way parents and educators dealt with such difficulties when we were children may indicate whether we view them today with fear or as a differential in our behavior.

So it pays to do this dive into the past and understand the possible effects that the education you received has in your present.

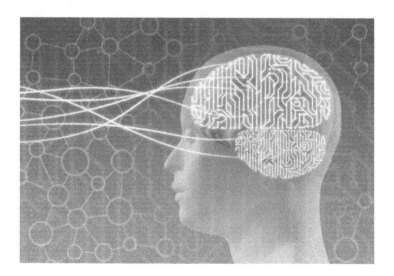

Chapter 23: Brainwashing

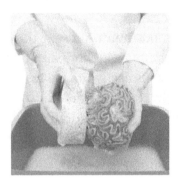

Brainwashing as a manipulation technique is far more powerful than both mind control and hypnosis, but it also requires far more training and expertise to be used most efficiently. While many of the concepts used in hypnosis and mind control overlap with brainwashing, there are also new techniques made available to you when you learn about brainwashing. Like hypnosis, brainwashing is a popular topic and plot device in many books, movies, and other media. Of course, as being the most powerful technique, brainwashing is also more high-profile than hypnosis and mind control. It has been used extensively in certain large-scale scenarios, including by certain governments, cults, corporations, etc. While brainwashing has been known throughout history by many different names, including thought reform, thought control, coercive persuasion, and re-education for the sake of simplicity, this will only refer to it as brainwashing.

By learning more about what brainwashing is and how it works, you will not only have gained a valuable technique for manipulating other people, but you will also be able to more easily recognize when you are being brainwashed by another person or by an organization.

The History of Brainwashing

One of the most well-known portrayals of brainwashing on a massive scale in fiction is found in the book 1984, which was written by George Orwell in 1949. In the book, a massive government entity maintains complete control over its citizens by creating propaganda, using surveillance to spy on people, rationing food, and even training people to use a different language.

There is no magical technology that allows the government to control its citizens' thoughts and actions directly. Still, through the laws it creates and how it enforces those laws, it can make its citizens think and act in only the ways that it wants them to.

Even though 1984 is a work of fiction, governments like the one described in the book have certainly existed in real life and continue to do so today. Of course, brainwashing has been used by other organizations than governments in its history, and different groups have used brainwashing successfully in different ways to further their goals.

While certain forms of brainwashing techniques have been in use for thousands of years, the public did not become aware of brainwashing on a large scale until the 1940s and the 1950s.

At that time, brainwashing was a major part of society in China under Mao Zedong, the Chairman of the Communist Party of China and China's leader overall. The term "brainwashing" comes from the Chinese phrase xǐnǎo, which translates to "wash brain" in English. Americans were not made aware of brainwashing as a phenomenon until after the Korean War had begun. During the war, American soldiers were captured as prisoners of war (POWs), and during their time spent in Chinese prison facilities, they were brainwashed by the Chinese government. The POWs that had been brainwashed were more likely to give over classified information to the Chinese and give false confessions, more willing to do what their captors wanted them to, and even defended the Chinese government's actions.

The United Nations commander at the time stated that "too familiar are the mind-annihilating methods of these Communists in forcing whatever words they want...The men themselves are not to be liable and they have my deepest compassion for having been used in this awful way." In other words, the Chinese were extremely skilled at brainwashing their victims, who would feel the effects of being brainwashed for years after it had been done to them. After American POWs were found to have been brainwashed, the United States Central Intelligence Agency (CIA) ran a series of experiments over twenty years that tested mind control and brainwashing capabilities, the most famous of these experiments being called Project MKUltra. To testing general brainwashing techniques, the CIA also experimented with drugs as a tool for manipulation and attempted to create a so-called truth serum that would be used for interrogation purposes.

From there, brainwashing took hold in the public's minds and began to play a large part in popular culture. Large audiences received stories involving brainwashing, and movies such as The Fearmakers, Toward the Unknown, The Bamboo Prison, The Rack, and The Manchurian Candidate were all inspired in some part by the experience of American POWs during the war or brainwashing in general. Starting in the late 1960s and extending through the mid-1970s, brainwashing as a concept was so deeply rooted in the public consciousness that it even seeped into the criminal justice system. Perhaps the most famous example is Patty Hearst, an heiress who was kidnapped and brainwashed by a terrorist group known as the Symbionese Liberation Army (SLA). She later joined the group as a member and was arrested during an attempted bank robbery.

Her trial was the first widely publicized instance of using brainwashing as a legal defense in court. While she was ultimately found guilty, the defense caused a renewal of interest and concern over brainwashing.

Since the 1960s, brainwashing has also been widely used in recruiting members to cults. The most well-known instance of brainwashing being used in cults is probably that of the Manson Family, founded in 1967 by Charles Manson. Manson was an extremely skilled manipulator, and successfully recruited nearly 100 people, mostly women, into his cult following. He had such a strong influence over them that he was able to convince them to commit several different crimes, from assault and robbery to mass murder. Nearly all cults use some form of brainwashing to influence potential recruits and convince them to join, from the most infamous to cults you have never heard of before. Some cults, such as Heaven's Gate and The People's Temple, used brainwashing to such a powerful effect that their followers were convinced to commit suicide.

Cults are especially important to study brainwashing because they demonstrate how far the power of brainwashing techniques can take people and are a good indicator of when things have gone too far. Suppose you are thinking of using brainwashing or any other manipulation on a person to make them inflict harm on themselves or anyone else. In that case, you should refrain from doing so and seek professional help for yourself.

But why is the history of brainwashing so important to learn about? After all, you are not a government entity such as the Communist Party of China, and you are hopefully not planning on dabbling in becoming a cult leader of any kind. Of course, there are valuable lessons to be learned from the history of brainwashing that you can apply to how you approach and implement brainwashing techniques in your own life. First of all, having a great understanding of brainwashing history should mean that you also have a good understanding of just how powerful brainwashing can be, even on the most unwilling targets. If American soldiers can be brainwashed into defending their captors, the country's enemies that they vowed to serve, then imagine what brainwashing can do for you if used correctly. Secondly, brainwashing history teaches the important lesson that anybody and everybody are susceptible to brainwashing techniques unlike mind control and hypnosis. If you focus on honing your talents and become a skilled enough manipulator, you can brainwash not just one person, but multiple people at a time into doing whatever it is that you want for them to do. The most talented manipulators can exert their influence over hundreds of people all at once, and every single one of their targets will be as thoroughly taught as the last one. This leads me into the final reason why the history of brainwashing is important to have at least some knowledge of because brainwashing is such a powerful and effective tool that can be used on so many people, it can be easy to take brainwashing too far, and force your targets into criminal or even life-threatening situations. By studying brainwashing history, you will know how horrible the effects of brainwashing can be for the target, the manipulator, and for anybody else who gets caught in between. While brainwashing as a tactic is not in and of itself harmful, when used with reckless abandon, things can quickly spiral out of control. As the manipulator, it is your responsibility to know when to stop before something terrible has occurred. Above all else, brainwashing history demonstrates the need to be safe, sensible, and responsible when using brainwashing techniques, as the consequences can be dire if brainwashing is used irresponsibly.

Chapter 24: 10 Steps of Brainwashing

Brainwashing phrases are mostly separate and can be generally divided into three levels. The first stage involves all the methods the abuser takes to tear down their prey; the second phase requires convincing the prey that there is a possibility of redemption; and lastly, the 3rd stage is where the target redeems itself and embraces his new self.

First Stage: Breaking the Target

Step 1: Identity Assaulting

To break down a predator's target, they may be the first target that makes the victim what they are: their ego or identity. Each human being has in his mind an idea of himself which is what they claim to be. This is the way they define themselves. Multiple identities are possible. You could be a mother and a career woman. You may be a smart businessman and an uncle. You may be a hard-fought student at the class. You just might be a Christian. You can choose between endless identities. That identity is your solution to the declaration tell me about yourself a little bit.

Suppose one day you wake up and someone advised you that you're not really what you believe you are. How do you manage to hear that? If this was deliberated in passing, you should possibly shrug it off and go on with your career. Or maybe you'd worry about it for a few hours or minutes, and maybe get frustrated for a bit, then push on. Now imagine someone comes to your home every minute of the day to remind you that you're not the guy you believe you are. How'd that help you feel? If it lasted through months or even weeks, then you will be out of your head by the end of it. You will be startled and left to question where to distinguish between fiction and fact.

If you'd thought about yourself as a great writer before, you'd start to doubt it. If you thought you were your children's biological father, you may start questioning him. If you've grown up thinking you're a real catholic, hearing daily contradictory reports would make you start thinking you might not be.

The first phase in the brainwashing cycle is when the entire dirty work starts taking hold. An individual who has planted the ugly seed of doubt in them is endangered to manipulation. We want to think the best of ourselves, as human beings. Also, we like having other people believe in us the best. Yes, some individuals may not care about someone else's validation and approval. That's admirable and we should all be working towards that. But at the last of the day, the guy who goes to bed thinking he is the worst of the bad periods of sleep more restlessly. Having high self-esteem and a strong sense of self, of course, saves you from the predators willing to attack you.

The result of the first phase of brainwashing is a completely-blown identity issue which the predator could prey on for the second step's purposes.

Step 2: Guilt Manipulation

Guilt, as it's been called, maybe a negative emotion, it is also a quite strong feeling. Guilt can start making you, as a person, promise things outside of your scope. Guilt will make you sit awake for hours wondering if you're such a bad human being because you're not. The human creatures around us are continually harnessing the strength of liability.

This is how the second phase of brainwashing tends to work: a brainwasher has indeed convinced its victim that they're not really what they've always assumed to be. Hence, the survivor is in a state of uncertainty because they try to address the issue of identification. Such that, if they aren't a decent guy, why are they then? The predator glides in at this point and begins to take them for their lives' entire sorrow trip. When you're uncertain who you are, it can be tempting to accept every falsehood you're getting fed up with about you. A brainwasher would also make a statement convincing their perpetrator that they are a nasty friend, irrespective of how this adverb is being used.

Steps 3 and 4: Personality-betrayal and breaking point

Even citizens themselves are intensely loyal. They're going to protect themselves and their behavior, and struggle to hear their words. Particularly the individuals who are afraid of speaking up for anyone also will speak up for themselves. A person having been brainwashed is the total opposite. Brainwashed people have no trouble rejecting themselves and anything else connected to them despite being continuously bombarded by signals about being the reverse about what they once considered themselves to be. This involves their family, associates, value framework, and all other relationships they might have that link them to the old identification that has been 'evaluated' by the brainwasher and found 'seriously missing.'

There are several reasons why a person who has been brainwashed can easily find himself in this step and cannot fight back. For beginners, they've already moved through the first 2 phases and come out in doubt and guilt, feeling drowning and disoriented. But frequently they don't have the strength to strike off. Remember that there is sometimes a risk of serious harm if conformance is not accomplished, so the goal may be too scared to contradict all the predator's replies.

Second Stage: Dangling a Salvation Carrot

Step 5: The Olive Branch

After the first 3 stages of brainwashing, a survivor of brainwashing sometimes feels so bad about themselves because they try to save themselves at whatever expense. The survivor is also in bad emotional health and has a weak self-image. Those who have forgotten their longtime sense of belonging and will clutch up on any straws offered to feel something again. At this stage, a victim becomes expected to experience a nervous collapse, and that is the signal for the attacker to leap in and deliver redemption.

The manipulator would also offer an olive branch after tearing down their objective for a long period so that the goal will slip into the pit of thinking there is hope at the last of a tunnel. An olive branch at this point could be something from a sweet word to a gift, or perhaps even some type of personal affection. This olive branch helps to demonstrate the goal that there is certain leniency to gain when they're on the right side of the manipulator. A manipulator is above all a 'normal guy' who wishes them the best. That is at least what they have learned since the start of brainwashing.

Step 6: Being Forced To Confess

Take into account: You have been confined for an amount of time to intense mental abuse by an individual. You have wasted your sense of belonging and feel confused and angry. You 're facing a psychotic collapse or already experienced one and can't make every part of your life head or tails. Since leaving the social network you have existed in solitary isolation and can't think of the last moment you had such a decent meal. Then, one day, this individual comes up at your door carrying a steaming coffee pot and freshly prepared muffins. They just say they want to chat. You are inviting them to your building. You just can't believe it. It's the only love you've been receiving in the longest period. What do you believe your former abuser will be reacting to this unusual kindness?

You'll experience a sense of sovereign debt more often than not. Human beings enjoy being kind enough to reciprocate that compassion. Whenever somebody does something good for you, then in exchange, it is natural and wants to do anything better. For a brainwashed human, the desire to pay back is much greater as they believe they still have to compensate for anything they are incorrect about. The brainwashed side, therefore, will be more than willing to offer away some type of kindness. This goodness would always come in the shape of a lie, in their troubled minds. The perpetrator would usually give the alternative of an apology as a means to get paid back.

Step 7: Guilt Channeling

A brainwashed survivor is frequently filled by so much crushing remorse that they still have no scope for any other feeling after weeks or months of becoming told they 're mistaken on anything. The goal has been swamped by so much abuser psychological torment they don't realize what we feel most bad for. The victim simply knows he's guilty of anything. In this misunderstanding, the manipulator glides in and persuades them that guilt is due to all the bad people they've believed in before. The predator, in other words, streams the guilt into the system of belief. The victim now begins to associate their beliefs with the guilt and the responsibility of dealing with the guilt. By fact, the abuser wants to help their prey continue to equate all the negative emotions of their history and let them think that if they select different values, there is a possibility to be rescued and feel stronger.

Step 8: Guilt Relief

The victim is beginning to feel a little relieved to recognize that he's just not deeply bad; perhaps, it is his perceptions that are wrong. He can be correct again, by detaching himself from his beliefs. He sheds his remorse by relinquishing anything related to his prejudices, even those nearest to him. He admits the mistakes of his previous ways and can embark on the current set of values that the brainwasher provides.

Third Stage: Reconstruction of a Brainwashed Self

Step 9: Harmony and Progress

At this stage in brainwashing, the target is keen to redeem itself and look very good in the brainwasher's eyes. Even so, they will start rebuilding a new identity based on the manipulator's offered belief system. After passing through the torture and suffering of the early phases of brainwashing, an offender is assured that only pain and guilt will come from their old belief system. They are glad to be rid of the former life and replaced with a new self that is their safe place from all their suffering.

Step 10: Rebirth and Final Confession

The survivor also experiences a sense of satisfaction upon embracing the current moral structure to be finished for their history and all of the resulting pain. Like the stereotypical last rope on a sinking ship, they must stick to their new identities as this is the only happiness they have experienced in a long period. At this stage, the brainwasher succeeded in obtaining a conversion, and might even be conducting a ritual to invite the latest conversion into the holy inner circle. It is typical for the majority of offenders to be separated from their families. They're going to get it in their heads that they're better individuals today and don't have to deal with their previous negative stuff.

Chapter 25: The Effects of Brainwashing on Individuals & Groups

The effects of brainwashing itself (and how effective it is a method of psychological control) have been called into question by different groups of researchers and experts who have spent

years studying the American soldiers who returned to the United States after being released from the war camps, but were labeled as victims of brainwashing at the time of their return. They claimed that the ones they did speak to were most likely converted through the physical torture and neglect they underwent and not the actual brainwashing process. Their main reason for thinking this is that of the tens of thousands of prisoners put through brainwashing experiments, and less than two dozen fell under the process of brainwashing. However, these are those soldiers who decided to return to the United States, and not those who were so turned against the home country that they decided to remain in the land of their captors even after the war was over and everyone was released.

Cults around the world have played a large role in the continued interest of brainwashing and its effects. From the outside, it is easy to say that cults are bizarre and difficult to understand why anyone would want to get involved in one. Still, the brainwashing, manipulation, and other influential psychological control practices by the leaders or recruiters of these groups are some of the most practiced and well-tested agents and manipulators in human culture. They accomplish this by targeting people who are most open to influence, making them special and part of a community and then convincing them through fake friendship or understanding that what they are doing or standing for is genuinely right and good.

Successful brainwashing can have several effects on individuals and groups of people in the long run. Some of the most common side effects that can be eased or reversed through a process of un-brainwashing (more commonly known as deprogramming) include:

· **Shattered sense of confidence**

This can often lead to a series of painful and damaging decisions after the fact such as dependence on alcohol or the use of stronger drugs

· **Inability to trust people**

From every random encounter to those they love with all their heart, people who have survived the brainwashing process (successful or otherwise) tend to retreat into themselves, unsure of how to trust people they are surrounded by after their ordeal

· **They see everything as a test**

A lot of life loses its excitement after a brainwashing process. The victim rarely has any interest in events or activities they once enjoyed, they have lost their drive and enthusiasm for the future

Each time they are offered an opportunity or invited to join in on a task, they hesitate and make sure to pull apart and analyze every detail before even thinking about whether or not it is something they want to take part in

How to Protect Yourself from Becoming the Target of Malevolent Brainwashing Techniques

Who is most susceptible to brainwashing techniques? Who is the most likely to become a victim of those seeking to improve their standing or just tear down others by convincing people to change their view of the world (sometimes a complete flip)?

One of the most common reasons people get drawn into cults or the control of a manipulative agent is that they have no idea what brainwashing looks like or what kinds of warning signs to look for. The first way to protect yourself from falling prey to these types of psychological predators is to recognize the traits they look for in potential targets:

·   Loners who have never found their place, but have not given up on finding where they belong or who they fit in with

This is one reason those runaway teenagers are often targeted by brainwashing cults and similar groups. They have not yet developed the emotional maturity or life experience to realize they are being taken advantage of in most cases.

·   They do not have anyone to stand up for them

This could be because they are anti-social by nature, but it is more likely because they are too stubborn to take the advice of others and have a tendency to get defensive when they are told what to do or that they should be more careful

·   They are searching for answers or a purpose

This is when potential targets are drawn in by friends, family members, mentors or others that they know or have come to respect and trust. In cases like these, the agent uses their familiarity with the target and their knowledge of how they see the world to gain control of them

Providing their target with a sense of duty to get them on board with the brainwashing process is the first step that is then followed by inspiring feelings of guilt and disappointment in the target when they have hesitations or fail at their assigned task

No one thinks they are susceptible to brainwashing. The concept itself conjures images of malnourished prisoners forced to watch propaganda videos until they accept them as truth and captured spies being injected with clear liquids that alter their mental state to change their reality by chemical means. However, brainwashing is not always as dramatic but can still be as harmful and dangerous. Once a person has determined whether or not they have the potential to become a victim, the next step is to look for warning signs that brainwashing is happening around you. Some of the most notable and widely established include:

- Unfamiliar, confusing and often increasing sense of fear connected to the world outside of their home or wherever they are currently living
- Constant feeling of inadequacy even when they know they have done their absolute best
- Feelings of mistrust and struggles with anxiety attacks over not impossible, but often improbable events like natural disasters striking out of nowhere, the fear of terrorist attacks at each place they visit from public restrooms in their local grocery store to the sidewalk corner across from their living quarters

- Abandonment of communication devices (no cell phone or social media allowed) and disconnect from people they are usually social with

These warning signs will be reinforced, promoted and even introduced if they do not develop on their own by the people doing the brainwashing. Any time you feel these feelings, particularly if you are experiencing multiple signs at once, look at the actions and behaviors of the people you consider your friends, your partners, and even your superiors. If they make the feelings worse through the things they do or say or mock you for thinking something is wrong, they may be running a brainwashing process. From here, the next step is the most difficult because it involves either denying what you are suspecting as just your imagination or that you are just going through a bad time, confronting the person about your suspicions (although this rarely leads to any kind of resolution, giving the agent in question only more opportunity to manipulate your emotions and feelings to whatever they want you to believe, most likely through guilt or through reminding you of your connection, or by removing yourself from the situation and severing ties permanently o until you have a better grip on your mental state).

Whether brushed off as fiction in favor of more solid mind control methods like physical pain and health neglecting or embraced as worrisome and complex method of psychological manipulation, brainwashing still has a lot to offer in terms of how the human mind works, how different people react in different situations and just how confident people can be in who they are and what they believe in. There is no limit of studying going on around the world and, certainly, experts on the subject have only just begun to peel away the layer of intricacy involved in the field.

Chapter 26: Deception

Deception is another key aspect that comes with dark psychology. Like many other tactics that come with dark psychology, it is sometimes difficult to tell whether one instance of deception is considered dark or not. But before we explore more into this, we need first to understand what deception is all about in our world.

Deception will be any word or action capable of making someone believe something that is not true. Fraudulently providing evidence for something false, implying falsehood, omitting the truth, and lying are all examples of deception.

Not all types of deception will count as dark psychology. Everyone will deceive others to some extent or another they may deceive others. They feel inadequate, because they feel embarrassed, or even as a kindness. For example, some studies have shown that many men are going to lie about their heights. This doesn't mean that they practice dark psychology. Besides, it is common for people to deceive themselves about various issues such as happiness, ambition, and health.

The Deception Spectrum

Deception can happen either on a small or large scale. Many people assume that deception has to occur on a large scale to be important. But dark deception is present in all parts of the spectrum, and it is important to be on the lookout at all times to ensure that you are safe.

Dark deceivers will often use the smaller deceptions to help them out as well. They may start with some of these small deceptions to test out the victim and condition that victim to believe the larger lies the deceiver uses later on.

Smaller deceptions can also be carried out to undermine the victim's trust in their powers of reason and logic. Suppose the manipulator can deceive the victim over a smaller issue, and the victim starts to question what is happening. In that case, the victim may conclude that their suspicion is irrational, and they cannot trust their judgment. Most people will start to conclude that it is their judgment that is at fault here, rather than entertaining the idea that someone else is deceiving them over some issue that seems so small. Of course, the dark deceiver is aware of this trust that people generally have and will try to exploit it.

A dark deceiver can work with a large-scale deception as well. One of the largest deceptions that they can use is to convince someone that you are someone else. Not in terms of just a personality trait or some other small detail. A true deceiver can even hide their entire identity. They will hide their date of birth, their name, and everything else. This is done to help push forward the goals or the agenda of the manipulator.

Deceptive Topics

Everyone has heard the saying "Money is the root of all evil." This may seem like an exaggeration, but money can often be the root of various deceptions. Deception and money more often than not cross paths. Some people will deceive in the hopes of attaining money; others will do it to hide their money, and so much more. Because money shows up as a topic so often when it comes to deception, we will take a look at it now.

Take a look at a professional beggar. These individuals will try to get money from the public, even though they have plenty of

149

their own. These beggars will use a few different dark psychological principles to get the money they want from their innocent victims. Such beggars are even willing to put some injuries on their bodies to look more desperate.

Personal marital status is another area where people are going to deceive. Sometimes, a person may try to hide their married background to seducing a new victim. This could be for sexual or financial reasons. Even other people have multiple wives that are spread out across the world, wives who have no idea about each other. This deception type has become even harder with the beginning of the Internet and can check in on people through social media. These deceivers can manage more than one wife from each other through many different means.

Some people may appear to be falsely married when they are not. A married couple is often seen as more trustworthy than one who is not married. The dark manipulator is aware of this idea and may choose to use it for their own end goals. Some people may try to have a pretend marriage to help with taxes and insurance. One of the most common deception types with this is when the deceiver creates a fictional dead wife or husband to sympathize with those around them and often their money.

A deceiver may also try to hide their criminal background. This is because it is hard to be trusted, either personally or professionally, to commit certain crimes. Many manipulators feel like they can use deception to hide any socially unacceptable or abnormal feelings. This can stop the victim from being alerted to the person they are dealing with until it is way too late.

For example, a dark manipulator may decide that they only want to use their victim for sex. But they know that if they focus on this topic, it will be a red flag and hard for them to get what they want. They then decide to deceive the victim. They may overtly lie and then imply that their true intention here is commitment and love. The victim will fall for this deception, the exploitation from that manipulator is done, and then the victim is the one harmed by the deception.

In a romantic relationship, the manipulator is often going to hide their true intentions. Deceptive actions and words will leave the victim feeling that the other person is exactly what they were looking for at that moment in time. This happens because the manipulator can identify someone who is vulnerable and then probe into their needs and weak points. The manipulator can then use this information and then cloak themselves so they appear to be something they aren't. This is a common beginning with the manipulator that can turn into more long-term manipulations that the victim isn't aware of.

Deceptive Tactics

The first deceptive tactic that can be used is lying. This is the first technique that the manipulator will choose as soon as they know that the victim is susceptible to lies and has trouble figuring out the truth. This is often because the victim is someone who trusts others. Or the manipulator may have worked on this victim for some time so that they lower their guard. The manipulator can also find ways to hide up the lies and then explain the discrepancies if the victim starts to notice.

Any deception that occurs with lying is likely to occur in a very subtle way and is thought out ahead of time. A deceiver is going to embed their lie into some truthful information. For example, the manipulator would start with a story that is about ninety percent true and ten percent false. Because it sounds legitimate and most of the story can be proven as true, the victim will think it is true.

Implying is another form of deception. Implying is when the manipulator is going to suggest something false is true rather than boldly stating it. If the manipulator wants to deceive a victim about how much money they have, they could either lie or imply it. A lie would be something like "Oh I'm a successful guy. I've made a lot of money," even though the manipulator knows this information is not true. But when they imply they are rich, they may say something like "it's so stressful trying to handle things with my accountant. Trying to get my tax bill down takes a lot of my time." The manipulator has acted and spoken in a way that makes the other person think they are wealthy, but they never state it.

Omission is another option for the deceiver. This is a failure to mention something, usually a fact that is pretty important, that is true. Omission doesn't use a falsehood to cover the truth like the other two options. Instead, this one is going to ignore the truth or just leave it out. Often this piece of information is important for the victim to know about to make an informed decision. The manipulator would leave this out to protect themselves and ensure that the victim didn't have all the information.

One way that the deceiver can use omission is to create their own emotional fence with that situation. This is a tactic where the manipulator implies that a particular period of their life, or some particular topic, is painful or uncomfortable for them to discuss. The victim, feeling bad and wanting to be considerate, will avoid bringing up this topic. This gives the manipulator a chance to avoid the truth while still making the victim feel guilty when trying to bring up that painful topic.

And the final form of deception will be the most elaborate, and often criminal, form. This is known as fraud. Instead of the deceiver simply lying about something from the past, this kind of deceit will have false stories, documents, and some other evidence to back up whatever their lie says. The deceiver is going to use these things subtly. They would never say something like "I'm a doctor; take a look at my certificate!"

Instead, they will use some subtle displays to show off to the victim. They will try to steer away from being too pushy with their fraudulent claims because they know that doing this will make the victim feel that something is wrong with the situation.

Fraud is becoming more common than ever because of the Internet. Deceivers can often work with professional software to make documents that look pretty realistic, no matter what type of document they need. This can make it hard to tell whether you are working with someone telling you the truth or deceiving you.

When this dark deception starts to enter the realm of fraudulence, it can be a bad sign. It shows that the deceiver is dangerous and they are committed to sticking with that dark psychology. They are risking serious criminal charges to do this kind of manipulation, and they are confident that they can do this without anyone noticing it at all.

Chapter 27: Hypnosis

What Is Hypnosis?

There have been many definitions of what hypnosis is. The American Psychological Association has defined hypnosis as a cooperative collaboration where the hypnotist will give suggestions to the person; he picks which he or she will respond to. Edmonton said that a person is but in a deep state of mind when in undergoing hypnosis. Therefore, hypnosis is when a person enters a state of mind in which a person finds himself or herself vulnerable to the suggestions of a hypnotist. Hypnosis is not new to us because many people have seen it in movies, cartoons or been to magic shows or performances where participants are told to do usual acts and they do it. One thing is for sure that, some people do believe that hypnosis exist and would do anything to avoid being a victim while others believe that its fiction.

Induction

Induction is considered as stage one of hypnosis. There are three stages in total. Induction aims to intensify the partaker's expectations of what follows after, explaining the role they will be playing, seeking their attention and any other steps needed during this stage. There are many methods used by hypnotists to induce a participant to hypnosis. One of them is the "Braidism" technique which requires a hypnotist to follow a few steps. This technique is named after James Braid. First step would be to find a bright object and hold it in your left hand and specifically between the middle, fore, and thumb fingers. The object should be placed where the participant will be able to fix their stare and maintain the stare. This position would be the above the forehead. It is always important that the hypnotist remind the partaker to keep their eyes on the object. If the participant wonders away from the object, the process will not work. The participant should be completely focused on the object. The participant's eyes will begin to dilate and the participant will begin to have a wavy motion. A hypnotist will know that his participant is in a trance when the participant involuntarily closes his or her eyelids when the middle and fore fingers of the right hand are carried from the eyes to the object. When this does not happen, the participant is begins again being guided that their eyes are to close when the fingers are used in a similar motion. Therefore, this puts the participant in an altered state of mind he or she is said to be hypnotized. The induction technique has been considered not to be necessary for every case and research has shown that this stage is not as important as previously had been known when it came to the effects of induction technique. Over the years, there have been variations in the once original hypnotic induction technique while others have preferred to use other alternatives. James Braid innovation of this technique still stands out.

Suggestion

After Induction, the next stage that follows is the suggestion stage. James Braid left out the word suggestion when he first defined hypnosis. He, however, described this stage as attempting to draw the partaker's conscious mind to focus on one central idea. James Braid would start by minimizing the functions of different parts of the partaker's body. He would

155

then put more emphasis on the use of verbal and non-verbal suggestions to begin to get the partaker into a hypnotic state. Hippolyte Bernheim also shifted from the physical state of the partaker. This well-known hypnotist described hypnosis as the induction of a peculiar physical condition that increases one's susceptibility to the participant's suggestions. Suggestions can be verbal or one that doesn't involve speech. Modern hypnotist uses different form of suggestions that include non-verbal cues, direct verbal suggestions, metaphors and insinuations. Non-verbal suggestions that may be used include changing the tone, mental imagery and physical manipulation. Mental imagery can take two forms. One includes those that are delivered with permission and those that are done none the less and are more authoritarian.

When discussing hypnosis, it would be wise if one would be able to distinguish between the conscious mind and unconscious mind. Most hypnosis while using suggestions will trigger the conscious mind other than the unconscious mind. In contrast, other hypnotists will view it as way of communicating with the unconscious mind. Hypnotists such as Hippolyte Bernheim and James Braid and other great hypnotists see it as trying to communicate with the conscious mind. This is what they believed. James Braid even defines hypnosis as the attention that is focused upon the suggestion. The idea that a hypnotist will be able to invade into your unconscious mind and order you around is next to impossible as according to those who belong to Braids school of thought. The determinant of the different conceptions about suggestions has also been the nature of the mind.

Hypnotists such as Milton Erickson believe that responses given are normally through the unconscious mind and they used the case of indirect suggestions as an example. Many of the nonverbal suggestions such as metaphors will mask the hypnotist's true intentions from the conscious mind of the victim. A form of hypnosis that is completely reliant upon the unconscious theory is subliminal suggestion. Where the unconscious mind is left out in the hypnosis process then this form of hypnosis would be impossible. The distinction between the two schools of thoughts is quite easy to decipher. The first school of thought believe that suggestions are directed at the conscious mind will use verbal suggestions.

In contrast, the second school of thought who believe that suggestions are directed at the unconscious mind will use metaphors and stories that mask their true intentions. In general, the participant will still need to draw their attentions to an object or idea. This enables the hypnotist to lead the participant in the direction that the hypnotist will need to go into the hypnotic state. Once this stage of suggestion is completed and is successful, the participant will move onto the next stage.

Susceptibility

It has been shown that people are more likely to fall prey of the hypnotist tactics than others will. Therefore, it will be noted that some people can fall into hypnosis easily and the hypnotist does not have to put so much effort. At the same time, for some, getting into the hypnotic stage may take longer and require the hypnotist to put quite the effort. While for some even after the hypnotist's continued efforts, they will not get into the hypnotic state. Research has shown where a person has been able to reach the hypnotic state at some point in their lives then it is likely that they will be susceptible to the hypnotist's suggestions and those who have not been hypnotized or it has always been difficult for them to reach that state then it will be likely that they may never be able to reach that hypnotic state.

Different models have been established to determine susceptibility of partakers to hypnosis. Research done by

Deirdre Barrett showed that there are two types of subjects that considered being more susceptible to hypnosis and its effects. The two subjects consist of the group of dissociates and fantasizers. Fantasizers can easily block out the stimuli from reality without the specific use of hypnosis. They day dream a lot and also spent their childhood believing in the existence of imaginary friends. Dissociates are persons who have scarred childhoods. They have experienced trauma or child abuse and found ways to put away the past and become numb. If a person belongs to this group finds him or herself day dreaming, then it will be associated with being blank and creating fantasies. These two groups will have the highest rates of being hypnotized.

Types of Hypnosis

A hypnotist can use different types of hypnosis a participant. Each of them will use different ways and will help with certain issues. Some types of hypnosis will assist in weight loss while others will be used to help a participant relax.

Traditional Hypnosis

This type of hypnosis is very popular and used by hypnotists. It works by the hypnotist making suggestions to the participant's unconscious mind. The participant that is likely to be hypnotized by this is one who does what he is told and does not ask many or frequent questions. If one was to self-hypnotize themselves, they will do this by using traditional hypnosis. Like we have said, this type of hypnosis is very popular and this could be attributed to it not requiring much skill and not technical. The hypnotist will just have the right words and just tell the participant what to do. This might pose a problem to the hypnotist where the participant is a critical thinker and can analyze a given situation.

Neuro-Linguistic Programming (NLP)

This type of hypnosis gives the hypnotist wide criteria for the methods they can use in hypnosis. The hypnotist can save time during the process as the hypnotist will just use the same thought patterns as the one that is creating the problem in the participant. If it is stress for example, the same thought pattern causing this stress will counter the stress.

Chapter 28: Reverse Psychology

This is a strategy used by people to get what they want by asking or demanding what they do not want. Scientists use another term: self-anticonformity because your demand goes against what you want.

Another way that psychologists explain reverse psychology is through the term reactance. It refers to the uncomfortable feeling that people get when they feel that their freedom has been threatened. The normal way to respond to that threat is the opposite of what has been demanded of you. It's the going against authority aspect.

Examples of Reverse Psychology

Reverse psychology is prevalent in many different types of professions because it can help people get what they want. It can be productive and successful if executed right. For instance, some sales techniques are based on this very principle, such as the Door in the Face technique. We have all fallen victim to this. Let's say that you are in a used car lot trying to buy a car. The salesman gives you this outlandish price that you would never consider paying. You want to buy the car, but you do not want to pay that much. So, you make a counteroffer for less. This is exactly what the salesman wants. You get the smaller price and the salesman makes the sale, which was his goal in the first place - putting you in a car.

The tactic can also be used in marketing. Here is an example of a store that sells high-quality merchandise. When we go shopping, we see advertisements and the name of the store on the outside of the store. We know where we are going. Well, what if the high-end store has no signs or ads on the outside of the store. It just looks like a regular building. You would have to know where the store was or have been there before to know that they did sell clothes. We all know that this indicates that the retailer is not trying to sell to just anyone. This enhances the mystery of the place and it makes it an exclusive venue. Those who do not want to be excluded or comfortable with the exclusivity will want to buy from the store.

This is a tactic that can be used for good as well. For instance, a parent might use it to get their kid to eat their broccoli. We all know the story; the parent tells the kid to eat their vegetables because they are good. But the kid doesn't like them and won't eat them. It is like a constant battle. So, what does the parent do? They use this tactic by getting the kid to want to eat them. How do you they do that? Haven't you ever bought some sweets that you didn't want the kids to eat. You put them in the fridge and tell the kids that those belong to you and not touch them? What happens? The kid finds a way to eat sweets because they can't have them. They're yours. Why not try that tactic with the broccoli? See how fast the kid jumps on those because they can't have them. We always want what we can't have.

Using this tactic in relationships can be a bad thing if the person using the tactic is trying to get something at their partner's expense. For instance, you asked your partner to go to the store. But instead of asking them directly, you tell them that they cannot handle the traffic right now. They might go just to prove you wrong. If this becomes a normal occurrence, your partner might stop trusting what you're saying to them, become angry with you and start to believe that you are trying to manipulate them to get what you want. This could backfire because they might believe what you say and start becoming dependent on you.

So, does reverse psychology work? That depends on the people involved. First, the victim has to believe that the culprit wants them to do something before they react to their demands and do quite the opposite. If they are aware that you are using this tactic on them, then it is never going to work.

Who Can Fall Victim To Reverse Psychology?

 Anyone can fall for any of these tactics because no one is safe from those who will do whatever it takes to get what they want from others. With this being said, those more relaxed and laid-back personalities don't usually fall for reverse psychology techniques.

So, who does fall more easily for reverse psychology tactics?

Those more irritable, stubborn, and overly emotional personalities will find that they fall for these tactics easier than others. Children are more susceptible as well because the cognitive parts of their brains have not fully developed yet. They might not perceive social cues that others can because they are less aware of what is going on. As they get older into their teen years, they might be able to sense what is going on, but they are also at the time in their lives trying to be more independent. However, they still have a strong urge to fight against authority and might do the opposite of what is asked of them just despite that.

How to Use Reverse Psychology

It might sound simple, demand the opposite of what you want. However, here are some steps for you, just in case.

1.   Your victim needs to have at least heard of both options.

2.   Argue against the option that you want

3.   Use nonverbal communication to back up what you are saying because it will make your case stronger.

Reverse psychology can be dangerous – especially if the victim finds out what you are doing, and if its motives are wrong. With that being said, it can be used for good – as shown above in the parent example. If you decide that you are going to use it, you should be careful and now what you are doing first and know the consequences of using the strategy. Sometimes a more clear, concise and direct approach could be better.

Chapter 29: Seduction

This talks about a psychological process that deals with how people get into an intimate relationship or lead people astray to persuade by corrupting or inducing a person to engage in a sexual relationship. Like it is in any other aspect of dark psychology, people seduce others in other to get them to do what they want so that they can obtain their selfish goals.

The strategies used in seduction include sexual scripts, conversation, paralinguistic gestures and non-verbal means of communication, and other short-term behavioral strategies. The word seduction originates from a Latin word which means "leading astray." This means that the word "seduction" can have either a positive or a negative meaning.

Attraction

To attract powerfully is a strong definition of seduction. This is a skill like any other. It can be honed and worked on with experience and practice. The things that attract us are indeed unique, however, some basic things attract us all. Like comfort and stability. Most find these things to be very attractive. Those who can provide it, or the illusion of it, can indeed persuade us. This is a form of allure. Allure is the quality of attraction. It is the thing that draws us. Allure is a powerful accomplice to seduction. They go hand in hand. Seduction being the act, and the allure being the draw.

In speaking of the act there is a lure when it comes to seduction. A lure is something that baits something. It is the morsel at the end of the string. When used properly, the lure can pull individuals from where they are to where the person on the other end of seduction wants them to be. And there are many forms of the lure. One being...

Temptation

To tempt is the attraction to the things that are not necessarily beneficial to us. This can be an indicator of darkness, although not necessarily. When we are tempted by something, we need to stop and look at what is tempting us and why. The temptation is the reasoning behind the attraction. It is often logical and explains the lure in an innocent light.

A more mellow version of the temptation is the entice. The entice is the offering of pleasure or advantage. It is more formal than the temptation, yet it is less pressuring. Enticement shows its hand by showing you what is possible. Enticement does not necessarily lead to seduction.

Beguile

When we talk about the enchantment of beguile, we begin to stumble into deception. This is a form of seduction for sure. It is not simply the seducing part of the process. Beguile is included with trickery to get what is needed. This can be considered very dark, and the ability to deceive is practiced by those who manipulate.

The saying is that flattery will get you everywhere and anything. This is the urge we talked about in manipulation and persuasion. This flattery is praise of the intent. Truth comes into play when it comes to being influenced. False flattery can show dark intentions. When we are being flattered, we are being moved by this flattery. Wheel, and flatter, it is the movement of seduction.

When we are unable to move, we are considered to be trapped. Ensnarement can happen during seduction in everything from actual handcuffs to the ensnarement of the heart and mind. It is the freeze of the hunted—ensnared by seduction. The cornerstone of seduction is charm. Charm is the charismatic ability to bring about almost everything listed above. From flattery to allure, charm can be the core of it all. We have talked a little about charm when it comes to manipulation. Charm combined with seduction is deadly. Seduction captivates. It is the essence that draws us so that we cannot look away. When considering everything from the gruesome to the sublime, captivation is encompassing seduction. When we are captivated, we are not necessarily ensnared. One captivated is not as secure as one ensnared. The captivated can most likely walk away. Then seduction pulls out another card and enchants. The spell. There is no science here, there is only magic. This magic of enchantment is yet another form of seduction. Yes, enchantment is a lure, and an enticement for desire. It has another form. It's a wonderment that there is something bigger than what we already know. When we are enchanted, we get lost in what we know and do not know.

Hypnotize and mesmerize are part of seduction when removed from the practice of the art. This means that these concepts are not just the practiced art of putting someone into an altered state for the process of suggestion.

Think about it for a minute. Yes, they are. They are part of seduction.

Yet another reason to have difficulty in measuring the science of hypnotherapy. This gray area... it is prime for dark psychology.

Back to seduction. Seduction is about the tantalize. It is the torment or tease. The offering of the unobtainable. Achieving this unobtainable thing is not the goal of the tantalize. It is the process of seduction that defines it. Entice is the promise during seduction.

Seduction titillates. Titillation is the excitement we feel when we are being seduced. This tingling can be a little tickle to a grand encompassing distraction. There is an effect seduction has upon us. The physical sensation mixed with the mental makes seduction the wondering and destructive force that it is. If we do not watch out, we can become bewitched. Alongside enchantment and delight there is bewitched. We are once again going beyond the normal into the magical. Believe in magic or not, being bewitched takes on a role beyond titillation or even basic seduction. There is the magic of control here. A surrender to a force that is not definable. Being bewitched takes us out of ourselves and puts us into a place of controlled magic.

Or it could just be another word for enchantment.

When we turn up the volume of seduction, we start to get into ravaging. When we ravage another, it is almost a devouring. This is starting to become an even more destructive force. Ravage is part of seduction. Some like to be ravaged, and in this there is a surrender that can be relatively harmful. When we are trapped or lead astray, this is a prime opportunity to become trapped. The trap is most certifiably a part of seduction. From the innocent capture of someone's affections to the forcible complete surrender of a trapped animal, the trap is the conclusion of seduction.

It is extremely interesting how often we go to seduction. There is a belief that it is a combination of things. From the basic core drive of us to be part of a society, to the desire to be wanted, seduction takes us there. It also allows us to surrender to it. There is a peace in the surrender to another. A high of being trapped.

When an animal gets caged or trapped—no matter how evolved we get, humans are animals—when trapped or tied up we eventually get to a point where we know we cannot escape and vacate from ourselves. It is in this surrender that we feel the swept motion. Seduction can take us there, the trap leading to the sweep, and for some that is all life needs. For those who practice in the dark, this area is a primal hunting ground. To take down prey with seduction fulfills a very primal understanding of what emotion is. When both parties participate and understand ground rules, seduction is a playful thing. With darkness and the psychological ability to control and manipulate, our moments of emotions during seduction become very vulnerable.

Control

What happens after this seduction takes place? Is there a moment where seduction is not enough to keep controlling the prey? Yes, seduction only takes us so far in control. It can be re-administered with a balance of charm to ensnare prey again and again. Yet there are greater tools that the dark use to keep control over others when seduction begins to wear off.

One of these tools is the lie. Lies are complex, convoluted and honestly not defined due to the unlimited ways they can be used.

Lies are a control mechanism of dark psychology.

So, we had better take a look.

Seduction Techniques

Below are three common techniques that are used in the art of seduction:

Switch between being arrogant and humorous:

This will work for a man that is trying to seduce a woman. Once you have successfully gotten her to talk to you, you can then decide to be both cocky and funny. This should be a very simple thing to do. Be a tease but while at it, spice it up with a bit of arrogance. Look for those things that you can use to mock or taunt her but keep in mind that this must be light-hearted as you do not want to come off as though you are castigating her.

This could also work for a woman to a man, but men typically use it more on women. Regardless of the gender of the user, it is important to apply caution, as the careless use of this method can produce ripple effects. The whole idea is to come off as a funny person, so you do not want to end up hurting the other person in any way.

Try to know more about the other person by asking for some personal details:

It is important to remember that you do not want to ask questions that will bore the other person, so you must ask him or her about them. Make sure you don't end up digging a pit for yourself by asking questions that will never contribute in any way to arousing their interest in you.

The truth is that the kind of questions you ask are always a reflection of who you are, so be mindful of the questions you ask. Your questions should make the person laugh, they shouldn't be boring, and they should make the person want to talk more. So, even after the conversation has ended, they will continue to think about you.

Make use of some subtly sexy words/language:

When you are trying to seduce someone, the best way to hook them is by adding some spice to their interaction with you. To do this, you must use some subtle forms to broach certain sexual topics. It is flat out wrong to start talking about sexuality, like how people should engage in sex. You are expected to make use of subtle suggestions that will put the person at ease with you so that they are not insecure or uncomfortable when they are in your company. You do not want to have them avoiding you because of something you have said.

Chapter 30: The NLP Negotiator: Effective Tactics

Life is full of negotiation, and you will have to negotiate for some reason or another at some point. Think of all the activities you do on a regular day and try to figure out if you could have gotten away with no negotiation in any of those activities. Like the breakfast you might have to prepare for the family, the simplest of things will require getting the consensus of everyone else. You may argue that that does not happen if you are alone, but you will have to negotiate with yourself on the choices you make for yourself even then.

So, if negotiation is that important in life, why should you not learn to employ the best techniques to negotiate? The power of negotiating gives you the satisfaction of being considered important and gives you self-worth. This is designed to provide you with a set of handy tactics you can use to succeed in your negotiation.

Six Golden Rules for Effective Negotiator

You may believe that the skill of negotiation is something that is innate for some and could be learned by others, but negotiation is not as complex as it seems. It is based on two fundamental aspects, logic and tact. The only problem is that you tend to camouflage these two aspects with all sorts of unwanted behavioral characteristics like ego that completely modifies them out of recognition. You do not want to get into an argument, and neither does anyone else. No one will have negative intentions, and you know that getting yourself into an unwanted scuffle over an issue that can be resolved amicably will only lead to you losing your mental peace. In an attempt to feel you are right or more importantly your opponent is wrong, you tend to forget that it would have been all the better to say, "See, I told you." This is where you need to use negotiation to attain peace and thereby lasting success.

Rule 1 – Identifying Common Ground

First, you need to understand that for a negotiation to occur, you need to find common ground. Take a common situation like a family deciding on a restaurant. Every individual in the family might have a different favorite diner, but their common goal is to have a relaxed meal. Understanding this common goal will reduce sibling rivalry in deciding a feasible dining place that caters to everyone's needs.

To arrive at common ground, you have to think of ways to outline the negotiation so that you can work in partnership to resolve the problem. It's important to remember that your problem is not the person in front of you but the issue in question. You must keep in mind that you do not oppose your opponent, but his stance on the issue. You need to understand that in negotiation, the objective is never to create a winner and a loser but to create a win-win situation for both. You should realize that by wanting to achieve this, you are letting go of that competitive mentality that gives rise to unwanted body language, the undesirable tone in speech, and unwanted words.

This will open doors to realizing the basic goals that you might want to work on in collaboration to meet the common core issue. This will also lead you to be open to others' rationales on the issue and take you forward to the next step proposed by Joseph O'Connor and John Seymour in their book "Stepping Up".

Rule 2 – Stepping Up

The next step in negotiating would be for you to step up. In stepping up, the intention is to identify smaller goals as stepping-stones to achieving a larger goal. For instance, let us say that your ultimate goal is to get an advanced degree in some particular field. You will have to break down your larger goal into smaller, much more manageable goals, such as finding a

171

school whose curriculum and timetables fit your learning requirements and busy schedule.

By stepping up in a negotiation, you see the bigger picture, tend to generalize intentions, and will be able to identify more options in solving the issue than just one non-compromising option. Another benefit of stepping up is that it almost always reminds you that the objective behind the disagreement is not the disagreement at all but is linked to something broader and common to both parties. Therefore, it is very important that when a disagreement arises that you step up before the quarrel evolves, leaving both sides in distress.

Rule 3 – Never Retort

The next technique that you need to keep in mind is never to retort. When an idea is suggested, it means that the person providing the idea had to invest in a lot of thinking before it was suggested. This would mean that they would be highly sensitive to any opposition that is likely to come their way. The best way to negotiate it through would be to give it some time, look at it from their perspective, and consider if the suggested idea has credibility. Instead of disapproving outright, it is better to show them the flaws of their proposal than to tell them. People tend to believe only through personal experience. Later explaining your position will make more sense than it would have, had you retorted in the beginning, and they will automatically see your reasons as to why you disagreed initially.

Rule 4 – Questioning

Questioning the opposition respectfully is the next important step in effective negotiation. If you find a flaw in the person's proposition, then phrase a question which will make the person realize his flaw. Instead of you stating it outright, which will only make the person defensive, intelligent questions are your negotiation weapons which can be used to break down the opposition's proposal in a polite manner while simultaneously leading them towards your idea.

The best possible manner to put forward a question is to  request permission before it, such as "Will you mind answering some questions to satisfy my curiosity?" This will hike up your image and respect in your opposition's eyes, not to mention that you will be guaranteed answers as they cannot elude responding to them once they have given consent.

Rule 5 – Hypothetical Scenario

If nothing seems to be working for you, try guiding the opposition away from the negotiation. You can do this by cleverly changing the discussion tracks towards a hypothetical scenario by using persuasive speech such as "under what circumstances will you consent to my proposition?"

This will corner your opponent into stating the condition(s) which will assure you a successful negotiation, provided you can meet them. If you are a teenager seeking permission from your parents to attend the prom and aren't having any progress convincing them, try asking your parents what they would require from you to consent. This will force them to give you a response, which you can then use to gain what you want.

Rule 6 – Resist Intimation

Learn the art of turning the tables on your opponent. This is necessary only if you are ridiculed for your stance. For instance, if you have proposed an idea that is totally off the wall and inconsistent with the others' suggestions, people will throw sarcastic comments at you to throw you off your feet. The most common phrases you might encounter include "Seriously? You would go ahead with such a plan?", or, "Really? Is that your justification for the whole situation?"

Normally what would happen is that you would try to scrabble together a different, more plausible explanation for your words. Refrain from doing so. Instead, be firm and stand your ground by responding calmly, "Yes, this is all I have to say", or, "Yes, you heard it right; that's my plan." This will throw your audience off their feet and get them scrambling for reasons to try and overthrow your suggestions. If you opt for the former reaction– trying to revise your idea to be more acceptable - you only portray a weak personality and an indecisive mind that will not hold in a negotiation.

Tools for Persuasion

How can you convince people that you are right in your stance? Below are two powerful tactics that you might argue are common habits in conversations yet could be used to steer your client's unconscious mind, spouse, or any opponent to accept your idea without a doubt.

The good option vs. the really bad option

An effective way of putting forward your suggestion would be to exaggerate its benefits in contrast to an amplified negative alternative.

Take the above example of deciding on a place to dine with your family. You might want to eat healthily, so you suggest a vegan restaurant. Your siblings might want to eat junk, so they suggest burgers. Normally you would all shout out your individual choices until you get on your parents' nerves and then end up dining at a totally weird restaurant picked out by your dad.

Here's how you change the scene to your advantage. Remember that the way you frame your suggestion has a profound impact on the outcome of the negotiation. An effective way of putting forward your idea is to compare the available options by portraying your idea as the best option and highlighting the drawbacks of other options. For example, "Do you guys want to eat a wholesome meal at Calorie Counter or eat burgers and increase your chances of developing high cholesterol?"

This puts a spin on the negotiation because it is no longer a negotiation of diners alone, but an option between well-being and bad health choices. Try this tactic once, and you will see how effective it is.

View the available options in terms of hypothetical everyday events.

Compare your options to everyday events in life. This gives context to your negotiation by adding a new simpler dimension to the whole discussion. For example, when you are trying to decide between two dresses, one which costs $100 and another which costs $75, you are most likely to calculate how many days' savings will be invested in this one dress. Another way of looking at it will be to equate the cost to a daily expense of yours, which can be sacrificed for a short while. So instead of looking at the expensive dress as something that will cost you 2 months of saving, try to look at it as taking a tube to work instead of a taxi for one month (the saving will be the cost of your dress).

Similarly, you can use this tactic when trying to persuade someone to buy a costly product, such as a food mixer. Instead of trying to engage in a never-ending bargain with your customers, it would be more effective to equate the product's usefulness to efficiency and time-saving features, which will appeal to clients.

Chapter 31: The Impact of Being in a Manipulative Relationship

Not all trauma causes physical scars. While physical scars can heal, emotional and mental scars run deep. These scars are not always visible, affecting the person for the rest of their life. Mental and emotional manipulation can lead to more problems with trust, intimacy, respect, and safety. If it is not dealt through therapy, the person suffering this trauma may live with this for the rest of their lives.

The short answer is that if any relationship makes you feel worthless, insecure, miserable, depressed, anxious, abused, or any combination of these, you need to get rid of that relationship. Pronto! No one should be the victim of another's agenda. If you've been a victim for far too long, it's time to pull the plug and put a stop to manipulation once and for all. You need to get out as soon as you can. Manipulation is pervasive, and because of that, it can sometimes be difficult to differentiate when a person might be manipulative, and when they might be persuasive. One telltale clue that you could look out for is that there will be a give-and-take, mutually beneficial or constructive relationship dynamic with persuasion. It's time to do some soul searching and seriously ask yourself: Why am I still engaged in this relationship? Why do I have such a hard time walking away?

Short Term Effects of Manipulation

When toxic people have hurt you, it can be difficult to learn to trust again. It is going to take time. The challenge of dealing with toxic people is hard. That is because they have a way of ruining your faith and belief in yourself and other people. To let someone in again and be able to trust them completely, to trust that they are not going to hurt you the way the toxic person did, can be a scary prospect.

Being around manipulators for too long is bound to leave some emotional and mental scars, both long and short term. Recognize that there is a problem. That is how you begin to fix it. To fix and heal yourself from a toxic relationship, you need first to acknowledge that you were in one. You don't have to be embarrassed about it. It's okay to admit that maybe this relationship wasn't the best. Among the short-term side effects of being under the manipulator's thumb for too long, including the following:

- Surprise and Confusion - When it's happening to you, you are confused and surprised that it is happening, and you wonder how someone so close to you can act this way.

- You Question Yourself - You will find yourself questioning yourself -whether you did the right thing, acted the right way, or wrong with you. You go through these mental questions because your manipulator has been questioning everything you do, making your doubt every single move you make.

- Anxiety and Vigilance - You become hypervigilant, sometimes paranoid about yourself and others. You become non-confrontational even when something is wrong, and you need to speak up, become timid although you're being treated unfairly, and not voice your concern.

- Passive - Passiveness becomes you. You feel that taking action leads to more arguments and pain, so your best solution is to be passive by default. This is frequently the case when someone is in an emotionally abusive relationship.

- Guilt and Shame - You often blame yourself or feel guilty. Your manipulators keep blaming you, and you start believing them, you take it out on yourself and feel even worse.

- No Eye Contact - You eventually stop looking people in the eye. You avoid eye contact and make yourself smaller to take up less space, so you feel you're less likely to be picked on by your manipulator.
- It's Always Walking on Eggshells - You don't know what would cause a meltdown or a spike in their behavior. You start overthinking every step you take to ensure that you don't do things that might anger or upset the manipulator.

Long Term Effects of Manipulation

The truth is, at times we just don't want to believe that someone we know or care about is taking advantage of us. The shock and disbelief lead many people to live in denial about the toxic relationships around them, especially concerning friends and family. Even when there are red flags and warning signs around them, they still find it hard to accept. They may like to make you feel guilty, but don't let the manipulator get inside your head and play on your insecurities by blaming yourself. Self-blame is one of those long-term side effects resulting from being around someone manipulative for far too long. Without therapy or early intervention in getting out of a manipulative relationship, a person may suffer from long-term manipulation consequences.

- Feeling of Numbness and Isolation - You become more and more isolated and numb. From reacting, you become passive, and eventually, you become an observer to the manipulation. You tend to feel nothing at all; you may feel hopeless and damaged and not feel any emotions again.
- Needing Approval - Needing or looking for approval and justification is seen in many different ways. It can be seen as excessively accomplishing a task, being overly nice to everyone, a people pleaser, or being extremely focused on appearance. You tend to feel like

you are not enough, and the way to compensate is to make yourself seem flawless and perfect so that other people will appreciate you more.

- Feeling Resentful - Resentment manifests in various ways, primarily irritability, constantly blaming yourself, frustration at not accomplishing a task perfectly, and even impatience. When you have been manipulated for a very long time, it is hard to see anything but bad things yourself.

- Judging Yourself Excessively - You may be holding yourself against very high standards as you feel like you are not good enough. You feel like giving yourself this high standard would make you feel in control. However, this often requires time and self-compassion to move from feeling in control after not being in control for a long time.

- Depressive Disorder and Anxiety - There have been plenty of lies that have been told to you that you believe them yourself over time. All of the above are ways that manipulation can do to oneself, especially over a long period. The great news is that all of these things can be healed. Granted, it can take time, and it is a tough hill to climb, but it is possible.

The process of recovering from manipulation starts with the simple task of appreciating yourself for the way you are. It is imperative to be considerate and kind towards yourself, but you should know that self-love is more than just a sentiment. The healing process is not something that is going to happen overnight. Nor is it something that you can accomplish all in one go. Change can be difficult, so you should do it in small stages. Beyond your capacity to tend to yourself, you must also remember that self-love is an intentional practice and has to be learned and cultivated. It gives you the ability to see yourself completely as yourself and recognize and value your weaknesses, strengths, challenges, and triumphs.

Is It Possible To Heal?

Yes, a resounding YES. Manipulation can be hard to identify, especially when it is among people we are close to. Nobody wants to be labeled as paranoid or crazy because we see and feel things other people don't. Worse still, if someone tells you to 'deal with it' or 'its nature to act that way.' No, it isn't. If you feel manipulated, if you feel wronged, if you feel like you are walking on eggshells all the time, if you feel worried and scared about your every move- that means you are not in a healthy relationship. It doesn't matter if it's with your mom, your dad, your siblings, boyfriend, colleague, manipulators can manifest anywhere.

If you do not detach yourself from manipulative behavior, it can lead to extremely serious mental health problems down the road, leading to depression and anxiety. The time to confront this issue is always now—and here are a few ways to go about the healing process:

- Speak to Yourself - Give yourself a pep talk by asking yourself a few questions. Do you feel like yourself? Do you feel like you are being manipulated? Do you feel unhappy when the person is around? What do you feel when you talk to your manipulator or when they are in the same room? Talking to yourself about these feelings or even writing them down can help you look back and assess things. It can also assure you that you're not the problem. If the same pattern from the manipulator keeps happening the same way in different situations, this is not okay.
- Decide If You Want to Approach the Individual - Keep in mind that this may not be ideal in every situation.

Manipulation can happen at work, at home, even in the gym. Depending on your degree of closeness with this person, decide whether it is worth talking to approach them. Sometimes you have no choice but to be around them or work with them. If this is the case, it may help limit your interactions or have someone you trust to be with you when you approach them for their behavior. If you can detach yourself from the situation, such as breaking up with a partner or ending a friendship- do this.

- Talk to People - You are at the center of this healing process. It's about self-love and self-compassion when healing from a manipulative relationship. Talking to someone you trust, someone who understands your position, about how you feel will help you heal. If you can't find someone you are comfortable talking about this with, seek a mental health professional or therapist.

If you can, though, you need to cut off all communication with them. Cut them out of your life for good; your future self will thank you for it. Block their number, delete their social media, ignore their emails and their phone calls. They will try to manipulate you to come back to them by trying to make you feel like they have changed or telling you that they're so sorry and to come back because things are going to be different. When you decide to leave a toxic relationship, it does not mean that you will wake up the next day immediately, feeling like a completely new person. Deciding to leave is just the first step. Healing is a process that takes time. Pain and heartache can be difficult, but these experiences help us grow strong and become better. It teaches us what we want and what we deserve. It sheds light on what you should not put up with and how to live your life to the fullest.

Chapter 32: Media Manipulation: Strategies and How to See Through Them

Some of the tactics and techniques used by various media outlets include psychological manipulation, logical fallacies, rhetorical questions, the use of propaganda, and outright deception. The main focus of this kind of media organization is on suppressing the information and the points of view of the target population while dictating what their options and thoughts should be. Some people will be forced to listen to specific one-sided arguments. People's attention may also be diverted elsewhere, away from the real issues.

There is indeed a huge number of people who may not be aware of "media manipulation." Although people lack basic knowledge about what media manipulation entails, some researchers have taken the bold step to come up with a list of different techniques used by deceptive individuals, such as politicians and media outlets that support them, since they want to control the public.

When looking into different media manipulation techniques, the main focus is on learning more about the techniques used when carrying out mass manipulation. Media manipulation strategies work to ensure that people are submissive, docile, obedient, and don't think for themselves. Additionally, some media outlets can support inequality, capitalism, and neo-capitalism.

Some of the popular media manipulation techniques are as follows:

1. Distraction

The distraction strategy is meant to deviate the target population from focusing on the important issues that pose significance in their lives. To ensure that people are distracted, media houses can flood the news with stories that revolve around trivial issues. The main objective is to ensure that the people are distracted by making sure that their minds are occupied. The result is that people will stop asking why the media is not looking into specific issues. In the process, people will even forget the real issues.

2. Problem-Reaction-Solution

This method can be likened to how politicians try to lure voters during an election period. The population is normally tested first. The first step is to spread rumors, and an evaluation will be carried out to assess how the general population reacts. After creating a problem, the second phase involves offering a solution to the problem. The public will view the manipulators as heroes.

3. Gradualism

This is the process of manipulating people by ensuring that they have accepted some socially unjust decisions. The population is manipulated gradually. The gradual manipulation may take place for many years.

4. Differing

Another strategy used by the media is differing; this is when people present some unpopular decisions, and they may emphasize that the decisions should be implemented since the general population will benefit significantly. The public may believe everything genuinely, and they may make some sacrifices, which they believe will bring forth some significant changes. For instance, the politicians may be the manipulators in this case, and they may trick the voters into thinking that they will lead a better life after the polls. At the end of it all, the people will realize that no changes have been implemented, and they lose faith and disengage from the system.

5. Treating People like Children

The media may be focusing on manipulating the public regularly. When they manipulate the public continuously, it is an indicator that they are treating people like children. The media will try to brainwash people through the use of sugarcoated arguments, intonations, and characters. In turn, the media will assume that people are immature, and they are incapable of handling the truth. The main goal is to ensure that the target audience is docile, submissive, and reacting. Media manipulation ensures that people cannot think like adults.

6. Appealing to People's Emotions

The media has learned more about how to appeal to people's emotions, and their main focus is on ensuring that people are unable to think critically. Various media outlets that want to push an agenda want to control people's thoughts. You should look into how powerful fear is as a tool.

7. Keeping the Public Mediocre and Ignorant

Some media organizations prefer dealing with people who are uncultured and also ignorant. By ensuring that people are isolated from various pieces of knowledge, the media can easily manipulate the public, which is also true for certain politicians. The media also ensures that a rebellion does not take place since people are ignorant.

8. Encouraging the Public to Accept Mediocrity

Ensuring that the public accepts mediocrity is similar to ensuring that the general population is ignorant. The media prefers to make use of such strategies when manipulating people. For instance, is the media airing the shows that people want to watch? Are some shows imposed on us by the media? In short, do we get to consume the content that we want, or does the media impose different pieces of content on us? At times it is clear that the media is brainwashing us, and we have ceased to care much about our surroundings. Also, we have been trained to be mediocre.

9. Self-Blame

The media usually encourages self-blame and ignorance and makes sure that people believe that they are responsible for their misfortunes. In short, the media will focus on self-incrimination and will make sure that the public will not mobilize at all costs.

10. Completing the Knowledge of the Public

To control the general public, the media has focused on learning more about its audience. The media can work together with other companies to learn more about every individual to manipulate the masses easily.

It is advisable to learn more about how to spot media manipulation. The resources talking about how to spot media manipulation are few; thus, we cannot delve into the topic in an in-depth manner. However, pay attention, and you may notice now when various media outlets are trying to manipulate people.

Conclusion

If you have made it this far in the book, congratulations. You have learned some of the most powerful and useful tools for manipulation and NLP. You are now prepared with all the tools you will need to be aware of people trying to manipulate you and get people to do what you want. There is only one more thing to do: develop a strong sense of self.

As you go over these techniques and learn about what it means to influence others towards your ends, it is easy to get lost in the concepts. You may start to feel like you have been manipulated yourself. You may feel that to deploy these techniques, you will have to start to believe in untruths.

This is not the case and following this train of thought can be very dangerous. It can lead you to forget who you really are and what you believe. When you ensure that, you not only become a kind of aimless wanderer in life but you also become a prime target for manipulation yourself. This is why it is infinitely important to develop a strong mentality and sense of self. Doing so will keep you from losing your original intent and identity. It will also guarantee that you are not made a puppet in someone else's marionette theater.

Victim versus Manipulator

It should be noted at this point that not all manipulation should be negative manipulation. Believe it or not, there is such thing as constructive manipulation. All of the techniques we have gone over can be used to help people. You can use any of the tactics to help someone quit smoking, for example. For instance, say you want to help someone eat healthier. You might use the overload pattern interrupt. You would push the subject's tolerance threshold regarding unhealthy foods to the point where they couldn't even look at junk food without associating with it unpleasant thoughts.

It is crucial to know how to use these powerful tactics responsibly. We are not condoning that you go out and try to scam every person you know. These tactics should be used sparingly and only when you really need them. They can be used responsibly to help yourself get out of a bad situation or relationship. They can be used responsibly when you are in dire need of help but have no one willing to lend a hand. They can be used responsibly by remembering always that the "subjects" you manipulate are people as well.

Speaking of "subjects," it is crucial to know the difference between subject and manipulator or victim and manipulator. The lines between these two concepts can be blurred in your mind without you even realizing. When that happens you are easy pickings. A skilled manipulator will be able to spot you from a mile away and take advantage. It becomes of chief importance to step out of the victim role and be aware of yourself and your surroundings not to manipulate yourself.

This is the best time to take an honest look at yourself through the lens of all the topics and techniques to see if you are being or have been manipulated in the past. Be fearless in your memory and introspection. Has anyone ever used these techniques on you? Is someone in your life using these techniques on you now?

Take responsibility for your actions. Even if you realize now that you have or are being manipulated, don't wallow in regret. Don't feel sorry or bad about yourself. Realize that everyone has been manipulated at least once in their lives. The essential thing is that you realize it now and can now take the step toward shedding the victim's role. When you remain in the victim mentality – thinking that you are "so dumb" for letting someone manipulate you or that you will only repeat these mistakes – you remain an easy target.

Stepping out of the victim role and into the manipulator's role is your first step in solidifying your identity and steeling yourself mentally. Own up to how you have been used in the past and move on from it. Just because it happened once or twice or three or even hundreds of times does not mean that it has to keep happening. Start thinking of yourself as a manipulator every day. Distance yourself from victim thinking and take control. Look at yourself in the mirror every day and say to your reflection "I am in control." It may feel silly at first but it is an effective way to program yourself out of victim thinking.

Developing a strong mentality will make it much easier for you to impose your influence on someone else and keep other people from doing the same to you. It is what you must do if you want to become a skilled manipulator. Learning the techniques is not enough. Manipulation is a mental exercise and keeping a strong mind will make you more successful at this exercise. Stepping out of the victim role is just the first step. There is more you can do to fortify your mind and identity.

MASTER YOUR EMOTIONS

Introduction

Emotions have a significant foothold in our behavioral aspect and how we approach the world before us. When considering a human's psychological makeup, emotions are the byproduct of many experiences we face in our lifetime. These are based often on past experiences, but certain emotions, such as fear, may be based on perceptions and assumptions of future adventures.

Emotional Attachments

Often, our psychological makeup is based on emotional attachments to our past. These are created and cultivated by our experiences and how we emotionally perceived them when they happened. Often, our emotions will be based on several things rather than the experience itself. For example, say you went to a local hospital to comfort a dying loved one in the past. You may have spent several hours, or even many days there comforting that person in the hospice ward. Later in life, you go there to the maternity ward to welcome a new family member into the world following their birth. Although the experience should be positive and enjoyable, your experience in that hospital was harmful and painful. Therefore, even though you are trying to enjoy the moment, you are likely to be plagued by a sense of sadness and grief because of the memories it brings up to you. This is because you have an emotional attachment to that hospital that is negative, even though it wasn't the hospital that brought you grief, it was the circumstances.

We develop emotional attachments for all types of things in life. Often, these emotional attachments are connected to something, places, and other tangible items. However, they may also be linked to circumstances. In many cases, it is a combination of both. As a result, we may have a naturally positive or naturally negative association with something in the future, even if we have no reason to feel that way.

Emotional Influence

Emotions influence us in many different ways. They control what we like and what we don't like, the parts of our memories that we want to hold onto and the others that we avoid, and even our values and beliefs. We often have a tendency to create and firmly hold onto beliefs we make when we are in a negative or upset mood and question the ones we generate when we are in a positive or happy attitude. This is because emotions we perceive to be harmful such as anger, fear, and sadness are often those that we experience in the face of stress. Our human psychology and biological makeup teach us to keep these experiences in the forefront of our minds to avoid stressful situations in the future. This is because, on an animalistic level, stress often indicates some form of danger: death, starvation, predators, attack, and so on. Even though we have evolved far past the reality of any form of stress indicating some record of immediate and potentially fatal danger is upon us, we still have these biological tendencies to see our priority in this way. This results in emotions, particularly negative ones, having a significant impact on our psyche and how we behave, approach life, and otherwise experience the world around us.

Influencing Behaviors

Understanding the importance of someone's emotions makes it easy to influence people to behave in almost any way that you want. When you can help said person associate desirable things with a positive, uplifting perspective, they become much more likely to remember it in a positive light. They want to experience it again and again. Much like humans keep negative experiences in the forefront of their mind to avoid stress, they also stay positive experiences in the forefront of their mind because they are addicted to pleasure. Therefore, if you can associate the behaviors you want them to choose with pleasure and the behaviors you want them to avoid with pain or stress, you can influence them to choose in your favor and ultimately do anything you want them to do.

Chapter 1:   What Are Emotions ?

Emotions are part of the human experience. We had just seen how much they influence us, but we still don't understand why. How is it that our emotions have so much power over us when we believe we are such rational creatures?

Why Emotions Are Powerful

When humans used to live in caves, they needed to be alert at all times. They needed to pay attention to their surroundings for predators. The slightest hesitation would mean that our ancestors would have ended up being a meal.

Back in those days, there was no time for rational thought. The very survival of the tribe or group of humans depended on how fast their instincts were. If they spent too much time rationalizing, chances are that they would not make it out alive. Which is why, rather than focusing on overthinking, they used their instincts.

Fast forward to the present. Today, we don't have to walk down the street worrying about saber-tooth tigers or angry woolly mammoths. However, our instincts are still present with us and they are still as potent as our rational thought. This is because our ancestors had paid more attention to their instincts, allowing them to be developed so well.

You might think it is a far-fetched idea to draw a link between our ancestors and ourselves. Just because they sharpened their instincts does not mean that we would automatically have heightened instincts.

On the contrary, one of the ways that instincts are transferred from one generation of organisms to another is evolution (Cudmore, 2017). Research has shown that instincts are deeply embedded in the scientific community's often considered learned behaviors. These behaviors become part of the DNA code and the information then becomes available for the offspring. This is why even a newborn spider can weave an almost perfect web without seeing a web before or being taught how to weave. Through the same way why human beings have a strong instincts.

But how are our instincts related to our emotions?

The reason is that our instincts are a subconscious factor. Our ancestors trained the subconscious part of the mind more than the conscious part by homing in on their instincts. Because of this, our emotions have had more time to experience, mature, and train than our rationality.

But, there's more.

According to a BBC (Petterle, 2009), humans are impulsive until the age of three. Being sudden means that we do not use our rational thought. We just work on whatever emotions guide us at that moment. We begin to gain the power of reasoning when we reach the age of five.

This means that no matter what you do, your emotional side is always the most experienced. You could be a savant who began training the rational mind from the time you were young. You could be the next Stephen Hawking or Nicola Tesla. But that still does not compare to your emotional side, which has been with you your entire life!

When you connect this with the fact that our emotional side has thousands of years of experience (since our ancestors), you are looking at a powerful force.

Just how powerful is the emotional subconscious?

No matter how much information your rational mind uses, your emotional subconscious does not miss anything. Our brains are capable of taking in nearly 34 gigabytes of information every day (Balbusso, Waterman & Lee, n.d.). And that is only during our leisure time. If you add in the information you collect when you are engaged in work, we take in more than 34 gigabytes of info! Yet visually, we only process 10 percent of the information that we see. But who does the processing? If you were to rationally and logically arrange every bit of information you receive, you would have to spend a long time on it.

Additionally, you are going to miss out on new information. This is why our emotional subconscious does the job for us. Every minute of every day, our subconscious stores information that may not be vital at that moment, but is a useful guide in the way we live our lives.

When we use our subconscious mind, we are making use of a powerful tool. Your subconscious mind is what instincts are based on. Your instincts are not extrasensory perceptions, a sixth sense, or anything else that might be considered mystical, pseudo-scientific, or mythical. They are simply the information collected in our subconscious mind made available for our use.

Every time you have that "gut feeling," it isn't divine intervention. It is merely your subconscious mind looking for patterns in your surroundings and situations. Using these patterns tries to build a cohesive structure, which eventually triggers your memories, or whether you should fight or flee. You also refer to them as fight or flight instincts, not fight or flight rational thought, which shows just how influential our emotional subconscious is.

When Do We Become Emotional?

For the most part, our emotions help us. Knowing that they have a significant influence over our lives, it is folly to think of them as a villain in a James Bond movie. Instead, you could say that they are like James Bond himself, figuring out various situations and giving us suggestions to deal with them. Our emotions also help us feel joy and other positive emotions that help us through the day.

But there are times when our emotions run amok. When they do, they often cause havoc that can happen in one of three ways:

- We experience the correct emotion for the situation, but the intensity of the emotion is too high. For example, we were right to worry about a particular situation, but there was no need to go into full-blown panic mode. Or you might have experienced a situation where you were stressed about something, only to realize in the end that there was no need to have so much stress at all.

- We experience the correct emotion, but we display it so that does not justify the situation. For example, we are angry about something but rather than talk about it, we go about giving the silent treatment, which does nothing but exacerbate the situation.

- And finally, we come to the most complex emotional reaction of all. When this happens, we don't have the right response at the right time; we are experiencing a completely 'incorrect' emotion. For example, after a particular incident, we realize that the intensity of fear we had felt was not the problem, rather the fact that we thought fear was the problem. Why were we afraid? What compelled us to feel fearful in that particular moment when it was not required at all?

Why would such unwanted emotions appear in the first place? Can we annihilate an emotional cause so that we don't have to feel angry unnecessarily? Or, can we modify the programming of our emotions so that rather than feel a negative emotion, we can replace it with something positive? For example, let's say that we are walking outside and someone bumps into us. Rather than feeling angry about it, can we wire our brain to create feelings of amusement or disinterest?

These are all important questions but they do not have a simple answer. This is mostly because we all react differently to specific scenarios. Some people fear heights while others are daredevils, choosing extreme sports that see them plunging off a cliff or jumping off a plane fearlessly. Some people mourned the death of Freddie Mercury like he was their distant relative, while others were playing "Another One Bites the Dust" for the first time on YouTube after hearing of his death. At the same time, certain emotional triggers create the same response in the majority of people. If someone were to find themselves in a close-collision with another vehicle, fear would be one of the primary emotions that they would feel.

We all have our unique emotional signatures, but at the same time share certain emotional traits with others. A loved one's death makes us sad, but spotting a bug in our room does not fill all of us with disgust. Certain emotional triggers are even specific to cultures. In fact, according to a recent study conducted at the University of London, certain situations trigger different emotions based on the culture people are from (Nauert, 2019).

So, When Do We Become Emotional?

One of the most common ways that emotions surface is when we perceive, positively or negatively, that something will affect our situation and welfare, whether that something has good or bad results.

A simple way to understand the above statement is through the example. Let us say that you have a job interview coming up. You are so confident that if someone were to dare you to go skydiving, you might probably say, "No, too easy. Throw me and the parachute bag separately!" Because of your confidence, you are feeling happy about the interview. Once the interview is over, you realize that you have pretty much aced it. But about a couple of days later, you get the devastating news that unfortunately, you did not receive the job offer.

In the above example, the interview is a factor that would affect your welfare. You perceived it positively because of your confidence. However, the situation itself had terrible results, since you did not get the job in the end.

Of course, emotions are not usually that simple. An excellent way to understand their complexity is by looking at how humans react to various situations. Aggression and anger come out when we are challenged. Fear is a reasonable response that warns us of threats in our surroundings. Disgust is our brain's way of letting us know that something — such as rotten food — is not suitable for us.

Chapter 2: How Are Emotions Created?

Your cognitive social behavior, personality, expressions, and decision-making come from the prefontal cortex of your brain. Emotions are chemicals released in the brain that activate individual sections; it takes about one-fourth of a second for the brain to recognize the trigger. In another one-fourth of a second, the chemical is produced and released. This process happens in under a second. The chemical is not only discharged in our brain but into our bodies as well; in about six seconds, we begin to have emotions which lead to feelings.

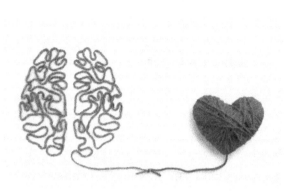

Now, let's talk about what sections of the brain this chemical is released to and which emotion it creates. There is a skinny layer between 1.5 to 5 mm outside of our mind, and six layers are covering the brain. It is divided into four parts, each part having a different responsibility. This part of the brain is created during the development of the nervous system. Your cerebral cortex has sensory and motor areas. Your brain's limbic system is beneath this thin layer of the cerebral cortex; it consists of a network that includes the hippocampus, amygdala, hypothalamus ,thalamus, cingulate gyrus and basal ganglia. These structures are linked to our prefrontal cortex.

The amygdala, a set of neurons shaped like an almond, is very small, but it holds the most extensive role in forming emotions, that of processing the emotions. The amygdala is part of the limbic system but is buried deep in the medial temporal lobe. Its task is critical: coordinating responses when it comes to emotional content. Behavioral, autonomic, endocrine and environmental stimuli are the major ones it responds to. The amygdala and septal nuclei have reciprocal connections with the prefrontal and limbic cortexes; the PFC translates the limbic cortex's data. Are you beginning to get a picture?

External stimuli cause most of the physiological reactions, which are, most of the time, caused by changes in your hormone levels. The hypothalamus delivers a message to the pituitary gland, which sits behind the bridge of your nose at your brain's base. It's a tiny organ, smaller than the amygdala about the size of the pea. This organ makes and stores different hormones and controls the emission of the hormones. The gland receives a message and produces hormones that affect many parts of the body: blood pressure, body temperature, electrolyte levels, and the rate of your heartbeat. It also stimulates other hormone-producing glands. Our senses – sight, hearing, touch, taste, and smell -- impact our hormonal levels, so taking care of ourselves is crucial. But it can also be affected by things outside our control – life-changing events, minor upsets, etc. Everything we do and experience activates this chemical. And since it takes less than a second or the brain to perceive a stimulus and produce the emotion chemical, we often react before we know consciously what we respond to.

Imagine sitting at your desk, getting ready to do something meaningful. Your brain and body are ready to concentrate on the task at hand – when suddenly, something happens. You spill your coffee on the papers, or the phone starts ringing. Despite your readiness to focus on the job before you, your brain releases that anger chemical and before the second is over, you are ranting about the mess. Your amygdala is busy coordinating this chemical to the limbic or prefrontal cortex, regulated by the PFC, which causes us to act before we even

200

know it. The hypothalamus delivers the message to our pituitary gland, storing the hormones this feeling just produced, and releasing hormones at the same time. It is for this reason that some scientists call our responses "learned behaviors."

Our brain food, sugar, caffeine, etc., is the fuel our brain needs for its neurons. When we don't eat, we feel, can feel okay, but usually don't.

What is the "ego" and how can it be good or bad? Your mind has this mediator; the ego's responsibility is to test reality and give us a sense of our identity. Our ego is supposed to prevent us from acting on basic urges we all get them as humans. There is Id, Ego, and Superego. Id is the only trait of personality we are born with. Ego comes along at about 3 and superego around 5 old, so children acquire this from us and the society around them, creating their sense of right and wrong. When toddlers act up and get yelled at or spanked, they absorb that lesson; when they see others doing it, they copy them. Your superego is instruction on making judgments, along with internalized morals, standards, and ideals.

Your personality consists of three elements, which develop at different points in your life. The id is there when we were born, for we don't know anything but ourselves. Ego shows up at our 3rd birthday, as we begin to comprehend more. At age 5, we develop superego, which is the feeling bad for doing something we know we shouldn't. Ego resides in the hippocampus. The Id is motivated by pleasure and it seeks instant gratification for all desires, wants and needs. When these needs are not met, the result may be anxiety or conflict with the calm state of mind. Have you ever felt an increase in hunger or thirst all of a sudden? Well, that is part of your Id, but all three of the elements in the personality clash with each other and the influence is powerful. Say for example you want to eat something, but you are busy and feel you don't have time. Your Id is saying, "I want that right now." But here comes busybody Superego telling you, "You must keep going; you can't take a break." Then Ego butts in with "Let's try and work this out together." Your conscience may punish Ego with feelings of guilt when Ego gives in to Id's demands; Superego delivers the responsibility.

I imagine you've heard the phrase, "He/she has a big ego." We mean that that person is seen as selfish and unreliable because they focus only on their own needs. This person can manipulate and consistently try and manage others and will make things difficult if things are not done to their satisfaction. Every situation needs to balance the ego-less person, who is unconscious to their own self needs and can be at risk from this type of Superego person. Ego can be useful to manage stress externally and internally and your ego helps you cope in difficult situations, so it is good to have a balanced ego. the opposite of ego is dignity and honor, so when someone pushes their ego aside, they are honoring or having more satisfaction.

It is not our ego that defines us unless we let it. Don't let a person with a big Superego bring you down, for your ego already does that. Realize that a person with a Superego hasn't figured out how to balance the three aspects of their personality, so don't let them control or define you. They try to control others; just don't let them do it. If you are struggling with your ego, it's essential to realize and make efforts to change. It's all about loving yourself and caring, and learning more selfishness; above all, understanding the process.

But over analyzing may make your ego falter and you may begin to feel anxiety, so be careful not to over-analyze how you are acting. We second guess and over-analyze due to expectations and doubt from others or our selves. They say if it's not broke don't fix it, meaning we are always trying to change or improve something that doesn't need it; we only think it does. Once something is already said and done, we cannot go back and fix it. It's not like gluing a broken plate back together.

Once something is in the past, it is in the past, and over-analyzing may bring it to the future, causing more – and possibly worse -- conflict. What is the point of becoming paralyzed over something we have no control over? Your ego is there to help you alleviate stress. The pie chart below is an example of the balance that is good to have. Look at how the Id is larger than all the others -- the ego is bigger than the Superego. We all feel some guilt at different times of our lives, but we must use it to improve not to punish.

Chapter 3: How You Can Control Your Emotions And Why Is Important?

Emotions are inevitable in our lives; we always feel them, either intentionally or involuntarily. We can also explore their extensive range, from the negative feelings of depression, anger, boredom, or irritation, to the beautiful ones, such as when we are happy, fascinated, or proud. We must always manage negative emotions and maintain good ones, but we need to understand that balance is essential in our emotional state. If we are still happy and kind, chances are people might take advantage of the situation. If we are doing others' work for free, they will send more work, overwhelming us. Hence, balancing our emotions is vital for our welfare. And this can only be done when we know to manage and control them. The following presents several control methods and measures. We can take and apply one or two from the list and see for ourselves if they are useful. If not, we can try different ones.

Learning and developing emotions is possible, and can also be risky. As we grow older, we become wiser and more sensitive to our own and others' feelings. Sometimes, we can use this to our advantage, because knowing someone's "soft spot" allows us to manipulate situations in our favor. But the opposite might also happen to us; others will take advantage of us because they know we are kind or patient.

Some emotional responses, like pain, fear, hunger, and sexual pleasure, are innate to humans. We don't need education or proper learning to feel these emotions. They just come out naturally to us whenever we are in certain situations. And as much as we want to eliminate them, they are already embedded in us. We just control or manage them to minimize their impact on our decisions and our lives in general.

As we undergo the growth process, we learn to associate certain emotions with certain situations. As a kid, I associate the evening or any dark place with fear, and toys with happiness. Some of these associations are irrational, like fearing situations that are not dangerous (e.g., public speaking) or becoming upset about things that we cannot control. As we grow older, our understanding of ourselves and our emotions deepens, and we begin to realize and adjust our reactions accordingly.

Some scholars believed that thought processes generate many emotional reactions. Most of the time, we act based on reasons, and reasons come from our minds. As humans, what is reasonable to someone might not be valid to other people. Hence, the aim is not absolute, but instead a relative factor. It's because human feelings are complicated, and emotions are caused by many factors, both internal and external to us. These factors are sometimes hard to control, but if we arm ourselves with the right knowledge and experience, there's a big chance that we can favorably manage them.

Understanding the direction of our emotional responses might not be simple. Still, it will undoubtedly help us find ways to alter or influence our and other peoples' feelings. Having greater control over emotions provides a lot of benefits. And I think these reasons are good enough to lead us to strive to control and manage our emotions and feelings.

The critical process of emotion control is to understand our feelings. Having the knowledge and awareness of why certain emotions exist and what causes their existence is crucial. This will enable us to identify specific emotions and the factors that drive our actions and reactions. Consequently, it is also essential to understand methods and exercises with which to manage emotions. This way, we can identify the best solution for any situation. Lastly, and most difficult, is to apply these techniques actively in our lives. We are often hesitant to change our behavior. But awareness of all these measures will be futile if we do not use them in real life. Managing and controlling emotions is dependent on a person's willingness to grow and adapt to change.

Studies and scholars have presented many ways how to manage emotions. Some might not be applicable, depending on our attitude or the situation that we are currently facing..

General methods of changing emotions are divided into five major groups: (1) creating preferred emotions; (2) decreasing undesirable feelings; (3) expressing emotions; (4) converting emotional energy; (5) other additional methods. Under these general methods are more specific exercises or activities used to alter and control emotions.

Creating Preferred Emotions

- Relaxation training. Many relaxation methods can be used, depending on what best suits your schedule or condition. Some research has suggested that relaxation reduces tension and helps overcome feelings of anxiety. It also counters fear and panic reactions, increases learning efficiency, and improves general health.
- Changing moods and feelings. All of us have memories or fantasies of being somewhere or with someone and feeling happy and carefree. Many believe that imagining doing things improves ability and self-confidence. It also grows self-esteem and helps develop a positive mental attitude. Internal serenity enables us to cope with harsh realities. It also creates greater awareness and concentration, along with increased motivation.
- Achieving happiness. Being happy involves many self-help methods. It means having some influence

in your life, having confidence in your self-control, and having the ability to handle unhappy feelings. Happiness can also be achieved by positively accepting any personal or relationship outcomes in our lives. Being happy reduces depression and sadness.

- Gaining peace of mind. Peace of mind is a beautiful mental state that can be achieved by accepting oneself and the world. It enables us to escape the stress of pressures or intense emotions. It also allows us to be calm and observant, and gives us a clear, accurate perception of things.

Decreasing Undesirable Emotions

- Meditation. Meditation is associated with religion, and it has stood the test of time. Recent scientific studies have revealed that meditation yields better self-control, more confidence, and a reduction of frightening ideas when done carefully and regularly.
- Self-desensitization. Keeping yourself calm reduces unwanted fear and stress. Some scholars have explained why desensitization is better than imaginary scenes, as real-life problems will have to be faced at some point.
- Flooding, or exposure to fear. The purpose of this exercise is to deal with any scary situation quickly. Another possible advantage is increased self-esteem, and the feeling of strength gained during the process.
- Self-inoculation. Self-inoculation is gaining awareness of what we feel. Having this awareness and understanding, we can learn ways to control emotions.

Expressing And Discharging Emotions

Certain emotions and feelings are so upsetting that our unconscious tries to suppress or repress them. We sometimes worry about the opinions of others. Hence, we avoid dealing with our intense emotions. However, there are various methods to reduce these fierce emotions, which can provide some relief to us. Venting or discharging emotions means strongly and completely expressing emotions such as fear, sadness, and anger, to the point that you feel "weakened." Then, the intense feeling is reduced, and you no longer feel a "heavy heart." Many therapists believe that repressing emotions can cause psychotic behavior, conflicts, and disorders, among other health-related risks.

Converting Emotional Energy

Stress affects our productivity. Some people are competent in handling stress, while others are unsuccessful. This method involves making a detailed plan on how to use emotional energy properly. This helps us get ourselves together while under pressure. This method's essence is to use emotions to increase motivation and not waste emotional energy on negative feelings.

Other Additional Methods:

- Distractions. Not thinking about unwanted feelings is one of the more useful methods of controlling emotions. Anger and depression can be reduced by watching a funny video or remembering a good memory. Other effective mood-changers include bonding with friends, traveling, and exercising.
- Changing the environment. Our environment affects our behaviors and feelings. Whenever we feel negative emotions such as depression, anxiety, and anger, we can change our setting by getting into a happier situation or changing our reaction to the environment. Also, reinforcing an environment with a definite idea (e.g., self-encouragement, reward system, etc.) can positively change emotions and behavior.

- Constant practice. We feel and become better when we practice. For example, you can overcome a fear of public speech by taking on speaking engagements. Practice does not make us perfect, but it makes an ideal method for controlling our emotions.
- Finding happy outlets. Engaging in friendly or happy activities frees up emotional baggage and helps us avoid dwelling on negative emotions. This can include traveling, visiting family and friends, helping other people in need, and many more activities.
- Drugs. There are several mood-altering drugs on the market. Some are prescribed and regulated, while others are illegal. But these only provide a temporary solution for our emotional problems. Hence, it is always recommended to remove the root cause of emotional distress, alongside any medication-based solutions..
- Skills. Acquiring new and better skills for managing difficult situations is an excellent way to control emotions.

There are countless other methods to change or control emotions. Some of these are very technical and applicable to certain people, such as implosion and rationale-emotive imagery therapy and paradoxical intentions. The segment above focus only on the methods that generally apply to everyone. Again, these methods do not guarantee effective control and management of emotions. The success or failure of these activities lies in the hands of the people who use them.

The bottom line is: we can alter and control our emotions given the right situation, method, and motivation to change. That is instrumental, because these methods will make us wiser at managing feelings and mastering our emotions, if we so decide.

Chapter 4:   Positive And Negative Emotions

We experience positive and negative emotions regularly. While it is suggested that feeling one is better than the other, negative and positive feelings can improve your life, this is often a difficult concept to understand. A large amount of negativity generally surrounds negative emotions, and they can often be more important than positive ones. As you will learn, negative emotions can have a powerful effect on your life.

The Difference Between Positive And Negative Emotions

There is a wide range of emotions that one can feel, and most situations cause one to experience several of them simultaneously. When these emotions are positive, like:

- Love

- Happiness

- Hope

- Gratitude

- Appreciation

- Trust

- Joy

We can feel more energized, motivated, relaxed, and excited about life. But when these emotions are negative, the opposite can happen. This can happen with primary and secondary emotions.

Primary and secondary emotions can often be viewed as adaptive, positive or negative, or maladaptive. Adaptive emotions help us grow, help us adjust and react appropriately in situations, and behave proactively. Maladaptive emotions are what makes us react most negatively. These emotions hinder our growth, keep us stuck, and lower our emotional intelligence.

Most people strive to have more positive emotions and tend to hide or ignore negative ones. This can be due to several factors. Negative emotions are looked down on, tend to cause more negative emotions, and tend to make matters worse. This makes people feel desperate, ashamed and filled with a feeling of lack.

Negative emotions tend to have the same social opinions as well. When you present yourself as a happy and optimistic person, you give the impression that you have your life together, that you are more successful, and satisfied. This can sometimes be a false image, as many people tend to feel that they have to give this impression to hide what is happening. This is not a healthy way to manage emotions.

What needs to be clearly understood is that negative emotions do not need to be managed. Negative emotions can be adaptive emotions when you know and deal with them appropriately. Negative and positive emotions can help motivate you and allow you to grow to be a better person. Negative emotions can help us teach us resilience and gratitude and give us clues about our lives that need improvement. In this sense, negative emotions can have a more significant positive impact on our happiness, health, and growth than positive emotions. But to use your negative emotions more positively, you must be able to recognize these emotions and understand how you tend to react to them.

Understanding the impact your emotions have on you helps you realize what emotions make you feel trapped and keep you living in the past. These emotions often go unresolved, which tends to be why you continue to have adverse reactions to specific situations, people, or events. But why do some emotions make us feel more energetic, while others make us feel exhausted?

Emotions carry their energy. Positive emotions make us feel good and therefore provide us with a sense of expansion. Since positive emotions allow us to relax our bodies, the energy they carry complements this state of relaxation. Negative energy, on the other hand, makes us feel constrained. This can make us tense our bodies and put us into a fight or flight mode that increases our stress levels. After experiencing negative emotions, we often feel exhausted and deflated. How it affects emotional energy is based on our perception of these emotions. Many see fear, anger, and other negative emotions as bad. This is why we feel so exhausted when we experience them.

- Anger

- Sadness

- Guilt

- Fear

- Anxiety

- Pride

- Resentment

- To regret

- Jealousy

When we experience these emotions, we automatically feel more shame and guilt around them. We often think that these emotions are a sign of weakness, so we usually try to suppress or ignore them.

Both negative and positive emotions are a natural occurrence. We cannot fully appreciate positive emotions if we never experience the negative. The main problem we have with negative emotions is that we think of them as negative occurrences. When you understand these negative emotions better and learn to accept and feel them, you can reduce your suffering.

How These Emotions Affect Our Lives And Our Health, Specifically Negative Emotions Such As Anger, Anxiety, And Negative Thoughts

When negative emotions are not adequately addressed and controlled, various health problems can arise. Constantly feeling helpless, depressed, stressed, anxious, and hopeless creates hormonal imbalances, depletes chemicals in the brain, and can damage the immune system. This can also lead to a shorter lifespan.

The Critical Inner Voice

The critical inner voice is the internal dialogue inside your head, filling you with discouraging, damaging, and dangerous thoughts. This inner voice can motivate and encourage those in good emotional health, but otherwise, it can lead to destructive behavior and uncontrollable emotions. This critical voice attacks ourselves and those around us, making it even more challenging to establish trust and find support. When unchecked, this inner voice can harm all areas of your life.

When your inner voice is negative and self-destructive, you can experience depression, anger, anxiety, and debilitating stress. If this voice begins to gain control, it could lose your self-esteem and confidence. This voice can leave you helpless and unable to set goals or find more positive ways to manage stress, which often results in resorting to unhealthy coping behaviors.

These negative conversations that take place inside your head are often the result of criticism or early experiences that made us feel inadequate. This dialogue may have been internalized by how her parents, siblings, teachers, or other figures to follow spoke to her. This does not always mean that the child was negatively spoken, but it can be a learned behavior when watching someone important talk to themselves about critically. No matter where the inner voice has influenced, it can be classified as self-hatred.

Chapter 5:   How Does Your Body Influence Your Emotions

Coping with destructive emotions is rarely straightforward and never easy. You can begin to identify your repressed emotions by listening to your body. When dealing with repressed emotions, especially anger and rage, the body is often affected as the mind. Repressed anger can cause chronic pain as well as

other emotional turmoil like high anxiety and depression.

Overall well-being isn't just about emotional and mental health; it is also about physical health. Your physical and psychological selves do not exist separately. They are continually interacting with one another. Keep reading to discover how your poor emotional health may negatively affect your body and your physical well-being.

Knowing how our minds work is part of the greatest mysteries we are yet to solve. A lot of individuals have dedicated their entire lives to understanding the mind, sadly to no avail. Understanding our mind and emotion's roles to our well-being is paramount as it puts us in the driving seat in controlling our lives. This is simply a little part of our quest to use the mind to control our feelings but must not be neglected. Like the relationship held by every part of our entire make-up, ignoring the interactions between our minds, emotions, thoughts, and feelings means we will ignore their roles. On a more serious note, this might be an aspect that we need to fix before taking further steps.

The mind and body do not function separately. They are not separate systems, and this can be observed when we are nervous. An instance of nervousness is a job interview or a first date with our long-time crush. Regardless of how calm and confident we would like to appear in such cases; we discover that we are both tensed and self-conscious at the same time. The muscles of our buttocks will be tightened as a result of the self-conscious feeling we are experiencing. We sweat more than usual, and might even feel nauseous in such events, not forgetting those periods we would fluff our lines when we want to try to be confident.

Our emotions constructed by the subconscious and highly influenced by the unconscious layer of our mind adds value to our thoughts. For instance, let us say you were raised to believe that tipping a salt shaker over is a sign of bad luck. When you observe someone tipping a salt shaker unintentionally or do so yourself, your mind sends thoughts which project emotions.

Our feelings are expressions of our emotional and mental state of existence. Generally tied to our physical and social sensory sense, they are used to react to joy, fear, love, disgust, sadness, hate, pleasure, and a lot of other emotions. In other to prevent extreme behaviors which usually comes at high costs, we must control and restrain some emotions and feelings.

Managing your emotions can be likened to developing a skill. It involves learning a better way of doing something. It requires change on our part. In reality, we struggle to accept change as humans. This is mainly due to many factors, but the mind's working is highly influential in this regard. Controlling your feelings will get you mentally stronger. The good thing is,

216

everyone can benefit it from controlling their emotions. Here is why you should keep your feelings in check.

Listen to Your Body

If your body is trying to tell you something, don't ignore it. It can be too easy to attribute physical discomfort to regular bodily changes, like aging, when, in fact, your physical symptoms may be caused by your emotional turmoil. It is also essential to notice when pre-existing conditions worsen for no physically identifiable reason. Chronic stress and anxiety can make things worse on our bodies when we face other diseases.

Get Involved In Healthier Activities

Keeping your body healthy affects your emotional health, just as your personal health affects your physical health. When you take the time to take care of yourself, you feel better about yourself, which results in more positive emotions. Find activities that make you feel good — this can include starting a new hobby, listening to music, being creative, and practicing physical activity.

These types of activities can often be combined, such as exercising while listening to uplifting music or finding a hobby that also allows you to be creative like painting, photography, or learning to play an instrument. Pushing yourself to try new things helps build your confidence, and when you have more confidence, you feel more in control and able to handle difficult situations.

Practice Deep Breathing and Mindfulness

All our emotions are experienced physically. When we are angry, upset or stressed, the feelings manifest themselves through our body. Our bodies respond on an evolutionary level (instinctively or involuntarily) like they would respond to a natural threat. Some physiological reactions to our emotions can be a speeding heartbeat, increased pulse rate, sweating, shallow breathing and more.

Exercise Daily

When you exercise daily, you can keep your body healthy and regulated. It produces hormones that will keep your body on schedule, happy, and healthy. It is recommended that people get at least 150 minutes of exercise a week to stay healthy and keep your body functioning regularly.

When you exercise regularly, you can lower anxiety, insomnia, and depression, keeping the body's circadian rhythm regular. Ultimately, keeping your body healthy seems to be one of the most effective ways to keep your sleep stable. Your body will thank you if you go for that after-dinner walk every day.

Your exercise can be anything. You could go to the gym and lift weights, swim, walk your dog several times a week, or even just buy a little desk cycle and pedal under your desk as you work. Anything is okay so long as you are getting the blood pumping regularly. It will keep your blood pressure healthy and alleviate the stress that might otherwise keep you awake at night.

Try Aerobic Exercises

Aerobic exercises can help you reduce fear and depression. You will be surprised to find out that you will be able to dissipate negative emotions as you move your body. Your calmness will return and you will be able to think again. These exercises affect your heart rate and also make your circulatory system continue to function the way it ought to work. Examples of such activities include taking a brisk walk or skipping with a jump rope.

Emotions are the way your body is communicating what's happening on the inside. It lets the people around you know how you feel through your body language, even if you don't say a word, and it enables you to see how you think if you learn to pay attention. When you're disappointed, your body communicates this through emotions like anger, fear, sadness and hurt. When you're happy, your body lets the rest of the world know through the smile on your face and spring in your step.

You feel energized and so happy that you can't contain your excitement for another minute. Although they're not always easy to deal with, one thing you can be sure of is that every emotion you experience matters. Even the less than comfortable emotions like shame, guilt or embarrassment. They all play an essential role in getting to know yourself better. For the sake of your wellbeing, you need to start listening to your emotions.

When you're just starting to learn about emotional mastery, as with anything new it is always best to start. In this case, begin by learning how to identify your emotions first. To detect the change in the various emotions and feelings you experience. It is also essential to learn how to separate your feelings from the people's emotions around you. You need to bridge that connected to yourself if you hope to understand what triggers your emotional responses and why certain things impact you the way that they do.

Some people have been lucky enough to grow up in an environment and supportive familial network that encourages rich vocabulary when it comes to emotions. Parents themselves are skilled at understanding, identifying, and helping their children link behaviors to the emotional state they feel. In other families, emotions are an uncomfortable subject that is either avoided, minimized or controlled. It is the children who grow up without the necessary emotional coaching that eventually go on to have a hard time understanding their emotions and feelings, let alone others' emotions.

Once you've identified what emotion you feel, the second step is to detect where in your body you feel this emotional change. Emotions manifest in your body and understanding where these changes occur is where you start to make the mind-body connection.

Try this exercise by sitting down in a chair or a comfortable place. Close your eyes, stay perfectly quiet and still, and remain that way until you feel something happening in your body. What is the first sensation you feel? An ache? An itch? Restlessness? The feelings you feel are how your body communicates with you, telling you what it needs and what you might need to do. If it is an itch, your body is telling you to scratch it to relieve the irritation. If it's an ache, stand up and stretch to ease the tension in your muscles.

Once you understand your body's signals, it's easier to know what needs to be done.You must learn to actively listen when your body is trying to tell you if you don't want to be run by your emotions for the rest of your life. Those who are run by their feelings have one thing in common: they will not progress far in life. If your emotions control you, it will always feel like you're stuck in a rut, and that the same old habits and behavior patterns seem to circle your life forever.

You'll only end up getting more frustrated and stressed with the way things are going in your life. Identifying your emotions and placing them in context enables you to determine where these emotions come from and whether it benefits you to feel the way you do.

Chapter 6:   How To Identify Emotions

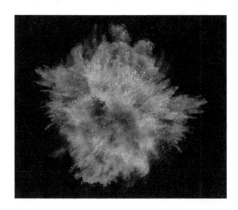

Emotions refer to the way you react to a situation. It is not an easy task doing so; it takes time and patience. Different people have different emotions, and you need to take time to identify the right feeling.

So, why should you even identify the emotions in the first place? Emotions come in three parts – the subjective, physiological, and expressive component. The emotional element refers to how you experience emotion. In contrast, the physiological component refers to how the body reacts to the feeling while the expressive part refers to how you behave when you respond to the emotion.

These elements play a big role in how you respond to emotion.

The Roles That Emotions Play In Our Lives

They Motivate Us To Take Action

The emotions dictate the way you react to the situation. For instance, when you are faced with an exam, you will feel anxious about how well you will perform and how the test will affect your results. Because of the responses, you might be forced to study better. The emotion allows you to take some action and improves the outcome.

Emotions also allow us to decide which actions to take; usually, the actions aim to help us experience more positive emotions while we reduce the probability of negative emotions.

Emotions Help Us Survive

Emotions are a way for us to avoid danger, survive ad reproduce. When we get angry, the next natural reaction is to confront what is irritating. When we are afraid, we will most likely run.

Emotions play the role of motivating us to quickly take action, which will increase the chances of success and survival.

They Help Us Make Decisions

Emotions can influence the decisions that we make. For instance, when we get annoyed, we look for a way to change the situation. Even when we have situations that require us to decide purely by rationality and logic, we still work by emotions.

Emotions Help Us Communicate

When we communicate with other people, we must give them clues that will better understand our situation. These clues involve emotions that we then display through body language. This can be in the form of facial expressions that are connected to specific emotions that we experience.

In some cases, it can involve us stating how we feel directly. For instance, when we tell someone that we are sad, happy, or frightened, we eat, giving them vital information that they can utilize to take action.

They Help Us to Understand Others

Just the way we give other people an idea of how we feel when we show them the emotions we go through, other people's feelings also give us an idea of what other people are thinking or planning.

When we know how to identify and interpret emotions, we can react to their feelings the right way. When we learn about feelings, we get to respond the right way to them, which means more meaningful relationships with other people.

How To Recognize Emotions

To manage your emotions, you first need to learn how to identify them the right way. A significant percentage of the people try to ignore the emotional reactions, letting the emotions build up. When this happens, the result is impaired ability to use their feelings productively.

Other people recognize the emotions but find it difficult to control them, and they find themselves at the mercy of the feelings.

To use your emotions the right way, you need first to identify the emotions the right way. Let us look at the best way to determine the feelings:

Understand the Trigger

The first step towards identifying the emotion is first to know what caused it. This will help you to describe the events that led to the emotional affair. In this step, try to stick to facts alone.

You can write down the event that led to the emotion to have it clear in your mind.

Why Do You Think It Happened?

The next step is to identify the possible causes that led to the emotional event. This is crucial because it determines the meaning that you give to the situation that happened. The type of emotional event that led to the issue will determine how you react to the event in question.

How the Situation Made you Feel

The next step is to determine how the emotional event made you feel both physically and emotionally. This will help you see whether the emotion resulted in a positive or negative reaction.

You need to notice both the positive and negative emotional and physical reactions you felt when it happened. Notice any physical feelings that you experience, such as tightness in the body.

What Was Your Reaction

You need to ask yourself this question so that you understand your urges. However, for the process to be effective, you need to make sure you are sincere. It might be painful to admit some of the desires that you felt when the event happened. When we face some situations, we at times get strange cravings to react differently. Some of the emotions that we go through might make us regret later on.

You need to compare your reaction at the moment that things happened and how you usually react. This will tell you whether you managed to control the urge or you failed to do so.

What Did You Do and Say?

The next step would be to understand what you said or did due to the emotions. Even though you didn't manage to respond the right way, you need to be honest with yourself about how you handled the situation. You also need to understand how the decision you made impacted on the case. This can be a good learning experience for you.

Once you evaluate your reaction, you can then use the situation to learn how to handle another situation that might arise.

How Did The Reaction Affect You Later On?

The final step in identifying the emotions is to understand the consequences of the actions that you took. If you said some words during the event, how did they affect you? On the other hand, if you acted in a certain way, how did it affect you later on?

So, if you find yourself being overly attached to your emotions next time, you need to ask yourself what happened and take the time to observe how you react when it happens. Go through these steps so that you can recognize your emotions. Once you practice and get used to these steps, you will be able to identify your emotions the right way and then choose the best way to respond to situations.

Chapter 7:   Factors Affecting Emotions

Sometimes, emotions arise for no apparent reason. Sometimes, it is due to some internal or external factors. The emotional state can be very dynamic, mostly if the person has not learned how to control his or her feelings.

One significant influence for your emotions is perception. How you perceive things or situations dramatically affects the chemical changes that take place in your body. For example, if you view an occasion as a problem for you, you will experience either hatred or fear towards the event. If you intend to speak or address people on such an event, you will probably experience anxiety during the session.

If you perceive the same occasion positively, you will appear more relaxed. You will also feel some excitement as the day of the experience approaches. These are two different kinds of emotions arising from the same occurrence. That means that how you view life and the events in it determines how your emotions behave.

The way you perceive others also determines how you interact with them. For instance, when you have a negative perception towards others, you may find that the responses you give them are somewhat hostile even if the question asked was a simple one. If you have a positive perception towards others, your engagement with them will be fulfilling, and you will leave them happy. It is, therefore, vital that you control your perception to ensure that you appear emotionally intelligent.

Your mental health can also affect your emotions. Stress and the lack of focus always manifest physically as well as emotionally. Physical manifestations of principle may include muscle aches and general body pain. Emotional signs are things like anger, sadness, and anxiety. Your stress levels significantly affect your mood. Therefore, you must learn how to manage your stress by identifying the source of the stress and dealing with it appropriately.

Lack of sleep impacts your general mood during the day. It is always enjoyed staying up late, especially when doing something fun. However, doing this continuously can interfere with the functional ability of your body. You may start feeling moody all the time, resulting in serious health conditions like stroke and heart problems. To relieve yourself from such occurrences, always ensure that you get enough sleep. The recommended hours of sleep for every individual is between seven and nine hours. If you are an early riser, you must sleep early enough.

Hormones can also cause emotions to fluctuate significantly. For example, women whose bodies have low estrogen hormone levels may notice drastic changes in their feelings. Testosterone hormone levels may also cause a mood problem in men. Tests can be carried out to determine if hormones are responsible for a person's mood changes.

Some foods may be responsible for mood fluctuations as well. For instance, chocolate causes a trigger in sugar levels and endorphins. This results in a feeling of pleasantness and excitement.

Each emotion always comprises of two components – a physical component and a mental component. These two also affect a person's mood and feelings differently. The cognitive part of emotions is characterized by:

- The ability to differentiate and choose between pain and pleasure
- The tendency to engage inactivity
- Memory thought, and perception of an individual. These three aspects define the social, mental, and material interests of human beings

- Ability to differentiate between muscular and organic sensations
- The bodily component of emotions, on the other hand, determines:
- Any changes in the body's internal organs as a result of emotional changes
- Movement of body muscles

The mental component is what comprises an emotional experience while the bodily component is what is known as emotional expression. Emotion is often triggered by the imagination, thought, or perception of a particular circumstance. It is not triggered by a single thing or event but a collection of mental activities.

External occurrences cause different kinds of emotions. For instance, seeing a leopard always triggers fear of getting harmed or losing a life. However, seeing the same leopard in a cage will not trigger the emotion of fear.

Every emotion is a response to a situation. It can be pleasant or painful, depending on your perception of the problem.

Emotions And The Environment

Your surrounding greatly determines the kind of emotions you generate. A home or place adorned with bright, shiny colors will always make you happy and at ease. The surrounding alone will improve your mood greatly. However, places like call centers or chat rooms with dull walls, and nothing colorful in place will always create a gloomy environment. Nothing is exciting about such environments. This explains why most workplaces do not get too many decorations.

Workplaces are not placing of excitement but places of serious business. However, your overall mood always affects how you respond to certain situations. For instance, if you are in a gloomy environment and a challenging issue arises, your response may not be quite good, especially if you have had quite a long day. If you have been confined in such an environment for long hours, you may feel frustrated by the new issue that has arisen and may get angry at everyone.

Negative emotions always harm your ability to perform your duties. Some environments can create a negative mood, and as a result, you may start developing negative emotions out of nowhere.

One example of individuals who get overwhelmed with the work environment is call center represcntatives. They are always faced with an expectation that some cannot meet. Customers always expect them to remain confident and joyful, regardless of how their day has been. However, this sometimes becomes impossible, and their emotions may run beyond control.

The color of the room also affects the mood of those in the room. You should thus understand which colors inspire a positive environment and which ones create a more productive atmosphere. Some of the colors associated with a great mood include:

- Blue – this is a great color for you if you wish to experience calm. The blue color is also known as a remedy for high blood pressure. It also stimulates the mind to think positively and causes individuals to become more productive. When balanced with other colors like yellow, it can also create a good setup for creative thinking, which is a catalyst for circumstances that require adequate problem-solving skills.
- Red – red is a very powerful stimulant. However, it should be used in moderation. Red is a good color for settings that promote serious physical activity. In environments that need some calm, you should use

red sparingly since the color is known to stir energy and action.

- Green – the green color also creates a calm environment. One great thing with green color is that it is found freely in nature. That is why people who need to relax spend most of their time outdoors. Green also acts as a source of balance for other colors, and it triggers productivity.

Besides colors, the lighting of an environment may also trigger negative or positive emotions. For instance, blue lights often promote a sense of creativity in the workplace and create a calm home environment. Studies show that being exposed to blue lighting improves performance significantly. Natural light also plays a big role in the home or work environment. It causes people to relax more, giving them better control of their emotions.

Emotions And Behavior

Some emotions cause people to react in a certain way, and this affects how a person thinks. This is always helpful when danger is involved. Sometimes, things happen, and there is no time to think before acting, but some emotions trigger a lot of thinking. For example, if you encounter a person undergoing a challenge, the feeling of sympathy or sorrow may cause you to start thinking about how you will assist the person.

Negative emotions mostly lead to negative thoughts, while positive emotions often lead to positive thoughts. That is why you must change your way of thinking. For example, if you sit an exam and fail it, you may start thinking that you will never pass the exam, and this assumption may cause you to stop working hard. When this happens, you should analyze the situation to understand better why you failed in the first place. This will help you improve on the areas that need development to perform better next time.

Most emotions often show in the person's face or actions. A good example is when you are angry. You will either raise your voice at others or make somebody's movements that suggest your agitation. The anger may also show on your face as frowns or clenched teeth. Some of these actions are predictable, while others occur without expectation.

Actions always indicate an expression of feelings. That is why it is not advisable to suppress your feelings, even if they are negative. Trying to suppress your feelings can cause mental and physical problems.

When it comes to behavior, emotions also affect the way a person makes decisions. Negative emotions always trigger negative decisions since they make people feel like they have very limited options available. When you are excited, you are always bound to make unrealistic decisions that are regrettable. That is why you shouldn't make decisions when highly agitated or highly excited.

As for the workplace, emotions can impact the motivation, personality, and temperament of a person.

They cloud a person's sense of perception and judgment. Emotions also play a major role in determining how you react to the stimuli that occur in your environment. When exposed to negative emotions for a long time, you may develop some sicknesses such as ulcers and heart problems. This also applies to stressful environments at work and home. Generally, having a bad mood always reduces individuals' performance since this makes employees make poor decisions that may affect the company's overall performance.

On the other hand, a positive wave of emotions boosts problem-solving and creativity skills of employees. As earlier stated, emotions are caused by a chemical balance in the brain. This chemical balance always determines an individual's mood and energy level. It also enhances or diminishes one's thinking and judgment capabilities. Therefore, individuals must seek to identify how their emotional state affects their behavior as a way of improving how they interact with others and respond to situations. Positive emotions always lead to satisfaction; therefore, it is always important to ensure that your emotions are adequately balanced.

Chapter 8: Advantages Of Mastering Emotions

Suppose someone asked me to choose the single largest factor contributing to a person's success in today's complicated and volatile world. In that case, I'd say emotional intelligence or the ability to control one's emotions without batting an eyelid.

Emotional Intelligence is our ability to manage our emotions by  discriminating among these feelings and using the information to guide our words, thoughts, and actions. To cut a long story short, emotional intelligence is an aggregation of your mental and emotional skills. Emotionally intelligent people enjoy many benefits in all spheres of life, including relationships, career, and social life.

Here are some ways your life can be impacted or benefited if you consciously focus on developing high emotional intelligence.

Greater Kindness In Everyday Life

One of the best benefits of high emotional intelligence is your ability to demonstrate compassion for others both in your personal and professional sphere. This compassion allows you to connect with people at much deeper levels so you can forge meaningful relationships. Compassion can be manifested in several ways, including helping someone dealing with a personal issue by taking on their responsibilities or making small everyday decisions for your employees' comfort/convenience.

Compassion helps you meaningfully connect with people both in your personal and professional life. You can reach out to people efficiently; forge more mutually fulfilling relationships and create an atmosphere of harmony and productivity. Emotional intelligence awards you greater compassion in dealing with people in various personal, professional and social scenarios.

Higher Employee Morale And Reduced Attrition

Morale may be an intangible concept in the corporate world, but its effects are highly measurable. You may not realize the value of high morale when it's there, but you will know when it's missing. Think about the lateness, early departures, attrition, and sick leaves your company suffers from. When leaders take the time to build emotional intelligence and connect with their team members, it reflects their morale.

Emotionally intelligent leaders who build stronger emotional ties with subordinate's witness improvement in the team's morale, lower measurable absenteeism, a higher team spirit and a greater desire to contribute to an organization's success. The emotional intelligence skill building cost can be minimal. However, the return on investment can be extremely high.

Let's get real here and call a spade a spade. Employees do not quit roles, they quit senior managers. It is about escaping people and not positions. Emotionally intelligent leaders, who recognize emotional triggers, quickly pick up emotional clues of their team members and "customize" their approach to each member's unique emotional make-up and motivation will experience greater success in retaining employees. This should not be mistaken with not doing justice to one's voice or feelings. It simply means presenting an accurate emotional response towards each team member to treat them with greater compassion, respect, and empathy.

The problem with most managers who do not understand the concept of emotional intelligence is they use a one size fits all approach for dealing with all employees, without understanding the emotional framework, motivators, and goals of individual team members. This one size fits all approach does not produce flattering results because personalities vary. Some people are more intrinsically motivated, while others thrive on extrinsic motivation. Some folks are quick to reveal their emotions; others aren't very comfortable sharing their feelings. Once you understand the emotional make-up of people, it becomes easy to deal with them more efficiently.

Increased Productivity

Emotional intelligence has a high correlation with an individual's work performance. Research has revealed that emotional intelligence is  twice as crucial as technical/cognitive abilities even among engineering professions. Emotionally intelligent managers, supervisors, and leaders effectively manage teams, motivating people and negotiating.

They create a more positive atmosphere with happier workers who are an asset to any organization. Happier workers translate into higher morale, low absenteeism, reduced attrition rate, and higher productivity. This leads to happier customers, more sales and higher profits.

Thus, emotional intelligence is an invaluable trait when it comes to success in the workplace. While everyone within an organization possesses more or less the same technical competency and educational qualifications, only a few rise up the corporate ladder because of their ability to manage people and their emotions.

An emotionally intelligent leader who understands the true value of identifying and managing emotions can empower his/her subordinates with these skills daily. Discipline or self-regulation is essential when it comes to keeping your emotions in check, avoiding panic, remaining calm and being an asset to the team.

Emotionally intelligent folks have little trouble recognizing and managing potentially destructive emotions that can create stress and lower productivity. The approach is calmer, more confident and efficient. Rather than experiencing a touchier view, these folks depend on their ability to possess a more realistic view of themselves and others.

Awesome Communication Skills

People with well-developed emotional quotient are more efficient when it comes to expressing themselves. They possess the ability to listen attentively to other people's verbal clues, while also being able to tune into their nonverbal communication. They know exactly what to say to channelize people's strengths. They use the right words and nonverbal signals to help people feel at ease. There is little scope for misunderstanding while communicating with a person who has high emotional intelligence.

Emotionally intelligent people are well aware of the most compelling emotional triggers of the people around them. They know exactly how to inspire people to act. People who can communicate by emotionally connecting with someone are far more effective than technically competent folks who fail to demonstrate empathy while communicating with people. Emotional intelligence awards you better response skills.

Dealing With Challenges

Don't you sometimes look at some people and wonder how they can stay afloat through the most challenging situations and emerge even more successful than before? Chances are, these guys score high in emotional intelligence. Emotionally intelligent folks can calm their bodies and minds to view things from a clearer and more objective perspective. Their acts are more mindful and less panic stricken.

Greater calmness, objectivity and clarity award you more resilience where life's challenges are concerned. Think about the Kungfu fighter who can take on the most powerful opponents by constantly working on martial arts skills. Emotional intelligence equips you with those skills to take on the toughest challenges that life throws at you with resilience.

Reduced Chances Of Addiction And Emotional Disorders

Addictions are generally a direct result of our inability to cope with emotions. People who struggle to come to terms with their emotions use addiction as a mechanism to avoid the more underlying and deeper prevailing issues. When you fail to recognize and manage negative emotions, there develops an unfortunate pattern of dependency on external factors such as food, nicotine, illegal substances, alcohol, porn and the like. Addiction is just a means to escape from emotions you aren't willing to deal with.

Emotionally intelligent folks are less prone to addiction because of their awareness of their emotions and their ability to manage them. They have a solid understanding of their feelings and do not struggle to deal with it. Since emotional intelligence makes you happier, more confident and balanced, there is a lesser propensity for dependence on destructive coping mechanisms.

They adapt more easily to challenges and changing scenarios in life. Emotionally intelligent people are competent in resolving differences and coming up with more positive solutions. Since they display such a high understanding of their own and others' emotions, it becomes easier for them to deal with conflicts.

Emotionally healthy people are less prone to be victims of drug abuse or binge eating disorders, predominantly from much deeper psychological issues.

Better Leadership Skills

Emotionally intelligent folks possess a highly evolved ability to recognize and understand factors that drive others, which makes them amazing leaders. They can make the most of this invaluable information to strengthen their loyalty and forge stronger relationships with people. A competent leader is intuitively tuned in to the most compelling aspirations and desires of his followers. He knows the "hot buttons" of his employees and exactly how to channelize these "hot buttons" to increase overall productivity and positivity within the work environment.

Emotionally intelligent leaders know how to channelize this information to extract better performance/productivity from people and keep them happy. People with a high emotional quotient excel at recognizing people's strengths and weaknesses and harnessing an individual's virtues for benefiting the team.

High emotional intelligence creates better leaders who can inspire greater faith and loyalty by using their teams or followers or emotional range. They are more aware of their emotions, which allows emotionally intelligent folks to create a harmonious environment. Practicing emotional intelligence makes you a better leader.

Did you know 67% of all competencies fundamental for high performance in the professional sphere are emotional intelligence? Take the example of the world's most successful CEOs. Amazon's Jeff Bezos passionately talks about getting right into his customers' hearts in a 2009 YouTube video while announcing the company's Zappos acquisition.

When Howard Schultz of Starbucks was a child, his father lost a health insurance claim. This turned him into one of the most empathetic CEOs, who is well known for showing his employees thoughtfulness by offering generous healthcare rewards. Little wonder then that these folks are as successful as they are. They understand the emotional pulse of their employees and customers and can keep them emotionally gratified.

Emotional intelligence helps build emotional maturity, boost social intelligence, prevent relationship problems, enhance interpersonal communication, help control emotions, deal with stress, influence leadership, help authorities make sound business change decisions, support staff, and control resistance to change.

Chapter 9: Mental Toughness And Emotional Mastery

Our emotions play a vital role in how we face challenges and setbacks. Our ability to function effectively when everything around us is going awry is closely linked to how we process our emotions. If we're unable to control them, our capability to perform under pressure suffers. If we can exert control, handling mistakes and distress becomes much easier.

This is referred to as our emotional intelligence. We can understand and manage our emotions in a way that allows us to perform effectively. Rather than stifling our feelings to toughen our minds against adversity, we should aim to do the opposite. We should try to recognize how we feel whenever we encounter challenges so we can learn to control our fear, manage our stress, and respond with purpose and determination.

The Value Of Self-Awareness

We must know what we feel deep down to become mentally strong. We need to be acutely aware of our thoughts, beliefs, and convictions. We must clarify our values so that our responses to unfavorable circumstances are purposeful.

Becoming mentally strong doesn't require that we detach ourselves from our emotions. On the contrary, we should embrace them. That's the only way to master them truly. By acknowledging our fear, frustration, and other negative emotions when things go wrong, we can evaluate them, determine their integrity, and regulate the unrealistic ones.

Increasing our self-awareness is the first step toward achieving emotional mastery.

Why Emotional Control Is Critical

Emotional mastery is often misunderstood as meaning to stifle one's emotions. But that belief is incorrect. Emotional mastery entails recognizing our emotions, understanding why we're experiencing them, and healthily managing them.

We don't want to disassociate ourselves from our feelings. That doesn't lead to mental toughness. Over the long run, disconnecting just makes us more susceptible to anxiety and depression.

Managing our emotions - that is, exerting emotional control - allows us to acknowledge them, confront them, scrutinize them, and decide whether what we're feeling is levelheaded given our circumstances.

For example, suppose you've completed an exam at school and received a poor grade. You may feel disgusted with yourself, presuming that you're dense and incapable of doing better. These negative emotions and overly-critical assumptions will wreak havoc with your ability to perform well in the future. Exerting emotional control allows you to honestly explore these emotions and assumptions and determine if they're accurate (spoiler: they're rarely accurate). It gives you a chance to realign your perceptions about your abilities with reality.

Mental toughness is directly connected to how we perceive ourselves and our ability to perform, regardless of our circumstances. Emotions that stem from distress, disappointment, and anxiety hamper us. They slow us down and can even cause us to abandon our intentions when things go wrong. This makes emotion management a requisite skill.

Mastering Your Emotions

Gaining emotional control takes time. Many of us devote our entire lives being greatly influenced by our emotions, even the ones that are irrational given our capabilities. So, it'll take time to learn to manage them. Following are a few tactics that worked for me. You may find that they work for you, as well.

- Reflect on your feelings, both positive and negative. Acknowledge them.
- Scrutinize negative emotions the moment they surface. Ask yourself, "Are these emotions reasonable?" If not, reflect on how these emotions hold you back.
- Meditate for five minutes a day. Observe your emotions without judgement. Mornings are best, but any time is fine.
- Confront your inner critic whenever it "speaks." Investigate its claims to determine if they're accurate.
- Recognize circumstances you can influence and circumstances you can't influence. Get accustomed to letting go of your frustration regarding the latter.
- Take action, even when you're uncertain of the outcome. This will train your mind to be proactive.
- Try to sleep well, eat well, and exercise. Our physical health influences our emotional health.

Be patient with yourself. No one achieves emotional mastery overnight. The good news is, if you take action every day, you'll eventually be able to manage your emotions

Chapter 10:   How Does Emotions Affect Your Health

How Negative Emotions Affect Your Health

Sometimes, our emotional distress manifests as physical distress, causing negative changes in the body. If you've ever been so stressed out that you found yourself so angry that your vision begins to go black and blotchy at the corners, then you understand how intense emotions can make us feel physically ill. Perhaps, you've had chronic stomach pain for years, but no doctor has been able to tell you why because it is not physical but psychological. This could be because it is your emotions causing your pain and not a physical ailment.

A common physical symptom of poor emotional health is a change in appetite. Many people who are suffering from depression experience a loss of appetite and subsequent weight loss. The body still gets hungry because it needs fuel to function, but even favorite foods may become flavorless and unappetizing. However, Sugar affects the brain's pleasure center, which craves the good feelings sugary foods cause. This may explain why people with depression sometimes gain weight and struggle with binge-eating.

Another common physical manifestation of intense negative emotion is digestive problems. The brain and the digestive tract communicate with each other all the time, which is why you may become nauseous when nervous. When you experience intense emotional distress, it causes disruptions in the natural contractions of your bowels. It also lowers immunity, which makes it easier for infection to take hold within the digestive tract.

You're Body On Anger

Anger itself is not always negative. It alerts us to something or someone in our life that is not right and motivates us to correct that and express our frustration. Incessant anger and rage, however, can be damaging to your physical health.

Chronic or mismanaged stress and anger can cause discomfort in the body and damage personal health in various ways. Here's a list of common physical symptoms caused by negative stress and anger:

- Accelerated heart rate
- Accelerated breathing rate
- Increased blood pressure
- General aches and pains
- Muscle tension and pain
- Jaw clenching/teeth grinding
- Stomach/digestive issues
- Lowered immune function
- Difficulty healing
- Dizziness and nausea
- Insomnia or trouble sleeping too much
- Loss of or increase in appetite
- Loss of sex drive
- Tinnitus/ringing in ears
- Eczema and other skin conditions

Stress and anger are not the only emotions that can cause you physical distress. Depression can wreak as much havoc with your physical health as it can on your emotional health, causing an array of symptoms and worsening existing conditions. Many people experience the physical symptoms of depression but may not realize that these symptoms have a psychological cause, which makes finding solutions to these physical issues much more difficult.

Impact Of Negative Emotions On Health

Aside from stomach challenges, negative emotions have several other health implications. There are illnesses and health issues you've had in the past that you thought were a result of diseases but were caused by your overindulgence on toxic energy.

Heart Health

Negative emotions have the same kind of impact that stress has on the heart. When you are anxious, you tend to want to do a series of things to help you feel better. Some of these things may not be healthy for you as they include reliance on alcohol, smoking, or overeating comfort food.

Eating Disorders

When a person is dealing with negative emotions, food. Not eating may or may not be intentional in that state. But anxiety always paves the way for eating disorders, and this is true because most people diagnosed with eating disorders struggle or may have struggled with stress in the past.

Eating disorders are illnesses. The people who experience them observe a sudden change with eating, which is usually caused by their anxiety over weight gain and how they look.

Unplanned Weight Loss

Anything toxic will affect you emotionally and physically; it will become evident that you are going through something, and one of the physical manifestations is weight loss. Yes, we all want to maintain a proper and healthy weight, but unplanned weight loss can be terrible, especially when dealing with eating disorders.

Your clothes will no longer fit properly. You will look exhausted and unhealthy, which will also cause people to ask a lot of questions. Even if you weren't a very chubby person before this challenge, the amount of weight you shed would be too obvious to ignore.

Unplanned weight loss can also affect a person's psychology because if you don't understand the connection between your emotions and weight loss, you will start to think you are very sick. Some people go to the doctor, hoping to get diagnosed for an illness they don't have.

Toxic emotions have a way of making you put the source of your worry ahead of yourself; you no longer take care of yourself or put your well-being first. In most cases, some people realize that they've lost weight after a long time because they weren't paying attention to their bodies.

Unhealthy weight loss will make you susceptible to illnesses and fatigue. You will always feel tired, and this can lead to unproductivity with everything you do. It is quite amazing to think that all these health problems started with just one wrong idea. So does this mean we can reverse the process with positive thinking?

How Positive Emotions Affect Your Health

When you feel good, everything else feels excellent, even your health. If you take the time to compare and contrast the state of your health when you felt anxious and when you weren't, you would agree that you felt healthier when you were happy.

But aside from the "feeling" of being healthy, it is a fact that positive emotions have an excellent effect on mental and physical health — people who are happy fall ill less often compared to those who are anxious or depressed.

Because of the impact of positive moods on health, there is a new term known as "positive psychology," which entails using different techniques that encourage us to identify and develop positive emotions for better health experiences.

Positive psychology emphasizes that attention should be placed on problem-free emotions while urging individuals to concentrate more on their strengths and not on their weaknesses. Anxiety is often a result of speculations about the worst-case scenario and fixating attention on the things you cannot do while anticipating disappointing results.

But with positive psychology, you are encouraged to look beyond the fear that causes you to have eating and sleeping disorders. You are also empowered to build the best things in your life and repair the worst.

As an individual, you need to thrive, and this also means you need to be in good health to achieve that, but good health is connected to your emotions, which takes us right back to the healing ability of good feelings.

If you are having trouble sleeping because you are anxious, try to be happy and worry less. You will notice that your sleep patterns will improve. If you love yourself above everyone else and appreciate your body, you wouldn't have eating disorders or be anxious about how you look.

Being healthy isn't the absence of illness, and that is what positive psychology seeks to express fully. In addition to being free from diseases, your newfound optimism will help you enjoy good heart health. It will cause you to enjoy a long and happy life where you aren't pressured to become anything other than you.

We are not concerned about the idea of longevity, which is all about how long we'll live. We are concerned with the impact and quality of life we have, which is what matters. However, the good thing about this thought process is that, while you aren't precisely focused on how long you'll live, if you do enjoy positive emotions, having a long life will surely be in the cards for you.

What Takes Place in Your Brain When You Are All about Positive Emotions?

Negative emotions cause you to be completely fixated on the cause of your anxiety, which also makes it difficult for you to be 100% aware of the other good things you have going for yourself. Sadly, the more narrow-minded you are with the problem, the more damage it does to your health.

The headaches you feel most times are because you find some things very complicated and challenging to handle. Still, when you have more positive emotions, stressful situations will be easier to handle. The ideas you labeled as "complex" will become easy because positive emotions help you build emotional resilience.

You should know now is that positive emotions act as a shield that protects you from challenges you may face with negative emotions.

Negative emotions constantly remind you of your problems. Think about it: whenever you started feeling anxious, most of the time, it was because you remembered something unpleasant or you thought of a problem that you would have to deal with later. Now, this doesn't mean that when you focus on good emotions, you become oblivious of issues. No, it isn't the case!

Don't focus your entire attention on the problem for too long, enough to get you upset, anxious, or afraid. With more emphasis on negative emotions, you would think that every day is horrible. You would think that you do not have anything to be grateful for at the end of it.

When we spend time to think about the effect of positive emotions and what complete reliance on it does to our health, we start to appreciate life more. We become open to conversations around being more positively driven.

You're Body on Positive Emotion

Scientists have been studying the positive effects of emotions for as long as they've been studying the negative effects. It is generally found that people who experience more positive emotions tend to be healthier and live longer. When we feel more upbeat and positive, it causes our bodies to become better balanced. Our autonomic systems (especially the autonomic nervous system) function properly without the interference of stress hormones and other physical consequences of negative emotion. When we experience positive interactions with others and ourselves regularly, we provide our body with a cycle of balance and health.

Chapter 11:   The   Benefits   of   Emotional Intelligence

Emotional intelligence is believed to be one of the fastest growing job skills, and for a reason. Those with high emotional intelligence have an advantage over others in the workplace mainly because they find it easier to work in multicultural environments ,cope better under pressure, and be good listeners and make potentially great leaders and emphatic colleagues.

Therefore, developing emotional intelligence makes it easier to cope with the demands of a stressful and fast-paced life of the 21st century. This is particularly important for those who see themselves in high-paid, prestigious, or leadership positions.

Therefore, the main benefit of having high emotional intelligence is that knowing how to manage emotions and easily understand and cooperate with others effectively makes you stand to be an asset to whomever you work for.

Besides, emotionally intelligent people process their emotions before responding to them. It means, they think before they speak. This may not seem very important but chances are if you have a habit of making ill-informed comments, you will sooner or later come to regret them.

This is perhaps particularly relevant for the Western culture where people usually don't like silence and tend to answer questions or make comments without thinking. Or even worse, believe that every silence has to be filled with a witty comment or a remark.

Words can both help and hurt, and your choice of words says a lot about you. One way of raising your emotional intelligence is to become more conscious of the implications of what you are saying.

10 Main Benefits Of Having High Emotional Intelligence:

People enjoy working for/with you

Emotionally intelligent people don't bully their colleagues or harass their staff. They know how to get others to do what they want without resolving to arrogance or aggression. Being flexible and open to suggestion, they make great colleagues or leaders.

People easily open up to you

Being empathic, emotionally intelligent people can tune in to others' emotions, so they easily understand others' point of view or circumstances that may have led them to do certain things.

You are the master of your emotions in any circumstances

The ability to identify, understand, and manage your emotions means you'll always be a step ahead over others when it comes to responding to challenging situations. Besides, being in charge of your emotions helps you manage stress better.

You effortlessly resolve conflicts

The step to successfully resolving conflicts is to deal with them before the situation gets out of hand. Your ability to manage your emotions, and easily understand those of others and triggers that may have led to them, makes it possible to respond to someone's behavior in a way that will diffuse a potentially difficult situation.

Because your interpersonal skills are good, you feel relaxed around people and are not easily thrown off balance in unpredictable and difficult situations, or with unfriendly or openly hostile individuals.

You quickly become a leader

Emotionally intelligent people have most of the qualities of highly effective leaders: empathic, confident, communicative, positive, and supportive.

You can work anywhere, with anyone

Great people skills, empathy, and social awareness mean that you will work well and get most out of every situation even under challenging circumstances or in a foreign culture.

You easily get a high-paid job

Being one of the most desirable skills in the workplace, high emotional intelligence can help you get the job of your dreams.

You don't do or say things you later regret

Knowing that you have to understand and process your emotions before releasing them, means that you will only act once you've had a chance to consider the situation. Sometimes, all it takes is having a few minutes to think things over and give yourself a chance to calm down and assess the situation, before making the final decision.

If there are occasions that you are too embarrassed to think about because of what you said, or did, it's probably because at the time you didn't have or didn't use your emotional intelligence, as a result of which you made decisions you lived to regret.

You are a valued friend and confidant

Emotional intelligence skills are just as valuable outside work. Some of your most important decisions and emotions take place outside the workplace, eg with your family, in your romantic relationships, with your friends, children, etc.

You are fulfilled

Having a successful career and being accomplished personally means you will have lived your life to the fullest.

So, through affecting your emotions, behavior, and interpersonal relations, emotional intelligence has a major effect on your life quality.

To continually cultivate and enhance these skills, you should never stop working on your:

Self-Awareness

Be constantly in touch with your feelings and learn to tune in to them.

Social Skills

Cultivate your communication skills and never underestimate the power of words. Besides, to become highly empathic, you have to try and develop humility. Although being humble is not easy in a society which encourages competition and individuality, ability to openly admit your limitations and mistakes, are traits of a true leader.

Emotional Regulation

Learn to control your strong emotions, particularly negative ones, and never act on impulse. Practice this by thinking of something that will make you feel hurt, angry, or exploited. Sit with the feeling, feel the humiliation, or anger, "digest" it, and only after you have calmed down "respond" to the person or situation that made you feel that way.

How Emotional Intelligence Can Help Out In Relationships

Have you ever made a snarky comment to your boss in a moment of anger during a heated discussion? Have you ever had a fiery argument with your spouse about a small issue blew up into something huge? Have you ever regretted making an important decision when you were upset? Don't feel bad if the answer is yes! All of us have gone through this. Why does this happen? When you cannot recognize and understand your emotions, you are controlled by them and react hastily. These are all problems of poor or low emotional intelligence.

People with high emotional intelligence are associated with the following:

- Increased creativity
- Change acceptance
- Good team worker
- Excellent work performance
- Retention at work

Emotionally intelligent people can understand four crucial, critical things:

- They can understand other's emotions, as they are smart in recognizing them. This particular skill is extremely tough when you are dealing with people who aren't emotionally open. You can easily identify that

254

someone is sad when they are crying, but how do you understand the person's grief if he or she is trying to hide it? People with high EQ can do it, and if you practice EQ, you can do it too.

- They are conscious of their own emotions and feelings. They are always in touch with their emotions and know what they feel, how they feel and why they feel. They don't push away the emotions by brushing it aside or giving it a wrong label. Regulating emotions is key, as there is a difference between showing your frustration during an official meeting or waiting for the meeting to finish to show your irritation. Consequences for the former can be dangerous and even spoil your relationship with your boss, while the latter gives you time to think over it so that you put it across in a much better way.

- Thoughts create emotions! Emotionally intelligent people understand this and work towards clearing and controlling the thought. Doing this can decrease the power of your emotions. Sometimes, your thinking process is affected by your feelings and mood, i.e., over-thinking. For example, your decision-making skills will begin to falter when you are upset, but when you are calm, you make decisions that handle the conflict much better.

- These people understand the correlation between their actions and the emotional reactions in other people. For instance, an emotionally intelligent man will know that breaking the promise he made to his wife can result in her feeling hurt.

Building emotional intelligence is a great way to improve your relationship with others – it can be a tough task, but it is doable. How do you build your emotional intelligence? There are several ways to do so, but we will look at the easiest and practical way.

- Observe your thought process.
- Watch the way your thoughts connect with your emotions throughout the day.
- The chemicals released in your brain will change the way you feel about things.
- Thoughts release these chemicals.
- Notice the connection between your thoughts and emotions.
- Work on decreasing negative emotions by not giving the power to the thoughts that create those emotions.
- Focus on increasing your thoughts towards positive emotions.

How To Determine Whether My Emotional Intelligence Needs Improvement

The act of loving someone calls for emotional intelligence – yes, you read it right! You require emotional intelligence to love, as you need to empathize, recognize problems and should be able to connect with the person on a much deeper level. The way you solve issues at home and your choice of partner indicates a lot about the connection between emotional intelligence and love. When you can harness the power of emotional intelligence successfully, you tend to see an improvement in your relationships.

The following are some of the classic signs that will tell you that you need to boost your emotional intelligence.

- Bursting into laughter or lashing out in anger in a moment signals your lack of emotional quotient. This is because you are finding it difficult to control your emotions.
- Having a tough time building and maintaining healthy relationships with colleagues and friends may indicate your problems with emotional intelligence. Lack of social skills.

- Are you finding it difficult to sympathize or empathize? If you want to have a lasting relationship, you should be able to empathize with others' feelings. It is a necessary part of a healthy relationship.
- You have an issue with your emotional quotient if you cannot connect with media, movies or books. Tragedy, comedy and horror – all these genres are meant to stimulate your emotions, but if media, movies or books don't move you, there is something wrong with your emotional intelligence.

It is crucial to understand that emotional intelligence plays a major role in every part of your life – it helps dictate a range of things, from a successful career to a contented personal relationship. For some people, emotional intelligence is naturally high while for some it is low. If you feel you have low EQ, don't hesitate to take steps to work on improving it. Self-improvement is a necessity in everything! Mindfulness is the basis for emotions – try meditating or getting into yoga sessions to improve your mindfulness.

The following simple steps will help you work towards improving your emotional quotient:

- Practice self-control. Pause, breathe (deep breath), count (for few seconds) and compose (think) a response. Don't react immediately.
- Abstain. If you are the one who responds indifferently to situations or makes inept jokes, give yourself time to listen to the opposite person before you frame a response. For example, making jokes at a funeral or other tragedy to lighten the grief.

Chapter 12:   Determining Emotions

Three key factors can determine our emotions. This is what is referred to as an emotional triad.

1.   Your physiology

Our emotions are the first waves of experience that our bodies usually feel. Therefore, whenever you want to be passionate, you can begin by talking faster or making your movements faster before adopting passion's physiology. On the same note, when you want to feel more confident, then it will be prudent for you to stand above all else, your ground, take a deep breath, and, if possible, speak with confidence. The same applies to negative emotions. You can stoop over, facing the ground, shallow breathing, and a frown, while speaking meekly. One of the perfect ways to put a phrase into this concept is that our emotions are typically driven by motion.

2.   What you focus on

Those things which we usually put our minds also affect how we feel. For any of us to have emotions of happiness, then it is essential to concentrate on those things that matter in your life. The things that you focus on are those that influence what you feel. However, remember that there will always be bad and good things happening in your life, and hence, you should learn to focus on the right things at all times.

3.   Your language

What you say and the words coming from your mouth can drastically change your feelings. Language patters such as "I am exhausted" or "it is challenging," will in the real sense, make you feel you have just uttered. Such sentiments might end up putting you at a disadvantaged position, disempowering you in the process. All words have different emotional states associated with them. This is how you end up being disempowered and, therefore, having negative emotions. Hence, we should always seek to choose our words, which include vocabulary, statements, and phrases that can impact our feelings big time. Invest in positive affirmations as these tend to have better results in producing the right and positive feelings on you than negative emotions.

It is believed that the choices we make determine our destiny. The same applies to happiness or any other negative emotions. Thus, it is up to us to determine what we want to feel and be.

4 Ways People Deal With Negative Emotion

Below are four manners on how you can deal with any negative emotions.

1. Avoidance

You can begin by sidestepping any negative feeling, which might spoil your mood. Avoidance does not, however, mean that you have to get rid of emotions or situations that you should face head-on. Learn to determine which feelings are worth avoiding and which you need to face.

2. Denial

It involves disengaging yourself from any negative feelings by ignoring them. Phrases like "it is not difficult" can assist you in this process. However, the major disadvantage with this kind of approach is that the underlying problem will not go away until you finally address it. This is just like in the avoidance way of dealing with emotions.

3. Competition

The concept of competition comes about when you seek to become different from the rest. You should compete against any negative feelings with positive ones as you try to win.

4. Learning and using negative feelings as a steppingstone

Lastly, we are always searching for ways to best learn from our negative feelings and channel them in the right manner or places. First of all, start by mastering them. Understanding them better can help make the service you better.

Conditioning Your Mind For More Positive Emotions

·   Observe your thoughts

You could always begin by taking care of your thoughts: out with the negative ones and in with positive. Look for ways to handle the constant negative thoughts nagging your mind as this is the first step towards being the best positive version of yourself.

·   Scan for the three daily positives

Your brain could be taught to always focus on those things, which are positive. It will help improve your health. When you focus on at least three positive things a day, you are more likely to develop a positive outlook in life.

·   Give someone a shout out

Always be grateful for everything that you do or receive. It brings about feelings of optimism. To best exercise gratefulness, remember to say thank you to those around you often.

·   Help others

It will help boost your emotions, enabling you to have a positive outlook in situations. Get involved in things such as charities or adopt a dog. Even the smallest act of help can make you understand and have a positive outlook in life.

· Surround yourself with positive people

You should always have people with a positive mindset around you all the time. Such individuals should be able to elicit feelings of inspiration, empowerment, and motivation in your life.

· Look after your body and mind

Studies have ascertained that when we are well-groomed, our physical and mental state is also enhanced. With this data in mind, make sure that you are always well-groomed and embrace good habits for your betterment.

· Subconscious re-training and inner healing

At times, to have a positive outlook, to heal faster, we must let go of any negative feelings within us. While you may have been hurt before, it will be vital that you learn to rewire your emotions to experience more positive feelings.

· Make time to do something that you love

You must create time to engage in those things that you love most, whether it is a recipe of your choice, road trip, or camping. Provided it brings out the best in you. Spare some thought to it.

Change Your Behavior And Your Habits And Change Your Emotions

When we change our habits, it thus makes us very much aware of our actions on our newly acquired behavior. We should be able to fathom that our emotional reactions are not valid at the back of our minds. However, by doing things differently, we end up changing our feelings, respectively.

Thus, our emotions can be described as a mental flow of energy, capable of influencing our characters with those we interact with daily. These are the feelings which propel us our communication with other people as well. Emotional roller-coaster can take into vary many directions. This is the authoritative nature of our emotions. Moreover, the hugest impediment to emotional change to enhance our minds so that it serves us better is when we try to put forth our will power solely to address our negative feelings

In more ways than others, we embark on this unconsciously, which might make us eventually frustrated due to mixed emotions going through our minds. In addition to this, one of the best approaches for handling such a scenario will be not to be resistant to them but to remove them out of our minds in an amicable manner, while at the same time, using the conflicting information more regularly.

Negative Emotions - The Short Term And Long-Term Solutions

We are continually experiencing both positive and negative emotions in our lives on a day to day basis. It is a regular occurrence, thus, it should not lead to any panic. However, for

some people, they can be significantly overwhelmed by such emotions in their lives. Such overwhelming feelings can include guiltiness, low self-esteem, being overburdened, frustrations, and being angry all the time.

The term emotion regulation describes one's capacity when it comes to managing and responding to emotions. In most cases, we employ this concept when dealing with cumbersome events in our lives. People use several tactics when it comes to adaptations to their surroundings. These tactics can either be negative or positive. The healthy strategies will not harm us in any way — helping us along the way to fully understand the genesis of our feelings.

You can break this cycle by looking for ways to change some components of this vicious cycle, bringing about additional positive changes. You should also teach yourself how to comprehend how your emotions, behaviors, and thoughts correlate. Look for what works best for you at the end of the day.

To address this, we can begin by paying close attention to how our emotions relate to our characters. You can also address some of these questions to yourself:

- Are there any thoughts, which can bring about negative feelings in us?
- Are there some that are so difficult to comprehend?
- How do I calm myself, and what strategies do I use?
- Is there any long term or short-term effects?
- Can I use these characters?
- Do I have any hidden thoughts or beliefs on myself or other people or life, which might trigger negative feelings?
- Do I have any perceptions, which I use to bring about positive emotions?

Chapter 13:   Assessing Your Emotions

Assessing your emotional state is a key step in honing emotional intelligence and having empathy in general. Some people may be constantly cued into their emotional states, while some others may go a day or a week without thinking about it at all.

Why Do Emotions Often Take Control Of People?

People Don't Recognize Own Emotions As A Staging Ground

Recognizing your own emotions is the staging ground for recognizing the emotions of others. This is why empathy and emotional intelligence do not consist of single emotional skills, but several. This should lead people to understand that successful emotional intelligence involves tying several emotional steps together to interconnectivity. If all you are doing is recognizing your own emotions, you do not understand others' emotions, and you are ultimately not behaving with emotional intelligence.

People Don't Know How To Control Feelings

Our feelings are expressions of our emotional and mental state of existence. Normally tied to our physical and social sensory feeling, they are used to react to joy, fear, love, disgust, sadness, hate, pleasure, and a host of other emotions. In other to prevent extreme behaviors which usually comes at high costs, we must control and suppress some emotions and feelings.

Persons who cannot generally control their feelings engage in unwarranted acts of violence, fighting, unprotected sex, and abuse of different substances which will undoubtedly put their lives at risks. There is a wide range of factors that contribute to such lack of control apart from the mind's feelings. These factors include environmental, genetically, social, and biological factors.

People Don't Understand The Impact Of Emotions

There is an active connection between how you feel and the physical problems you experience, and this is because you are not different from how you feel. Most of the challenges you experienced in the past or those you are facing now have solid connections with your dominant emotional pattern.

When emotions are used in the right way, they can become a tool for empowerment, and when they are misused or repressed, they can become a gateway to suffering. Many people are afraid to maintain a positive emotion for a long time. They have accepted the mistaken idea that life cannot be so exciting enough for anyone to be happy all the time.

You need to start dealing with your emotions so that you can identify and get rid of the negative ones while embracing the positive ones. All these discussions we are having about feelings and problems are so important.

Signs of Emotionally Unstable People

Feelings, especially intense feelings, can often be autonomous, which means they are automatic and subconscious, developing due to an external force or trigger.

To take control of our emotional selves, we must learn the signs of emotionally unstable people.

Denial

Denial is the rejection to accept the truth of a situation, and in short-term use, it is a healthy and effective coping mechanism. It allows the unconscious mind to deal with the situation before the conscious mind must deal with it. However, persistent denial can cause severe emotional distress; we all know that ignoring a problem will not solve it. Denial prevents us from dealing with our emotions and seeking support because we cannot face the issue. It is so powerful; you may not even realize you are in denial until someone else helps you see it.

Being Overly Serious

Being too serious detaches you from your coworkers and friends. Nobody wants to say something funny they found online to you, because they would come off as not serious. You unknowingly miss out on the beautiful things in life, and it might begin to reflect on your family and kids.

Going through Your Phone in the Middle of a Conversation

This is a very disrespectful act that is unfortunately very common nowadays. Some people are so attached to their phone that they can't bear to take their eyes off it for an hour; hence they tend to go through their phone even when an important meeting is going on. This can mess up your relationship because it makes the person think you're insensitive. Bringing out your phone and going through it in the middle of a conversation is not only insensitive, but it's disrespectful too. You're telling the person that whatever they were saying to you, as important as it was to them, is unimportant to you, and that can make the person feel insignificant. You should discontinue using your phone in the middle of a conversation.

Calling The Names Of The Important People You Know

If you cannot go through a conversation without mentioning the names of the important people you know, this is you trying to make yourself look better than every other person sitting in that room at that moment, and you do not necessarily have to drag that kind of attention to yourself. You have met the president—nice. Your father's brother is the one on TV—yeah, that's nice. Not everyone needs to know. Instead of making you look interesting, you come off as a braggart in want of attention and that sincerely puts people off. Name dropping might make you feel better about yourself, but how do you think it will make others feel about you?

Subtle Bragging

Subtle bragging, or humble bragging, is the act of bragging in a way that is not exactly noticed as bragging. You don't realize you are bragging when you practice humble bragging, because by your standards you are just modest. This is something we do among friends, sometimes innocently.

Screaming At People

No one likes a screamer. No matter how much the person deserves your screaming, it's not necessary. You make people feel small and insignificant when you scream at them, especially when it is a constant habit to scream when you are mad at others.

Gossiping

When you gossip about another person, it says more about you than it does about the person you talked about. It doesn't make sense to base your discussion on another's life; relationships that thrive on gossip have a very shaky foundation and are bound to crash sooner than later. Gossiping is a horrible habit, and it depicts a very low state of emotional intelligence.

Talking A Lot More Than Listening

When you talk more than you listen, it limits your chances at learning and unlearning things. You are shoving your opinion down others' throat without giving them the time or the chance to air theirs.

Listening most times helps you to make a better decision. Not listening to people when they talk and being too concerned about airing your own opinion will make you look ignorant. At some point, you will begin to say things that do not make a lot of sense because you were not listening in the first place. You will suddenly begin to look ignorant, and no one wants to associate with an ignorant person who is also unwilling to learn.

Posting Too Much Of Yourself On Social Media

 A lot of people are guilty of this action. It depicts a want for acceptance, and it's usually captured by the phrase "putting it all out there." Well, news flash, you do not have to do this. You do not necessarily have to tell the world all the dreams you have or everything you do after you wake up and before you go to bed. You do not have to be validated by social media and those online. They don't care that much about you. They should not know so much about you. It's needless throwing these things in their faces. Save some information for yourself. Remember, the internet has a good memory; it never forgets.

Saying Too Much Of Yourself Too Early In A Relationship

Not everyone needs to know all the information you spill to them when you talk to them for the first time. Sharing too much too early makes you come off as an attention seeker. It seems like you want the person to think you are real and open and want them to like you almost immediately. It's a lot better to let the relationship flow organically, and then the rest of the information will come out naturally without stress. It's also better to relax and know the other person better while building trust in the relationship. Sharing too much of yourself is rushing things and does not give the other person a chance to be comfortable.

Being Closed-Minded

This is a huge problem. You must view things with an open mind. Keeping a closed mind makes you unapproachable. It also means that you already have a formed opinion about a certain thing. When you are approached, you are unwilling to listen and make changes to your initial thoughts, making you inaccessible. It's very practical to keep an open mind and be open to changes. These habits are associated with people with low emotional intelligence, and they should be stopped now. They are harmful to you, the people around you, and your emotional intelligence growth.

Avoidance

Avoidance is similar to denial, but it is much more conscious. It happens when we cope with certain events, emotions, or thoughts by avoiding them altogether. For example, a person experiencing high levels of work stress may stop showing up for work. We avoid stressors in hopes of eliminating that stress, but this causes more stress and more discomfort because we are not dealing with the emotional trigger.

Social Withdrawal

Many people experiencing emotional turmoil will withdraw from family and friends. This is not to be mixed up with simply needing some alone time, which we all need sometimes. Social withdrawal happens when we feel too exhausted, overwhelmed, or insecure about being around people whose company we once enjoyed. Human beings crave connection, but it is easy to fall into withdrawal, increasing negative emotions like loneliness and self-doubt.

Compulsive Behavior

Compulsive behavior is the repeated engagement in an activity despite sense and reason, usually to the point of obsession. We engage in this behavior because it can provide temporary relief against negative emotions like anxiety, stress, and grief. Still, it can exacerbate these problems by leaving us feeling out of control of our behaviors. Examples of compulsive behavior include binge-eating, over-exercising, hoarding, gambling, and sex. For those struggling with Obsessive-Compulsive Disorder, these activities may seem very simple and insignificant, like hand-washing, checking (doors, gas taps, light switches, etc.), ordering/organizing, and counting.

Self-Destructive Behavior

Sometimes, we find relief from negative emotions through behaviors that are temporarily pleasurable but ultimately self-destructive. A great example of self-destructive behavior is smoking cigarettes despite knowing it can cause health problems later in life. We are often conscious of this kind of behavior's negative consequences, but we engage in it anyway for the relief it provides. Common self-destructive behaviors include smoking, alcohol abuse, drug abuse, binge-eating, and self-harm.

Chapter 14:   How To Use Your Emotions To Grow

Emotion is a psychological state generated subconsciously. Certain internal or external bodily responses stimulate it. Sometimes, people interchangeably use the words' emotions and moods together, but there are differences in meaning. An emotion is intense, short-lived, and has a cause. On the other hand, a mood may not have a definite cause, is milder, and could last longer.

Basic Emotions And How To Use Them To Grow And Change Our Lives

Emotions come in different types and influence what we do and interact. Most decisions we take are based on our present emotions. Psychologist Paul Eckman in the 1970s identified six universally basic emotions: anger, surprise, fear, disgust, sadness, and happiness. Later on, he added excitement, embarrassment, shame, and pride.

He later came up with another theory that worked like a color wheel blending some of these basic emotions to create others, such as trust and joy to create love.

Below, we identify some of these basic emotions and their effect on our daily lives and behavior.

Happiness

Most people strive to achieve this emotion called happiness. It is an emotional state of feeling pleasant brought about by feelings of well-being, satisfaction, gratification, joy, and contentment. It is expressed through:

· A smiling face

· Having a relaxed stance

- Pleasant tone on your voice

Happiness is considered as a basic human emotion. Things that influence happiness in people are normally culture. For example, attaining some high standards in life like owning property and having a good job could result in happiness. However, the truth is that happiness is dependent on personal belief, and what may bring happiness to one may not necessarily mean anything to another.

Happiness and health are related. Ill health can deprive one of the emotions of happiness. Both mental and physical health contributes to emotions of happiness. Also, to be noted, marital satisfaction is a great contributor to emotions of happiness.

Emotions of happiness are linked to poor health, anxiety, stress, loneliness, and depression. This has brought about lowered immunity, inflammations, and a decrease in life expectancy to such individuals.

Sadness

Sadness is a transient emotion characterized by bad feelings of disinterest, hopelessness, grief, disappointment, and dampened mood. Emotions of sadness happen to everyone from time to time. If prolonged, it can lead to depression.

Sadness is expressed in various ways including:

- Crying

- Withdrawal from people

- Lethargy

- Quietness

- Dampened mood

Depending on the root cause, people can be assisted to cope with its severity to not sink into deeper complications like depression. Also, this emotion can be prolonged resulting in negative thoughts, if not well-managed.

Fear

Fear is one of the most powerful emotions and an important role in survival. When something causes you to fear, you are likely to develop a fight-or-flight response. All of a sudden, you become tense, your respiration and heartbeat increase, your sensory organs become alert, prompting your whole self to either fight back or run from danger. This response can cause you to do the unplanned in a way you cannot explain.

This kind of emotion can be expressed as follows:

·   Facial expression: widening the eyes, opening your mouth, pulled back chin

·   Action: run, fight back, and hide

·   Physiological reaction: accelerated heartbeat, breathing heavily, panting

Different people express themselves differently in incidents of fear. Some people can become numb and even collapse in incidents of fear depending on the cause. For instance, a snake's sight may cause one to run, another to fight back, and another to become numb and motionless.

Fear can also result from thought regarding a potential danger, resulting in anxiety not knowing what exactly to expect.

Some other individuals love attempting fearful ventures, like extreme sports ventured by people who enjoy the feeling of attempting fearful things.

If consistently exposed to a fearful situation, it could lead to familiarity hence reducing the feeling of anxiety and fear. An example would be one who fears hearing gunshots. If they move near a barrack where gunshots from training soldiers are the order of the day, then gunshots' fear reduces with time.

Disgust

It can be displayed in the following ways:

· Turning your face away from the scene of disgust

· A physical reaction like vomiting

· A facial expression like closing eyes and wrinkling your nose

Disgust can be brought about by an unpleasant sight, smell, or taste. Food that has gone stale can cause a disgusting emotional reaction.

Other things that may trigger a disgusting emotion include decomposing body, rot, blood, untreated wound, and poor hygiene. The sight of immoral actions can also be disgusting.

Anger

Anger is also a major powerful emotion characterized by feelings of frustrations, agitation, hostility, and antagonism. Same as fear, anger can cause body fight-or-flight response to respond promptly. When feelings generate emotions of anger in you, you are likely to arise to fight back or defend yourself.

It is normally displayed through:

· Facial expression: glaring or frowning

· Body language: staring strongly at the source or turning away from the source

- Voice tone: yelling or speaking gruffly

- Physiological response: turning face color, sweating, shaking

- Aggressiveness: throwing objects, kicking, hitting

Most of the time, anger is presumed as a negative emotional reaction. Still, it can be constructive because it helps one express themselves in full, expel all the stored pain from within, and clarify your dissatisfaction with anger. Expressed anger hits the 'enough' button, and the situation has to be addressed.

However, anger can become uncontrollable leading to an unhealthy, dangerous, and harmful way of expression. For example, the aggregated can hit the other with an object leading to injury or even death. This is where uncontrolled anger turns to violence, abuse, and aggression.

Some health conditions in individuals can lead to uncontrolled anger when provoked. Such cases should be handled soberly, bearing in mind that it could run out of hand leading to unprecedented events.

Due to uncontrolled anger, some people have resulted in having diseases like coronary heart disease and diabetes, while others have found themselves in behaviors like smoking, alcoholism, and aggressive driving.

Surprise

This emotion is normally brief. It is a physiological startle response resulting from an unexpected response. This kind of emotion can be negative, positive, or neutral. Example of a negative surprise could be arriving home and finding your pet dead, whereas a pleasant surprise could be an award from your boss for a well-done job.

It is characterized by:

- Facial expressions: raising eyebrows and opening the mouth
- Physical response: jumping up and down
- Verbal reactions: gasping, screaming, and yelling

Surprise emotion can also trigger a fight-or-flight response. There is a burst of adrenaline that causes the body to either flee or fight.

Surprise moments tend to linger more in the mind standing out in memory. Surprise news can get hold of people attention, and that's why newsmakers are more inclined to breaking news.

Other Significant Types of Emotions

Other significant types of emotions that may not necessarily trigger expressions include:

- Amusement
- Shame
- Contentment
- Satisfaction
- Excitement
- Guilt
- Contempt
- Pride in achievement
- Embarrassment
- Relief

Advantages of Emotions

Emotions have three components, namely:

- Subjective (experience)
- Physiological (body reaction)

- Expressive (behavior response)

1.   Motivate to take action. Let's take for example when one is about to do a final exam that determines whether they step up or re-sit, there is a definite feeling of anxiety. The most emotional response will be to study. The motivation to study will outdo the anxiety to ensure you stand out with good grades.

Naturally, everyone will strive to engage in activities that bring positive emotions and avoiding those that are likely to trigger negative emotions.

2.   Boost our survival tactics and help us avoid danger. Charles Darwin believed emotions drive both humans and animals to manage and reproduce. Anger drives to confrontation, fear may cause us to move to safety areas, and love may cause us to look out for our mates for reproduction purposes.

Emotions are adaptive drivers taking us to a place of action that guarantees survival and success.

3.   Help in making decisions. Our emotions are major influencers in our decision making, right from what we take for breakfast to the leaders we choose during political elections.

Even though logic, rationality, and statics are key factors in making decisions our emotions determine the final move. Emotional intelligence has been proven to play a major role in our decision making.

4.   You are understood through your emotions. You should not be afraid to express yourself through your emotions. You can express your emotions through body language such as facial expressions of whatever emotions you are going through.

You can also express your emotions verbally, hence your listener will know your position on a particular issue and be advised how to react or help.

5.   Through emotions, you can understand others. Just as expressing our own emotions can help convey valuable information to others, likewise, we can understand others through the emotions of their display. It's important to be able to interpret and respond to others through the emotions they display. This enhances effective communication in dealing with different people as you consider their predicaments through their emotional expressions.

Charles Darwin, an early scientific researcher on emotions, indicates emotional display can save anyone from impending danger. For example, a spitting and hissing animal indicate that it's angry and possibly defensive, so the best thing is to back off and avoid it.

Understanding others through their emotional display will help us know how to respond calmly and amicably.

The Significance Of Both Positive And Negative Emotions To Daily Life

Some of the common positive emotions may include:

- Awe
- Serenity
- Happiness
- Amusement
- Interest
- Contentment
- Satisfaction
- Joy
- Love

Negative emotions include:

- Annoyance
- Melancholy
- Loneliness
- Rage
- Sadness
- Disgust
- Anger
- Fear

Both positive and negative emotions happen and for a good reason. For example:

- Disgust – we can reject unhealthy stuff.
- Trust – you can connect with genuine people.
- Sadness – you get to connect with our loved ones.
- Joy – it reminds us of what is important.
- Surprise – have a focus on new situations.
- Anticipation – you can look forward and plan.
- Fear – it protects us from anger.
- Anger – it enables us to fight against problems.

Unpleasant negative emotions are also important in our lives. Some seemingly positive emotions can be a major contributor to stress. For example:

- Planning for a wedding
- House moving (exiting at the same time stressing)
- Having a baby
- Starting on a new job

The above activities are positive and exciting but can bring negative emotions with them; hence both positive and negative emotions are inevitable.

Chapter 15:   Building Solid Relationships

Emotions are a tricky subject because it involves matters in which people tend to assess their emotions quickly without knowing its actual meaning. Frequently, terminology about emotion is used incorrectly, or it is used so that it has been stripped of its real meaning. We may say that certain people are emotional, but it is not clear what that means. Even the person who uses the term emotional might be using it differently than how the person hearing it interprets it. Because emotional intelligence involves interactions, it is easy for emotional intelligence to be hindered because people use improper terminology or allow themselves to be misled by terms that have acquired a negative connotation.

Typically, when someone is described as emotional, this is intended to be taken in a negative light. Emotional people are often regarded as impulsive, difficult to talk to, difficult to work with, unscientific, irrational, loud, or resistant to being spoken to. But this characterization is based on assumptions about emotional people. Indeed, labeling someone as emotional is a simple and almost devious way to neutralize and invalidate someone by immediately labeling them as something they may or may not.

Words have power and in using words incorrectly and communicating them to people, we allow those words to become a part of that person because others will associate that person with those words that we have chosen to label them with. In labeling someone emotional, we have now doomed them to being interpreted in a specific light by others that they will be interacting with. This prevents them from being able to build social relationships and sustain them in a way that is healthy and beneficial for both.

Building social relationships is the end goal of emotional intelligence and highly emotionally intelligent people have been shown to have better social relationships with others. This leads to highly emotionally intelligent people being more successful in objective measures of success. "Emotional" people are thought to be better at relationships, but this is because "emotional" people are considered to think about emotions more than others do.

This perception has to do with the idea that thinking about emotions too much is something negative. These dysfunctional perceptions have led to some people eschewing in any emotion, while others have taken the opposite side and have become advocates for emotion and emotional thinking. But this is a downward spiral that results from terminology not being used appropriately in emotion. Showing compassion for someone is a sign that you feel emotion. All religions are infused with emotional feeling and people become better friends, better family members, and better lovers because they care.

Emotion is the basis for meaningful social relationships. Having emotions does not mean that you are bogged down by them, which is how some characterize it. By rejecting emotion or mischaracterizing emotion, we create a society where people either have distorted emotions because they do not understand them correctly or they feel no emotion at all because they have been taught to be wary of emotion based on misconceptions about emotion.

An easy way to think about emotion as the basis for building relationships is by thinking about how we relate to one another. When you engage in an act that is beneficial to someone other than yourself, you show emotion. Perhaps it is part of your spiritual or religious belief to engage in acts that show charity or kindness towards others. Perhaps you have donated clothes to a charitable organization or have assisted at a soup kitchen. These are all ways that you show care and concern for others.

Caring, concern, worry — these are all feelings that fall along the spectrum with sadness, anger, guilt, disappointment, hope, and all the other feelings that are part of being human. These are things that people should not run from but should embrace as they are essential to partaking in social relationships with others.

Suffice it to say that research proposes that highly emotionally intelligent people have better relationships and more successful group interactions than people who do not demonstrate emotional intelligence. Of course, these benefits stem from all aspects of emotional intelligence. People who have empathy, have better self-regulation skills, or demonstrate compassion will generally be liked and valued by their peers compared to those who are not.

One of the goals of this is not to approach emotion from the standpoint of two camps: those in favor of emotional thinking and those against it. This dichotomy approaches the subject from a distorted standpoint as it does not accept that feeling emotions are a normal part of being human. Indeed, lacking emotion or irregularly demonstrating emotion is a criterion for some psychiatric conditions in the Diagnostic and Statistical Manual. The goal of this is not therefore to lead you to see this subject from the standpoint of being an "emotional person" or an "unemotional (or rational) person." We all feel emotions and we need to claim them.

By understanding how having emotions ties into the many aspects of emotional intelligence, we can healthily approach the subject. Some of the stigma that comes from so-called emotional people is that people labeled as emotional may not engage in the associated steps of understanding other people's emotions, self-regulation, and empathy. This was touched on in the discussion of narcissism. Still, those who healthily embrace their emotions also embrace others' emotions and know how to regulate their emotions if they begin to get in the way of social interactions.

Social relationships, therefore, require that all the components of emotional intelligence be used effectively. Indeed, the topic of healthy social relationships helps tie together the power of emotional intelligence as a tool as it does not focus merely on one area. To build and maintain social relationships, an individual must:

- Demonstrate compassion and tolerance for others
- Have empathy
- Assess one's emotions and the emotions of others
- Understand the emotions of others
- Make an effort to relate to others
- Regulate one's own emotions

Social relationships are complex, whether they are romantic in nature, friendships, or employer-employee relationships. By tying together all aspects of emotional intelligence, men and women can create and maintain important relationships. This is not just true of individuals in the workplace. Research has shown clearly that going through the different intelligences that comprise emotional intelligence is important for adults in their relationships and children in the school setting.

Non-Verbal Communication

Non-verbal communication is essential to social interactions in humans. Although human beings do have the capability of producing speech, the cues that we send that do not involve words are just as important in conveying our feelings, desires, and intentions as the words that we say. Non-verbal communication is almost a form of mind-reading, which can be both positive and negative. By communicating without words, sometimes we can express how we feel more accurately and more deeply. As a song from the 90s goes: "Words are meaningless, especially sentences." It is not always easy to describe what we are feeling with words.

Non-verbal communication is sometimes overlooked because everyone does it so it is easy to take it for granted. Overlooked or not, non-verbal communication is important as it allows to be cued in to what we are feeling or thinking. Recall that empathy and emotional intelligence, in general, requires that the other person be able to gauge our emotions and experiences accurately. This means that non-verbal communication comprises a set of non-verbal cues that others will use to be able to gauge what we feel accurately.

This is important because it means that we must be keyed in the non-verbal cues of others and our cues that we are sending. This is distinct from the self-regulation that is part and parcel of emotional intelligence, but there are some similarities. Sometimes it may be important to curtail our negative cues or cues that may push people away even if they reflect how we feel. Although this may seem to some like dishonesty, it is just a recognition that interactions with others are important and that sometimes we have to coordinate and control our cues to be able to interact with others. The assumption here is that others will be engaging in a similar dance of regulation of non-verbal cues, which is all a part of normal human interaction.

The question then becomes what the non-verbal cues are that others are responding to. There are many gestures, movements, postures, and other things that we do as people to indicate what we are feeling internally. Some of these are gestures that naturally crop up due to our internal state, like the furrowed brow that indicates worry. In contrast, others are acquired postures that we pick up sometimes without knowing, like placing your hands on your hips when you are irritated, angry, or in a hurry.

No matter where our gestures originate, it is important to be conscious of them so that we can think about how others may interpret our gestures. Although the argument can be made that we should not alter these non-verbal cues as they accurately reflect how we feel, sometimes it is necessary to control our own emotions (or indications of our emotion) as part of showing sympathy or empathy others.

Therefore, being conscious of our non-verbal cues becomes an essential part of the social interactions that we have with others. People who frequently show non-verbal cues that indicate negative or frustrated emotions will likely be perceived more negatively by people than those whose gestures are more positive. Although everyone goes through trying times and everyone naturally feels anger, sadness, frustration, tiredness, and the like, paying attention to our social cues can help us get along better with others and have more fruitful outcomes from our interactions.

Although most people will be acquainted with the sorts of non-verbal cues that indicate our internal emotional state, it may be helpful to some people to review them here. Some of these non-verbal cues include:

- Body position
- Facial expression
- Hand position
- Yawning
- Laughter
- Hands on hips
- Speed of speech

- Tapping of the foot
- Vocal Tone
- Looking away or not making eye contact

By paying attention to the cues listed above, you can effectively show sympathy, have empathy, and set yourself on the path towards becoming a highly emotionally intelligent individual.

Chapter 16:   Overcoming Negativity

Mental preparation is the key to overcoming negativity.

Some of the most successful people in the world start their day every morning by mentally preparing themselves for the day.

They meditate, recite their goals to themselves, use positive affirmations ,or even listen to motivational podcasts on their phones or other mobile devices.

Essentially, they do whatever it takes to prepare their minds to focus on blocking out and minimizing the impact of any kind of negativity they are going to encounter.

Life is going to put you through a countless emotions. You're going to experience everything from excitement ,fear, stress, pressure, passion, determination and more.

There is a thing that will help you get through it all and come out triumphant on the other side–overcoming negativity.

•   Think About It

When a negative thought pops into our heads, we don't stop to think enough if this is a thought that should be taken seriously.

Is there a cause for alarm? Or could be perhaps be exaggerating the thought in our minds, making it sound worse than what it is.

External factors trigger some negative thoughts and emotions.

You might be tired, hungry, exhausted, overworked or already feeling tense at the time of the negative thought, which probably aggravated the situation.

When you're already not in the best frame of mind, a small issue can seem worse than what it is.

The next period you find yourself dwelling on a negative thought, stop and think about it for a minute and ask yourself if it's justified.

- **Have an Action Plan**

There are always going to be unpleasant challenges. We can't run away from it, even if we wanted to.

But viewing those challenges from a negative perspective is only going to make things much worse for you.

On the other hand, having a plan of action about what you can do to manage the unexpected un-pleasantries that life may occasionally throw your way will keep you moving forward and no longer be held back despite the negativity that you feel.

When Plan A fails, have a Plan B, a Plan C, and as many back-up plans as you need.

Be as adaptable and fluid as water, ever ready to twist and turn to continue forging a path forward, because that's the only way to go forward.

Having a plan instead of having no plan at all, helps you manage the way you feel.

- Think About What's Helpful

Whenever you've experienced a setback, the last thing you might be thinking about is how this situation is helpful to you.

As bleak or negative as a situation may be, one trick mentally tough individuals use to help them maintain their optimism is to think about what helpful lesson they can take away from the setbacks they experienced.

It could be one lesson, it could be two, it could be as many lessons as you'd like.

No matter how bad things seem, there's always a silver lining, it's up to you to find it by asking yourself the right questions.

Questions like what have I learned from this experience? What can I do to make it better moving forward? What's one positive takeaway from this situation?

- **Observe Your Surroundings**

Your environment has an enormous impact on the way that you feel. The place you spend most of your time is going to weigh on your mind subconsciously. You may not be actively thinking about your surroundings, but it's there in the back of your mind.

If you find it hard to remain positive throughout the day, do a quick scan of your surroundings and observe the negativity sources.

Your cluttered workstation? The toxic colleague who is constantly complaining and talking negatively about other colleagues behind their back?

Maybe that pile of paperwork you've been postponing for a while now and haven't gotten around to doing yet.

Once you've identified a potential source, ask yourself what you can do to rectify the problem.

Can the source be removed entirely? If it can't what else could you do to spend less time around this negative source in a week?

- **Stop Feeding into Your Thoughts**

Feeding into your negative thoughts is only going to fuel it to become even more out of control.

A thought may start small, but the more you continue to obsess and dwell over the matter, the bigger that thought eventually seems to become.

The expression making a mountain out of a molehill is completely applicable to this situation.

We sometimes build up our fears so much in our minds that they seem disastrous until we eventually face them and come to realize it wasn't so bad after all.

- **Find Inspiration Daily**

The perfect way to cultivate a positive mindset and minimize negativity is to wake up each morning and make the first thing that you see something that is going to inspire you.

Pick a quote or a saying, stick pictures of inspirational quotes on your mirrors, in your cubicle at work, a note on your phone, make it your wallpaper on your computer, and just surround yourself with it so it's hard to miss.

Starting on a positive note will help set the tone for the rest of the day, so wake up each morning and let positivity be the first and dominant feeling that helps to start your day right.

Every day is another chance, another opportunity to begin anew, and it is what you do today - not what has happened in the past - that matters most.

- **Cultivate Positive Dialogue**

We've established by now just how powerful your thoughts can be. If your thoughts can influence negativity, they also have that same power to do the opposite.

You need to start tapping into that force and begin creating a more optimistic mindset.

You must push every negative thought you have about yourself out of your mind and start replacing it with something positive instead.

Imagine your negative thoughts as physical boulders in front of you, and you need to forcefully push those out of your mind and clear the path for newer, better things.

For every negative thought that you find yourself thinking, stop and immediately replace that thought with a positive one.

• Reshape Your Failure Perspective

Instead of thinking about them as failures, see them as lessons instead.

They're not failures, they're learning experiences that teach you what not to do, and what needs improvement.

We are constantly learning something new, always growing and developing into a better version of yourself.

Nobody can do everything perfectly, or always get it from the first go without taking a few stumbles along the way.

Every successful person out there today that has made their mark and becomes a household name didn't get to where they are without taking a few tumbles and stumbles along the way.

They too made plenty of mistakes before they got to the pinnacle of success.

Change your mind set by changing the way you see these failures, don't focus on how you failed but instead, start thinking about how you can improve next time or what you can do differently.

• Keep Your Company Positive

Negative people will only weigh you down. They'll drain you of energy, become a mental and emotional burden that you don't need.

When you attach yourself to people who think positive, you'll slowly adapt the way you think to emulate them as their wisdom, outlook, stories, and affirmations slowly seep into your way of thinking.

Examine the people in your life right now, and if any individuals

 in it are toxic with their negative outlook, it's time to start distancing yourself from them.

How To Overcome Negativity

You need to believe in yourself. Believe that you are stronger than you give yourself credit for, believe that you deserve to have a better, happier life.

You'll never truly achieve the level of positive mindset you hope for if you still have those nagging thoughts at the back of your mind that make you doubt yourself every step of the way.

Whenever you feel your emotions receiving the better of you, stop and take a breath.

Focusing on your breathing will help you shift your focus and mind from feeling anxious, nervous, scared or angry to calm, steadiness and peace.

By believing you can achieve it, you've already put yourself one step closer to making it happen for real.

Chapter 17:   Importance of Empathy

Empathy plays a dominant role in our society's ability to function, promoting our needs, sharing experiences, and desires among one another. Our neural networks are set up to connect with others' neural systems to both see and comprehend their feelings and separate them from our own. This makes it possible for people to live with each other without feeling that someone is in control.

Empathy is vital as it helps us comprehend and understand the feelings of others, and what they are going through, so that we can be able to respond appropriately to the situation at hand. To a greater extent, empathy has been associated with the social behaviors. There is plenty of research supporting this argument. Thus, the higher the degree of empathy a person feels, the more they tend to help others. Notably, an empath can also control actions or even go to the extent of curtailing immoral behavior. For example, someone who sees a car accident and is overwhelmed by emotions upon witnessing the victims in severe pain, might be far more inclined to help the victims or call for help.

Additionally, having strong empathetic feelings can also lead to negative effects. When a person demonstrates strong feelings toward people or causes, negative emotions may be stirred in others due to their insecurities. A perfect example of this can be seen in the way charlatans such as so-called fortune tellers exploit the insecurities of individuals. As a result, they may be able to trick empaths into actually believing that the end of the world is upon us and so forth.

Interestingly, people with a more pronounced psychopathic trait are said to show a more pragmatic response to events where there are moral dilemmas, such as the "footbridge dilemma". In this thought experiment, the conductor of a runaway train has to make a choice: since the train has no breaks it is heading toward five people crossing the tracks. Alternatively, the conductor may switch tracks and hit only one. Thus, the dilemma lies in whether you choose to kill one or kill all five people crossing the street. Hence, a pragmatic approach would lead to killing the least number of people whereas an empathetic approach would lead to killing none.

Measuring Empathy

Quite often, a self-report questionnaire is used in measuring empathy. This is in the Interpersonal Reactivity Index (IRI) or the Questionnaire for Cognitive and Affective Empathy (QCAE). In measuring empathy, the person is asked to indicate how much they accept the statements that are set to help measure the different types of empathy that one might be having.

One will find statements like "It affects me very much when one of my friends is upset," which QCAE test uses to measure empathy. QCAE plays a key role in identifying cognitive empathy by the use of statements the likes of "I try to look at everybody's side of a disagreement before I make a decision."

With this method, it was discovered that people scoring higher on affective empathy have more grey matter. Grey matter is said to be a collection of nerve cells in the anterior insula, an area of the brain.

This zone is regularly associated with directing positive and negative feelings by coordinating external stimuli, such as seeing an auto crash - with automatic and programmed sensations. Likewise, individuals utilizing this strategy gauging compassion have found that high scorers of sympathy had a progressively dark issue in the dorsomedial prefrontal cortex.

The activation of this particular area occurs when there are more cognitive processes; this includes the Theory of the Mind. As stated earlier, this theory calls for the individual to understand the beliefs, intentions and motivations that drive them. As a result, the individual is then able to immerse themselves in the mindset of others fully.

Can Humans Lack Empathy?

Several cases have proven that not all humans have empathy. For instance, walking down Minnesota, you bump into a homeless person shivering in the cold. You will notice that few people will express sympathy or compassion for the homeless person. There are many cases in which passersby express outright hostility towards such people. So, what could be the cause of expressing what seems to be selective empathy? Various elements come to mind: how we see the other individual, how we characterize their actions, what we attribute their misfortunes to, and our past encounters and desires. These all become an integral factor in our ability to express or repress empathy.

Furthermore, the two main things that contribute to experiencing empathy are socialization and genetics. And while the "nature vs. nurture" debate is far from being conclusively settled, the fact of the matter is that our preconceived notions tend to influence the way we act and react when confronted with a situation that requires us to express compassion in a fellow human being.

Here are the top reasons why we sometimes lack empathy:

a) We fall victim to cognitive biases

In this factor, our cognitive biases, that is, our judgments, lead us to pin the misfortunes on an individual on themselves. We tend to attribute their pain and suffering to their shortcomings instead of being compassionate and attempting to aid the victim whenever possible. These biases can be the result of societal and cultural perceptions.

b) We dehumanize victims

Quite often, we tend to view victims as people who are different from us. For example, the common "that will never happen to me" concept creates a barrier that separates us from our fellows. In this regard, we not only dehumanize the victim, but we don't necessarily assume that they are in pain and suffering. This is generally when victims are viewed as number and statistics rather the flesh and blood beings who suffer and experience sorrow.

c) We blame victims

This is one of the most common responses when analyzing someone's misfortunes. We tend to see them as victims of their consequences. And while there are situations in which that is true, the fact of the matter is that a true empath does not care how a person got to be in their situation. All they care about is how to help the victim feel better or even solve the issue they are in.

True empaths can filter out logic and reason insofar as assigning blame and responsibility and looking at the reality of what others are experiencing. So, even if it is the victim's fault, it doesn't matter. What matters is that the person needs help. That means that the rest can be sorted out later on.

Moreover, blaming a person's misfortunes on themselves tends to take away any responsibility from others. That is, if the victim is responsible for their lot, then they should be the ones to solve their problem. As such, why are they asking for help if they were the ones who caused the problem in the first place? Such attitudes create a significant barrier for empathy.

Can Empathy Be Selective?

It is good to note that we don't generally feel empathy for the people who are directly responsible for their actions in such times. The brain reacts very differently when we see people suffering from what we perceive to be an injustice. However, if we feel that their pain is justified, the brain nullifies empathy.

These perceptions also extend to ethnic and social groups. We see the suffering of people from varying social groups in a very different light. For example, the poor have little to no empathy for the rich; the rich may view the poor solely responsible for their lot. Thus, empathy tends to become skewed in one direction or another.

Consequently, it is encouraged to practice empathy regardless of social class or ethnicity. While this is hard to do, it is a skill which can be practiced and developed over time. Nevertheless, the true empath will not find it difficult to identify with others.

Determining If You Are An Empath

Here is a simple trial that can help you define if you are an empath or not. You can go through it, giving a simple "yes" or "no" answer to each question.

- Have I in any time been labeled as sensitive, introvert, or shy?
- Do I get anxious or overwhelmed frequently?
- Do fights, yelling, and arguments often make me ill?
- Do I often have the feeling that I don't fit in?
- Do I find myself being drained by the crowds, and by that then do I mostly need my time alone to revive myself?
- Do odors, noise, or nonstop talkers get me overwhelmed?
- Do I have chemical sensitiveness or low tolerance for scratchy clothes?
- Do I prefer using my car when attending an event or going to a place to be free to leave earlier?
- Do I use food as my source to escape from stress?
- Do I feel afraid of being suffocated by relationship intimacy?
- Do I easily startle?
- Do I have a strong reaction to medications or caffeine?
- Do I have a low threshold for pain?
- Do I tend to be socially isolated?
- Do I get to absorb the stress, symptoms, and emotions of the other people?
- Am I mostly overwhelmed by doing several things at a go, and do I always prefer handling one thing at a go?

- Do I replenish myself generally?
- Do I need a long time to get better after being with tough people or energy vampires?
- Do I always feel being in a better place while in small cities than the big ones?
- Do I always prefer having one on one interaction and small groups and not the large gathering?

You can now try to know who you are by calculating your results.

- If you agreed to at least five of the questions, then you are partly an empath.
- If you agreed to at least ten questions, you are at a moderate level.
- If you agreed to eleven or fifteen questions, you are a strong empath with strong tendencies.
- If you have agreed to more than fifteen questions, then it's without a doubt that you are a full-blown empath.

The determination of your degree of an empath is important as it will make it easy for you to clarify the types of needs and the type of strategy you will need to adapt in a bit to meet them. With the determination, then you will be able to find a comfort zone in your life.

Chapter 18:   Self-Awareness

Self-awareness describes a heightened state of understanding that helps you become closer with yourself on a deeper level. You begin to see the obstacles that stand in your way and what you can do to overcome them. By living a life of progress and development, you can feel proud and confident in your journey. By deciding which parts of your personality you want to shine, you can effectively create the life you want to live.

Signs Of Low Self-Esteem

People who live with low self-esteem usually develop it years before they realize what is going on. Some may still be struggling from problems they had in their adolescence. Other people may begin struggling with their self-esteem in adulthood, as they try to build a life that they can appreciate. Regardless of when feelings of low self-esteem begin, the first step is identifying that you are struggling.

Here are the common signs of low self-esteem:

- Constantly thinking negative thoughts about yourself
- Focusing heavily on your flaws and weaknesses, without the intent of inspiring change or fixing a problem
- Difficulty handling stressful situations
- Fear of failure
- Difficulty accepting compliments or positive feedback
- A need to have the approval or reassurance of others
- A need to establish social status or show of possessions to seem more appealing to others
- Difficulty trying new things

- Behaviors like promiscuity, drinking, using drugs, and acting impulsively

If you recognized at least 3 of the behaviors above, you may struggle with self-esteem. You can also consider your overall feelings about yourself. If you feel confident in yourself and feel that you have a purpose, you probably have good self-esteem. However, if you are unsure of your purpose in life, you might be struggling with self-love.

Signs Of Low Self-Confidence

Lack of confidence can drastically impact your life. It affects the people you are comfortable approaching and the situations that you put yourself in. There are many signs of low self-confidence, including:

- You cannot leave the house without doing your hair and makeup or otherwise priming yourself
- You back down in disagreements to avoid conflict
- You use your phone frequently in social situations
- You are indecisive, even when making simple decisions like where to eat
- You have trouble sharing your opinion with others
- You have trouble accepting constructive criticism
- You have poor posture
- You compare yourself with others
- You have trouble accepting compliments
- You give up on goals easily and have trouble trying new things

If you have 4-5 of these characteristics, you may struggle with self-confidence. Remember that confidence can be situational. You may feel confident at work, for example, but struggle in social situations.

Becoming Self-Aware

Self-awareness is something that occurs in levels. Studies show that a person generally becomes aware of themselves and how they differentiate from the people around them beginning around age 18 months. For children, a heightened state of self-awareness is developed by age 4 or 5. At this time, they understand their movements in a mirror are their own and they can identify themselves in pictures and videos. There is also an understanding that they exist from the perspective of others as well. This self-awareness continues through life, but it is the way that it is used that affects the role that being self-aware has in our lives.

Public Vs. Personal Self-Awareness

People eventually develop two types of self-awareness. The first type is public self-awareness, which is a heightened awareness of how other people perceive you. Public self-awareness is the reason people make certain decisions in public to go along with social norms. It is most common in times when people are the center of attention, such as when they are telling a story to their friends or giving a presentation at work.

When people focus too much on adhering to societal norms, it can cause anxiety or distress. They may worry too much about how people will respond to them, so they hang back in social situations and avoid trying new things because they are afraid of how they react. When you have too much public self-awareness, you can question your own decisions and actions.

Private self-awareness describes the way that you are aware of yourself. It is not usually physical aspects since it describes an internal and personal awareness. It may be the physical symptoms like butterflies in your stomach when you see someone you are attracted to or the panic that sets in when you realize you have not studied for your test. Even though nobody around you can tell that your palms are sweating (unless they are physically shaking your hand), you are personally aware of your nervousness.

How To Use Personal And Public Awareness

The goal of self-awareness is not to make yourself self-conscious. You should not put yourself in a position where you are incredibly anxious or questioning your decisions. Be aware of everything. Be aware of your strengths and weaknesses. Be aware of those times that you have succeeded in tough situations and the mistakes that have taught you lessons. When considering public awareness, be aware of how people's perceptions of you affect your relationship and the offered opportunities.

The proper way to use self-awareness is to use it in a way that better yourself. Someone who does not share their ideas in the office because they are afraid of others' judgment will miss out on opportunities like leading a project or taking on a high-profile client. Their boss perceives them as someone who does not have innovative ideas or lacks self-confidence and thus gives the more important roles in the organization to someone they think is more capable of handling the situation.

As you become aware of the strengths and weaknesses, you can learn to harness those strengths to help build on useful skills. You also learn which areas you can improve in. Another benefit is better quality relationships. When you are aware of personal relationships and how the other person feels about you, you gain insight into making the relationship better. For example, someone may be aware that their mom is sad at the end of their visits. This perception might cause them to ask her what is wrong—she just might be sad because they don't visit often, and she knows she won't see them for a while.

Finally, becoming self-aware helps you learn how to nurture yourself. Your goals become clearer as you realize the things that make you happy and fill you with purpose. The benefit of certain relationships in your life will also become clearer. You'll learn which relationships to give your energy and attention to, as well as which relationships are bringing you further from your life's path or that harm your life. Overall, you'll have a better insight into what you need to do to make your goals a reality.

Increasing Self-Awareness With Meditation

Meditation is often grouped with spiritual habits or religion. However, meditating regularly does not have to be about religion. It is about discipline. Meditation is a form of mental discipline that quiets the busy chatter many people have in their mind. Think back to the last time that you were eating or taking a shower. Do you spend your lunch break at work enjoying your food and taking a much-needed break so your mind can refresh? Or are you thinking about the things you want to finish before going home for the night? Are you stressing over life when you are in the shower? Or are you taking the time to enjoy the water's warmth after a tiring day and the pleasant feeling of getting clean?

The average person lives a busy life. It is generally believed that if you want to be successful, you have to stay busy. There is always something else to be done and it is not uncommon to spend time that should be spent relaxing worrying about those unfinished things. This is the reality of life for many people, but it creates an unhappy existence. When you do not give yourself the time to slow down and reflect on your life, you are not giving yourself the time to prepare yourself for self-improvement. Then, you may find yourself stuck in the same pattern without having a specific goal all through your life.

Benefits Of Meditation For Self-Awareness

Meditation is often referred to as 'the path to enlightenment'. Self-aware people know themselves on a deeper level and this allows them to shape their life. The goal with this meditation, however, does not have to be religious. When you meditate for self-reflection, you are looking within to understand yourself because you are your life's creator. You are the only person who can choose if you keep working a dead-end job or take the steps to further your dreams. You are the only person who can choose if you want to spend the rest of your life with the person you are dating or pulling you away from your life's path. Here's a look at how self-reflective meditation can change your life.

- Building a foundation of truth- People do not always know who they are at their core. Other times, they may have strayed so far from their beliefs that they have lost the meaning of what they were. Meditation reflection helps you see those areas where you have deviated from your value system.
- Better use of talent- Sometimes, we end up pushed down life's path with little thought to what we are good at. Consider someone who has an art degree from college—but works in a factory because it was the first open position they found after graduating

college. Even though they are talented as artists, they are always tired from work and don't work to advance that talent. They get stuck in this job even though they despise it and eventually end up staying on because of their loyalty. However, they are miserable with their lives and their passions are going to waste. When you reflect on things that make you happy, it allows you to see the talents that you have tucked away. By reflecting on these strengths, you can find the inspiration to grow them and use them in a way that benefits your life.

- Improved goal-mindedness- When you do not set goals for yourself, you move through life aimlessly and without direction. There is no pressure for doing something, so it is easy to say you will start 'tomorrow' or 'next month'. If you do not hold yourself to it, however, you will never see results. Reflection gives you time to think about your goals and the path to achieving them. It also lets you set time aside to consider your accountability in meeting your goals and whether you are actively trying to reach them.

Chapter 19:   Responses   to   Your   Emotinal   Triggers

Feelings, especially intense feelings, can often be autonomous, which means they are automatic and subconscious, developing as the result of an external force or trigger. If someone cuts you off in traffic, for example, the anger that bubbles up in your gut is generated without conscious thought or intent.

To take control of our emotional selves, we must learn to be aware of our emotional triggers and our natural responses to those triggers. The perfect way to do this is to practice mindfulness.

What Is Mindfulness?

Sometimes, intense negative emotion causes us to become disconnected or detached, moving through daily life without engaging with our emotions and experiences. This feeling of being disconnected is very common in people struggling with depression and high anxiety or stress. To combat this emotional distress, we must learn to become more present within our lives, live with our eyes open to what's going on around us, and impact our emotional well-being. To put things as simply as possible, we need to turn off "auto-pilot" and begin to be aware of how we feel and why.

As emotional beings, we are naturally mindful. Still, it can be difficult to be fully present when dealing with high anxiety or anger or other negative emotions. When we practice mindfulness, we force ourselves to face these emotions, consider them and learn to understand them. We can cultivate mindfulness through a variety of techniques, the most common and widely practiced being meditation.

What Is Meditation?

Meditation is an excellent relaxation technique that also helps us connect with our inner truths. Meditation aims to quiet the mind and body, remove insignificant thoughts, and develop inner balance by interacting with our emotional selves without the constant external and internal chatter. Meditation itself is a rather simple activity, but calming the body and mind is easier said than done. By introducing meditation into your routine, you will get better and better at it, and you will begin to crave the positive and peaceful feelings it can bring out.

How Does Meditation Promote Mindfulness?

When we meditate, we steer our awareness away from the external and turn it inwards, paying attention to what the body and mind are doing without life's external noise. Meditation promotes relaxation, which relieves the body of stress and stress hormones and allows it to function more easily. When the body is less stressed, there are fewer physical distractions from what is going on in the mind. When we are meditating, we are naturally more aware of our thoughts and emotions, and we are open to the insights we have within ourselves.

How Do I Meditate?

When I first read about meditation's possible benefits, I was hesitant to try it, mostly because, well, what if I was doing it wrong? It turns out, I didn't have anything to worry about, because there is no right or wrong way to meditate. It all depends on what works best for you and what is most comfortable. If you don't know where to begin, here's a step-by-step guide to meditation.

- Set an intention for today's practice. Your intention may simply be to practice meditation, especially at the beginning. As you become more accustomed to meditation, you may set a more specific intention before you begin, such as seeking intuition regarding a struggle in your life. If you choose to set a specific intention, begin with a question. How do I deal with _____? Ask yourself this question and see what answers you get.

- Find a quiet, comfortable place to sit. The most important thing is that you find a comfortable seat that will not strain your muscles. Cross your legs, or if this is not comfortable, spread them out in front of you to relax into the floor/couch/bed/comfy spot. If your hips do not like this position, try elevating your butt with a pillow or folded towel. This can relieve tension in the hips.

- Relax your body into an upright position. You don't want to strain your muscles; allow your body to relax into your spine's natural curvature. Relax your body from top to bottom, starting with the face. You can relax your face by focusing on relaxing your forehead and jaw muscles. Let your arms fall parallel to your body, and rest your hands on your legs. Work your way down until your body feels tension-free (or as tension-free as possible) and grounded into your seat.

- Close your eyes or focus on a single point. It is common to close one's eyes during meditation, but that can make it easier to fall asleep. If you do fall asleep, don't beat yourself up. It happens, especially when meditation is new. If you don't want to close your eyes, choose a spot in front of you to focus on. You may focus on a spot on the floor in front of you, light a candle, or set up a calming landscape poster.

- Take calming breaths and notice your breathing. It doesn't matter how you breathe as much as it matters that you pay attention to your breaths. Feel each inhale and exhale move through your body. Focusing on your breathing encourages mindfulness of the body and allows the mind the quiet.

- As thoughts enter your mind, allow them to pass through. When a thought comes up, you want to try to release it, let it flow out of your head as quickly as it flowed in. By emptying the mind, we allow our inner voice to be heard through intuitions. Your mind will probably wander, but that's okay. What you're trying to cultivate is an ability to be present at the moment and connect with yourself in a judgment-free environment.

- Consider setting a timer. Especially when you are first starting with meditation, you will probably have limited stamina. Begin with short, five-minute sessions, working up from there to spend longer and longer periods meditating. By setting a timer, you can avoid the distraction of how many seconds or minutes have passed and instead focus on your practice.

- Consider using a mantra. When you think about mediation, do you imagine a monk sitting cross-legged uttering "om" over and over? This is called a mantra, and you may choose to use one if your thoughts are particularly lively. Choose a neutral or positive word or phrase and repeat it throughout the exercise. You may say your mantra aloud or in your mind.

Using Mindfulness To Recognize Your Emotional Triggers

For the most part, our intense negative emotions manifest automatically due to some internal or external trigger. This could be a negative thought, a traumatic event, or even just an unexpected change. What triggers emotions in you will not necessarily trigger others, and what triggers emotions in others may not do the same for you. This is where mindfulness comes in. When you find yourself caught by the tide of negative emotion, try to identify what exactly caused you to feel this way. Here's a list of some possible triggers for common negative emotions:

Stress

- Change in the environment (a big move, a new job, etc.)
- Change in family life (marriage, divorce, a new baby, etc.)
- Changes in social life (discord among friends, someone moving away, etc.)
- Change in health (new or worsening illness, an injury, etc.)
- Change or increase in financial responsibilities (losing a job, etc.)
- Change in the workplace (tension among coworkers, getting fired, etc.)
- General disorder (a cluttered home, child and pet messes, etc.)

Anger

- Betrayal by a trusted person or entity
- Being disrespected, challenged, or insulted
- Being physically or emotionally threatened
- Being patronized or condescended to
- Being lied to/given misinformation
- The injustice done to you or others
- Discrimination/prejudice

Fear

- Threat of death
- Threat of injury or pain

- Loss of perceived safety/security
- Dark or unfamiliar environment
- Imagining a threatening event
- Reliving past fear or trauma
· Feeling exposed/vulnerable

Anxiety

- Anticipating failure or discomfort
- Feeling unprepared or insecure
- Feeling inadequate or worthless
- Negative self-talk/self-deprecation
- Upcoming event, performance, or challenge
- Social and familial conflict
- Remembering bad experiences
- Personal strain (due to finances, travel, etc.)

Sadness/Grief

- Major illness in a friend or loved one
- The death of a friend or loved one
- Temporary separation from loved ones
- Feeling rejected or unwanted
- A loss of identity or self-worth
- Anticipating future tragedy
- Disappointment in self or others
- Involuntary memories of loss or disappointment

Once we know what is triggering our emotional distress, we can begin to put together techniques and strategies to cope with it healthily.

Using Mindfulness To Recognize Your Emotional Responses

To gain mastery over your emotions, you will need to practice recognizing how you respond to your emotional triggers. If you're angry at your significant other because of something that was said, consider how you're responding and what made you angry in the first place. Do you shut down and avoid the conflict? Do you explode into screams and rants? Practice recognizing how your body and mind respond to intense emotions, and consider which reactions are positive and negative.

The Role Of Self-Talk

One of the most important aspects of mindfulness is being aware of how you talk to yourself. You must learn to pay attention to how you interact with yourself within your private thoughts because poor self-talk exacerbates poor emotional health. Self-talk is constant, and it can be easy to get in the habit of speaking to oneself from a place of judgment. We more readily notice our shortcomings than we do our skills, talents, and successes, and when we focus our self-talk around these negative things, we influence how we feel negatively.

Consider how you talk to yourself. Here's a list of common ways people engage in negative self-talk:

- Self-defamation (I look fat, I am stupid, I can't do anything right, etc.)
- Self-criticism over a past event (I should've done, should've said, etc.)
- Doubting own abilities (the ever destructive "I can't")
- Dismissing own abilities and good qualities
- Focusing on own perceived faults and failures
- Personalizing things that are out of our control
- Thinking in black and white (in terms of extremes)
- Assuming we know what the future holds

By practicing mindfulness, we can acknowledge the destructive ways we communicate with ourselves to be more empathetic and forgiving of our emotional struggles. Once you get in the habit of practicing mindfulness, you can begin to build coping strategies to remove your emotional triggers and change your responses to the triggers you can't get rid of. You may even begin to do this naturally once you are more aware of your triggers and reactions.

Chapter 20:   Emotional Intelligence In An Angry World

Anger is something that we all feel from time to time. But as a society, we're generally not very good at handling our anger. One cause why this happens is that we tend to think of anger as a negative emotion. The thing is, anger is a neutral emotion. It's what we do with it that makes it either positive or negative. Some people have done great things when faced with anger, righting the wrongs that they see, marched for good causes, and advocated for better things that they have been angry about. Other people, though, have done some pretty terrible things in a fit of rage. They've become aggressive, destructive, even violent, all examples of how anger can become negative when used for the wrong reasons. Anger is one of our core emotions as a human being, used to describe how we feel, and it helps us identify and connect with what is happening around us. What you do with anger is entirely up to you. It can be used to propel you positively, or propel you in the opposite direction too.

On its own, though, anger is neutral, but like most people, you've probably thought of anger in a negative context. Most people are either afraid of this emotion or try to deny the emotion altogether. It's easy to see why anger has developed an unpleasant reputation. In moments of anger, we make poor decisions. We lose all sense of rationale, and our emotional intelligence ceases to exist. All we feel is pure rage (in extreme cases), the blood pounding in our veins, and our muscles become tense and angry. Anger is a raw emotion that can lead you to do things you ordinarily would not do. Anger seems to hijack all our common sense and make it impossible to make good decisions when consumed by this emotion. All we end up doing is either hurting ourselves, the people around us, and feel full of regret with how badly the situation was handled.

Understanding Your Anger

Different people would have different emotional triggers that set off this reaction, and there could be several factors that cause you to feel angry. Some examples of these triggers include:

- You feel powerless.
- You don't feel accomplished.
- You experience an unfair treatment against you or someone else.
- You've been lied to.
- You are ignored or mistreated.
- You think you're being neglected.
- You experience verbal or physical assault.
- You think your colleagues are not pulling their weight.
- You secretly resent having to take on more responsibility.
- You witness an injustice.
- You're disappointed.
- Promises are broken.
- Things don't go your way.

There is also the fact that some people generally have a shorter fuse than others do. Other possible reasons behind why you find yourself losing your temper more often than you should include:

Your Personality and Temperament- Competitive personalities tend to have shorter fuses because those with this personality type generally insist or demand that things go their way. We're not wired the same way. Some act quicker, while others need more time to process their next move. Some jump to action without thinking twice, while others need more time to ponder the consequences. Some people are more outgoing and adventurous; some are more laid back and introverted.

Your Role Models - Did you have parents or other family members who were quick to anger? Sometimes the cause of our short fuses is because the role models we had are what we can identify with. We don't know any other way because this is how we were raised. If one or both of your parents tended to be quick to anger, chances are you're likely to have that same tendency too. If that's the type of environment you grew up in, you're probably not going to see anything wrong with it until it's pointed out to you.

Mood Disorders - An undiagnosed personality disorder could trigger your short fuse without even realizing it. Bipolar disorder, depression, anxiety are all potential triggers because it won't take much to make you angry. If you suspect you may have any of these mood disorders, it is best that you seek professional help and don't leave it undiagnosed.

Higher Stress Levels - No surprises here that stress could be a cause for your short fuse. Being under a lot of pressure could lead to abrupt outbursts, temper tantrums, and irrational behavior. It is your body's way of reacting to the stress that you already feel.

Inability to Communicate Expressively - When you have a hard time making yourself understood or expressing yourself, it can often lead to a lot of feelings of frustration. Poor communication skills can lead to a lot of misunderstanding, which could lead to arguments which cause your temper to rise because you feel like your point is not getting across. Poor communication skills are yet another potential trigger for why you may have a shorter fuse than others.

Sleep Deprivation - A lack of sleep could also act as a potential trigger for a short fuse. Have you ever noticed how things seem

317

much harder or require more effort when you're feeling tired and exhausted from lack of sleep? You feel cranky, irritable, and even the smallest of things seem like a big deal. Your body is tired, your nerves are frayed, and a lack of sleep makes you less efficient than what you normally would be. Therefore, it doesn't take much to trigger your temper when you're sleep-deprived.

There could be so many possible scenarios and situations that could cause a person to get angry or upset about it. One of the things that you would need to do towards learning how to manage your anger would be to identify the triggers that set you off to learn to recognize them. We can break our anger-response to hormonal levels. The amygdala triggers a response to irritating information or frightening situations. Our "fight or flight" response to annoyances is related to the hormones the brain releases, primarily epinephrine (adrenaline) and norepinephrine (noradrenaline). These hormones result in emotional and physical responses to make us alert and energized. We sometimes call the resulting sensation an "adrenaline rush."

Typically, four responses occur when anger is triggered:

Assertiveness - You're appropriately managing and working through your anger. You're in control and retain your ability to communicate the way you feel towards the person who might have triggered these emotions inside you.

Aggression - This happens when your anger is being unleashed.

Passive-Aggressiveness - On the outside, you're agreeable. On the inside, you're seething and angry but doing your best not to let it show.

Passive - On the surface, you appear calm, and that's because you're storing all your anger and stockpiling it.

Left unchecked, anger could, directly and indirectly, affect your health. It is causing your health problems without you even realizing it. Some examples of how anger is indirectly affecting your health, including increasing your risks of a heart attack because of the constant stress that you feel. It also increases your blood pressure and cholesterol levels, making you prone to having health-related problems because of that stress. It could cause obesity. The way it directly affects your health is by hampering your decision-making process. You can't make rational, appropriate decisions when you're blinded by anger all the time. It drives you to physical injuries too. For example, you could punch something in anger, which ends up hurting you. Or worse, you could punch someone else, which causes physical injury to another person. Neither of which is good, of course. Anger could drive some towards alcoholic tendencies, lead to road rage, make it difficult to concentrate, and more.

Besides, constant, chronic anger will only increase your chances of contracting heart-related diseases like high blood pressure or heart attacks. Anger is connected to the heart because norepinephrine and epinephrine contract your blood vessels, making your heart pump more difficult. These two hormones also happen to be responsible for increasing glucose and fatty acids in the blood, which only leads to damaged arteries and speeds up atherosclerosis. Luckily, there are healthy ways of learning how to control that anger.

Chapter 21:   Anger Management

Just like all other basic emotions, anger is designed to convey a specific message to us. That message could be our disapproval of something that has happened or something that someone has done. However, if our first response when angry is to vent or become raging mad, the message gets lost in translation. For this reason, a calm mind and level-head are essential when dealing with anger. Being in a tranquil state of mind allows you to take a step back and objectively evaluate your anger from reason. It also allows you to acknowledge your feelings and validate them without letting them control you.

Keeping calm when angry, however, is easier said than done. It takes a lot of practice, patience, and maturity to keep yourself from acting out of character when something that triggers rage in us happens. If someone offends you, it is much easier to revenge. In a way, we derive some pleasure from causing suffering to perceived opponents when we feel like they have wronged us. However, in reality, these solutions are illusory, since they do not deal with the real issues and cause of our anger. They can be more detrimental to us and our relationships in the long run. In light of this, we must find healthier ways to control our anger, even when we feel justified in it.

So, what is anger management, and what does it entail? Essentially, anger management is the process of identifying signs that you are becoming angry or frustrated and taking the necessary steps to calm yourself down to deal with your anger more productively. Many people have the misconception that anger management is meant to keep you from feeling angry. Others even think that it is designed to help them suppress feelings. Both of these are poor understandings of the role of anger management. Like we found out earlier, anger is a universal human emotion that all living humans experience at some point in their lives. Also, we already saw why suppressing anger is counterproductive as a long term strategy to manage anger.

The role of anger management is to help you become better at identifying signs that you are becoming frustrated and equip you with the necessary skills to keep your anger under control. A lot of literature has been written about anger and how to deal with it more effectively. Therefore, one can learn the right skills for dealing with frustration from reading books such as this one. However, the most common way people learn anger management is by attending an anger management class or therapy with a counselor.

You will get to learn how to identify the warning signs when you get frustrated, and how you can effectively calm yourself down to approach your anger from the point of strength.

You may be questioning yourself right now, " How do I know if I need anger management classes?" Here are the signs that you need to attend anger management classes to keep them in control.

- You Constantly Feel Like You Need to Suppress Your Anger

While expressing your anger through fits of rage is not the appropriate response for anger, hiding your anger is not a healthy way of coping. If you constantly feel like you need to bottle up your anger, this may point to a lack of proper coping strategy. It may also be that you are afraid of being vulnerable with other people and showing them your true feelings.

Vulnerability is very important in any relationship, as it helps to build trust among individuals. Refusal to be open about one's feelings usually leads to isolation, fear, and distrust. These are not only weak foundations on which to build a relationship, but they can also trigger more feelings of anger and frustration. Therefore, it is essential to take it upon yourself to learn the right coping strategies instead of hiding your feelings of rage.

- You Always Focus on Negative Experiences

Granted, life is very challenging, and everyone will experience negativity in their lives at some point. However, it is important not to allow the bad things in our lives to rid us of our joy and vitality. If you constantly focus only on your life's negative experiences, you get distracted from actually living your life to the fullest potential. You may also find it a lot tougher to appreciate everyday living's simple pleasures, such as having a comfortable roof over your head and people who love you. You, therefore, need to learn the right coping strategies when angry to prevent your anger from becoming habitual.

- You Constantly Struggle with Feelings of Hostility and Irritation

If you constantly struggle with uncomfortable feelings of irritation and hostility towards others, you need to learn anger management skills. While life is not perfect every day, many things make it worth the experience. If you are perennially irritated by the state of affairs in your life, this may point too deep-seated anger issues that need to be resolved as soon as possible.

- You Constantly Find Yourself in Arguments which Further Trigger Your Anger

There are many instances in life when you will find yourself justifiably angry at someone for something they did. However, if you always find yourself in heated confrontations with people, this could sign an underlying anger problem. It could also simply be a sign that the strategies you use to deal with your anger are ineffective. Perhaps your first response when angry is to blame the other person or throw a temper tantrum. Maybe you even find yourself engaging in abusive exchanges with the objects of your frustration. These strategies of coping with anger are very inappropriate since they only trigger more angry reactions from you. Instead, it is important to find a way of calming yourself down enough to deal with the issue with an objective mind.

- You Engage in Physical Violence when Angry

While anger is a very normal reaction that may provoke feelings of aggression, using violence to deal with anger is inappropriate. Physically abusive responses when angry can be very damaging to your health, reputation as well as relationships. It can also lead to very serious legal consequences, such as getting sued or imprisoned for abuse. If you find yourself prone to committing acts of violence when angry, you should immediately seek professional help. Through counseling and attending anger management classes, you can break this cycle of poor anger management and learn to express your frustration in healthier ways that do not involve violence.

- You Manifest Out-of-Control Behavior when Angry

Perhaps you are not outrightly violent towards other people when angry. However, you may tend to smash or break things when angry. This is still not an appropriate response or strategy to deal with anger and frustration. This type of behavior fails to address the real cause of the anger, and only reinforces the idea that showing aggression will make the anger go away. The truth is that it doesn't work. The only effective way of dealing with anger is getting to the root cause and harnessing the emotion in positive ways.

- You Avoid Certain Situations Because of Fear of Getting Angry

Another tell-tale sign that you need lessons in anger management is you find yourself constantly avoiding scenarios that may trigger your anger. Perhaps you don't like going to parties with your spouse because they always leave you alone to chat with the other people. Maybe you avoid talking to one of your close friends because you feel they are too judgmental.

Whichever the case, the temptation to avoid any scenario that may trigger your anger can be too strong to resist. However, opting out of certain situations due to fear of getting frustrated is not an effective way of dealing with your anger. For one, it shifts the responsibility to the other person, thereby diminishing your power to take responsibility for your emotions. It also only covers up pent up frustration, which continues to simmer without your awareness. This can eventually erupt in very damaging ways, both to you and your relationships.

Anger management classes are typically designed to help people develop the skills to notice when they get angry and take the necessary steps to deal with the emotion appropriately. Usually, the classes are conducted as one-on-one sessions or group sessions with a counselor or therapist. Depending on your needs, the anger management program may take a few days, weeks, or even months. Therefore, you need to be patient and consider the whole experience as a learning process.

When you first begin attending anger management classes, the first thing you will learn is how to identify stressors and triggers of anger. By identifying the early warning signs of anger, you can begin to understand its causes and figure out how to control it. Stressors are typically those things that cause frustration in your life and trigger pent up anger. These may include frustration with a child who behaves poorly, financial problems, or coworkers who constantly gossip about you.

Apart from identifying the triggers, anger management classes will help teach you how to pick up on anger symptoms. As we found out earlier, physiological symptoms of anger vary between individuals. You may, therefore, not manifest the same symptoms as someone else when angry. While one person may experience an increased heart rate and sweat when angry, another person may feel a tight-knot in their stomach when upset. Anger management classes will help you identify the physical symptoms of anger as they present uniquely in your body.

Beginner's anger management is also meant to help you recognize the signs that your anger is on the rise. Perhaps you may feel like you want to yell at your anger's perceived object, or you feel the need to keep quiet to avoid a heated confrontation. Being aware of the physical reactions happening in your body will allow you to take a step back and carefully evaluate your anger before proceeding with an appropriate response.

Chapter 22:   How To Heal Your Body And Soul: Emotional Freedom Techniques

What is emotional freedom? And why do we need it? Who is it helpful for, what does it help with? Is there a place in the fast-paced serious world? And how is it achieved?

Emotional freedom is that much-desired and increasingly difficult state of harmony and peace. A state in which we are free from the influence of our negative emotions on our psyche, our decisions, our deeds, our communication. We do not stop to feel emotions, but we can distinguish ourselves from them and their influence on our  decisions, reactions and actions. We are already independent of the filter of emotions that distorts our perceptions and experiences!

Why do we need emotional freedom? When we are free from the effects of increasingly stressful external factors, we are independent. Throughout our life, the accumulated experiences, starting from childhood—traumatic experiences, disappointments, insults—create several sabotaging and limiting beliefs in the subconscious. The unpleasant feeling always experienced is strongly associated with the nervous system, with the body's entire internal biochemistry and becomes an integral part of us. It arises with a new limiting force in every situation, resembling that past unpleasant moment. When we are under the influence of a negative emotion, we are dependent on it because of an experience in the present or the past. They establish our mood, self-esteem, decisions, and actions or inactions. Emotion creates a filter on our perceptions that distorts reality. We interpret and feel what is happening from the standpoint of painful memories and beliefs of the past.

So we are dependent on our fears, on the feeling that we are not good enough, that people do not accept us and reject us, humiliate us, and threaten us. Or are we just unsure that we won't do it, that we don't deserve it. Or they get us into a real hell of panic, anxiety, and obsessive thoughts. Self-sabotaging subconscious beliefs can truly upset our lives. Often, unresolved emotional conflicts, when seeking a solution, manifest themselves as illnesses in our physical body.

Release from negative experiences, perceptions, emotions, fears, and sabotaging beliefs allows us to have a better quality of life. We feel better physically, communicate with ease, and meet our daily challenges. We can improve every area of our lives. Emotional freedom enables us to recognize challenges, work consciously. and direct our emotions.

EFT encompasses everything that happens simultaneously in the mind, emotions, and body to release and transform it. EFT and other energy psychology techniques are often used to achieve excellence in business, sports, or in personal. They reveal and eliminate subconscious internal conflicts and limiting beliefs that hinder our success and realization.

The EFT has one great advantage—because of its simplicity, it is quickly mastered by anyone and easily applied in all situations and at any time—true freedom at the tip of your fingers! As its creator says: "Try it on whatever comes to your mind! Especially when nothing else helps!"

Everywhere in the civilized world—for over thirty years—leading specialists, therapists, and medical professionals have been using EFTs in individual and group practices. EFTs are becoming more accessible, understandable, and easily applicable not only by the world's greats in sports, politics, and business. EFTs are gentle, easy to understand, and easy to implement by anyone!

What is the evidence that it works? EFT and Matrix Rearrangement have been the subject of serious research. The method is based on fully scientifically recognized and proven approaches—from acupuncture to cognitive therapies and perceptions from different psychotherapy units and new medicine. Measurements and studies with apparatus recording changes in brain activity and stress levels have recorded a remarkable turn in the course of one or more sessions.

The results from practitioners around the world are amazing. It deals with people experiencing disasters and huge losses, with war veterans, with children with attention deficit disorder and hyperactivity disorder. Therapeutic sessions improve and heal the following: anxiety, allergies, panic attacks and anxiety, addictions, inability to cope with life's challenges, weight loss, lack of faith and purpose, complete change and release of negative memories, depression, terminal illnesses, successful conception and childbirth after unsuccessful in vitro procedures, clearing of severe birth memories and relationships, intolerance to life, consequences of sexual abuse, withdrawal from bad habits, and traumas—the events that have left a swelling in life . . . the memory has changed.

Who needs emotional freedom? Emotional freedom techniques are one of the most popular and accessible methods of energy psychology. Created by engineer Gary Craig in 1995, energy psychology is a line of collective psychotherapy methods, coaching, and other healing approaches based on the tradition of healing the body-mind system, dating back five thousand years ago. The EP blends the bio-energy foundations of these traditions with best-in-class psychological practice, and has in the past thirty-five years been further validated by clinical experience with millions of clients around the world and supported by research at numerous universities.

The energy psychology methods gently and quickly release the body-mind system from negative perceptions and stressful events frozen over time in it. These events are the reason for the negative way in which one sees the world and the people around him, or the basis of outdated programs on how to experience and regulate his emotions and how to enter into relationships with other people.

Also known as Tapping Techniques, Meridian Tapping, EFT Tapping, and more, they combine the achievements of cognitive (analytical) therapies in Western medical science with ancient Eastern knowledge of the body and the subtle energies that flow into it. While modern Western medicine underestimates the impact of thoughts and feelings on the onset of illnesses, and verbal psychotherapies ignore the body's physiological reactions when experiencing negative emotions, TEC focuses on what is happening simultaneously in the mind and body to release it.

Techniques For Emotional Freedom

Emotional freedom techniques points based on ancient acupuncture, the technique is a tapping of ten acupuncture points on the face and body while experiencing negative

emotion, which helps to quickly, within minutes, release the unpleasant feeling. Medical research has found that this tapping sends a soothing signal to the brain's center responsible for our fight or flight response. This signal breaks the link between the thought, feeling, and physical sensation of the body that corresponds to that negative feeling or physical pain. The erasure of negative feeling restores the capacity for rational thinking and the ability to find solutions. Based on the EFT, much deeper and with astonishing results, is the Matrix Rearrange technique.

Chapter 23: Stress And Worry

Stress alone is responsible for tens of thousands of deaths every year. Stress does more harm than many diseases and leaves countless families grieving the loss of a loved one. This is why you must take active steps towards reducing your stress levels.

Taking Responsibility For Your Stress

Stress is something you have some control over and, therefore, must take responsibility for. The more you take responsibility for it, the better you'll be able to reduce it.

Stress happens for various reasons and manifests in numerous situations. The traffic jam on your way to work, a business presentation, tensions with your boss, or frequent disputes with your spouse all constitute potential stress sources. There are two ways you can reduce stress:

- By avoiding situations you perceive as stressful, and
- By becoming better at dealing with stressful situations.

We'll see how you can use these methods to reduce your stress levels.

How You Can Use Stress To Grow

Exercise - Make a list of your major sources of stress

Let's look at specific situations that are sources of stress for you. Using the workbook, write down what causes the most stress in your typical week. Come up with at least ten things.

Reframing Stress

Emotions arise as a result of your interpretation of events. The mere fact you experience stress (or any other emotion) means you've added your interpretation to what is happening. Otherwise, you would have a stress-free life.

Now, look at your list of stressful situations. For each situation ask yourself the following questions:

- Is that situation stressful in itself?
- What do I need to believe to experience stress in that specific situation?
- What would I need to believe to reduce or remove stress in that particular situation?

Let's say you're stuck in a traffic jam and you find it stressful.

Is that situation stressful in itself?

No, not necessarily. The traffic jam exists and there is nothing wrong with it, per se.

What would I need to believe to experience stress in that specific situation?

I would need to believe:

- There shouldn't be any traffic jams, and therefore, something is wrong.
- The traffic jam is a stressful event in itself.
- I should be where I need to go, instead of being stuck in traffic.
- I can do something about it.

What would I need to believe to reduce/remove stress in that particular situation?

I would need to believe that:

- A traffic jam is a normal event like anything else.
- I don't necessarily have to experience stress just because I'm stuck in traffic.
- I'm here caught in a traffic jam and I don't need to be there (wherever I want to go), for a while.
- I can't do anything about it, so I might as well enjoy it, or at least don't stress over it.

Dealing With Worry

Worry differs from stress as it isn't the result of something you experience in the present, but a concern you have regarding events from the past or events that may happen in the future. You experience stress when you face a stressful situation in the present moment.

For instance, a stressful situation would be being stuck in a traffic jam or having your boss yell at you. Worrying would be remembering (past) or anticipating/imagining these stressful situations (future). Interestingly, most of your worries are unnecessary for the following reasons:

- They happened in the past and there's absolutely nothing you can do about them, and
- They may happen in the future and you can't control the future.

Exercise - Make a list of your worries

Make a list of things you worry about (past or future). They may be similar to the things you wrote in the previous exercise. Examples of things you may worry about are:

- Your health
- Your financial situations
- Your work
- Your relationships, and
- Your family.

Now, write at least ten things you tend to worry about in a typical week.

Sorting Out Your Worries

Constant worry results from trying to control events over which you have no control. When you do so, you create unnecessary stress in your life. To deal with stress and overcome chronic worries more effectively, you must learn to sort out worries. An effective way to do this is to separate the things you have control over from the things you have no control over. You can divide your worries into three separate categories:

- Things you have control over
- Things you have some control over, and
- Things you have no control over whatsoever.

1. Things you have control over:

This category includes things such as your actions and behaviors. For instance, you can choose what to say and how to say it. You can also decide what actions you'll take to achieve your goals.

2. Things you have some control over:

There are things you have only limited control over such as a competition or a job interview. You can't be certain you'll win a tennis match but you do have some control over its outcome. For instance, you can choose to train harder or hire a great coach. Similarly, you can prepare for a job interview by conducting extensive research about the company you apply to or doing a mock interview. You don't, however, have absolute control over the outcome of the interview.

3. Things you have no control over:

Unfortunately, there are also many things you have no control over. These are things such as the weather, the economy, or traffic jams.

Exercise - Sort out your worries

Look at your list of stressful situations. Next to each item, put C (control), SC (Some control), or NC (No control). This simple act of sorting out your worries already helps reduce them. As you identify things you have no control over, you can let go of your urge to worry.

Now, for things you have (some) control over, write down what you could do about it. What concrete actions could you take to alleviate them?

For things you have no control over, can you let go of your need to control them instead of accepting them?

Taking One Hundred Percent Responsibility For Your Stress And Worries

What if you had more control over your worries than you believe? Look at the situations you have no control over and ask yourself, "If I had control over them, what would I do? What would it look like? And how could I prevent them from happening?"

Often, you'll realize you have some control over these situations. This can be by changing, reframing or eliminating them from your life.

Let's say you identified traffic jams as something you have no control over. This sounds reasonable. Once you're caught in the

335

traffic jam, you can't do much about it. But, could you do things differently? For instance, could you leave home earlier or take a different route?

What about reframing the situation? Instead of escaping the situation mentally, you could choose to be fully present by making traffic jams a productive part of your day. You could then make the most of it by listening to audiobooks. Imagine how much you could learn if you listened to audiobooks every working day for an entire year.

Go over your list and look for things you have no control over. Write down what you could do to change, reframe or eliminate these events.

Chapter 24: Why Self-Discipline And Self-Control Are Important?

Relationship Among Self-Control, Self-Discipline, And Willpower

Willpower is your inner strength to take action, decision, and execute any task until it is done regardless of your outer and inner resistance, difficulties and discomfort. It helps you overcome temptations, negative habits, and laziness and carry different actions even though it requires effort and unpleasant experiences.

Self-discipline is the rejection of your instant gratification to achieve something better or to achieve a better goal. A person also can stick with thoughts, actions and behavior which can lead to success and improvement. Self-discipline is also self-control which can be manifested in physical, emotional, spiritual and mental discipline. However, self-discipline is not living in a restrictive or limiting lifestyle. It is also not being narrow-minded. Self-discipline and self-control is one of the pillars of willpower and success.

You need self-control and self-discipline to make daily decisions and actions. You also need it in making important decisions and reaching major achievements in life. Self-discipline and self-control are needed to continue studying, start a business, lose weight, maintain long-lasting relationships, change habits, meditate, have self-improvement, and keep promises.

Willpower, Discipline, Self-Control

• Developing mental strength

Every tip given till now, every piece of advice, links back to using your mental prowess to overcome sloth. The unfortunate part is that everyone wants to be productive and successful. Still, very few want to invest in developing a strong mind – with which they can control their destinies.

What's mental strength? Your mind can listen to you in the face of temptation or inaction. And it's a combination of your willpower and self-control, tempered by discipline. Indeed, the first two are almost synonyms of each other, while the third is the outcome. It can be safely said any one of them is incomplete without the other two.

Let's understand these attributes in detail.

Defining Willpower

Willpower is considered as the ability to overcome instant pleasure, and resist temptation in the short term to achieve goals in the long term. Most of us have heard of the 'marshmallow experiment' in which a kid is left in a room with a single marshmallow for an hour. If he resists the temptation to eat it in that time, he gets two marshmallows later. More kids waited for the second marshmallow than settle for just one.

Strong willpower helps you overpower feelings and emotions while empowering you to ride through logic. Many individuals develop it consciously as a tool to regulate their actions. Psychologists contend that willpower is a limited resource, to be used carefully. However, this premise hasn't been corroborated by research yet.

Willpower is the force that gives you self-control, with which you can avoid succumbing to momentary impulses. It empowers us to pause and think – so that you can look at optional responses. It also prevents you from jumping into things that could be regrettable later.

Scientifically speaking, willpower resides in the right brain in a section called prefrontal cortex. Willpower is known to use up glucose, causing depletion of the ego. When this happens, our reserves are low and our guard is down, and we tend to indulge and overeat. This explains why people going through stress tend to put on weight easily.

In layman's terms, willpower can do something even if you don't feel like doing it. Research studies have shown that kids who grow up with more self-control become adults who're stable and secure, not to mention scoring high in self-discipline. This, in turn, leads to better performance academically and happier lives. Self-control is the one single contributor to the long-term success of an individual.

Willpower is like brainpower. Use it less and it weakens. Employ it more and more and it gets fitter and stronger. If you've always lived a life of surrender, it would be tough for you to develop willpower. Some psychologists also liken it to a muscle – neglect using it and it sags. Keep stretching it and it gets more resilient.

Needless to add, self-control is the key to overcome fears and obsessions, and to prevent unwelcome behavioral traits. When practiced well, it puts you in charge of your life, developing your tolerance and patience, improving your relationships, and repeatedly succeeding. It also empowers you to avoid excesses and attain moderation; assists you control your moods and reject negativity; and strengthens your self-esteem and inner strength. Self-control helps you to become a complete, well-rounded personality.

But for willpower to work, you need to make it work – and you should be determined for it. Temptation appeals to the sub-conscious while willpower resides in the conscious, so you need to make constant, serious efforts to improve it. Here are few simple ways to add more muscle to your will.

Try To Resist Temptation At Every Opportunity

We've all heard the cliché: 'Where there's a will, there's a way.' Temptation is all around us – in different sizes, shapes and intensities. From enjoying a cake to watching a thriller, everything is temptation. When faced with one, attempt to ward it off. Tell your mind to fight it and immerse yourself in some other activity. It may not work the first time, or even the second, but gradually you'll gain the strength to fight it. Just say No and stay with your decision.

If At First You Don't Succeed, Postpone

This works like magic. If you can't say No to the cake right away, tell yourself that you'll have it tomorrow. When tomorrow comes, say the same thing. Keep putting it off, and eventually you'll realize that you're not tempted by it anymore. This is because your mind can't accept No for an answer. But if you tell your mind that you can have it later, it agrees. Postpone temptation forever.

Point to remember: Don't tire your will by constant negation. If you constantly deny it the pleasure it's seeking, its edge gets blunted. Since willpower isn't considered to be infinite you've got to expend it with care. Hence the next point.

Remove All Temptations From Your Vicinity

If cakes are your weakness don't store them in your refrigerator. Prevent temptations from entering your home, then there's no way you'll fall for them. If the television is a temptation, unplug it or – better still – disconnect the cable connection. Out of sight is out of mind, and you don't miss what you don't see (in most cases). Guarantee that your immediate environment is free from such attractions; your willpower will thank you for it.

Equip Your Body To Resist Temptation

If you're serious about boosting your willpower, you need to get your body prepared. See that you eat nutritious food, get enough exercise and sleep well. Regular workouts help you to fight stress better, leading to better self-control. And the good news is, you don't have to spend hours in the gym every day. Even light exercise like taking a walk or doing basic yoga can enhance your resilience.

Make Affirmations Work For You

Self-affirmations can lead to better self-control. When your affirmations are positive and confident, and repeated often, they have a lasting impact on your mind. There's a world of difference between "I can't have that cheese pizza" instead of "I don't want to have that cheese pizza". The former suggests your limitation while that latter indicates confidence.

Whenever you feel the need to boost your self-control, say these affirmations over and over again:

- I am in full control of myself.
- I am in full control of my reactions to external stimuli.
- I am in full control of my behavior.
- I am the master of my life.
- I possess the power to choose my thoughts and emotions.
- I understand that my self-control gives me inner strength.
- I am, with each passing day, enhancing my abilities to control myself.
- I practice self-control because it's a lot of fun.

Simple Self-Discipline Workouts

We refuse to do several things in our everyday life, purely because we lack the mental strength to do them. These could be small acts, seemingly insignificant, but with the potency to enhance our inner muscle and make us better individuals. We hesitate to do them for a variety of reasons, including laziness, low confidence and self-esteem, low mental strength, shy and ,timid or plain procrastination. A part of us may want to do it, but we stagger and lose the opportunity, only to regret it later. This is where our mind plays a role in increasing our willpower.

- Your sink is full of dirty dishes and you're surfing the Internet mindlessly. Force yourself to reach for the Shut Down button, close the computer, and head towards the sink. Don't fall for any more procrastination. Start with cleaning just one spoon and soon you'll find yourself cleaning up the entire sink. It's your win against your sloth.
- A pregnant woman enters the subway carriage and no seat is empty. You have the choice to give her your seat but you hesitate. Don't. Do it for yourself, not for her or for the sake of being nice. Give her the seat and record a minor victory.
- You come back home from a tired day outdoors. You know you need to wash. But your mind tells you that you're fatigued beyond repair, so you just sit in front of the television watching senseless stuff. Don't believe yourself. Don't let yourself be taken for a ride. You do have the strength to walk into the shower and bathe. You'll feel so fresh that you'll be glad you did. More importantly, you would have triumphed over yourself.

Look around and find dozens of similar instances where you're offered a choice – one, the usual easy route and the other, the unusual difficult one. Choose the difficult route always. Take the stairs instead of the elevator, walk instead of seeking a lift, hit the gym instead of sleeping early in the morning. Each such act of yours strengthens your willpower a little more. Become a strong personality, not a weakling at the mercy of your faint heart. Conquer yourself and you can defeat the world.

Solutions Snapshot

Develop mental strength through willpower, self-control and discipline.

A strong willpower is behind self-control.

Willpower is like muscle; its strength can be enhanced through practice.

There are many benefits of willpower. It helps you become happy and successful.

Have the will to make willpower work. Here are some tips:

- Attempt to resist temptation at every step.
- If you can't say No right now, postpone yielding to temptation.
- Remove all enticements from around you. Out of sight, out of mind.
- Eat healthy food, get exercise, sleep well – all help fight temptation.
- Use self-affirmation to develop inner strength.
- Test your mental prowess during simple everyday events.
- You can't conquer the world if you fail to conquer yourself.

Chapter 25: The Sustainability Of An Excellent Emotional State Of Mind

We will now discuss a fundamental concept for all the thoughts and ideas that you have learned. An attempt to completely change the anxiety narrative and present a complete solution-driven model that will help you overcome emotional issues permanently all relies on one word—sustainability!

It is so inspiring to learn new ideas about the steps you can take toward better anxiety management, but what is better than learning is the idea of sustaining what you learn. Anxiety is a feeling, and like all other feelings, it can creep up on you at any time even when you seem to know what to do.

So the best approach to imbibe is the sustainability approach that enables you to make the lessons gained a vital part of your life. With the sustainability approach, you will be taking decisive steps that will help you go beyond wanting to change negative thoughts to positive ones and just being 100% positive all the time.

Yes, it is possible to have positive thoughts all the time. It requires a lot of work, commitment, intentionality, and dedication to the process; but it is possible.

Emotional Resilience

For you to sustain the answers, you've discovered that you will need to be emotionally resilient. Resilience is like a muscle. You've got to flex it enough to so it can take on more emotional punches. Resilience isn't about winning the battle of emotions; it is about the strength you display every time you are faced with an issue.

Some persons discover answers to their anxiety; they apply the solutions and erroneously believe that they wouldn't have any other issue going forward. So when they are hit by something more significant than the initial anxiety, they buckle under and fall into the pit of depression.

But an emotionally resilient person doesn't give up. They are aware of the repetitive cycle of emotions and are prepared to take it on at any time, regardless of how hard it might be.

Listen, regardless of what you've learned, there will be moments when you feel like you haven't learned anything at all; and in those pivotal points, what you need is emotional resilience. You will need the kind of emotional toughness that will cause you to strive on and maintain a positive outlook about life.

Emotional resilience also helps you bounce back from stressful situations that may have otherwise held you down and become worse. Resilience is not an "I can bend but not break" trait; instead, it is an "I know I am broken, but I can pull myself back together again."

When you are emotionally resilient, you do not only adapt quickly to stress, negative emotions, or disappointment but also gain insight into some of the best ways you can avoid the kind of situations that lead you right back to that emotional space.

So how can you build emotional resilience?

First, you must be self-aware, which is the ability to stay in tune with your feelings. This will help you avoid the pitfall of blaming the world for your challenges. Instead, you will learn how to look within for answers. You can also build emotional resilience by being persistent. You develop that never-giving-up attribute, which keeps your internal motivation alive.

Emotional control is another way of ensuring that you've got emotional resilience. When you think carefully before making a decision, you will most likely protect yourself from many issues later.

Emotionally resilient individuals are also very flexible with their thinking patterns. They have a mix of rationality, positive thinking, and adjustability, all essential parts of positive mental health.

The attributes will help you build emotional resilience, which will be instrumental in the sustenance of a positive mindset. If you aren't emotionally tough, you will have many moments where you break down and stay down (which is the lowest form of the impact of anxiety).

We are saying here that it is okay to fall, but don't stay down. When you build emotional resilience using the ideas provided thus far, you will be able to get over negative emotional situations and build yourself strong enough to inspire others going through a similar challenge.

Have A Support System

Emotional resilience is crucial, and in addition to that, you must have a great support system around you. We all need support, especially when dealing with sensitive issues, but we will enjoy the best kind of support from people who genuinely care about us.

When you feel overwhelmed, sometimes you may not be able to do anything to help yourself at that particular moment. This happens when you are dealing with something very painful or an event that has such a huge effect on your emotions.

What you need at such times is to rely on someone else who will help make the emotional burden light. You may need a hug, a smile, or someone to talk to, regardless of what you need. Support systems are essential to helping you sustain a positive mindset.

Most people do not get to bask in the feeling of having support systems because they don't share their challenges, and when they are asked if they are all right, they go with the natural response, "I am fine."

When dealing with anxiety, it isn't the time to lie to yourself or others. If you do have people who love and care for you, that is an added advantage you must utilize to solidify your built mindset.

Well, now is the time to put that lesson to good use by not only being expressive to yourself but being expressive with others who may be able to help you through moments of mental crisis.

There is an erroneous belief adopted by many persons that states that if you share your struggles with others, you will become vulnerable, and they may take advantage of you. Well, the reason this idea is erroneous is that if you are with people that love you, then you wouldn't worry about someone taking advantage of you.

Do not allow the statements made by other people to shut yourself off from others. You've got to open yourself to sharing so that you can derive joy in great company.

Sometimes when you share, you don't need advice. You might only need to get some things off your mind, and you are bound to feel better afterward. Try not to isolate yourself from others. You never know who might become that accountability partner that will pick your telephone call in the middle of the night when faced with an emotional crisis.

Your support system may include very close friends, family members, or your romantic partner. Some people join emotional support groups that consist of people dealing with anxiety, and they come together to help one another. If you've got the right people around you for support, then great. You can also join a support group if you feel reluctant to share the details of your anxiety to those dearest to you.

We are building a sustainable pattern with the solutions we have offered, and support systems are a part of that pattern. If everyone has people in our lives, we can lean on; the world will surely be a better place for it. There will be fewer cases of people who feel alone with their challenges and more success stories of people who come together and stay connected over a common goal, eradicating adverse emotional problems.

Reach Out To Someone Else

When you have a great support system and the right mental tools to beat anxiety, what can you do to make it all better? Reach out and help someone else who may be unable to get out of that place. Listen, the best way to become extremely good at something is to share in the experience with someone else.

Some people are going through this challenge and have no one to hold their hands. There is little or no hope for such individuals, and you can contribute in your way to make it better. Now you may not be able to reach out to many people, but you can reach out to those within your sphere of contact.

Use all the ideas you've discovered and the ideas that have worked for you on this journey to help someone else. You wouldn't know someone is dealing with anxiety by just waiting for them to burst into tears or have a moody look. You need to interact with people on a deeper level. Ask questions and remain connected with them before some of them open up to you.

When you help others, you will also be solidifying the solutions you've imbibed because you will be required to do some of the solution-driven activities with these people you help. As you improve on your emotional strength, the people you help will lean more on you and get better.

Anxiety is a demoralizing challenge for anyone to go through, but what makes it better is knowing that you've got someone with you through it all and deriving motivation from that person.

When we speak of volunteering and helping those on the streets, everyone (the rich and middle class) is often encouraged to participate; they are often told to give willingly regardless of how small their gifts are. Well, it is the same with helping someone who struggles with anxiety. You don't have to become an expert on dealing with stress before reaching out.

Sometimes it might be a visit you pay to the person's home to listen to them; it might be a hug, a gift of this book, or a kind smile to a stranger. There are countless ways of reaching out to another person; you need first to become sensitive to others and try to see their pain beneath the smiles and pretense at being "fine."

Be very patient with the people around you. Some people may not be willing to share their challenges with you even if they believe you can help. You have a responsibility to persist respectfully and be a shoulder for them to lean on. Helping others also makes it possible for you to look beyond yourself and seek ways to make positive contributions to the world in your small way.

You don't have to start out helping a lot of people at once. Start with one person. Succeed with the individual. Ensure thorough feedback. Then reach out to someone else. Being charitable with your time and emotional effort will cause you to become increasingly conscious of your own emotions and others. You will be able to perform the dual function of being a caregiver to yourself and other people.

Don't just read through this book, then put it down, and forget to use the content to impact others. You can be an agent of change in the world today in your unique way.

Chapter 26:   Embracing Our Feelings

Feeling An Emotion

To change the difficult behaviors that occur when we are emotionally reactive. It is necessary to replace the behaviors with new and more functional one. This may result in an increased awareness of our feelings. Habitual behaviors serve to take our attention away from underlying feelings that seem overwhelming. When these behaviors stop, the smoke clears and the underlying feelings become more apparent to us.

To handle the feeling component of an emotion, take the opposite approach. Instead of stopping the feeling, allow it. Instead of changing the feeling to something more positive, embrace it as it is.

The healthy response to feeling is not changing it, moving away from it, or distracting attention from it. Instead, embrace the feeling with awareness. Feeling is a natural response of our bodies to a situation or how we perceive that situation. Problems that we have with our emotions lie in distorted perceptions, not in feelings. Feelings demand to be fully felt. If we push the feeling away, we replace it with numbness and repression or self-destructive actions that distract from feelings. Avoidance of feelings is the source of painful symptoms and defenses. This is why it is so important to embrace feelings, even when we are being emotionally reactive.

Many people run away when confronted with uncomfortable feelings. They are unpleasant; they seem negative. To embrace them is like doing a 180-degree turn. Why embrace unpleasant feelings--like the feelings that accompany emotional reactivity? It is important to understand that they are not destructive. Rather, the behaviors that are used to avoid these feelings are the destructive element. For instance, a person may feel sadness over the loss of a friend, and instead of feeling the sadness will drown his sorrows in drink. In this scenario, drinking is destructive. Embracing the feelings of grief, however, will eventually lead to their transformation.

Throughout a lifetime we develop numerous, unconscious methods to avoid painful feelings. By embracing our feelings, the compulsion to act these strategies out is short-circuited, and we take the wind out of the sails of defensiveness. If one's tendency is to avoid feelings of hurt by becoming angry, once that hurt is embraced and allowed, then the strategy of avoiding hurt by getting angry has no more purpose. The underlying pain and hurt is faced and transformed.

Painful feelings often become associated with painful events. We believe that if we allow the feelings to arise, we will be vulnerable and hurt again. But the feelings we experience now are not those of past experiences. They are merely changes in our physiology and are not necessarily harmful. What is harmful is running away from our feelings. By embracing painful feelings instead of pushing them away, we can heal.

A feeling is made up of sensations in our bodies as nerve cells become activated. Blood flow changes, adrenaline increases and other chemical changes occur when we are emotional. Feeling is the awareness of these many sensations being stimulated and an evaluation of pleasantness, unpleasantness or neutrality. Negative feelings in themselves cannot be horrible or overwhelming, only unpleasant. The true negativity resides in our beliefs and thoughts about them. Understanding this can be a powerful reminder that feelings are okay and are not monsters to be avoided.

Learning To Soothe Ourselves

One analogy we can use is comparing our emotions to an infant's responses because infants are highly emotional and have not yet developed the defenses or intellects of adults. They are very sensitive on a feeling level. When an infant is upset and runs to her mother, the mother needs only to hold the infant and attend to her to calm the infant's high emotional arousal. Being held by a loving caregiver creates a situation where the original emotion changes, sometimes to its opposite. The child may be laughing and smiling within a few minutes. Feelings require similar attention. We need to soothe ourselves by holding the feeling and staying with it until it changes - until we feel soothed and calmed down.

The ability to soothe ourselves emotionally is a principal skill in mastering emotions. We learn this from our caregivers when we are infants. Those unable to soothe themselves may experience distressing emotions for longer periods. Often dysfunctional behaviors serve as distractions from these uncomfortable feeling states. By learning to embrace the feeling component of our emotions and soothe ourselves, the impetus for these negative behaviors decreases dramatically. The troublesome behaviors may remain a habit, but the compulsion to act them out loses much of its power.

It is of primary importance that we change our view of our emotions. We need to stop trying to change them or avoid them, instead, let them come to full awareness. If we can make this discovery — that feelings are our friends and have important information for us — we can build the necessary skills to master our emotions and reactivity.

Steps For Embracing Our Feelings

1.   Move your attention to the feeling rather than away from it.
2.   Bring your awareness fully to the feeling without backing away or getting distracted. Stay with the feeling.

3. Explore the feeling. What does it feel like? Are there images that occur to you as you explore the feeling? Note the images but keep your attention on the feeling.

4. Notice the specific parts of your body that are affected by the feeling. Where in your body are you feeling this? See if you can break the feeling down into its parts. Notice what specific sensations are in your body.

5. Let your breathing relax. Take a deep breath. As you do this, imagine that you are breathing directly into the area where you are feeling the emotion.

6. Be aware if the feeling changes, and notice its energetic quality. Whether the feeling is anger or sadness, it is just energy. Stay with the feeling and see what changes take place.

7. This exercise should be soothing. If it is not, some fears or memories hold this feeling in place and not allow it to move.

By staying with the feeling and experiencing it in our bodies, we contain it and own it. It does not own us. Knowing that feelings are sensations in our bodies allows us to form a container around them. Awareness is the container that surrounds the emotion and it is larger than the emotion. Awareness contains everything that we are experiencing in the moment: sights, sounds, thoughts, sensations in our bodies. We may be feeling extreme anger in every cell of our bodies, yet our awareness is greater. We can see the trees and the sky, and they have nothing to do with our anger. Instead of seeing anger as a force that sweeps us away, reduce the anger to its true size. Notice how the emotion appears in your body whenever a strong emotion occurs.

As we learn to embrace and experience feeling, a significant transformation takes place--the feelings change. Our feelings have one basic need — to be felt. When we receive this message, it fulfills its task. The feeling may then move to calmness or some other more positive emotion as long as there is no distorted thinking to support its continuance.

Another thing that takes place as we embrace feeling is a change in our deep belief structure. Negative beliefs about experiencing intense feelings fade. We realize that we have embraced the most intense feelings. Yet, nothing horrible has happened to us, which helps us break the deep associative ties between these feelings and previous experiences of abuse and distress. We learn that by feeling the feelings, we may soothe ourselves and calm ourselves down. Embracing our feelings now leads to a positive and healing outcome. This is a key method of healing faulty emotional learning during abusive situations and comes to the surface when we are emotionally reactive.

Numbness And Embracing Feelings

As cited earlier, there are three basic ways of expressing emotional reactivity: conflict, caretaking and avoidance. All three of these methods avoid feelings to some extent. Let's explore how avoiders can come into greater contact with their emotions.

The avoidant style can be so pervasive for some that it becomes part of their personality style. Because it is difficult for them to experience strong emotions, they avoid them altogether and rarely allow themselves to feel. It may appear that they are not emotionally reactive because they seem calm and peaceful. Still, this calmness is due to avoiding situations that trigger their emotions rather than true peace of mind. They are engaged in a pre-emptive strike; their avoidant behavior itself is their emotional reactivity.

The avoidant person needs to learn to identify avoidant behaviors and to stop them. Awareness of these behaviors is difficult because the rationalizations behind them are so complete. The individual engages in excuse-making, judgments, and other defense mechanisms to justify avoidance and disguise it. A person may even get so far away from his emotions that he no longer feels them, even in situations that would typically trigger intense emotions. Some people talk about serious abuse in their childhood as if they were reporting on someone else's childhood. Sometimes a person may express bizarre behaviors, such as laughing when describing how they were physically abused as children. This dissociation from one's feelings occurs in many people who have had overwhelming trauma.

Chapter 27: Reflect On The Bright Side Of Life Everyday

You Can't Change The Past Or Predict The Future: Live In The Present

Living in the present can be a difficult feat to achieve for many. Whether it is through their upbringing or as a result of various environmental factors, most people have been conditioned to dwell about the past and to worry about the future. Even today's technology contributes to one's inability to focus on the present.

Take, for example, the notifications you receive from your phone. You may be fully engrossed in whatever you are doing at the moment. Still, when you hear your phone go off, the mind tends to automatically switch to either an experience or a future event related to the notification you have received.

Other factors that can keep you from staying in the present include:

· the natural tendency of the mind to edit out the positive aspects of your previous experiences, thus making the past seem more negative than it was; and

· the uncertainty of the current situation you are in, which generates feelings of anxiety, negative thoughts, and worry.

Many people find it difficult to overcome these elements and start living in the present. Some do not even know what it means to be in the present. They cannot imagine how it feels like to be free from their ruminations about the past, and their apprehensions about the future. Most of the time, they simply do not have enough personal will to focus on what is currently happening to them.

Fortunately, there are various ways to get over the challenges of being in the here and now. Through the right mindset and a positive attitude, you can start living in the present and make better life choices.

When you live in acceptance of what has already happened, and what will come to pass, then you will begin seeing things for what they truly are. You will be able to forgive yourself and others for the mistakes that have been made in the past. You will also be able to free yourself from feelings of anxiety and worry about the things that may come your way.

Let me share my personal experience on this subject!

So, it just happens that I had made at some point in my life, quite too many financial mistakes and bad financial investments that did cost me some huge chunk of my savings for the supposed pleasant life I looked forward to living. Not once, not twice, not even thrice. Under these circumstances, I should have typically read the signs on the wall, right? and know what investment is good and bad, but duh! (laughs), I kept sinking in much money in more investments, but this time around, to recover my previous financial losses. However, I ended up losing more and more. At a point, I lost it and went into bouts of anxiety, negative thoughts, and worries about the mess I created in my finances and how I should have known better after the initial three losses incurred. I would overthink what would become of my financial status, especially at the point of my life where I was somewhat out of a job. I was scared, unhappy, and angry every other day I lived. This feeling went on for as long as I could remember, and then, on one Tuesday morning, I laid woken right on my bed and looked up, gazing into the ceiling before me, and I asked myself, a life-changing question.

"How has my overthinking of the past financial mistakes, what I could have done differently, and what the life I hoped to live in the future has helped me achieve?".

I decided that I was going to leave the past mistakes where it belongs, "the past"— I was going to focus on living in the present by making the most out of it— and that I wasn't going to beat myself up about what the future holds. Consciously deciding on this gave me a great sense of relief and peace.

No matter how much we try, we can't change the past simply because it is out of our control, and no matter how we wish we could predict the future, we simply can't because the universe operates on its terms and conditions. So then, the obvious choice you can make, one which you have control of is to live in the moment and enjoy what each day brings. It sure helps.

Change The Way You Think: Gratitude Vs. Regret

Everyone has felt regret at different points in life. You may have

gotten over them by now, but you have surely experienced how heavy regrets can be.

Regret can be something you have done—whether deliberately or unintentionally—to hurt yourself or somebody else. You may also regret after making a snap decision that resulted in something less favorable than it should have been had you only taken your time.

Having regrets is a normal human experience. However, obsessing over them is not healthy or productive, and would most likely result to overthinking, which in turn would produce bouts of anxiety, negative thoughts, and worry. There is no way to go back in time and change the circumstances that have led to those regrets. The only way to go is forward.

To overcome a regretful mindset, you must learn how to adapt and apply gratitude in your life. Rather than ruminating about what has happened and what could have been, you should switch your attention to the good things in your life.

Changing the way you think is not something you can do half-heartedly. You must learn how to practice gratitude whichever way you can. You can do it by literally keeping track of the fortunate instances you have experienced in life. Others find the habit of writing down positive things to help keep them grateful, especially during tough times.

You can even take this further by being thankful for the lessons you have gained from your past, no matter how painful or hard they are. Be thankful that you have managed to live through them, and you have then been allowed to learn from your past mistakes. You are now a step closer to enlightenment and becoming a better version of you.

Once you have chosen to adopt a grateful mindset fully, then you will be able to:

- feel contentment about the blessings in your life;
- gain an optimistic point of view;
- better appreciate the people around you;
- find ways to help those in need; and
- have a higher level of self-awareness.

Take note that successfully overcoming your regrets does not happen overnight. You must be patient with yourself, and continually practice applying gratitude in all aspects of your life.

The more you practice it, the easier it becomes to access a grateful mindset, even during trying times.

Act With Confidence: Stop Asking "What If"?

Torturing yourself with the question "what if" gives you nothing but unnecessary feelings of anxiety, negative thoughts, and worry. There is no way to know what will exactly happen by choosing to act in a certain way. It is a waste of time and energy to think about the uncontrollable aspects of the future.

More often than not, obsessing over your actions' possible outcomes will only make you feel upset. Having no definite answer since there is an endless number of possibilities can be particularly unsettling.

To stop asking yourself this question, you must:

- focus on the here and now of the situation;
- identify the things that are within your control; and
- think of each situation as an opportunity to learn.

If you do end up acting upon the wrong decision, the only healthy thing to do is learn from it and move on. Do not let your mistake define your present and what your future would become.

Reallocate the time and energy you would have used in overthinking about the what-ifs of the situation into something more productive. Use that as a motivation to make better decisions the next time you are facing a similar circumstance. Remember, you can take more control over your thoughts and actions if you simply believe you can do so.

Do Away With Negativity And Embrace Positivity

There are days when nothing seems to go your way. The moment you wake up, you just know everything that can go wrong will go wrong.

Since you are already expecting it, any disappointment that comes your way further strengthens the negative vibes you feel. When this happens over and over again, those vibes solidify into a perennial negative mindset.

If this scenario sounds familiar to you, then know that you have the option to turn things around for the better. You are in control, and you can choose how you will approach important matters in your life.

From here, you can start nurturing a positive mindset centered around your personal growth and development. You can reframe your outlook in life, thus giving you hope and motivation to overcome the challenges that may come your way.

It should be noted that you should actively work on embracing positivity. Once you have acknowledged that you have the right to be happy and ultimately responsible for your happiness, you may then apply this positive mindset in your day-to-day life and the achievement of your goals.

Chapter 28:   Ways To Attract Good Energy

Positive energy can improve how we feel and communicate with the people around us. In our daily dealings with other people, we receive the kind of energy we send out. This energy is usually within our entire body, spirit and mind and, when it vibrates out, it's usually felt by others around us.

The way we feel about the people around us results from the kind of energy we carry around and the energy that we pick up on from them. We may feel free and cheerful around some people and feel awkward and cold when we're around other people. Maintaining positive energy will improve our total well-being and help us to communicate more positively with people.

On the other hand, negative energy negatively affects our entire well-being due to the feelings of resentment, discord and unhappiness that accompany it. So, your ultimate goal should be to resist negative energy and embrace positive energy.

You can achieve this by increasing your energy level and surrounding yourself with positivity. Here are nine daily ways to boost your inner vibration and help you feel the energy flow around you.

Pay Attention To The Energy You Release

If you're releasing lots of negative energy, there's no way you'll attract positive energy. How others feel when they are with you tells a lot about the kind of energy you discharge. Do people feel calm and happy or gloomy and sad when they're with you? Your answer to this will help you know if you have to work on boosting your energy or not.

Negative energy will always impact your relationships negatively, and your attitude towards others is a reflection of who you are. Ask yourself: What kind of impression do I make on people?

If you're the type that always reaches out to people and creates great relationships, you may be releasing positive energy. If you're the type that people avoid, you may be releasing negative energy. Therefore, you must focus on emitting positive energy.

Change The Way You Think

If you spend most of your time thinking about negativity, you'll become a pessimist in no time. But if you spend most of your time thinking about the positive aspects of your life, no matter how hard that can sometimes be, you'll easily attract good things. Always ensure that the positive thoughts guide you in all you do.

If you're battling a bad situation, resist the urge to slip into pessimism. Instead, tell yourself that it's only a phase, and it will soon pass. Always engage in positive affirmations, especially when things go wrong. When you receive bad news, try not to dwell on it or catastrophize. Replace negative thoughts with positive ones. Let the inspiration for your actions come from positive and realistic thoughts about yourself.

Discard Negative Influences

Quit surrounding yourself with negative people, things or places will take away your happiness and total well-being. Some people are toxic, and you should be far away from them. These are people who always try to discourage you from everything you do and look for every means to bring you down constantly. If you're not observant enough, you may begin to pick up bad habits from these toxic places, people or things.

When you disengage yourself from these negative influences, you'll be able to design the kind of life you want for yourself. At times, disentangling from these influences may seem difficult because they're a part of your daily life. If this is the case, avoid them at all costs and prepare yourself mentally if you cannot avoid running into them.

Increase Your Circle

As you discard negative influences, increase your circle of positive influences. Surround yourself with people of like minds that can influence you positively and inspire you to be the best you can be. Ensure that you hold these relationships in high esteem and nurture them.

These people should be able to be honest and authentic with you, but it shouldn't be done to spite you or make you feel less sure of yourself. The positive energy that radiates from this group will help you live a happier life.

Be Kind And Compassionate

Some little acts of kindness can have a significant impact on the receiver and the giver. Being kind and compassionate towards others has been proven to attract lots of positivity and good relationships. So, the more you give and show compassion to others, the better your physical and mental well-being will be.

Being kind is also a great way to motivate the people around you and inspire them to be kind to others. Smiling to people around you, serving someone a cup of tea or doing anything that makes people around you happy sends loads of positive energy to you, which boosts your inner happiness.

Be Grateful

Each day, if you dwell too much on negative thoughts, you'll find it hard to see the things you ought to be grateful for. Devote most of your quiet time to thinking about the little things in your life and be thankful for them. Doing this will help you let go of harmful and toxic emotions.

Think of the good things and people in your life and why you are grateful for them. Doing this for a few minutes every day will help you a great deal. If you can't think of any right now, you can begin by keeping a gratitude journal and jotting down a list of things that make you happy and feel contented. Being grateful will help you reflect on the bad times you've had and how you overcame them all.

Discover Your Inner Strength

Taking your focus away from all the negative thinking that may erode your confidence level and cause feelings of insecurity and self-doubt and shifting to positive thinking that boosts your self-esteem and confidence is essential to developing inner strength. Inner strength is what will make you resilient in the face of stressful situations and help boost your energy level so that you can handle whatever comes your way.

Align Your Current Self With Your Future Self

The things you spend your time and money on will determine how far you'll go in life. These choices you make today will shape your life tomorrow. Ask yourself: What do I desire most in the world? Work towards being the person that your future self will be proud of by building healthy relationships and a healthy lifestyle.

Develop a picture in your mind of who you would like to be in the future and start taking steps to make it a reality. Doing this will help you exert more control over your life, and the more positive actions you take, the more positive the reality you will create for your future self.

Act In Good Faith

There's a general belief in business that both parties act in good faith as they work together. We all benefit from treating one another fairly, but only a few people understand that this principle should be followed as we interact daily personally or professionally.

Endeavour to be nice to everyone you meet and treat them with respect, and in most cases, you'll receive the same gesture. Even if someone wrongs to you, avoid retaliation as it won't make you feel better. They may be having a bad day and react negatively to you for this reason. So, when you act nicely to everyone, even when they react harshly to you, you can be sure to attract positive energy, and this will help a lot.

Chapter 29: Daily Emotional Management Rituals

To truly master your emotions, you will need to go a lot further than just engaging in sporadic emotional management practices, anytime emotion is triggered within you. You will need to be willing to intentionally work with your emotions every day so that you can acknowledge, process, and release your emotions on a day-to-day basis. In doing so, you are allowing yourself to release your emotional reserves to not hold onto them longer than necessary. You also allow yourself to create space for you to learn from your emotions and discover new ways to deal with them more healthily and productively. As you will discover over time, your emotions are something that you will continually learn from every single day. The process of learning how to navigate emotions healthily and productively is one that lasts a lifetime, largely because every time an emotion is triggered, it will be under different circumstances. The more emotion is triggered, especially under different circumstances, the more you become aware of how those emotions feel for you, and how you can navigate those emotions more effectively.

There are many ways that you can create a daily emotional management ritual for yourself, with no one answer being right or wrong. The key to finding a ritual that works best for you is to identify what your life tends to look like from an emotional point of view and to create a ritual that works best for you. An ideal ritual should address how you feel and help you learn from and release those emotions all at once. If you are dealing with a particularly troubling emotion, your daily ritual should include some form of activity intended for helping you process that emotion, too. This way, you are always working within your needs and supporting your overall and day-to-day emotional wellbeing.

Stay Committed to Your Daily Mindfulness Ritual

The first thing you can do for yourself, from an emotional capacity, is staying committed to your daily mindfulness ritual. Mindfulness is going to help you in countless ways, including processing and releasing emotions. A great way to incorporate mindfulness specifically into your daily emotional management ritual is to use mindfulness to help you recognize what emotions you are experiencing and to navigate them in an intentional capacity. The more mindful you are, the more you will find meaningful ways to address your emotions during your emotional release.

One great way to incorporate mindfulness into your emotional management routine is to take the time to investigate any emotions you have experienced throughout your day mindfully. You can start by noticing one to three emotions you may have experienced that day that was particularly strong for you. Do not work through any more than three at a time, though, as you do not want to overwhelm yourself and make it more challenging for you to address your emotions.

Once you have noticed these emotions, give yourself time to analyze why they occurred, what happened once they did, and how the aftermath of those emotions was experienced. If you can identify the trigger of the emotions, understand your thoughts and feelings in response to those emotions, and recognize how they lead to your behavior. This will give you a greater understanding of how those emotions affected you. Likewise, if you can acknowledge your emotions'emotions' consequences, you can create the opportunity for you to understand how your emotional responses affected you in the long run. Be sure to do this for both negative and positive emotions, as this will give you a chance to identify opportunities for growth while also giving you a chance to celebrate yourself for growth you have already implemented.

Take Up Journaling

Journaling is a wonderful practice for many different reasons. Aside from helping you keep a little log of your life, journaling allows you to express your true thoughts and emotions outside of yourself, where you otherwise may not have been able to. Many people talk about what they truly think and feel seems impossible, even if they are talking to someone such a therapist where it seems like you "should" be able to speak honestly about what you are thinking or feeling. Having a private journal that you keep to yourself can be a great way for you to openly admit to how you were truly feeling, what you were truly thinking, and anything else that you may have hidden during your day. You can also honestly reflect on what you think and feel after the fact.

Releasing your thoughts from your mind and physically getting them out onto paper may not be quite the same as talking to someone about your emotions, but it will provide you with a great opportunity to get a sense of release. In many cases, the sooner you can release your feelings by admitting them, and the more honestly you can do so, the easier it will be for you to let go and move on in the long run. However, if you get into the habit of acknowledging your emotions and then repressing them, it will become more challenging for you to release how you feel about that particular situation. Hence, the pent up experience begins.

If you are not someone who typically journals, rest assured that there does not need to be a right way or a wrong way for you to engage in journaling. You do not have to be thoughtful, emotional, curious, or well-articulated to keep a journal. You also do not need to worry about spelling, grammar, punctuation, or other writing errors. You don't even need to worry about writing full form sentences, sharing things in story form, or otherwise being exhaustive in what you are thinking and feeling. Even just keeping bullet-point styled notes about what you were thinking and feeling and how that impacted you can be plenty to help you sort through what is going on in your brain. Use your journal in a way that works for you, and trust that this will be plenty to help you fully accept, learn from, and release any emotions you have experienced on a day to day basis.

Give Yourself Frequent Stress Breaks

I firmly believe that stress breaks should be a mandatory part of everyone's daily activities. Day to day life can be stressful, even if you are doing the same thing every day. The demands of work-life, family life and other parts of life can all be overwhelming, even on the best of days. Giving yourself stress breaks means that you are willing to acknowledge your emotional state and make choices that will nurture your wellbeing. When it comes to emotional management, there is no one size fits all. Spending just one session working on your emotions each day will not result in you having effortless or healthy emotional expressions for the rest of the day. It will improve your chances. However, you still need to make choices that will keep you in a healthy state of expression during the day. You can improve your expressions on a day to day basis by being willing to give yourself stress breaks so that you can decompress.

A stress break could be an intentionally scheduled break where you get to do something different from your normal activities.

However, a stress break can also be accomplished by giving yourself 5-10 minutes to decompress anytime you find yourself feeling particularly stressed or emotionally charged during the day. You can also give yourself 5-10 minutes to decompress if you find yourself feeling drained or overdrawn from your day. During those 5-10 minutes, allow yourself time to simply breathe, be mindful, and engage in a relaxing routine that will allow you to feel more at peace after your day. Through this, you will find yourself flowing much more peacefully and harmoniously throughout your day.

Work In Harmony With Your Nature

Whenever you try to do something, it is always best to work with your nature rather than against it. In particular, with emotions, working with your nature means rather than denying your emotions or trying to force them to change, you learn to incorporate them into your daily experience. Incorporating your emotions into your daily routines could include fitting certain parts of your routines into certain parts of your day and scheduling your days based on how your feelings behave.

When it comes to scheduling with your energy, consider how you tend to have energy during the day and schedule your activities based on that. This way, you are not trying to force yourself to engage in things when you do not have adequate energy for them. Therefore you have no reason to feel pressured or stressed in those activities. For example, if you know that you tend to have more energy in the morning and less in the evening, you could exercise in the morning and do your mindfulness routine in the evening. If, however, you are the opposite and you tend to have less energy in the morning and more in the evening, you might benefit from doing your mindfulness practice in the morning and exercising in the evening. This way, you are working with your nature to create harmony and flow throughout your day, and you are not amplifying your stress for any reason.

You can also schedule your days based on how you anticipate you will feel. For example, let's say you are trying to schedule your week out, and you know that you have a stressful project to complete on Tuesday. Based on this knowledge, you might make Monday and Tuesday relatively relaxing days and save other things, such as cleaning the house or engaging in other demanding activities later, once the project has already been finished. This way, rather than forcing yourself to get anything done when you already know that you won't have the energy, you work with your nature instead.

As far as emotional fulfillment efforts go, focus on learning tools that allow you to release emotions in a way that can easily be executed on a day to day basis. Exercise, art, listening to music, relaxing, talking to a loved one, and other similar measures can all be used to release your emotions in a healthy, productive manner. Suppose you tend to experience many rapid emotions during the day. In that case, you might even consider carrying a journal with you and quickly jotting things down anytime you come across a large feeling. This way, you can quickly release that feeling at the moment, and you can reasonably circle back to it later on in the day. This would be far healthier than, say, stuffing it down and allowing it to ruin the rest of your day.

Conclusion

Mastering and regulating your emotions are a question of choice. You either want to do it or you don't. There's no shortage of information about the subject of emotions, yet many still struggle with control over this aspect.

Learning to master your emotions is like learning a new skill or habit. Having to change the way that you've been accustomed to doing something is not easy.

You know you don't want to be at the mercy of your emotions forever.

So, it's time to work on what you can do about it. When emotions hit you like a tidal wave at the beach, the first habit you need to put a stop to is instinctively trying to dismiss them.

Stop sweeping your feelings under the rug or trying to run away from them. Your emotions need your attention. Instead of fleeing your emotions, you need to face them with self-control and emotional resilience.

In an overly stressful situation, your ability to effectively regulate your impulsive behavior, control it, and not succumb to the temptation reacting in a way you know to be negative, that is emotional self-control. Without emotional self-control, it will be easy to end up in a lot of trouble because of your poor reactions. In a professional setting, a lack of emotional self-control will be extremely damaging to your career prospects. Would you elect someone emotionally volatile into a leadership role? Or task them with more responsibility? The answer is no, not when you know they could have an emotional meltdown at any moment.

Being mindful and aware of your emotions will serve you well in the development of your emotional self-control capabilities.

That's the reason self-awareness is the first core EI skill that needs to be developed. It enables you to cultivate the necessary awareness needed about the sequence of events leading to the emotion you feel.

The key to emotional self-control is to learn how to manage your emotions. Manage, being the focus word here to clarify that this is not about suppressing your emotions. Exercising self-control over your emotions is giving yourself the time and space needed to work through your challenging emotions so you can stay calm even in the face of emotions that threaten to destabilize you.

Learning control in this aspect matters more than you think. As the brain's radar in charge of detecting potential threats, the amygdala has the power to "hijack" your brain and take over when it goes into overdrive. In this hijacked state, the only thing that your brain can focus on is what is causing you distress. You can't focus on your job, you can't focus on a conversation, you can't focus on anything except the perceived threat that the amygdala has zoned in. When you can't focus and think clearly, that's when mistakes happen.

As you learn to develop your emotional self-control, each successful attempt will boost your confidence, reinforcing the belief that you can do this. A boost in confidence leads to the development of self-esteem. There's a feeling of pride and a sense of accomplishment that follows when you know you've overcome what you thought you couldn't do. To successfully wrestle control back from your emotions and put yourself in the driver's seat again was not easy, but you did it anyway and you should be proud.

Emotional intelligence is not a subject you're going to find taught in schools, although it should be, given what a beneficial skill it can be. In a world where anxiety and stress are at in its prime, EI skills are by far the most important skill anyone can learn because of its strong connection to your sense of self. When everything in life doesn't feel like an emotional roller coaster that's threatening to spin out of control, it transcends into your life's other aspects. Your relationships are better, you feel better, and you're infused with a strong, healthy sense of self-esteem because of that newfound control.

Emotional management is also an incredibly powerful tool to help you begin to experience true happiness and fulfillment in your life. So often, people get stuck in negative cycles where their emotions feel overwhelming and seem to take over, and that can lead to massive levels of guilt, embarrassment, and shame. The more you feel those emotions, and reinforce them through your emotional expressions, the more you will find yourself struggling to feel true happiness and fulfillment in your life. When you learn to change those behaviors, however, you begin to create space for you to heal from past emotional expressions and enjoy healthier and more fulfilling new ones. Through that, you begin to experience emotional freedom, as well as true happiness and fulfillment in your life.

Low self-esteem invokes negative feelings and emotions. When all you can think about are the worst things about yourself and all the things and life, you fail to regulate your emotions properly, and dwelling in unhappiness for too long is how your self-esteem starts to diminish. Your emotions are not the only powerful thing at your disposal. Your mental toughness is also a very powerful asset that you possess. By constantly pursuing betterment in your life overall, you'll find more things to be happy about, which leads to higher levels of satisfaction. The way you feel about yourself starts to improve and with it, your self-esteem.

Developing Greater Self-Esteem, Self-Awareness and Emotional Resilience

Life is always going to be full of ups and downs. Even if you're happy in general, there may be some moments where you encounter difficult or trying times. In the face of these challenging situations, there are only two options to choose from:

·   Option 1 - You can either run away and let your emotions strip you of happiness.

·   Option 2 - You can choose to be emotionally resilient and bounce back from these trying times. To see the challenges as an opportunity for self-improvement.

Emotional resilience is what emotionally intelligent people turn to when hard times befall them. Instead of letting their emotions consume them, they choose to learn from them. Emotionally resilient people don't let their unhappy emotions define who they are, and they use emotional self-control and self-esteem to do it. When times are the hardest, resilience keeps you going.

Self-esteem is an important component of resilience. When you lack it, it makes a big difference in your perspective of life. When self-esteem is present, it's easier to feel optimistic, cheerful and overall more positive outlook towards the different areas of your life. Positivity is the key to successful resilience. When times are hard, that's when you need positivity and optimism to fall back on or it would feel all too easy to succumb to the temptation of giving up. Without self-esteem and a strong belief in yourself, it will feel impossible to weather the emotional storms that come your way. Believing that you can make it through the battle is halfway towards winning it. Like your emotions, self-esteem is going to fluctuate. Some days you might feel more confident than others.

Building a strong foundation of self-esteem and self-control is how you master emotional resilience, and here's what you need to do to start mastering these skills:

- Find A Healthy Outlet - Find a healthy outlet that works for you to channel your emotions. This outlet should be something that makes you feel good about yourself again and feel better after an emotional time. It could be yoga, meditating, listening to music, exercising, catching up with a loved one, etc.
- Build A Support System - Talking to someone you can trust who won't judge you in return can be the antidote to an emotional, troubled soul. Not everyone may be lucky enough to form these close relationships, so it is okay to seek professional help if you feel you might benefit from having someone to talk to.
- Persevere - Resilience is about not giving up no matter how much you may be tempted to. Build on your resilience, self-esteem, and self-control by pushing yourself to keep taking one step forward, no matter how hard it feels at first. Trust that you're getting better with each step forward and you'll emerge victorious, confident and resilient at the end.
- Give Yourself Time - Even the most painful wounds can heal when given enough time. Without self-esteem, resilience, and self-control, emotions get out of control when you're hurt and pain. Be patient, take each day as it comes and remember that you will get through this and feel better. All you need to do is give yourself time.
- Happiness Is Your Choice - It is a choice that only you can make for yourself each day. Emotionally resilient people choose to prioritize their happiness

over every other emotion, and they're a lot more confident and in control because of that choice.

Thank you for taking time reading this book and I hope you learn so much on how to master your emotions!

HOW TO
ANALYZE
PEOPLE

Introduction

How do I analyze people? Do I need to follow any formula to do this? Is there a particular approach that is helpful to understand people? When it comes to understanding a human being's personality traits, there are many different theories and models, which can be followed. You can understand one's personality based on his or her body language, inborn personality traits, facial features, etc. Some say you can even get to know about a person by the way he or she walks.

All the above-cited theories are 100 percent true. But there are so many other factors to be considered when it comes to analyzing people and their underlying behavioral traits. You will need to have a deeper knowledge on many other things before concluding on a person's personality and character.

Let us try to understand on how to analyze one's personality using a practical illustration.

Practical Illustration on Analyzing People

There was this guy in the gym that was always punctual. He used to come to the gym every day at the same time. Well, what is so great about that, you ask? If you are not looking at the smallest of the details, you will end up losing the basic and important personality traits of a person. Coming back to our gym guy, the detail cited might seem unimportant. But for someone who knows how to analyze people, this simple detail can mean a lot.

This guy's punctuality shows the following personality traits in him:

- Self-motivated

- Strong willed

- Well organized

- Knows the importance of time

All the above-said traits are visible because of how he handles time to be punctual not just once but regularly. He is not a procrastinator but a doer.

The next important thing that was noticeable in this guy was he always wore clothes that showcased his muscles. The exercises and the workout process he followed were also quite strange. It was not the common one's people usually do, but there was an odd style to his routine. This meant that the guy was quite a show-off and wanted to be the center of attraction. Further information confirmed that he was the only child in the family.

When you try to analyze one's personality, it is important to note how their birth order affects the personality. When a person is the only child in the family, they are usually showered with loads of love and attention during their childhood. Sometimes, this continues even after they grow up. Since they are used to being the center of attraction in their family, they expect the same wherever they go.

Another important thing about this gym guy was that he always wore black. I guess he loved to wear black! Though he often kept changing his clothes during his workout routine, all his clothes were black or had black shades in them. Even the cover of his mobile was black.

While analyzing one's personality, it is important to understand that people will go to an extreme if they try to escape from something. It was the same with the gym guy too. Wearing black revealed that the guy wanted to appear dangerous, tough and evil. He wanted to look like a bad boy.

Further information on the guy confirmed the reason for this – the other kids bullied him when he was a little boy. He felt weak. While growing up, he ensured he concealed his past by playing tough. Working out regularly at the gym and donning black were the two steps he had taken to help him run away from his childhood.

It is important to connect all the dots when you are analyzing someone's personality. You need to keep in mind that these dots are the ones, which will lead you to the finishing line.

If our assumptions are true, our gym guy wanted to be powerful and tried all the other means that would help him become powerful. So, he should be doing other things apart from going to the gym. The guess was right – our gym guy was interested in martial arts and was practicing this regularly.

When a person wants to move towards an imperative goal, he gets interested in things that help him in the process. In other words, he or she would want to get away from the identity he hates, i.e., being weak, being scared, being anxious, etc.

Is It Easy to Analyze People?

It would be foolish if it were told that reading couple of articles on analyzing people would help you understand anyone and everyone's personality and behavior traits. The good news is that all the knowledge required for you to analyze people can be found in books and articles. All you have to do is understand the basics and implement them in the right way.

The first and foremost thing you need to do is – read all possible articles on human psychology, personality analysis and behavioral traits. You will then need to test your knowledge by analyzing your personality. When you are successful at doing this, you can try the approach with your best friend or spouse or siblings. Try to analyze him or her.

When you are confident and know the outcome is correct, you can start implementing what you learned from other people – especially strangers.

Another Example to Understand the Concept Better

There was this girl in our project who was always seen accompanying guys rather than other girls. She was, in fact, more comfortable talking with the opposite gender and loved discussing guy-related topics. She enjoyed the conversation and always came out with accurate details on whatever topic she discoursed. A normal girl would have found those topics boring, but for her it was different.

While analyzing her behavior, it was confirmed that she didn't like her feminine role because of which she was trying to mask herself with another role. What would be the reason for doing this? Collecting further information on her background gave us the answer we needed.

She grew up in a house where women were valued less than men. Since her childhood, she saw the men in the family being treated differently compared to women. This was the core reason for her to protest against her gender.

The most crucial thing you need to understand while analyzing people's behavior is – to study their childhood, the way they were brought up, their experiences as a kid, etc. The experiences one has during their young age can permanently affect their future behavior.

Coming back to our girl, she often kept saying that she was particularly interested in zodiac signs, as most of her traits resembled what her zodiac sign said. We often try to compensate the things we lack by focusing on things we always wanted. In this case, the girl lacked self-understanding because she had developed this extreme interest in zodiac signs. She wanted to compensate for the lack of knowledge she had about self.

The important factor you need to note when you are analyzing people's behavior is that humans tend to turn their attention toward something that helps them compensate for their weaknesses.

More analysis on the girl's behavior:

This girl always used to challenge people and was extremely competitive at work. She ensured that anything she started was always completed on time and to a good standard. Being the youngest kid in the family, she was always surrounded by siblings who had already proved their mettle in a specific area. She had to stand out from those capable grown-ups. This led to the extremely competitive behavior, which was necessary to compensate for her weakness.

While analyzing people's behavior, it is necessary to relate to their birth order. This will help you understand the basic traits of the person. Another peculiar thing in this girl's case was, even though she was a strong-willed, extroverted and competitive woman, she got married to a guy who was a complete opposite to her character. Her husband was reserved and shy. He was not very confident when compared to the girl.

This proves that our analysis has been true so far. Since her childhood, she was taught that women were weak and not as important as men. This made her hate being a woman. As she grew up into an adult, she specifically became attracted to weak men as that would give her the chance to be the dominant member in the family.

The last and final thing one should note while analyzing people's behavior is that most humans are not aware of their personality dynamics. In the case of this girl, she could never understand why she was attracted to weak men. The reason is all these personality dynamics happen at a subconscious level.

Personality and Behavior

You don't need to spend months or years with a person to know their personality. All you have to do is understand the simple principles about a person's behavior. This will help you to start noticing their underlying personality, which gets revealed in many circumstances. It can be tiny actions, which are usually not given importance by others. There will not be any change in these behaviors even though the time passes.

For example, if your best friend loves bungee jumping, it means this person will never hesitate to take any kind of risk. It doesn't necessarily need to be only physical risk. He can even quit his job because he simply didn't like the job. He won't wait to find another job even though his financial security is at risk.

On the contrary, if a person sits at the same place in the same food court every day, he might fear change. He will get restless or anxious when it comes to a new routine or new environment. He will maximize efforts to resist the change when it is about to happen and find an escape mechanism. For instance, if he is moved to a new team or a new work profile or gets a new boss, he will most likely resist the change.

Let's say a person keeps looking toward both the sides of the road many times before she decides to cross the road. Then the lady would most probably be very cautious. She would be careful and reserved when it comes to decision-making. And even if she takes a risk, it will be a well-calculated risk.

If a person likes to stick to a particular job without wanting to change it, it is possible that he or she would be loyal and stick to his or her partner until the end.

These tiny and minute details, which seem to be of no value, provide good clarity of a person's behavior in serious and difficult situations.

Chapter 1: Behavioral Psychology

From a psychological viewpoint, human behavior concerns the full spectrum of emotional and physical behaviors that humans engage in that include social, biological, and intellectual actions and are impacted by attitudes, culture, ethics, rapport, and genetics, among other considerations. Human behavior is a complex interplay of cognition, actions, and emotion. Correspondingly, actions are behavior as actions capture everything that can be observed. Actions can be captured through eyes or physiological sensors. An initiation or transition from one state to another is an action. Actions as behaviors can happen at various time scales starting from sweat gland activity to muscular activation, sleep, or food consumption.

For cognition as behavior, cognition defines thoughts and mental images that one carries and can be both nonverbal and verbal. For instance, "I have to work on my book" can be treated as verbal cognition. On the other hand, imagine how your project will look after reworking on it is considered as a nonverbal cognition. As such, cognitions consist of skills and knowledge by knowing how to apply tools in a constructive manner, such as memorizing a jacket's color or singing songs.

When viewing emotions as behavior, emotions are considered a relatively brief conscious experience marked by intense mental activity and a feeling that is not influenced by either knowledge or reasoning. Emotions normally happen from a positive to negative scale. Increased arousal can cause other aspects of physiology that indicate emotional processing, such as enhanced respiration rate.

Emotions can only be inferred indirectly akin to cognition through monitoring facial expressions and tracking arousal, among others.

Understanding Behavior from a Psychological Viewpoint

Investment Model

Human behavior can be understood in terms of work effort focused on creating change. For instance, whether Hilda is headed out due to the need to watch the movie or wants to be with her boyfriend, the act of going to the movie is a form of investment. In this manner, human behavior occurs due to the need to get a particular outcome. The return of this investment can be found from the movie Hilda watches or a kiss from her boyfriend at the end of it.

In this aspect, behavior involves considering the investment in terms of calories, time, risks, and opportunity costs. The motivation of where to invest our actions in spurring a particular behavior to emanate from evolutionary influences that have made us prioritize sex, food, safety, territory, and higher social status over other states of affairs. Genetics also impact certain behavioral traits, such as dispositions and temperaments. For instance, extroverted people find stimulating social situations more satisfying compared to introverted people. Against this backdrop, the learning history of an individual impact the investment value system. For instance, if Hilda loved the first two Star Wars movies, we can expect her to show a strong desire to see the third.

An illustration of human behavior's investment model is where one is seated on a sofa gazing at the television when an advert of a cookie triggers in you the desire to pour a cup of milk. You have had a tough day, and you are feeling burnt out. In your mind, a small computation takes place where you weigh on the value of getting up and pouring yourself a glass of milk. Eventually, the thirst wins out, and you decide to get a glass of milk from the refrigerator. Unfortunately, a quick look in the fridge indicates there is no milk, which makes you take a glance at the rubbish you have, and you see that you've already used all the milk bottles.

The feeling that follows this disruption in your ability to fulfill your desire is irritation, and your first thought then is to overcome this obstacle by running to the store and getting a bottle. You then juxtapose this idea with the cost in terms of time, effort, and money that would cost you, and you drop the idea. Still, you must satiate your desire for a drink somehow, so you decide to drink some orange juice instead. In detail, the investment model for understanding human behavior views behaviors in the form of energy and labor required to realizing a particular outcome — the behavior costs in the form of time and energy computed in the form of benefits and costs. Human behavior is largely a cost-benefit analysis according to the investment model of animal behavior. Most animal documentaries on animals' behavior can help you realize how inherently animals make the cost-benefit analysis.

Take the case of wildebeests in African savanna plains that need to drink water and cross the infested river with hungry crocodiles. In this environment, water and grass are scarce, and wildebeests desperately need water and grass. Simultaneously, the wildebeests have to watch out for marauding crocodiles lurking under the surface of the water, ready to devour the wildebeests. Eventually, wildebeests have to invoke an investment model of behavior to maximize the possibility of living, drinking water, and crossing the river to graze. Under this model, most wildebeests cautiously approach the river, ensuring that they near the river bank when drinking water, which would enable them to retract sporadically at the hint of any threat that might put them out of control and in danger.

In this manner, human behavior is a sort of transaction with the environment. The human being actions are primed to maximize benefits from the environment. The mind is a critical component of behavior as it stores a history of what has desired outcomes and computing the cost-benefit analysis before one-acts. It can be argued that the investment model of behavior affirms the assumption that human behavior is conscious and well thought. Additionally, actions lead to lost opportunities, and one has to pursue an action that best maximizes the intended outcomes. For instance, if an animal spends time defending a territory, it loses out on finding food.

Social Influence Model of Human Behavior

Human behavior can be viewed from the understanding that a human being is a social animal. Human behavior happens in the context of a social matrix. A social influence entails the actions that influence the investment of another person. For instance, when Hilda was going to the movie, she asked her boyfriend out, or the boyfriend did ask her out.

In most cases, social influence processes involve cooperation, cooperation, and whether the transactions move people closer or make them drift apart. Social influence also manifests as a resource. As a resource, social influence concerns the capacity to move other people in alignment with our interests. Social influence in this context refers to the levels of social and respect value other people show us and the degree to which they listen, care about our well-being, and sacrifice for us. For instance, if Hilda is attracted to his boyfriend and agrees to go to the movie with her, this indicates social influence. If the boyfriend breaks up with Hilda, it is a potent indication of a social influence loss.

Additionally, social influence is determined by the amount of attention from other people. In line with this understanding, a person's actions will seek to attract attention from people or sustain the attention of people. Probably you have colleagues or public figures that consistently act to attract and sustain admiration from other people. On a personal level, one is likely to act in a manner that invites admiration from colleagues, friends, and other people. The behavior and likely behavior of an individual is likely to optimize admiration from others. Furthermore, within the social influence model of human behavior, people are likely to act in a manner that invites more positive emotions than others' negative emotions. In a way, the need to attract more positive emotions from others is related to attracting admiration from others, but it is highly related to emotional intelligence. One can only enhance the likelihood of getting a positive emotional reaction from others if they have requisite emotional intelligence levels.

Through emotional intelligence, one learns to show empathy and pay attention to how others are feeling. Against this backdrop, human behavior is likely to be reactive to how others are feeling. It is likely to be highly considerate of others for the motivation to attract positive emotions from them. This can also become highly performative, as human behavior also makes people sacrifice their needs for other people to gain more influence through it. People who can gather a lot of social influence are generally able to have power over others to have hundreds of people who will willingly sacrifice their own needs for them. This means that this person in power is also aware that there are so many people who would do anything to associate with their influence, and their behavior stems from this knowledge. On the other hand, the influential people's followers are likely to take the actions of the individual as guidance or a message of how one should act and live.

Justification Model of Human Behavior

First, human behavior requires justifications by legitimizing it. For instance, when you shout at someone, there are chances that one will qualify the behavior by stating that they were upset. In reaching a justification, one assesses the behavior and the ideal outcome. For instance, the ideal outcome may have attracted admiration from others, but one ended up embarrassing themselves in public. Expectedly, the individual will feel angry for not only failing to attain an ideal reaction from the audience but also degrading the status quo. In this state, the individual will justify subsequent undesired behavior by drawing attention to the disappointment they got earlier on.

Using the Hilda and the movie example, Hilda may have felt justified to make her boyfriend tag along to the movie and allow the boyfriend to show romance because of what lovers do. The justification of her behavior and the boyfriend's behavior emanates from observation and learned patterns of what lovers do and not necessarily how they feel. Justification of behavior can be simply that others do, so the individual is obliged to emulate the same. Try watching court proceedings for you to realize how people place significant value of justification for their behavior.

At the corporate level, organizations have invested significantly in assessing human behavior during recruitment stages and assessing workers. Human behavior is complex, and organizations seek to have the best bet to recruit and retain fairly predictable workers. Most of the personality tests administered during hiring and appraisal processes are meant to help profile workers and have a predictable look at how they may behave. There have been attempts to determine a formula for human behavior as a simple system, but it has been satisfactorily concluded that human behavior is dynamic.

Chapter 2: How You Can Analyze the Behavior of People

Studying people is not reserved for psychiatrists but any other person even though psychiatrists are best positioned to analyze people. Analyzing people requires understanding verbal and nonverbal cues. When studying people, you should try to remain objective and be open to new information. Nearly each one of us has some form of personal biases and stereotypes that blocks our ability to understand another person correctly. When analyzing an individual, it is crucial to reconcile that information against the profession and cultural demands on the target person. Some environments may force an individual to exhibit particular behavior that is not necessarily part of their real one.

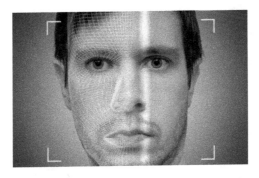

Start by analyzing the body language cues of the target person you are trying to read. Body language provides the most authoritative emotional and physiological status of an individual. It is difficult to rehearse all forms of body language, which makes body language critical in understanding a person. Verbal communication can be faked through rehearsal and experience, and this can give misleading stand. When examining body language, analyze the different types of body language as a set. For instance, analyze facial expressions, body posture, pitch, tonal variation, touch and eye contact, as a related but different manifestation of communication and emotional status. For instance, when tired, one is likely to stretch their arms and rest on the left and right tops of adjacent chairs, sit in a slumped position, stare at the ceiling, and drop their heads. Analyzing only one aspect of body language can mislead one to come up with a conclusion correctly.

Additionally, it would be best if you give attention to appearance. The first impression counts, but it can also be misleading. In formal contexts, an individual's appearance is critical to communicate the professionalism of the person and the organizational state of mind of that individual. For example, an individual with an unbuttoned shirt indicates he hurried or is casual with the audience and the message. Wearing formal attire buttoned and tucked in suggests prior preparation and seriousness that the person lends to the occasion. Having unkempt hair may indicate a rebellious mind, and this might be common among African professors in Africa, for instance. In most settings, having unkempt hair suggests that one lacks the discipline to prepare for the formal context or is overworked and busy. Lack of expected grooming may indicate an individual battling with life challenges or feeling uncared for.

It is also important that one should take note of the posture of the person. Posture communicates a lot about the involvement of an individual in a conversation. Having an upright posture suggests eagerness and active participation in what is being communicated. If one cups their face in the arms and lets the face rest on both thighs, it suggests that one feels exhausted or has deviated from the conversation completely. Having crossed arms suggests defensiveness or deep thought. One sitting in a slumped position suggests that he/she is tired and not participating in the ongoing conversation. Leaning on the wall or any object suggests casualness that the person is lending to an ongoing conversation. If at home, sitting with crossed legs suggests that one is completely relaxed. However, the same posture at the workplace suggests that one is feeling tensed and at the same time concentrating.

Furthermore, observe the physical movements in terms of distance and gestures. The distance between you and the target individual communicates about the level of respect and assurance that the individual perceives. A social distance is the safest bet when communicating, and it suggests high levels of professionalism or respect between the participants. Human beings tend to be territorial as exhibited by the manner that they guard their distance. Any invasion of the personal distance will make the individual defensive and unease with the interaction.

For this reason, when an individual shows discomfort when the distance between communicators is regarded as social or public, then the individual may have other issues bothering him or her. Social and public distances should make one feel fully comfortable. Allowing a person close enough or into the personal distance suggests that the individual feels secure and familiar with the other person. Through reading, the distance between the communicators will give a hint on the respect, security, and familiarity between the individuals and the likely profession of the individuals.

Correspondingly, then try to read facial expressions as deep frown lines indicate worry or over-thinking. Facial expressions are among the visible and critical forms of body language and tell more about an individual's true emotional status. For instance, twitching the mouth suggests that an individual is not listening and is showing disdain to the speaker. A frozen face indicates that the person is shell-shocked, which can happen when making a presentation of health and diseases or when releasing results of an examination. A smiling face with the smile not being prolonged communicates that one is happy and following the conversation. A prolonged smile suggests sarcasm. If one continually licks, the lips may indicate that one is lying or feeling disconnected from the conversation.

Relatedly, try to create a baseline for what merits as normal behavior. As you will discover, people have distinct mannerisms that may be misleading to analyze them as part of the communication process. For instance, some individuals will start a conversation by looking down or at the wall before turning to the audience. Mildly, mannerisms are like a ritual that one must activate before they make a delivery. Additionally, each person uniquely expresses the possible spectra of body language. By establishing a baseline of normal behavior, one gets to identify and analyze deviations from the standardized normal behavior accurately. Against this understanding, one will not erratically score a speaker that shuffles first if that is part of his behavior when speaking to an audience.

Furthermore, pay attention to inconsistencies between the established baseline that you have created and the individual's gestures and words. Once you have created a baseline, then examine for any deviations from this baseline. For instance, if one speaks in a high-pitched voice that is uncharacteristically of the individual, the person may feel irritated. If one normally walks across the stage when speaking but the individual chooses to speak from a fixed position during the current speech, the person is exhibiting a deviation that may suggest that the individual is having self-awareness or is feeling unease with the current audience. If an individual speaks fast, but usually the person speaks with a natural flow, the person is in a hurry or has not prepared for it.

Correspondingly, view gestures as clusters to elicit a meaning of what the person is communicating or trying to hide. When speaking a person, will express different gestures and dwelling on the current gesture may make you arrive at a misleading conclusion. Instead, one should view the gestures as clusters and interpret what they imply. For instance, if a speaker throws the hands randomly in the air, raises one of their feet, stamps the floor, and shakes his or her hands, all of these could suggest a speaker feeling irked and disappointed by the audience or the message. As such, different aspects of body language should be interpreted as a unit rather than in isolation.

Go further and try to recognize the strong voice. A strong voice suggests the authority and confidence of the speaker. If the speaker lacks a strong voice, he or she is new to what is being presented or has stage fright. Having a strong voice that is not natural suggests a spirited attempt to appear in charge and confident. A strong voice should be natural if the individual feels composed and confident in what he or she is talking about.

Relatedly, observe how the individual walks. When speaking to a target person, they will walk across the stage or make movements around the site where the conversation is happening. From the manner of walking, we can read a lot about the individual. Walking up and down while speaking to an audience may indicate panic or spirited attempts to appear in control. Speaking while walking slowly across the stage from one end to the other end indicates that one is comfortable speaking to the audience. If a member of the audience poses a question and walks towards the individual, it suggests interest in clarifying what the individual is asking.

It might be necessary to scout for personality cues. Fortunately, all people have identifiable personalities, but these can be difficult to read for a person not trained in a psychologist. However, through observation, one will get cues on the personality of the individual. For instance, an outgoing person is likely to show a warm smile and laugh at jokes. A socially warm person is likely to want to make personal connections when speaking, such as mentioning a particular person in the audience. Reserved individuals are likely to use fewer words in their communication and appear scared or frozen on stage when speaking.

Additionally, one should listen to intuition, as it is often valid. Gut feelings are often correct, and when reading a person, you should give credence to your gut feeling about the person. When reading a person and you get a feeling that the person is socially warm, you should entertain this profiling while analyzing the person's body language. While considering gut feeling, you should classify it under subjective analysis, as it is not based on observable traits and behaviors but an inner feeling.

Expectedly, watch the eye contact. Creating eye contact suggests eagerness and confidence in engaging the audience. Avoiding eye contact suggests stage fright and shyness and lack confidence in what one is talking about. A sustained look is a stare, intended to intimidate, or may suggest absentmindedness of the individual. If one continuously blinks eyes while looking at a target person suggests a flirting behavior. An eye contact that gradually drops to the individual's chest and thigh suggests a deviation of thoughts from the conversation.

Additionally, pay attention to touch. The way a person shakes hands speaks a lot about their confidence and formality. A firm handshake that is brief indicates confidence and professionalism. A weak handshake that is brief indicates that one is feeling unease. On the other hand, a prolonged handshake, whether weak or strong, suggests that the person is trying to flirt with you, especially between opposite sexes. Touching someone on the head may suggest rudeness and should be avoided.

Lastly, listen to the tone of voice and laughter. Laughing may mean happiness or sarcasm. Americans are good at expressing sarcastic laughter, and it is achieved by changing the tones of the laughter. The tone of the voice states if the person is feeling authoritative and confident or not. Overall, a tonal variation infers that the individual is speaking naturally and convincingly. A flat tone specifies a lack of self-confidence and unfamiliarity with the conversation or audience and should be avoided.

Chapter 3:   Deconstructing Behaviors

Human behavior is the reaction of a human being to internal or external stimuli; this means that your behavior is how you react to your environment, whether internal or external. It is made up of all the physical activities and emotions that you express as you respond to these environmental stimulations. The human behavior is transient, and changes as the person grows until it becomes more rigid. Behavior is how we can look into your mind, figure out what you are thinking, and think those thoughts. It helps us see your attitude towards certain circumstances and respond individually and then collectively as a human. Humans all share similar behavior and have individual expressions. Behavior also can help us into your culture, social interactions, values or paradigms, ethics, persuasions, views that you hold dear to you, which is the authorities that influence your thought patterns.

Now that we have defined what behavior is, we also need to understand certain behavioral measurements that we have. If an organism expresses itself, we want to be sure the organism is expressing itself in the confines of acceptable and customary behaviors. We have common behaviors, unusual, acceptable, and some that we cannot tolerate at all. How do we know certain behaviors are acceptable? These things are defined for us by our societies. The society forms the framework by which our habits are screened through the popular thought "do we do this here?", "Is this what people of our society do?" "Is this out of place here?" these form some of the basic thoughts that go into the acceptance or rejection of certain social behaviors. For instance, cannibalism is acceptable in fewer cultures today, even cultures that practiced it before, have abolished the practice. It means eating meat raw could be seen as awkward and out of place. Psychology, sociology, anthropology, and economics are centered behavioral fields. They deal with human behavior concerning social interactions.

Because our environment highly influences behavior, it is possible for it to change, if those environmental factors that trigger them are absent. For instance, if staying in a hot environment would always force one to detest wearing clothes. If this individual moved to a colder region, the individual would have to adopt a new way to survive due to environmental factors. Behavior changes as the individual moves through life and encounters myriad environments and niches that incite certain reactions. Even though behavior could change, there are some intrinsic parts of the human that cannot change. After all, the behavior is a reaction of the person to his environment. If that's the case, then behavior can also be influenced by genetic and physiological traits. These traits have moved psychologists to classify behavior into different catalogs with their different reactions.

Let's quickly look at the factors that influence our behavior

The manner at which a person handles a situation personally, or maybe in a gathering, is influenced by many factors, but we would look at those key ones; those that have a primary role to play in how a person relates with another reacts to a situation.

Abilities

Abilities cut across talents and skills, and whatever you can do that fascinates. Skills are things that a person learns from his environment, while talents are intrinsic and innate. Examples of talents are singing, dancing, drawing, etc. talents are normally things you are not taught to do, they are things that just flow naturally or don't need so much natural input to spark up. This means that if it is a talent, while learning, it would be easier to absorb than when it is not. A skill, on the other hand, is gotten through hard work and consistency. For instance, you have driving as a skill, or writing, etc. these things are not innate. They are learned. You can transform your talent into a skill, in what way? By refining it till it becomes marketable. They don't just stop at being skills and talents, and they are more abilities that we humans possess, abilities like intellectual and physical abilities. Your intellectual abilities tend to influence your behavior so much; how you process information and how you conclude would affect how you behave. Let me add something about learning here; if you have a scenario with an educated person and a non-educated person, they will react differently. You would rarely have an educated person eat of the trash because he/she knows the dangers. Verbal, reasoning, memory—cognitive abilities greatly influence one's behavior.

Gender and Genetics

A human's genes are the basic building blocks for existence. What this means is, locked up in your genes is information on how your body would form. From the moment the spermatozoa of your father were released, it carried in its genetic information that would impact how you would look and how you would behave. In them were codes that contained the entire wiring of your human being. Genetics are the reason for gender. Gender, in general, is whether a human is male or female as defined by society. What this means is that societal accepted parameters define our genders. For instance, a human with a penis is called male because of the presence (majorly) of the penis, and a human with a vagina and breasts is called a woman, because of the presence of her sexual organ. Our gender affects our behavior. Men have the way they act, and women have the way they act. The truth is, because of the presence of certain hormones in excess in our system, like the presence of estrogen makes women act in a certain way, and testosterone makes men behave in a certain way.

Race & Culture

Culture is the eyes through which we see the world. Our culture greatly influences how we react to the world. Our culture is our way of life, not just us, but the way of life of the people who live with and around us. It is the way of life that we have come to see and accept as safe and important. Although some cultural practices have been rendered obsolete due to enlightenment, another culture can be born and practiced. For instance, if a person belongs to a culture where they do not allow women to take up leadership roles, they would react to women as secondary. If he belongs to another culture where the women are allowed to lead, and his supreme leader is a woman, he would not be taught to subjugate women. This is the impact of culture. It forms our worldview. We see the world from our cultural lens; if a person is African, he relates to the world that way. This is what makes nature beautiful, the fact that we all have different cultures, and if a person looks at the world from these different perspectives, the world takes on a new shape. It can broaden your mind and your perspective. Looking through various cultures can help you value humanity and what humanity has to offer. It gives a less selfish perspective.

Perception

Perception is the method the mind engages in changing stimuli into meaningful information bits that it can use. This means that if you see something, or hear something, perception is how you take that thing you heard and transform it into something very useful to you. For instance, if you hear your name that is an external stimulus or sound from your environment, your brain would take that stimulus and translate it into something you can understand—your name—and you would respond.

Perception can be dividing into six parts, namely:

Sound perception: this is the ability to perceive/interpret different sounds and sound waves in the environment and is aided by the ears and the brain.

Perception of speech: this is the ability to interpret sound to hear into meaningful bits of information that can be used in communication.

The perception of touch is how humans use their bodies to identify objects and relate to their physical environment through touch.

Perception of taste: Humans can identify different flavors by tasting with their tongue and smelling with their nose. There is an apparatus called taste buds that are used for sensing and identifying tastes in the tongue.

Perception of smell: this is the ability of a human to identify different scents of objects or odors in the environment through their nose. This helps the human receive stimuli from the environment and translate it into a smell. Why do we need to smell? Imagine you were in a room full of chemicals that could harm you, but you could not identify them as harmful from their smell?

Perception of sight: this is the ability of humans to sense objects as they move through light. It is the eye's reaction to light to reveal our environment to us. This ability helps us navigate our environment to avoid obstacles and identify threats.

Religion and Spirituality

Religion is one of the world's greatest influences. It has influenced

 men so much, and many can kill or die for what they believe. This deep-seated awareness that a creator exists and a need to worship him has changed our behaviors all through the ages. Religion is a deep part of our culture; in fact, most cultures are built around religious beliefs. For instance, the Christian faith frowns at murder,

marrying more than one wife, engaging in intercourse before marriage or outside of marriage.

Types of Behavior: there are two broad types of human behaviors. That is, there are just two ways human beings interact with the world in a broad sense. The first is the extrovert, and the other is the introvert. There are other ways to analyze human behavior that other psychologists have identified. Some identify four behavioral types, other identify six. Still, the underlying factor is that amongst all the behavioral expression, they are either very expressive (extroverts) or they aren't as expressive, they are more of the enclosed personality type (introverts). The basic tools in analyzing any behavior first is to know what these behaviors look like. How does an introvert act like, and how does an extrovert act like? If you can figure these out, it would be easy to analyze them according to their behavior.

For instance, it already an obvious fact that an extrovert is expressive, and an introvert is not. It is also obvious that specific behavioral terms cannot fit some people. Some people act like introverts in some situations, and in some other cases, they are extroverted. You must also know that there are degrees to these things. Some people are extreme introverts, and some that are not. These behavioral patterns have their strengths and weaknesses. As you read along, find those strengths and build on them. If you focus on the weakness, you might hurt your growth and progress.

Chapter 4: How to Use Emotional Intelligence to Analyze Anyone?

What Is Emotional Intelligence?

Emotional intelligence is recognizing emotions and leveraging on personal information in making healthy choices. Emotional intelligence is the capacity to acknowledge our emotions, regulate them, discern others' feelings, and differentiate between varying emotions, and using emotional intelligence, you can facilitate thoughts and behavior to achieve the desired results.

Since emotional intelligence involves recognizing emotions, it is essential to understand what emotions are and what types of emotions there are.

What Are Emotions?

These are mental states or feelings that occur spontaneously and not by intention. Physiological reactions often accompany these feelings. These occurrences respond to our perception of what is happening or what we see or hear per-time. Emotions help us understand our experiences. We would never know that a loved one's death is a painful experience if we have never felt sadness. We would never know that someone destroying our lawn is an annoying experience if we have never felt angry. Feeling emotions help us categorize our experiences and react accordingly. Positive emotions register an experience we are having or are about to have as good and worth having. When we say we look forward to the experience, it is not the experience we look forward to per sé. It is more the emotions associated with that experience that we look forward to having.

On the other hand, negative emotions alert us of unpleasant or potentially unpleasant experiences. We know we should do certain things or not do certain things if we would avoid such experiences. For example, when faced with a sudden threat, we feel fear of loss or pain. The emotion of fear triggers a fight or flight reaction. What we are trying to avoid is the loss or pain, not the occurrence itself.

Without emotions, there would be no emotional intelligence. Without emotional intelligence, we would not tell precisely the kinds of experiences we want to have and the kinds we don't want to have.

According to author David G. Meyers, "Emotion is made up of three components; physiological arousal, conscious experience and expressive behaviors." Physiological arousal means the person feeling a particular emotion will become physiologically alert. This is a point where the sense organs are stimulated to perceive. A brain primarily controls physiological arousal called the reticular activating system (RAS).

Expressive behavior refers to a behavioral reaction to the perception of what is happening or what is seen, heard or thought. This often involves verbal and non-verbal communication of a person's emotions.

Conscious Experience refers to the awareness of a person's environment, what he sees, hears and feels, and his thoughts.

Emotional intelligence is impactful in every part of your life. These are four areas it can affect.

1) Your performance at work

Most people keep their emotions at the door when going to work to appear more professional, although it used to seem that way. Emotions have always been in the workplace, but they were kept in check, with people pretending not to feel while they are working.

2) Your health physically

If you're unable to put in control your stress levels, it can manifest physically, and it can lead to serious health issues. Uncontrolled stress can cause an increase in your blood pressure, it can weaken the immune system, it can increase the risk of heart attack and stroke, it is also one of the leading causes of infertility, and ages on quickly.

The first step to improving your emotional intelligence is to learn how to relieve stress. Learn How to take breaks when you are under pressure.

3) Your relationships

If you understand your emotions and control them, you will be better at expressing how you feel and understanding how others are feeling.

This allows you to communicate more effectively and form stronger relationships, both at work and in your personal life.

How Improving Your Emotional Intelligence Can Be Beneficial To You

Being able to maintain control of your emotions will help you in every area of your life. It helps you manage your emotions and feelings when you are in stressful or emotional situations and avoid unnecessary dramas. You'd be able to make decisions without being influenced by your present emotions. You'd be able to make logical decisions devoid of emotions.

To improve your emotional intelligence and decision-making abilities, you need to understand and learn how to manage your emotions by developing critical skills needed to control and manage overwhelming stress, and communication effectively. If you can control your feelings, you can control your life

Indicators of High Emotional Intelligence

There are different measures of EI depending on which model you are looking at. Some companies have their human resources departments run the tests on applicants and employees as a requisite for hiring or retention. While this is so, there are still criticisms about the accuracy and methodology of the diagnostic tools. However, in practical terms, experts have come up with their lists of what traits or characteristics people who are highly emotionally intelligent have.

Among the more commonly listed qualities include:

Ability to Label His Emotions Correctly – there are many possible variations and combinations of the basic emotions. Being able to accurately label these emotions lead to more rational choices and decisions. Misunderstandings and counterproductive reactions are avoided.

When you gain mastery of your emotions, you can describe your less than cheery mood as more than just "down" or "sad." You will be able to say that you are "dejected," "lonely," or "nostalgic." All these variegations of "sad" have different meanings. When you label your emotions accurately, you can get deeper into the cause of your emotional state.

Awareness of What He Can and Cannot Do– self-awareness is one of the foundations of emotional intelligence. When you have a high EI, you will have a heightened awareness of your strengths and weaknesses.

People with high EI accept that they have limitations and can devise a plan to work around those limitations not to accomplish their goals. They capitalize on their strengths to propel them towards success faster. They are confident enough of their capabilities to laugh off mistakes and joke about themselves.

Natural Curiosity About the People Around Them– people with high EI care about other people and want to know what they are going through. They have the empathy required to relate with others effectively. This also makes it easier for them to understand other people and be a good judge of character. They can read people accurately and see the motivations behind their actions and behavior. To these, they can react accordingly.

Gratefulness– there is always more to be thankful for than to feel wrong about. This is what people with high EI subscribe to. Thinking about what you are grateful for instead of what you do not have is a great mood booster. Studies support this with findings that indicate a 23% reduction in cortisol, a stress hormone, in people who have an attitude of gratitude. As a result, they have more energy and are mentally and physically more capable to do their tasks

Ability to Decide When to Stop and Take A Break– it is not wrong to take a little breather from time to time. People with high EI can muster the self-control to say no to just another hour more of overtime at the office, to taking work during their off days because there are just too many items in the office pipeline, or to taking phone calls in the middle of the night because the graveyard shift personnel do not know what to do.

Emotionally intelligent people know that they need a break from all the stress to function optimally. They can stop and step back from their routine and give their minds and bodies the chance to rest and refocus. This results in an emotional, mental, and physical state ready to get back to things from where they left off.

Belief That No One or Nothing Is Perfect– again, this comes from recognizing that people make mistakes and there are no exceptions. They accept that not all things can be as they expect them to be. They accept the flaws and deal with them in a manner that will give them the best outcomes. They are not too hard on themselves when they make mistakes. Instead, they learn from their mistakes. They adapt and then move on, avoiding the same mistakes along the way.

Ability to Let Go of Excess Baggage– negative thoughts and emotions can be a heavy burden to carry along with you on your road to success. A person with high EI does not hold grudges. He does not allow ill feelings to linger and impair his judgment.

Even toxic people can become excess baggage for you if you do not have the EI to handle them properly. They can weigh you down and infect you with their being "toxic." People with high EI can keep a good head on their shoulders and less steam blowing out of their ears and nose.

Healthy Mind and Body– as negative emotions are kept at bay; highly emotionally intelligent people are less likely to turn to unhealthy coping habits like smoking and drinking. They know that their bodies need proper care if they are to perform at their best every day.

They do not rely on coffee to keep them going as they have enough supply of healthy happy hormones to give them the energy to get through the day. They ensure that their minds and bodies can get the nourishment they need from a balanced diet and lifestyle.

Even when they are "forced" to be around negative people, people with high EI do not let them affect their happiness. They are confident enough with who they are and what they can do and thus do not let other people's opinion cast a cloud over their sunny disposition.

How Emotional Intelligence Is Helpful to Analyze People

Emotional intelligence is beneficial when it comes to dealing with other people. Yes, the general intellect is useful, but you need a substantial level of the EQ to handle social relationships.

EQ is required also in businesses; it helps you understand a better way to close that deal. You'd get to understand your clients better.

It's possible to have a high level of EQ and IQ at the same time. Since IQ deals with your mental capacity and EQ deals with the ability to relate with people, you can very well have it both ways.

Emotional intelligence helps you draw on your reserve. You get to focus on your mental and emotional health and keep an eye on others emotional health.

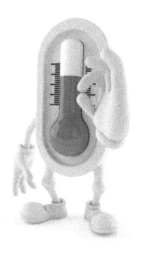

Chapter 5: Components of Personality

Components

What are the components that make up or define a personality? When we look at the definitions, you'd think that a person's character is made of pieces of patterns and traits. While this is true, it is not entirely what makes a personality. Some other core components of nature are:

- Psychological and physiological: while most approve that personality is a product of psychological form, research also points to nature being influenced by biological needs and processes.
- Consistency: there are a recognizable order and regularity to the behaviors seen. People generally behave or act in the same ways no matter what the situation.
- Multiple expressions: when we speak about personality, it extends above and beyond behaviors. Personality is also perceived in our feelings, thoughts, social interactions as well as our close relationships.
- Behaviors and actions: personality also has a massive effect on what causes us to act, behave, move, and response in specific ways.

Psychology Applications

How personality changes and develops over a person's lifetime is a fascinating element of life that one can study. This study and the results gained serve as an essential tool to understand the real-world practical applications, why people act and behave a certain way, and what motivates the behaviors and thoughts.

In most cases, to study a person's personality, personality assessment tests are usually done to help people understand and learn more about themselves and their weaknesses, preferences, and strengths. These assessments may focus on how people level on certain traits on whether they rank high on conscientiousness, extroversion, and openness. Some reviews, though, focus on specific aspects of personality changes over a course of time, whereas detailed assessments are used to help people determine the kinds of careers that go well with their existing personality and how they can perform specific job tasks.

How Do They Answer Questions?

One important thing to pay attention to when trying to gauge people's personality type is how they answer questions. Extraverts often answer questions quickly and tend to think out loud. This means that they will likely verbalize several thoughts before officially giving their final answer. Alternatively, all of these thoughts may work together to create their overall solution. Introverts on the other hand are far quieter. They may use a filler word such as "um" or "uh" while they think about it, but they are less likely to provide as much information about the thought process. Instead, they will quietly mull it over in their mind until they have an answer for you.

Are They Focused on The Past and Present, Or the Future?

These people are more concerned about right this minute and use the past to create their overall outlook on life. In other words, they combine the past and present to create their perception of reality.

The other type of person is known as an intuitive. Intuitive types are people who are more focused on the future. While they are presently living in the moment, they are likely to be looking for what is coming next, rather than mulling over what has already happened.

How Do They Consider Others in Decisions?

If you want to know what drives a person, pay attention to how they consider other people when making decisions. People who make decisions quickly without considering how the outcome will affect others are known as thinkers. These are people who are more focused on the logical, rational, and thought-based side of things. They are likely not intentionally ignorant toward how the outcome affects others. Instead, they are simply driven by thought. The opposite of this includes those who are driven by their feelings. These people are more likely to pay attention to how the outcome will affect themselves and the other people in their lives. They want to know what the emotional repercussions will be and are very careful to make sure that no one gets hurt due to their actions.

How Do They Adapt to Change?

Some people adapt well to change, others don't. Knowing this element of a person's personality type can significantly help you when it comes to understanding them as a whole. If a person tends to be open to options and is willing to look at all different solutions for a problem, they are more likely to be comfortable with change. They can adapt to any chosen solution and are typically more interested in selecting the best answer for the question than the best solution. The other type, then, is someone who is not good with change. These people choose the solution that answers the question and keeps them feeling comfortable in the solution. They are unlikely to want to change their decision and will typically defend their solution quite gravely.

Combining the answers to these four questions is the best way to gauge how a person is in various situations. You will be able to understand and predict how they are most likely to act under a variety of different circumstances, making it much easier to understand their personality type. Remember, everyone has a different placement on the personality spectrum. Some may be louder and more outgoing than others, whereas others might be quieter and more reserved. They may, however, share qualities from opposite ends of the spectrum. The best way to gauge exact personality type is to look at each person individually and build their baseline with this knowledge.

Chapter 6: Personality Types

We use the different types of personalities to know the strengths of each person. Let us look at the different kinds of people that you will come across.

Most people have a general idea of being shy, daring, outgoing, or charismatic. But this is not all when you understand the personality type you get to enjoy many benefits:

Knowing Other People's Preferences

Every person has his or her preferences, and you can judge these by knowing the personality type.

When these people operate within the preferences, you get them to be more effective and efficient. However, operating outside the preferences requires more type and energy.

Knowing if you are within the boundaries can improve efficiency, productivity, and even grow management skills.

Avoid Conflict

Understanding the type of person by depending on the personality type helps you avoid any conflict.

You get to diffuse them way before they come up. If you know that your personality makes you intense whenever a situation arises, you will adjust the behavior to be more receptive to the issue.

When you are usually the one to accept responsibility even when you aren't the one that messed things up, you get to train yourself to become more analytical and take time to evaluate the situation before you handle it.

Helps You Appreciate Diversity

Once you know your personality type, you have the chance to interact with other people and appreciate how diverse they are.

When you are in a work environment, the chances are that you will hit a roadblock and end up failing to handle some situations.

When this happens, it is good to have a mind to take up the issue on your behalf and implement it.

Find the Right Career

The personality type you adopt plays a massive role in the kind of job that you are suited to.

It also affects how you handle the job that you are given.

The type of personality you have helps you find the right career to give you proper job satisfaction. For instance, if you are an extrovert, you will find it hard to work in a position that requires you to work alone.

On the other hand, if you are an introvert, you will find it hard to work in a position that doesn't allow you to work alone.

Make Better Decisions

How you make decisions is based more on what you see and experience.

You know that you will either end up with something good or lose out when you take a particular decision.

It also bases on sensing and intuition.

If you decide to make a decision based on sense, you will engage all your fixe senses to gather information, analyze it, and make the right decision.

On the other hand, if you use intuition to decide, you will most likely feel the situation before you can make a choice.

The only downside to analyzing issues before you decide is that you will tend to explore the problems longer than necessary, which in turn decides to take longer than expected.

The theory behind having a personality type is that we get born with it. Then we live with it before finally dying with it.

When faced with a situation, we have the chance to apply the personality type the right way spending on the scenario or experiences

The personality types are based on Myers-Briggs theory developed by a partnership between a mother and daughter combination.

Let us look at the combination pairs that make the theory applicable in all situations:

Extraversion and Introversion

This is concerned with the way you direct your energy.

If your energy is mostly directed towards dealing with people, situations, and things, you are an Extravert (E).

On the other hand, if you direct your energy towards your inner world, you are a perfect example of an introvert (I).

Sensing and Intuition

This looks at the kind of information that you end up processing.

If you are one to look at facts, analyze them, and then come up with a decision from the points, you are a sensor (S).

On the other hand, if you are one that makes your decisions without having to analyze facts, then you are intuitive (N)

Thinking and Feeling

This looks at your personality type, depending on your decision-making style.

If you base your decisions based on logic, taking time to analyze and come up with the best approach, then you prefer Thinking (T).

If on the other hand, you prefer to use values, which means you make decisions based on what you see is essential, then you are in for Feeling (F)

Judgment and Perception

This is the final pair that you can use to determine your personality type.

If you plan your life in a structured way, you prefer Judging (J).

If on the other hand, you have a preference of going along with the flow, responding to things as they come along, then you are in for Perception (P).

To determine the kind of personality you are, you need to take a test that will use the information you give to determine your personality type.

The 16 Personality Types

The Inspector – ISTJ Personality

When you first meet them, ISTJs are usually intimidating.

They look formal, serious, and organized; they uphold tradition and old-school values that make them work hard, be patient, and honour any responsibility that they are given.

They don't make a lot of noise; instead, they are quiet, calm, and reserved.

The Counselor – INFJ Personality

These are ideologists and visionaries that ooze with creative imagination and a lot of brilliant ideas.

They have a good way to look at the world and have a depth to how they think, never accepting things the way they come.

They are usually looked at to be amusing or weird due to their outlook towards life.

The Mastermind – INTJ

These are usually introverts that are reserved and quiet, always comfortable being left alone.

When they socialize, they drain their energy, making them get to recharge.

They don't like coming up with plans and strategies, always being exact at what they do.

The Giver – ENFJ Personality

These are focused so much on other people.

They are usually charismatic, idealistic, ethical, and highly principled.

They know how to connect to other people so well regardless of the background and the personality.

They usually rely on feelings and intuition and mainly rely on imagination rather than the real world.

The Craftsman – ISTP personality

These are usually logical and mysterious but very enthusiastic and spontaneous.

Their personality traits aren't easily recognized, and many people can't anticipate the way they react.

They are usually unpredictable, but they find a way to hide the traits in the world.

The Provider – ESFJ Personality

This is the extrovert.

They are social animals that feed their need to interact with other people and make them happy.

They are usually popular among their circle of friends. These are traditionally sports hero and cheerleaders.

Later in the year, they are the center of planning social events and organizing them for the families.

The Idealist – INFP Personality

These are usually reserved and quiet.

They rarely talk about themselves, especially when they meet with a new person.

They spend most of their time alone and in a quiet place to make sense of the things happening around them.

They don't make decisions before analyzing the situation.

The Performer –ESFP Personality

These are seen to be the entertainers in the group.

They are usually born to be at the front of the group and tend to capture the stage.

They like being in the spotlight and love learning and sharing what they have learned with others.

The Champion – ENFP Personality

These have individualistic characteristics and don't like being forced to live outside what they believe in.

They love being around other people and have a lot of intuition when it comes to themselves and others.

The Doer – ESTP Personality

They have that need for social interaction all the time, and a need for their freedom.

They usually make decisions before they think and are always fixing issues as they move ahead.

The Supervisor – ESTJ Personality

They are honest, organized, and great believers in all that they do.

They always believe that what they indulge in is socially acceptable.

They usually opt to take the post of being the leader of the pack.

The Commander – ENTJ Personality

They focus on the external aspects of things that they deal with rationally and logically.

They are naturally born leaders that take everything to a whole new level.

The Thinker – INTP Personality

They thrive in an environment where the situation needs logic ad brilliant thinking.

They love working according to patterns and have an eye for discrepancies.

The Nurturer – ISFJ Personality

These are usually ready to pay back generosity for generosity, and they believe in making sure that things work the way they need to do.

They value cooperation and harmony when they meet with people.

The Visionary – ENTP Personality

These are rare in the world.

They might not thrive in social situations, especially those involving people that are different from them.

They are knowledgeable and intelligent with the need for mental stimulation most of the time.

The Composer – ISFP Personality

They are introverts but don't behave like one.

They usually have issues connecting with other people at first, but they are fun to be within all situations once they do.

Chapter 7:   How to Analyze a Person for Their Photos?

"The camera is an instrument that teaches people how to see without a camera"- Dorothea Lange

There are no escaping people's pictures in the age of a continually  buzzing social media feed. Like it or not, people are going to picture of themselves. However, the good news from a person analyzer's perspective is you can gather plenty of clues for speed reading people even before you meet them, only by learning to read their photographs.

Imagine gaining some clues about a prospective employee before they come down for a face or face interview or learning more about a client before negotiating a significant deal with them. How about picking the right date by gathering insights about their personality through their social media images? Every image of a person holds a fascinating amount of information, meaning, and an indication of his or her emotional state. We only have to be conscious enough to watch out for these clues. Sometimes, we are so overcome by the aesthetics of the image or the photography that we miss entirely the image's emotions.

This attempts to offer you some insights about how people's photographs can be used for interpreting their values, personality, and behavioral traits. There are some obvious and some subtle pointers about decoding an individual's personality through their photos. You'll learn to find meaning and context within the images rather than view them as random shots.

Do Not Rush

Since photographs capture moments where time freezes, you need to study the image carefully to avoid any biases or inaccurate readings about something that may have happened in a microsecond. This may be contrary to the fast-speed, short span of attention, limited energy, and the multi-tasking disposition we display. Hit the brain's pause button, do some deep breathing and get yourself into slow motion before you begin analyzing people through their images. You need to approach the art of analyzing people with both curiosity and compassion.

Don't leave out any details. Look at the entire image. What is it that holds your attention when you first look at the picture? What are the conspicuous aspects of the image? Slowly move your attention and awareness to the other parts of the photos. Look at it from different angles and perspectives.

Pull the image closer to your vision to detect elements that would otherwise go unnoticed. There are plenty of subtle details that your eye may miss if you don't view it near. Turning the image upside down or sideways allows you to view it from an unusual perspective, changing your entire viewpoint about the image. You'll end up noticing things you wouldn't have otherwise seen.

Subjective Reactions

What strikes you the most about an image when you see it for the first time? What emotions, feelings, thoughts, and sensations overcome your mind when you look at the picture intuitively? Think of a single descriptive word or phrase as a caption or title for the image that captures your spontaneous reaction.

Do you think the picture represents pride, anger, anxiety, relief, frustration, confinement, exhaustion, success, happiness, exhilaration, smoothness, rage, sadness, and other compelling emotions? Your gut-level reaction offers a clue on what you are thinking about the person.

While observing or analyzing people through their photographs, one of the most important considerations is your instant or immediate reaction. However, you'll need to go beyond the first impression. You'll have to apply some amount of free association to analyze the person. Through free association, you are focusing on all elements of the image. Here are some questions you can ask yourself to facilitate more significant free association to analyze people through images.

What does the picture remind you of?

What is the predominant emotion expressed by the person in the image?

What memories, incidents, and experiences can you pull out from your state of awareness on looking at the image?

How would you title the image?

However, when you are analyzing people through their pictures, beware against what psychologists' terms projection. Projection is an unconscious process through which our feelings, emotions, experiences, and memories distort our perception of other people we are analyzing. You may invariably end up projecting your feelings and experiences to them than trying to identify their personality. This is especially true for more ambiguous images. You don't know if you are rightly empathizing with people reading them correctly or simply recalling your own experiences.

Sometimes, our subjective reactions get in the way of reading people accurately. However, overcome this tricky situation and identifying when your own experiences and biases are getting in the way of analyzing people will help you be a more effective people analyzer.

Facial Expressions

Human beings are innately expressive when it comes to tuning in to other people's facial expressions. What is your first reaction on looking at the person's face in the photograph? Psychologists have recognized seven basic emotions in a person – surprise, contempt, fear, sadness, anger, disgust and happiness. Keep these seven basic emotions in mind while analyzing people's expressions in images. At times, the expressions are underplayed or subtle, making it challenging to pin down the basic emotion.

Look for pictures where the person may not be aware that they are being clicked since that can be a more accurate representation of their subconscious mind.

Relationships

Again, you can tell a lot about the relationship between people by looking at their photographs. If a person is leaning in another person's direction, there may be attraction or affection between the people. Similarly, if people are leaning in the opposite direction from each other, the relationship may lack warmth. If you notice a person clinging on to their partner's arm in almost every photograph, they may most likely be insecure about losing their partner. It may reveal a deep sense of insecurity or fear of losing their partner.

Try to predict the relationship between people through their body language in images. This can also be done in any public place where you have some time at hand to check people's body language, relationship equation, and reactions. What are their feelings, emotions, thoughts, and attitudes towards each other? Is there a pattern in how people touch, lean towards each other or look at one another? Does their body language reveal a lack of connectedness?

One of my favorite pastimes when it comes to analyzing people is looking at celebrity couples' photographs and trying to read the nature of their relationship and/or their personality through their body language and expressions. I try to analyze if the image reveals intimacy, affection, and positivity? Or it demonstrates tension, disharmony, and conflict? Akeret, a well-known psychologist, believes that a photograph can also predict a relationships' future.

Some signs of comfort include smiling, holding hands, titling head in the direction of their partner. Hip to hip posture may indicate things are going great between the couple. How is the palmer touch? If it is touching with the full hand, the partners are close and affectionate. On the other hand, fingertips or fist touching can be a sign of being distant and reserved. Crossing legs may mean that they weren't very comfortable or open when the picture was

434

taken. If you find a person crossing their arms or legs in almost every photograph, they may be suspicious, doubtful, cynical, and unenthusiastic by nature.

Profile Pictures and Personality Traits

A big body of research suggests that human beings tend to assess one another's personality through a quick glimpse. This is exactly why first impressions are so lasting. It takes us only three to four seconds to form an impression about a person through verbal and non-verbal clues. Sometimes, they may not even say anything and we can subconsciously tune in to personality.

A recent research study reveals that you don't even have to meet a person once to form an opinion about them. All you need is a glance at their Facebook or even Tinder profile picture to gauge their personality. Here are the big five personality traits that are revealed through a person's profile picture.

The big five is pretty much the same to a scientific classification of personalities as Briggs-Myers is for recruitment. This personality approach classifies personalities based on five fundamental traits: introversion-extroversion, agreeableness, openness to new experiences, conscientiousness, and neuroticism.

A glance at your social media profile picture is sufficient for you to rate people correctly on the five fundamental dimensions. In a research conducted by PsyBlog, it was observed through a scientific analysis of the profile pictures of thousands of social media participant personalities that there were very specific and consistent patterns when it came to each of the five personality attributes.

For example, people scoring high on conscientiousness used natural, filter-free, bright, and vibrant images. They were not afraid to express a large number of emotions through their pictures. If fact, they displayed a higher number of emotions through their images than all other personality types.

You'll also find people scoring high on openness taking the most amazing shots. They are creative, innovative, and resourceful. They'll play a lot with applications and filters owing to their creativity. Their pictures will be more artistic, unique, and feature greater contrasts. Generally, people who score high on openness have their face occupy more space than any other feature in the photograph.

Extraversion folks will have perpetually broad smiles plastered on their faces. They will use collages and may surround their profile picture with used vibrant images. On the other hand, simple images with very little color or brightness is a strong indication of neuroticism. According to the blog, these pictures are likely to display a blank expression or in extreme cases may even conceal their face.

Agreeable people may often seem to the nicest people to get along with among all personality types. However, turns out, they aren't great photographers. Agreeable people are known to post unflattering images of themselves! However, even with the poor or unflattering images of themselves, they will be seen smiling or displaying a positive expression. The images will be vibrant, positive, and lively.

Chapter 8:   Read the Facial Micro-Expressions

The micro-expression is an expression that lasts about 2-5

milliseconds derived from an unconscious emotion. By unconscious, we mean that it is understood that the individual only realizes it after expressing it.

The Face May Reveal the Opposite of What a Person Says

The emotions are the same whether you're a housewife, a suicide bomber, or a politician in Japan. The truth may not be what you're talking about. The truth is in the face. A detective arrives from the United States with a revolutionary method in the suitcase. It analyzes facial micro-expressions. And it catches liars.

"Bill Clinton, former president of the United States. He tried to deny the case to the trainee, right? He does not synchronize speech speed with the movement of hands. Usually flashes ten to fifteen times a minute," says Detective Wanderson Castilho.

"Somalia, a Botafogo player, went to the TV to declare that he had been kidnapped. If you notice, the blinks are fast. But then they slow down because the brain does not want to see that lie told," says the detective. "The brain knows the truth."

Cristiano and Carlos, people like you or me, will tell you the most exciting moment they have ever experienced in life.

"The most striking moment of my life was the birth of my son. Because I got into the operating room and she had a cardiac arrest in the middle of that surgery. I see that whole run, I do not understand anything, I just see that. At the same time, it was striking and very tense," says Carlos.

"The most exciting moment was in my wife's delivery, where I went to watch in the operating room. It was a joyful moment, I felt numb, and I took lots of pictures. But even then, something different was happening. My wife was going into cardiac arrest, but I was so anesthetized with my son's remarkable moment that I failed to realize that she was going through a problem. But the situation was circumvented and thank God everything went well," says Cristiano.

"Of course, the two did not live the same story. Only one of them lived through the experience. We asked them to tell the same story so Wanderson could detect which one is lying. Watching the video, do we have any micro-expression that we can detect? At one point, we can see some of Carlos's denials about the story. The face does not fit the case, what happened?" says Wanderson.

The study of human behavior in psychology is a complex task, the techniques to understand other people unfold to cover the most diverse forms of human expression. However, no technique is in itself sufficient to face the complexity of human communication.

Verbal communication accounts for only 7% of human communication. In reality, 93% of human communication occurs nonverbally, through tone of voice, intensity, posture, micro-expressions, gait, etc. Results from more than 40 years of research show evidence that makes interpretations of non-verbal behavior more objective and helps psychologists improve their skills in searching for understanding of the other.

Also, the application of knowledge about facial expressions has been consistently useful for various domains ranging from clinical to business. One objective of this book is to explore the scientific production of facial expressions as a technical possibility for the psychologist's current work, say for example, in Mozambique.

We will seek to discuss research foundations from the work of Paul Ekman, elected one of the 100 most important psychologists of the twentieth century by the American Psychological Association (APA) and considered the greatest scholar of facial behavior.

For elaboration, bibliographic research methodology in the molds designed by the APA was used to research documents and relevant information published in books, videos, newspapers, research reports, dissertations, photos, and interviews from the Paul Ekman Group database library.

Micro-Expressions: Revealing Hidden Frauds and Emotions

Unlike macro-expressions which can last for up to four seconds, micro-expressions are very fast facial expressions that last only a fraction of a second and are recognized in cross-cultural studies. They occur when the person, deliberately or unconsciously, tries to hide their feelings. They were

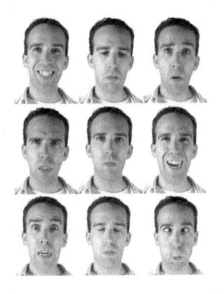

initially described in psychotherapy with depressed patients. Researchers proposed that these expressions occur when people have repressed feelings (hidden from themselves) or deliberately try to hide their feelings (deletion). however, it cannot be determined by the expression alone whether they originated from repression or suppression.

More than 99% of the population cannot identify these signs, including professional groups, psychologists, psychiatrists, neurologists, and police, except secret security agents who show better test performance. However, Ekman and Friesen showed that with training, people can recognize them in real-time. These studies suggest that, by enabling professionals (e.g., psychologists), they are better able to perceive signs they did not perceive before, which directly influences how they conduct or approach the situation.

Physiologically, micro-expressions represent signs of stress, that is, when the cognitive and emotional systems enter into a neural conflict, giving rise to the avoidance of brief physical manifestations. For example, this happens when the person does not believe what he says or feels something different from what he shows. An experiment with university students in the USA showed evidence of evasion of micro-expressions to hide unpleasant emotions linked to experience.

Several behavioral scientists and others have been concerned with fraud detection and the method of understanding this type of behavior. These works interested not only the psychotherapeutic community which is concerned with understanding human emotions but also sectors of the army (like the powers of the I and II GM), criminology, and law.

The traditional form for detecting frauds or lies is based on torture and intimidation, which in turn generates physiological responses of stress, and there is always a risk of error and damage to the subject.

The polygraph is an instrument designed to detect lies, evaluating the tension and pulse of the fingers. Changes in this tension and pulsation rhythm from readings taken at baseline would mean lie signals, which trigger an electric shock to the head as an unpleasant stimulus (punishment). However, the physiological reactions to the test itself are considered problematic, so their validity is questionable.

Humans are considered the best tool for detecting frauds (lies). Studies and statistics show that humans achieve up to 90% accuracy in detecting signs of fraud when trained. The observation of physiological signs, lack of spontaneity in expressions, voice hesitation, skin resistance, and other clues represent measurable signs associated with the contrast between cognition and emotion.

Importance of Expression

Knowledge of recognizing the facial expressions of emotions and micro-expressions is of great importance for understanding intrapersonal management, interpersonal relationships, and the development of emotional intelligence and empathy. A study by Helen Reiss et al. showed that the ability to recognize emotions through brief facial expressions results in better empathy ratings as reported for study group patients than for the control group.

Training in facial expressions also increases awareness of internal emotions, allowing us to recognize when we become emotionally vulnerable, enabling better management of emotions.

Facial Expression and Micro-Expression Application in the Real World

Knowledge about facial expressions has practical multidisciplinary application, the disciplines in which it is important to have the capacity to read the emotional states of others include: psychological assessment for screening of criminals in communities, airports, and terrorism prevention; fraud detection in interviews and or police inquiries, clinical support, and evaluation; marketing and sales; research; television industry, etc.

We will discuss some of these applications in detail as they can be implemented in our context:

A) Police training, inquirers, and criminal issues: Fraud, often carries increased emotional expressions than normal situations (micro-expressions).

However, micro-expressions do not say in themselves whether the subject is lying but point to discrepancies between what is said and what is emotionally experienced by the individual. Around

the world, security agents and police officers from the USA,

Portugal, Brazil, the UK, and several other countries have training on recognizing micro-expressions and body language in their training modules.

Considering the explosion of criminal acts of abduction against civilians in Mozambique, these techniques can be useful as evaluation and behavioral monitoring (e.g. on patrol, inquiries) for law enforcement and public safety agents.

B) Profiling at airports: Several universities which study technology have developed, based on Ekman's studies, tracking systems for facial expressions that allow monitoring of terrorism, drug trafficking, and other suspects. Airports security agents are also trained to obtain these cues through direct observation of body language and facial expressions in particular. This can be taken as a standard of prevention of organized crime and security enhancement, especially considering the precautions that international airports recommend following the September 11 attacks.

C) Health professionals: These professionals can develop a better rapport with patients, interacting in a more humane, empathetic and compassionate way, contributing to the achievement of more accurate diagnoses by obtaining more complete information.

D) Nonverbal language in education: The crucial aspects of student-teacher interaction are non-verbal. Teachers can read their students' facial expressions to get suggestions on lesson progress and plan a more effective process. Likewise, school managers who read their teachers' emotions are more likely to reduce burnout and increase their effectiveness.

E) Development of social skills for special populations: Individuals on the autistic spectrum have benefited greatly from the training that helps them recognize micro-expressions through the ESET (subtle expression training tool). At the opposite end of the spectrum, individuals with schizophrenia tend to have an increased ability to recognize emotions than control groups.

F) Psychological and medical evaluation: Ekman's studies evidenced micro-expressions in interviews of the detachment of depressed patients who attempted suicide. Stuart recalls that most psychopathologies in DSM IV are linked to some kind of emotional alteration (APA, 1994). In the modern conceptualization of emotions it is necessary to consider that changes in nonverbal behavior may be associated with the course, signs, and symptoms of the problem.

Chapter 9: Verbal vs. Nonverbal Behavior

Language is incredible. As humans, we have an incredibly heightened ability to communicate with one another. This level of communication is a part of why we have been able to advance so far in our evolution. The advancement of our communication results in advancement in our society. We will discuss how our communication is more advanced and the intricacies behind verbal and nonverbal behavior. More importantly, we will define nonverbal and verbal behavior and also give two differences between the two and learn how to analyze the statements that other individuals make verbally. More specifically, we will learn how to analyze these verbal statements using nonverbal language. We will also go into the details of analyzing the nonverbal behavior of those around us.

Defining Nonverbal Behavior

Nonverbal behavior or communication is the subconscious or conscious relaying of ideas or emotions through physical motion or well-known and understood gestures. Messages can be transferred non-verbally through a variety of signals and methods.

The first of these defining signals are methods known as proxemics. Proxemics essentially means the distance between two individuals. The distance between two individuals or proxemics carries a lot of weight in terms of nonverbal communication.

The second method of nonverbal communication is known as kinesics and is simply another word for body language. Kinesics or body language is the transmission of ideas through gestures and often unconscious motions of the body.

Meanwhile, another defining method is known as haptics. Haptics is another word for the act of touching something. In the world of nonverbal behavior, the way that somebody touches something carries a lot of weight in communicating their emotions to another individual. A soft touch on the arm can mean many things, which becomes very different in comparison to a firm grasp of one's hand. Not all touches are equal, and every touch—depending on its longevity, intensity, and location on the body—has many different meanings behind it.

Another form of nonverbal communication is our appearance. People use their appearance to communicate their personality in a variety of ways. Most of this is a conscious decision made by the individual, but some factors are almost entirely caused by our parents that aren't necessarily chosen by us but still say things about ourselves. Most likely, the biggest and most common type of nonverbal communication using our parents is simply judging whether or not somebody cares about their appearance. By just looking at another person, we can instantly tell whether they care about how they appear to them. This carries a huge amount of weight in the snap judgment we make about people every day. The final common form of nonverbal communication is the use of eye contact. Eye contact is extremely important in us as humans. Humans are very focused on an individual's eyes, which is often one of the first things that a person looks at when they see a new face. Your eyes are often considered the windows to the soul, which is true in the sense that they can reveal many factors about yourselves. By looking into someone's eyes or measuring the amount of eye contact they give, we can understand a vast amount of information about their personality. Do they have strong eye contact? Do they avoid eye contact? Do they have intense eye contact? The answers to all of these queries give us different definitions to a person's personality. As humans, we put a lot of weight on an individual's eye contact as a defining portion of their personality. This is why we must keep eye contact in mind when attempting to understand someone's nonverbal communication.

Defining Verbal Communication

Verbal communication seems quite obvious when spoken out loud. Verbal communication consists of any form of speech or language used to relay ideas or thoughts to another. Verbal communication includes much more than simply speaking to a person. The way we string together ideas and thoughts with words shows a lot about their personality in the words that we choose in the cadence that we choose to put them together. There are multiple ways that we can express ourselves through verbal communication. The first and most evident way to express ourselves through verbal communication is by speaking to those around us. By stringing together words and sentences, we create cohesive thoughts and ideas that express our feelings to those around us.

In addition to being able to accurately and positively express our emotions and feelings to those around us, the act of speaking is also quite easy to use to persuade or to alter our true meaning. It is much easier to lie to a person verbally than to lie to a person with our body language. Because of this, we often find people who lie very easily vocally to a person but whose body language cues do not match their words.

The second form of verbal communication, writing, may surprise some people reading this text. While not technically verbal, the act of writing still comprises verbal communication because it uses common vocally spoken language simply in written form. The difficulty in this is that a person reading a text has a much harder time guessing and understanding the cadence of the person who wrote the text. Because of this, written ideas and emotions can be misconstrued because people cannot quite tell the intonation of the author of the text through the words.

Another form of verbal communication is an underlying feeling within our words known as denotation or connotation. The connotation is considered as the feelings or emotions associated with the meanings of certain words or phrases. This is not to be confused with its antonym, denotation, which is the literal or primary meaning of a word, opposite to the emotions or series that the word suggests. To convey these important forms of verbal communication, a person must use our neck form of verbal communication.

The next form of verbal communication that we will be discussing is tone and volume. When talking to another person, an individual's tone can express a lot about that person's inner thoughts or feelings. The tone is a very difficult form of communication to pin down and explain to people. For some individuals, the tone is very easy to control and change in their language—while for others, it can be very difficult. You cannot describe the tone based on the inflection that an individual puts on to certain words at certain times. The tone is very interesting because every person can understand the meaning behind other people's tones almost in perfect connection with one another. Still, it is very difficult to explain to others. In connection to this, a person's volume also holds a great deal of significance in their verbal communication. Since childhood, we have all learned about the difference between an inside voice and an outside voice. Do volume levels show a lot about our emotions? We can read a lot about how someone feels in a certain situation based on their volume at that time.

It is important always to remember that you have to use both verbal and nonverbal forms of communication together in parallel to understand the total outcome of a person's ideas and theories. A common misconception amongst individuals is that verbal communication and nonverbal communication are contradictory. This is not the case. Verbal and nonverbal communication must go side-by-side when communicating with those around us. The combination of these two complex forms of communication makes the translation of our ideas and theories the most effective. One cannot exist without the other—in most cases. Body language specialists often assert that nonverbal communication can play one of five roles when trying to read another person. These five roles are known as substitution, reinforcement, contradiction, accentuation, and regulation.

Substitution - certain types of nonverbal communication are started as a substitution or placement for verbal communication. Examples of this are nodding your head for yes or shrugging your shoulders for "I don't know."

Reinforcement - nonverbal communication can often be used to reinforce a previously given statement. By reading an individual's body language and judging it consistently, you can almost entirely ascertain whether they are telling the truth or not.

Contradiction - this is the opposite of reinforcement. If a person's body language appears to be contradicting something that they are saying, then by the rule of contradiction, they are almost certainly lying—depending on their environment, of course.

Accentuation - body language often serves as a method of accentuating something that a person says vocally. Examples of this include smiling when someone says that they are happy or shivering when somebody says that they are cold. This can also be used to put a greater level of importance to a statement that somebody has given out. An example of this is creating the quotation mark symbol with your fingers while saying something sarcastically. By adding body language to your making statement, you are reaffirming and showing importance in your statement.

Regulation - an individual's body can also serve to regulate that person's vocal language.

Chapter 10: Personal Beliefs

A belief is something that you hold as a fact or truth. Each person has something that they believe in – some good and others bad. A personal belief is a collection of ideas that a person sees as true. In most cases, things that contradict your personal beliefs will often make you angry, frustrated or uncomfortable.

Beliefs come from several sources. These include:

- The environment – your environment is capable of shaping you into believing some things about yourself, others and life in general
- Knowledge – information obtained from people, books and quotes
- Personal experiments and experiences
- Cultural and societal norms such as religious beliefs
- Events – these may help you to establish beliefs. For instance, attending an event may change your perspective about life

In most cases, potential beliefs will stay in your mind until you can embrace them as truths and make them part of your belief system. Before people make these potential beliefs part of them, they take time to find reasons to allow such beliefs on their list. Once an individual accepts a certain belief, they can stand and defend that belief with all the pieces of evidence available.

There is a large difference between beliefs and values. Values represent long-standing beliefs that have proven to be of importance to an individual. Therefore, beliefs are the building

blocks of values, which become standards of operation that people use to define their lives and choices. Only beliefs that are important to a person can grow into values. These can then be categorized into various types depending on their role. For instance, you can have values that are related to career, family, wealth or happiness. Being able to differentiate your values is important since you will understand where to apply them in your decision-making processes.

Together with values and beliefs, there is also, what is known as attitude. This is the feeling people have towards each other and the present circumstances. A person's beliefs and attitude contribute greatly to his behavior. People derive their attitude from beliefs and values.

Importance of Personal Beliefs

Beliefs define behavior. Most of the things you do can be easily traced to your beliefs about your surroundings and the world. Beliefs may also influence your reaction to the behavior of others. This is why it is important to ensure that you always choose the right beliefs since they are not private aspects of your life. Below are some roles played by your personal belief:

1.   Influences your behavior

Most of your personal beliefs often affect how you perceive and react to some situations. For instance, you may feel offended and react in anger when a person tries to challenge what you have as part of your belief system. Most beliefs affect the human mind and how it responds to certain circumstances.

2.   Influences perception

Your beliefs can also impact your perception about everything that goes on around your life. For instance, if you are a person that values the law and observes it, you will always treat those who break the same law as the guilty ones.

3.   Influences your choices

Have you ever wondered what influenced your choice of career, spouse, neighborhood, course or diet? There must be an underlying belief somewhere that influenced this decision. It is never a matter of chance or inner wisdom. You only had to think or believe that one choice is better than the other is and that is how you reached your decision. When faced with several things to choose from, people tend to settle for that choice that closely matches their belief. So, your choices greatly reflect some of your beliefs.

4.   Influences your personality

People with strong beliefs always display strong personalities. Your belief system determines your personality more than any other factor. For instance, a person who believes that lies are wrong will always endeavor to remain true to others without minding the consequences.

When beliefs are exercised and chosen correctly, they greatly impact a person's character. They also contribute to your growth and development. The more you exercise a certain belief, the more it becomes part of you. Eventually, this belief becomes a component of your nature and you will not need to struggle to implement it. Personal beliefs help individuals to perform better in their personal and corporate worlds. They give you a sense of identity and convict you any time you are about to decide that is contrary to your belief system. When faced with a challenge, your beliefs can act as a motivation that steers you into fighting for your rights. It always becomes peaceful when people know that things are being done based on their belief system.

Beliefs and Human Behavior

Most people tend to go about their daily businesses without understanding what contributes to their behavior. Yet, human behavior's motives are often based on several beliefs that people have created about themselves. These beliefs often determine how people react to situations and how they respond to their emotions and the emotions of others. In a nutshell, your beliefs determine what you do daily and influence how you do it.

Personal beliefs are always very strong. They are responsible even for the career you choose, the relationships you get into and the things you achieve. When asked what beliefs influence their lives, most people are always unable to respond to this question. They would not even know where to begin since they do not have their personal beliefs defined. However, most beliefs are in-born or implicit. This means that other people cannot identify them, yet they do exist and influence a lot of things that go on in the lives of human beings.

Personal beliefs are different from other types of beliefs like religious, secular or political beliefs. These include guidelines that build individual capabilities. Most people seek to gain conscious awareness of these beliefs to influence the outcome of their behaviors. To understand this better, let us look at some of the personal beliefs that influence the totality of a person's wellbeing.

- **Control**

The first and most influential personal belief that human beings have is the degree of control on their future and destiny. Beliefs that revolve around control normally direct you to pursue or stop pursuing some goals for one reason or the other. When control beliefs lose their power in you, you will start linking your accomplishments to luck, fate or circumstance. Individuals who focus on external influencers for their behaviors often avoid setting big goals. They always remain at their comfort level since they are ready to embrace any outcome that results from their behavior.

On the other hand, individuals who have strong control beliefs always command their actions and outcomes. They believe that they can influence the results of anything and focus on their personal growth and development. They understand the role beliefs play in determining their success; therefore, they emphasize the place of self-belief in all their activities and performance. They can tie their successes and failures to certain aspects of their lives and seek to improve their performance each time.

- **Competency Beliefs**

These also influence your behavior in a very big way. They include assessments of your ability to obtain the required outcome. They also indicate the assessment of some abilities and skills necessary to accomplish a certain assignment or purpose.

Competence beliefs may arise from a person's past performance while others may arise from present challenges. People who tend to assess their level of competence do this based on their knowledge and skills and some competency beliefs that include how others perceive an individual. The effectiveness of competency beliefs can be used to determine a person's self-worth. They can be used to determine how a person will perform on a particular role and how he can overcome challenges. Competency assessments are commonly used to determine the capability of a person in a certain skill or ability.

- **Value-Based Beliefs**

Another attribute that influences your personal belief is the amount of value you place on some tasks' outcome. This value differs among individual and cultural standards. It also changes based on the level of social, moral and cognitive development that a person needs.

When you place very little value on a certain task or goal, you will not sacrifice your effort on it. For instance, if a certain career goal is of no value to you, you will not spend time building that career. If you have enrolled in a class associated with the career, you will not see the importance of completing that class and obtaining a certificate over it. Another example is when you are participating in a race and the first position is not of value to you, you will not deliver your best in terms of your pace. You will go at a comfortable pace for you, so long as you reach the finish line.

Assessing values involves understanding how it impacts the person's beliefs and outcomes. There are two types of values that you need to understand.

1.   The intrinsic value which is measured by the level which a person enjoys completing a task

2.   The utility value which refers to the usefulness associated with mastering and completing a task

Personal beliefs that assign very little value on good behavior contribute greatly to some moral disengagements that ruin individuals and organizations' reputations. People with less value on ethics and honesty will always engage in unpleasant personal and business practices without being mindful of the environment and the people around them.

Goal Orientation

Personal belief is also related to how you define and pursue your goals. Goals define a person's capability as well as their purpose for engaging in a certain activity. Setting goals enables you to come up with certain

performance targets, which you must meet within a stipulated amount of time. For instance, you may decide to enroll for a course for personal development, for appearance purposes, or just because you want to master a certain skill. These are three different goals.

When you pursue a goal to improve your appearance, your focus is always on being good in your colleagues or friends' eyes. Most people that go for this goal are those that keep comparing themselves with others. They are often driven by the desire to outdo others and do not focus on results.

Epistemological Beliefs

These are personal beliefs that are related to intelligence and natural knowledge. Some research indicates that some individuals believe that they can improve their intelligence by acquiring new knowledge and expanding their viewing things. Understanding this helps explain some individuals' behavior when it comes to negotiation, persuasion, and other skills that are tied to cognitive and emotional intelligence.

Chapter 11: Golden Rules for Analyzing People

It is so easy to get things wrong when analyzing people. What you see, the nonverbal cues, might mean and translate differently from what you think. Reading body language is more than the basic gestures. To avoid making wrong assumptions, these three golden rules will help mold your skills.

Don't Read Individual Gestures

Here's one of the first mistakes you can make when analyzing people. It is often wrong to analyze gestures individually. Most times, individual gestures usually have no meaning and are inconsequential to the overall body language of the person you want to analyze.

Like verbal languages, body languages come with all the rudiments of grammar—words, punctuation, and sentences. Each gesture is like a word, and as we all know, a word can have a myriad of definitions. For example, scratching the head comes with lots of meaning—dandruff, forgetfulness, lying, or just a childhood habit. Perhaps the subject's mother may have patted his head a lot during childhood, and the habit stuck as he or she grew up.

Therefore, it is only until you put the individual gestures (words) into clusters (sentences), that you will reveal the truth about the person's feelings. Never forget that you need to have a cluster of body languages before you can accurately analyze people.

Let's examine a body language cluster of someone interested in what you are saying to support our point on clusters. Imagine you are sitting across an interviewer whose body language exhibits the hand-to-face gesture. This body language involves sitting with your legs crossed (defensive position), your index finger pointing up the cheeks, your thumbs supporting the chin, and another finger covering the mouth.

When you combine these individual gestures to form a body language cluster, you can safely conclude that the interviewer doesn't like what they are hearing. What's more? The cross-legged position shows that he or she is holding back negative feelings. At this point, you should know that there's little chance of winning over the person.

Search for Harmony

Do you remember the phrase "Actions speak louder than words?" Yes, your actions speak about ten times louder than your words. Therefore, when your body language is not consistent with what you say, conscious people, are likely to spot the discrepancy.

Let's go back to the example in the first rule. If you were to ask the interviewer to give an opinion on what you said earlier and he replied that he disagreed with you, his body language will correlate with his verbal statement. In other words, his body language is in harmony with his verbal sentences. However, if he said he agreed with what you said, there's a high chance that he's lying since his body language is not in harmony with his words. And that is one of the steps in detecting a lie.

Why don't we look at another scenario before we proceed to the next rule? Suppose a speaker is standing on a stage, speaking confidently with his arms crossed (defensive position) and his chin pointing toward his chest (hostile position). In this position, if the speaker is telling us about how open and receptive, he is to new ideas, would you believe him? What if he tries to assure you of his caring and gentle nature with his fists clenched and repeatedly hitting the lectern? By observing the disharmony between his verbal sentences and his body language, you will detect that he is insincere.

Read Gestures in Context

What would you think of when you see someone sitting at a park with his chin down, and legs and arms crossed? You might probably say he is being defensive and being insincere. Well, congrats, since you now understand how to read body language clusters.

But wait a minute! Before we put the final stamp on your conclusions, why don't you observe the environment's gestures? What if it was a cold and windy day and the subject was trying to shield himself from the elements? So, when you take the environment and circumstance into consideration, you will create an accurate analysis of people. What if the subject assumed the same position in a library? Then you can safely assume that the subject is being defensive.

Recognize and Decipher Quirky Nonverbal Cues

There are universal body languages that are not specific to a group of people. These universal signals are easy to detect and analyze.

You should know that there is a second type of nonverbal signal that's limited to an individual. This is referred to as a quirky nonverbal cue.

Mind you, these less popular signals are hard to detect and are often associated with behavioral patterns formed out of habit. To detect quirky nonverbal cues, you have to search for behavioral patterns in the people you interact with frequently. It's hard to detect these with those you are meeting for the first time. The more you interact with someone, the better your chances of discovering that behavioral pattern upon which you would base your analysis.

For instance, if a colleague always scratches his nose and bites his lips before going into your boss's office, it might be a reliable quirky nonverbal cue that speaks of his nervousness. Undoubtedly, these nonverbal cues have become his gestures to show how nervous or flustered he is.

Try to Establish Baseline Behaviors

Establishing a base behavior is a critical rule in analyzing people. When you interact with people in your workplace, parties, hangouts, or family gatherings, try to grip on their baseline behavior. In simpler terms, try to understand their normal phase—how they act without any pressure or external stimuli.

Start by studying their normal sitting posture, their feet' usual position, their common facial expression, their posture, and the tilt of their head, where they place their personal belongings, and so many other nonverbal tics. Mind you, this is not for you to start acting all creepy around those you interact with, or else they will tense up around you.

The goal is to know how to differentiate their "normal" face and stressed-out face. This rule is not limited to those you are familiar with; you can also apply it to strangers. At the start of your interaction, you should note the "starting point." Establishing a "starting point" or baseline will help you gauge if the person has deviated from it.

Study Behavioral Changes That Could Lead a Change in Decision

Let's paint a scenario: You have been working on a deal for quite a long time, and you've finally gotten the invite to pitch your ideas to a company's executive. A few minutes into the meeting, you start receiving positive vibes from the executive. "This is already a success," you tell yourself. However, the boss receives a call just before he makes his final decision. While on the call, you noticed a difference in his mood.

You observed a change in his body language from being receptive to defensive. At this point, the signal you are getting from the company executive is called an intention cue. These are signals that reveal what a person is about to do, and it gives the observer the time to act fast.

Watch Out for Misleading Nonverbal Clues

You will undoubtedly come across fake or misleading nonverbal clues in the course of analyzing people—it's unavoidable. It takes a lot of experience and practice to differentiate between real nonverbal clues and counterfeits.

Veteran readers can also fail to spot the difference between the two. Therefore, you need to carefully observe before making your judgments.

Distinguish Between Comfort and Discomfort

Let's face it, there are many nonverbal signs to watch out for. The list is endless, and it might lead to confusion if you try to actively look for them all. Therefore, I've created a trick for you to easily detect and understand the nonverbal language you are dealing with.

When in doubt in evaluating a body language signal, all you have to do is ask yourself if it looks like a comfort behavior, such as happiness or contentment, or if it looks like a discomfort behavior, such as unhappiness, stress, anxiety, or disappointment. Most of the instances, you will be able to place nonverbal signals into these two main categories.

Don't Act Like a Creep When Analyzing People

Nonverbal language enables you to assess people and decode their emotions accurately. One thing you should avoid is making it noticeable that you are observing people. Observe with subtlety.

Most folks tend to stare at people when they first try to read on their emotions and thoughts. Analyzing people aims to analyze them unobtrusively because people tend to clam up and restrict their body language when they notice an intense stare. So, work on perfecting your observation skills, and you can get to that point where your efforts will be subtle and successful. Remember, it's all about persistence and practice.

So Why Do You Misread?

Remember, it is possible to make mistakes when you read people. Many body language books teach you that someone has a weak character if he has a weak or limp handshake. But ask yourself this: what if the person is suffering from arthritis or any ailment that might affect his hand grip? What about artists, sculptors, surgeons, and therapists who rely on their hands' perfect condition to get their work done? These people might prefer giving you a weak handshake to prevent unnecessary damage to their hands.

When it comes to analyzing people, there are many factors involved that people might often overlook in a bid to act as the next Sherlock Holmes. Tight-fitting clothes might restrict some people's ability to exhibit certain body language. For instance, ladies with short skirts often have to keep their legs closed, making them less approachable. Although these circumstances only apply to a minority, it is important to consider the effects of a person's physical restrictions on their body language.

So, if it is possible to misread body language, can people also fake it? This is where I set the facts straight; you can't fake body language. Your body will always betray you to the trained eye. A trained body language analyst can detect disharmony between your spoken words, main body signals, and micro signals. You just can't fake the micro signals. These are the involuntary signals that you give off unknowingly. For example, if someone tells you a lie with a smile on his face while holding his palms out, his micro body signals will give him away. His mouth may twitch, or the corners of his eyebrows may lift, which contradicts the message he's trying to pass across.

Chapter 12: Why Analyze People?

We're inherently curious about why others think and feel the way they do. If a friend behaves unusually, we are quick to develop theories about the motivations and intentions behind their bizarre actions. Some people even pride themselves on being an excellent judge of character. Unluckily, we tend to rely merely on our past experiences and intuition when analyzing people, leading to inappropriate assumptions. There's a need to have a more precise way of interpreting the meaning behind the changes in a person's physiology. Learning the basics of analyzing what a person's body language says about their emotional state holds several benefits:

Control Social Situations

Humans are social beings, and there's no way around it. We instinctively crave for community and connection. Learning how to analyze others will enable you to understand them better on a deeper level. We are constantly broadcasting our identity through the way we present ourselves publicly. For instance, the clothes we wear can say a lot about how we would like others to view us. Underneath these superficial qualities,  there's also sub-communicated information about our identity without our conscious awareness. For example, how we dress may express how insecure we are about ourselves because we're trying to cover up our personality's imperfections.

When you begin analyzing people, you'll notice that you start to uncover more interesting and more revealing information about others that's chiefly responsible for how they behave and feel. Possessing the ability to observe and interpret social cues will also better equip you to handle all interactions with tact and diplomacy. As you incorporate these tips and techniques, your relationships, both professional and personal, will flourish as you deepen your understanding of the universal language of humans that is body language.

As of late, there's been an epidemic of self-proclaimed socially awkward people in the last decade. The current era of Facebook, text messaging, and Snapchat has shaped how an entire generation has developed socially. That's not to say that they have been stunted in their social development. Communicating through these new mediums is the quickest, most convenient way to express ourselves. However, when we communicate through these new mediums that solely rely on words, we lose the non-verbal aspects of communication. Also, unlike with non-verbal communication, we can easily lie with our words.

Even in this digital age of shopping for groceries on Amazon, some activities require us to have face-to-face interactions. In a world filled with people who are more accustomed to typing or texting behind a screen, learning how to analyze body language would give you a huge advantage in social situations. So, until absolutely everything can be accomplished from the comfort of your home without speaking to another human being, it's an excellent investment to work on your social intelligence.

Increase Emotional Intelligence

After learning how to read the body language of the people around you, you'll naturally begin to become more self-conscious. It can be quite overwhelming to comprehend how the smallest of actions can expose how we feel at any given moment. This idea that people are equipped with the ability to read anyone's minds just by looking at them practically would make anyone feel extremely vulnerable.

The perfect course of action would be to take measures to control our body's physiology to convey to others how we want to be perceived. This requires us to be self-aware enough to know when we're sliding back into our default body language and then modifying it to portray ourselves the way we would like to be portrayed. You'll begin to recognize that our emotions can be influenced by how we position our bodies. The idea of deliberately placing ourselves in socially dominant stances to feel more self-confident has become a popular theory in the last decade.

Stances such as "The Wonder Woman," which require one to spread their feet a little wider than shoulder-width apart and place their hands on their hips, can make a person feel just as powerful and confident Amazonian heroine herself. When we modify the way we stand, we are proactive in managing our emotions. The truth is, so many of us allow our emotions to control our lives that we forget that we have emotions and that we are not our emotions.

By changing how we feel internally, it can transform our thoughts, beliefs, and behavior. To produce lasting changes, manipulating your body language as an emotional management technique requires diligence and practice, especially to turn this skill into a habit. At first, it'll take an overwhelming amount of effort to monitor our emotions since we haven't been conditioned to manage them. One way to accelerate this process is to integrate it into our social life to the point where it becomes our natural way of reacting to the world. It's easy to regulate your emotions when you're alone. It's much more challenging to practice this in the company of your friends and family.

Sometimes, our friends and family may say or do things that we don't agree with. It's not our responsibility to change these things about them, but we are always responsible for emotionally reacting to them. If you keep tabs on your feelings at any given moment and dissociate yourself from them in the toughest of scenarios, you'll make smarter decisions and take more deliberate action.

Spotting Deception

Everybody lies; the question is, how can we recognize when people lie before we suffer the consequences of their dishonesty? The ability to read people and figure out when they're lying is like a superpower that you can have. All it takes is to learn what to look out for in a person's body language and hone your observation skills, so you notice the signs every time they occur. The majority of the population is not aware that their dishonesty can be broadcasted publicly by their bodies. However skilled you may be at lying, it takes a lot of work for the brain to lie. We essentially need to hold on to two realities in our head, the reality of truth, and the reality we've conjured with our lies. It reaches a point where the brain is too preoccupied to ensure that the body's

469

communication is in agreement with your lie, so it carelessly places your body on autopilot. Your body acts as an inadvertent tattletale when you lie while trying to ensure nobody knows that you're lying.

An illustration of this is when somebody is unable to maintain eye contact. When a person displays this behavior, there's a slight possibility that they are not telling the truth. This is the body's way of protecting itself from those who can potentially "punish" the individual if they're caught lying. If the eyes are the windows to the soul, constantly breaking eye contact suggests that your soul has something to hide. Sometimes, the body fails to suppress certain behavioral tics that indicate that what you're saying may not be in harmony with the truth. For example, if your coworker compliments the way you've dressed for work, but the facial muscles used for frowning slightly twitch, this may indicate that they are disingenuous with their compliment.

This sample brings up whether every lie is "sinister" and if you should expose every attempt at deceit you encounter. Would it be so terrible to go about your day believing that someone expressed a positive interest in the way you dress? Not at all! Some may prefer to live a life of blissful ignorance and wouldn't prefer to peek behind the curtain for fear that they'll regret learning the truth.

Chapter 13: Analyzing People via Their Verbal Statements

Our analysis and observation skills would be incomplete and inefficient if we ignore the significance of verbal statements. Verbal statements hold a myriad of keys into the doorways of our personalities, intentions, and emotions.

You can glean a lot from the words that you hear. Analyzing people through their verbal statements requires less effort and astuteness than that of nonverbal behaviors. We will take an in-depth look at how our words reveal our intentions, emotions, and personalities. I will include common speech clues you will come across in your daily interactions with those around you. Let's delve into this significant aspect of communication.

Understanding the Relationship between Words, Behavior, and Personality

Everything you do (nonverbal) or say (verbal) speaks volumes about your personality. When you become adept at analyzing people, you will realize that there's a synergy between our actions, thoughts, and beliefs and that each aligns to provide a full picture about who we are. Even though it seems insignificant compared to body languages, the words you use can tell a great deal about your desires, strengths, insecurities, and emotions.

How Words Reveal Your Personality

"Hey! Did you get taller overnight?" At first glance, this statement looks like a friendly banter, and it reveals no negative vibe. Now, if you look at the statement from another perception, you will realize that it allows us to glimpse the speaker's mind. In this context, the speaker cares a lot about the height difference. How did we know that?

If you think about snakes all day because you are scared of them, then you might easily confuse a skink for a snake.

In other words, we notice the things we care about. When you observe the friendly banter, you will realize that the person may be concerned about his height. This concern helped him to notice the height difference of his friend.

This statement could also stem from the speaker's insecurity about his height. Remember, when it comes to analyzing verbal statement, you need to consider the various factors at play, including watching the body language. In totality, both aspects of communication—verbal and nonverbal—are incomplete without the other.

Learn to Unclothe the Veil around Jokes

Two teenagers went to a restaurant. When the waiter came around to take their orders, one of the kids jokingly replied, "I want anything that costs a million dollars." To a casual observer, it is a normal and bland banter. To an astute observer, this kid is worried about money. Perhaps his family might be passing through some kind of financial crisis, or his parents and loved ones might have taught him the importance of money.

There's always a hidden message in every joke. Therefore, learning to analyze these jokes will give you a glimpse into the speaker's deepest desires and personality. You should know that the words people use have a deep meaning, irrespective of how well-crafted they are. A person might tell a joke to you without realizing he is revealing much more about his intentions. That is why it's easy to analyze those who make hurtful jokes to demean you.

Before we move to the next section, here's some advice: Never analyze a single phrase on its own. To not get incorrect results, try to observe the whole sentence, how the speech is conveyed, and the accompanying body language.

As a side note since we are talking about jokes, do you know the best sign that someone is intelligent? Humor. If you're looking to make connections with the smartest person in the room, find the one who makes others laugh the most.

Stories Are Powerful

It is easy to recognize a biased story, either verbally or in written form. You can effectively glimpse into the storyteller's psyche by listening to him or by reading his work. Here's an example for us to dissect:

From subject A's point of view: Last night, I was walking down a lonely street with my friends, and a large and muscular dark man appeared out of the neighboring bush and seemed to come toward us to attack. But he changed his mind in the last second and walked past us.

From subject B's point of view: Late in the evening, I took a stroll when I misplaced my keys in the nearby bush. It was already getting dark when I noticed I didn't have my keys on me. Time wasn't on my side since I needed to get home quickly to prepare for my date, so I searched and searched through the shrubs until I felt the keys. I jumped out onto the street in excitement and started running home. In my excitement, I nearly bumped into a group of frightened teenagers.

Both stories gave us different alert about the incident. The first point of view was from a teenager who didn't see the look of excitement on man's face. Rather, he emphasized the words huge, large, and dark. So why did he emphasize the physical attributes of the man who jumped out of the bush? Well, it's because that's the part that concerns him the most. He was scared because of the man's sudden appearance and physical size, which had a huge impact on the story. We have a full and clearer picture when you take a look at the other man's point of view, and that is the power of perception in stories.

So, when someone tells you a story, I want you to dissect the story and note the emphasized points of the story. By doing this, you will know how to analyze people effectively.

An Insight into How the Brain Process Words

There's something we have all come to agree on: the human brain is very efficient. We only use verbs and nouns when we think.

For instance, "I walked" or "I jumped." Adjectives, adverbs, and other speech parts are added during the latter phase of converting thoughts into written language or spoken words. The words that we add at this stage provide an insight into who we are and what we are thinking.

The basic and simple sentence consists of only a subject and a verb. For example, the verbal statement "I walked" consists of only the pronoun I (subject) and the verb's object. Any other word added to this basic sentence only modifies the verb's action or the quality of the noun. These deliberate additions or modifications provide insight into the writer or speaker's behavioral characteristics and personality.

Word clues help us to make behavioral guesses or develop hypotheses regarding the personality of others. Take a look at the verbal statement "I quickly walked." The word clue in this sentence is quickly since it serves as a modification of the verb walked. This word clue infused a sense of urgency in the statement, but it did not explain why. An individual can "quickly walk" because of the urgency of an appointment.

People who utilize this phrase are regarded as meticulous. Meticulous people are reliable and hate being late for an appointment since they respect societal norms and want to live up to expectations. These set of individuals will also make good employees since they don't want to disappoint their employees.

Conversely, you can also quickly walk when in a dark and lonely area with a bad reputation. Bad weather could also be the reason that you quickly walk.

In summary, people might make use of the word clue quickly walk for a variety of reasons. It's important to always read verbal statements about the circumstance surrounding the speaker or writer.

Word Clues You Need to Know

"I Labored Hard to Accomplish My Dreams"

The clue in this sentence is labored hard, and it shows that the person's dreams were difficult to accomplish. Perhaps it took him longer and harder to accomplish this particular dream than the other goals he has accomplished. When we delve deeper, you will discover that the word clue labored suggests the person holds the belief that dedication and hard work can produce great result.

"I Bagged Another Contract"

The word clue is another, and it reveals that the speaker or writer has won so many contracts and this is just the latest accomplishment. You can deduce that the speaker wants everyone who cared to listen to know that he won so many awards from the above sentence. He is trying to bolster his self-image by appearing successful. To an astute observer, this person seems self-conscious about what others think. More so, he needs the admiration of others to boost his self-esteem. Others who noticed this character weakness might try to exploit it for their gains.

"Jim and I Remained Friends"

The word clue in this sentence is remained. From the sentence, you can deduce that the speaker and Jim have gone through trying times. Perhaps the fabric of their friendship has gone through different difficult situations. They probably weren't supposed to be friends under normal circumstances. The speaker is trying to defend why she remained friend with Jim. The speaker doesn't feel convinced about her choice and, therefore, feels the need to defend her decision.

"I Patiently Sat Through the Meeting"

Here, the word clue patiently holds a plethora of hypotheses. For instance, the speaker might be bored with the lecture but felt obligated to sit through it for various reasons. Perhaps the speaker had to use the restroom but felt self-conscious or trapped from standing up to go the restroom. You could also deduce from the statement that she might have had an urgent appointment somewhere else.

Gauging from this statement, we can accurately say the speaker is someone who adheres to social etiquette and norms, irrespective of other pressing needs. Those with no social boundaries would have left the lecture to attend any other issue requiring their attention. People with social boundaries like the speaker would make good employees since they know how to follow the rules and respect authority.

Conversely, those who leave during the lecture to attend to other pressing needs are perfect candidates for jobs that require out-of-the-box thinking.

"I Decided to Buy That Dress"

The modifier or world clue here is decided. It indicates that the speaker weighed several options before settling for that particular dress. This statement shows us that the speaker is not impulsive. Rather, she weighs her options and takes the most logical step. More so, there's a high chance our speaker is an introvert since introverts tend to weigh their options before taking a step.

It's not a sure analysis, but a hypothesis about the speaker's personality. Conversely, an impulsive person would say, "I just bought that dress." The word clue just represents an impulsive decision.

Chapter 14: How to Analyze Yourself

Through self-awareness, you gain an understanding of yourself and your personality. You can also get to know your behaviors and tendencies. Part of this process is coming to accept the unsightly corners of your mind that you would rather keep locked away. It is through embracing our whole being (even the darkness) that we can achieve true contentment. Some strategies listed below will allow you to take a closer look at the person you have become.

Be Aware of Your Feelings

Notice Your Thoughts

Your thoughts are essential in defining who you are. They will assist in guiding how you feel and your attitude and perceptions of situations. You should keep in touch with your mind. You need to be able to tell whether they are harmful if you are pinning yourself down, or within which areas you are hard on yourself? This reflection to encompass all of your perceptions, even the ones that need to change.

Keep a Journal

Keeping a journal can be a wonderful way to stay in tune with your patterns. Emotions and reactions will be documented. You can review the pages to gain an objective perspective on your values and consistency.

Be Conscious of Your Perceptions

Your perceptions can lead you astray, making you to come up with wrong conclusions about what occurred or what you saw. For instance, you can blame yourself that your friend was mad at you during lunch break; thus, you will think that you did something wrong. When you are conscious of your interpretation of her mood, this can assist you in knowing why you concluded that she is mad at you.

You are supposed to take your time to study your moves and beliefs about what happened with such situations. Write down what you saw, heard, or had feelings about that made you understand the situation the way you did. You must be able to get answers about what made your friend moody, and if there are any outside reasons, you should be aware of it.

Identify Your Feelings

The feelings you have will readily tell you the person you are, from how you react to situations you have at hand and the people around you. You are supposed to analyze your feelings and how you respond to different topics, interactions, tonal variations, facial appearances, and body language.

You should be able to tell why you have certain feelings and why you experienced such emotional responses. You should understand what you are responding to, and what directed you to make such choices. You are allowed to use physical cues to assist you in understanding how you feel.

Scrutinizing Your Values

Know Your Values

When you are aware of what you value, this can give you an overview of who you are at your core. Many of your beliefs are based on your individual experiences. They will change, the more you get to know about yourself. You may find it very difficult to identify your values at times. The concept can be intangible and unclear.

Identify Your Values

Values are the beliefs that you remain loyal to. They are usually based on morality. There are some things that you believe that others may not agree with. One of your core values may be to never steal. This is an idea you have thrown meaning behind, and you hold to this sentiment even when theft would benefit you in a significant way.

Your values describe the type of person you are. The caliber of friend or partner you are (to someone else) may be based upon these ideals, which you consider important. Defining unmoving moral mission statements can take some work! Imagine knowing off-hand, every aspect of yourself that you consider to be worthwhile. Most people aren't able to do this.

Start identifying your values by inscribing answers to questions like:

- Think two people you admire, what qualities do they have that make you admire them? What particular thing do they believe to make you admire them?

- Think of the person you hope to be in the future and write down all the positive aspects of their character.

- What are you passionate about?

- What good thing have you done, even when it would have been easier to walk away or take advantage?

Plan Your Core Values

When you have answered the above questions, you should have an idea of the qualities that you consider important. Writing these values down will allow you to create a map. Pick one or two of these at a time, and form a plan for being the sort of person who better embodies these beliefs. You have always been completely in control of the person you are. It can be so easy to forget that we are steering this vessel. Our daily grind can fog up the lens of our abilities. YOU decide all of the things that you wish to embody.

Do you look up to brave people? Right this moment, plan an activity that places you outside of your comfort zone. Do you want to be charitable? Call that homeless shelter, right this instant, and offer your services. You are being the steering wheel. You can be as cool, well-red, honest, or kind as you want to be.

Discover Yourself

Write Your Story

Writing down your story can be both fun and rewarding. This is your chance to document the events that changed you and the beliefs that you hold dear. Not only is this a brilliant way to pass the time, but it can also allow you to look back on your life, like a spectator. Can you imagine the feeling of accomplishment that will come from completing a project of this nature?

Evaluate Your Story

After writing down your story, you should be able to evaluate yourself by asking yourself questions like:

· What are some of the themes that recur in your narrative? Are you always saving people or you are the one who is always saved? Is your story based on a topic? Is it a love story, drama, comedy, or some other genre?

- What is the title of your story?

- What are the chapters your story is divided into?

- Have you labeled yourself and others in the story?

- What kind of words are you using to talk about yourself and the others? Are you using positive language?

Resolve What Your Analysis Means

You have to decide what your story means after writing it down. What is interesting about authoring your account, for review, will be referred to as narrative therapy. It will highlight your moments in life when you felt essential or worthy. It will also show you how you see yourself and the path of your life up to where you are.

For instance, you can tell your story as if it were a drama, due to a feeling that your life is dramatic and very intense. If it was written as a comedy, then you will think that your experience has been full of fun up to where you are. Or maybe it feels like a cosmic joke? A love story could indicate that you are a romantic.

Put it in Your Mind That it Takes Time

You can follow all the steps, but you still have to remember that it will need to take time. You should be aware that its vital to analyze yourself and put your ideas into action. The person you are will change in the days to come.

Track Your Sleeping

When you lack sleep, exhaustion will have some negative impacts on your body. This can encourage stress. You should be able to look at the hours you spend sleeping every night. Amount of sleep needed for an individual varies. This can result in your anxiety levels getting higher than they should be. When you don't sleep:

- You will think and learn slowly.

- There will be an increase in accidents.

- A lot of health challenges will be experienced.

- Increase in depression and forgetfulness.

- Lower libido.

- You will age faster.

- Weight will fluctuate.

- You will have impaired judgment.

You should have a list of things to help you to enhance your overall life experience. This will aid you in a thoughtful self-analysis. Brainstorm ways to promote growth. You should always see yourself evolving and changing based on your ambitions and life experiences.

It's extraordinarily vital to take your time and engage in self-analysis. This will assist you in changing into the person that you are meant to be. You can live by your values. You can make the rules and steer yourself toward realizing your goals.

Chapter 15: Judging by the Cover

We've all been fed on the belief that judging a book by its cover is not the right way to do it. However, in a time and attention pressed world, where we rarely have the time to read people comprehensively, we seldom have an option but to analyze and speed people to make quick decisions. Reading a book by its cover or speed-reading people may not be such a bad thing today. People's outer appearances can often help you make solid and reliable conclusions about their personality. The subconscious visual that you form about an individual through their appearance is often accurate.

I know plenty of psychologists who believe that making snap judgments about people based on their appearances is an extremely narrow way of looking at it. However, the way a person treats themselves just as he/she treats his/her immediate environment can reveal a lot about their inherent personality. It can help you gain a deeper understanding of their personality to make communication even more meaningful.

The way a person dresses or maintains their outer appearance can reveal a lot about their internal feelings. Their exterior can often be a near accurate indicator of their thoughts, emotions, and feelings. Ever noticed how you don't bother about how your hair or face looks when you are completely dejected or sad. You don't have the inclination or zest to look good.

Similarly, when you feel more positive and upbeat, you will invest extra effort in looking good and feeling wonderful about yourself. People are well-dresses or sport a neatly-groomed appearance to gain respect or validation from others. They may want people to perceive them in a more positive light. It can also be a sign of high self-confidence, power, and authority. People in positions of power and authority may also be wealthy, which gives them the resources to be expensively dressed and groomed. It can be a sign of influence, power, and confidence. These folks are viewed in a more positive or flattering light by other people.

Here are some tips for reading people through their cover or outer appearance to make a near-accurate analysis of their personality or behavioral characteristics.

Good Influencers and Negotiators

Imagine a scenario where a plain-looking person is selling you something you don't need. He/she is plain looking and not very attractively dressed or groomed. Would you buy from him or her? The person doesn't appear like they are in a commanding or influential position when it comes to negotiations.

Now imagine another scenario where an extremely attractive, well-dressed, and nattily groomed salesperson walks up to you and introduces themselves to you. Again, you don't need what they are selling but you still listen to everything because they are cute-looking, friendly, and speak with oodles of charm. By the end of their sales pitch, you realize that you can use their product.

Attractive and well-groomed people have the power to influence people's decisions, however hollow it may seem. Of course, it isn't simply about wearing good clothes and looking good and ignoring everything else. There is a natural confidence and ease with which these people operate. Other factors such as friendliness, conversational skills, intelligence, and other things matter, too. This should explain why some people invest a bomb in maintaining their wardrobes and appearance.

Introverts and Extroverts

Extroverts thrive on adventure, new experiences, and risks. Their brains process dopamine starkly different than it is processed in a person who is more inward driven or introverted. These thrill-seekers think fast, act faster, and be more impulsive when it comes to decision making. They will move and walk fast, which means they are at a greater risk of injuries.

This can be slightly stretched to conclude that people who have more injury scars or casts have higher chances of being extroverts. Their thrill-seeking disposition and brain make them more prone to accidents and injuries. Yes, these people won't think twice before jumping out of a window to escape an adulterous confrontation.

Similarly, while introverts are more likely to observe your shoes and look at your feet while talking, extroverts will look you directly in the eyes while speaking. Since introverts are more inward driven and reflect upon their options before deciding, they tend to seize/observe people. There is a tendency to look down at a person's feet because of the awkwardness involved in looking away from a person while speaking rather than looking into their eyes. To avoid this uncomfortable situation of looking everywhere around the eyes, introverts will glance at a person's shoes or feet while thinking.

Since extroverts are more outward driven and focused, they will look people in the eyes while talking. There is a tendency to experience rather than think, which means all their efforts are directed towards experiencing or listening to people instead of thinking about what people are talking about. They'll seldom look in different directions (unless they are lying or there's another clear reason for the mismatch in behavior) and will have their eyes firmly fixated on their speaking.

Blue eyes and light, blonde hair has almost always been closely linked with introversion. However, there isn't a conclusive study to support this view. More than anything, it is a popularly peddled media notion that is completely supported by the Hollywood and Disney brigade.

There is a definite bias towards light eyes and hair each time a character has to be represented as an introvert. Ariel, Belle, and Hercules are all Disney characters who've been portrayed as introverts with light hair and eyes. Today, you can't go about judging people's personalities through the color of their eyes or hair because people are dying their hair and changing colored contact lenses faster than you can say personality.

Reading People through Their Clothes

How a person dresses reveals a lot about their personality. Neatly dressed and groomed people may have an inherent need to be respected and accepted within their social group. They may have a deep need to fit in or be validated by others. At times, dressing excessively well or paying too much attention to one's appearance can sign narcissism or self-obsession. The person may also be suffering from a deeply-rooted inferiority complex or low self-esteem that they are trying to compensate for by dressing well.

Sometimes, people who pay too much attention to their grooming and appearance may believe that they aren't good enough for anything and may use their looks to cover up for the perceived inadequacies in their life.

One of my friends could never match up to her older sibling when it came to intelligence, social skills, and talent. While the parents lavishly praised her older sister for being an intelligent and talented student, she (the younger sibling) wasn't believed to be striking or extraordinary in anything. She believed she wasn't good at anything throughout her growing up years and sought constant validation from people through her looks and clothes. She became obsessed with her appearance and spent huge sums of money on grooming, beauty products, beauty treatments, and makeovers.

Thus, an excessive need to look good and dress well can also be a clue to an inferiority complex marked personality. Know more about a person before you make snap judgments about their outer appearance. However, appearance and other nonverbal clues can offer you plenty of insights about an individual's subconscious thoughts, feelings, and preferences.

Chapter 16: Is Someone Uncomfortable Around Me?

One thing that we need to take a look at when we are analyzing someone is how comfortable they are with us. If they are comfortable, their stance is going to be more relaxed. They will offer us more information about themselves; have more open expressions, and so much more.

But when someone is feeling uncomfortable with you, this will spell out some trouble for you as well. This is going to make it harder for you to talk with them. They may even inch away from you in the hopes of ending the conversation before you have a chance to get to know them.

So, one of the first things you need to explore is whether someone is comfortable or uncomfortable around you. As soon as you notice that someone is uncomfortable with the situation or with you in particular, you can start to take the proper steps to get them at ease and feeling better.

Now, how do you make sure that you can meet up with someone and ensure that they are as comfortable with you as possible? Some of the signs that you should watch out to tell if someone is uncomfortable with you or in that situation will include the following:

The Flinch or Wince

When we find ourselves in an awkward situation, it is never fun, and it is going to cause people to wince literally. When someone feels uncomfortable, but they don't want to let others know, they may wince or flinch a bit. This is going to be a quick contraction of the torso away from you. And the wince is going to be like they stubbed their toe, or got a paper cut. They often don't realize they are doing it or don't want you to know about it because they are polite. But, if you do pick up on this with the other person, take note of what is causing that reaction.

They Back Away from You

When someone feels uncomfortable, they may take a step back from you without realizing what they are doing. If they aren't able to move away from you or the situation, they will see how much they can close themselves. This can include turning away, crossing the arms and legs, and retreating in the torso.

This process is known as blocking body language. This is something we can do without thinking about it as a way to protect ourselves. Suppose you are with another person and notice that they are doing these actions. In that case, it may be a good idea to respect their personal space (remember that each person has a different idea of what their own space is and how large it is), consider taking a step back, and allow them the space they need to get comfortable.

Their Words and Gestures Get Faster

Any time you are around another person who does not feel that comfortable, they may have a sense of fight or flight. And in this situation, they are going to start moving their arms wildly. And in some cases, they are going to start talking faster. This is because the person feels that their breath and the beat of their heart goes faster. When this happens, it will include their speech and gestures accelerating because it allows them to get the conversation done with.

Their Laughter Is Nervous

Nervous laughter is another thing that we need to take a look for when trying to figure out how comfortable someone is around us. We have all heard the difference between real laughter and nervous laughter. This nervous laughter is often going to erupt, and it is a way for us to release some of the tension found inside. This is why they may giggle or laugh at things that would seem odd to another person.

The Tone of Their Voice Changes

One of the first things that we will notice when we are talking to someone nervous around us is the tone of their voice. We can notice this if we know the person from before, and we know what the usual tone of their voice is, but we can also see this with someone we have never talked to in the past.

When someone is nervous, it is sometimes going to appear in a loud and squeaky voice. This is because we have an increased amount of stress because of that situation. The voice is often going to rise in pitch, and it will sound shriller than before. As the stress rises in the individual, the tension will rise, causing some issues with the vocal cords.

They Have Trouble Maintaining Their Eye Contact

If someone is comfortable with you and doesn't mind spending some time talking with you, they will have no problem talking to you and maintaining good eye contact. But when someone keeps looking at their watch, glancing over their shoulder, or seeming like they can look everywhere besides at you, this is a good sign that they are not enjoying the conversation.

This one often needs a few more signs to go along with it. It could mean that they are not interested in the conversation. It could mean that you are dominating the situation and the conversation, or it could mean that there is something with you or the conversation or the situation around you that makes the person feel uncomfortable.

When this does happen, it is an excellent time to pause and take a break from the conversation. You can stop talking and then ask the other person what they think or what views they hold on the subject. Then, give them some time to talk to you without interrupting. The answer that they provide will help you know if this is a conversation that the person is interested in continuing or something you need to stop and move on with.

The Answers They Give Are Only One or Two Words Long

If someone is comfortable with you and is enjoying the conversation, then their words are just going to flow out of them. This is true even if you and the other person have just met each other. But, if you get into a conversation with someone and you find that they are only giving one-word answers, then this is a sign that they aren't interested in the conversation, that they are distracted, or that they are shy and don't know how to make the conversation go more.

This may take a bit more work to get the person to open up and talk with you a bit more. If the person is shy, you need to change your tactics to get them to be more comfortable and open up a little more. For example, make sure that you show interest in them, and see if it helps only ask questions that need a more detailed answer, rather than ones that can be answered with yes or no.

Their Ears Get Red, Or They Scratch Their Nose

These are signs that someone is not that comfortable in the situation, but they are more subtle signs that are easy to miss out on or assume are not that important at all. When these shows up though, you know for sure that the other person is not feeling at ease in the situation and that you need to approach them differently.

If you are talking to someone who seems to blush when they feel embarrassed or nervous, you already have a good idea that having a red face is a big sign of someone not being comfortable with the situation. But some people are going to blush in a less obvious manner. This means that you need to watch out for places other than the face that starts to red. You want to watch the ears in particular because this is an early sign that the other person feels out of place.

In addition to watching the color of the ears of the other person you are talking to, it is also a good idea to watch the other person and how often they are scratching their nose. If they only do this once in the whole conversation, then this is not a big deal. But if you see them doing this all of the time, then this is a good sign that they are feeling nervous, and that you may need to lighten up the conversation and help them feel more at ease.

One thing that a lot of people don't realize is that an increased amount of blood flow to the face is going to cause the nose to feel itchy. The nose is going to have a ton of blood vessels in it. And when we are under stress, which can happen when we feel nervous or like we don't belong, the flow of the blood can increase, and a lot of that will end up in the blood vessels of the nose. This causes it to itch and can be a sign that there is some uneasiness going on.

As you can see from this, along with some of the other topics that we will explore in this guide, body language will do a lot to tell us what the other person thinks and how they are feeling. It even helps us to know if someone is feeling a bit uncomfortable around us or not.

If you find that you are the one who is the source, although sometimes, it could be another person, the situation, or something else, then you may find that giving someone a bit of space and offering up a quick apology for it can help them to relax. Saying something like, "I'm sorry if I'm a bit much. I get onto a topic and get so excited that I overdo it. I would love to hear your opinion on XYZ!" This helps to let the other person know that you are not trying to make them feel uncomfortable, and can get things back on track for you.

Chapter 17: Lies

Do you know that you are lied to more than ten times a day by the people who are close to you? When people lie, they make something that is not true and seem to be the naked truth.

Everyone looks at lying as a bad habit, but this does not stop them from lying. The lies start when we are still kids, and it goes on into adulthood. The sad thing is that when lying goes beyond the boundaries, it becomes a destructive habit to many people. Let us start by looking at the different types of lies.

Types of Lies

White Lie

White lies are more of an excuse not to do something and are told with the intention of font spoiling your relationship.

However, telling white lie after white lie will lead to conflict later when the person realizes that you have been lying to them. You will end up losing credibility in front of the family and friends.

Broken Promise

When you promise someone something, you need to go ahead and fulfill it. Broken promises refer to a commitment that you fail to a jeep. If you did not have the intention to fulfill the promise, you end up making things worse.

Fabrication

Fabricating something is telling someone something, which you do not know for sure if it is true. You just come up with something then you say it. When you spread a rumor, you will be like stealing another person's reputation.

Bold-faced Lie

This is a lie that you tell, and everyone knows that it is a lie. The signs will be there that you tell a lie, but since you know, it is a bold one; you just say it while maintaining a straight face.

Now that you know what types of lies are there, the next thing you need to know is why people lie in the first place.

Why Do People Lie?

Fear

People lie because they are afraid of the consequences of the truth. They will tell a lie because they know that they have done something that you do not like. So, they try to cover up the crime so that you do not get to know what they did.

Manipulation

A person will tell you lie so that they can manipulate the truth. The lie is motivated by the desire to get someone to say something or to do it, or to make a decision that will favor the liar in one way or another. Many people lie to get something, such as money, sex, status, or power.

Pride

In many instances, the person will lie because they are too proud. They use the line as a way to display a favorable image. They will exaggerate so much that you will not know what is true.

Why Is Lying such a Big Deal?

Why is it that we focus on lying so much? The truth is that when you lie, you change so many aspects of yourself for someone else. Let us look at the disadvantages of lying.

Lying Can Affect Your Health

People that lie have to keep the guilt for a very long time. They will keep unpleasant secrets that can even lead to health complications.

You Will Live a Stressful Life

People that lie get to release stress hormones.

It Makes You Lonely

When you lie, people tend to alienate you because they cannot trust you. You will face the punishment that people will not believe you, and you will not believe anyone. When people alienate you, you end up having no one to share with.

It Becomes a Habit

When you lie, you will make it a routine such that even the things that do not need you to lie end up being lines in themselves.

You Have to Remember a Lot

When you lie, you have to think of what you said about the lie, how you said it, and how you said it. If you have many lies, you will find it a huge bid on you, and it might cause a lot of unnecessary stress. By the time, you start remembering what you said and how you said it, you will be open showing that it was a blatant lie.

You Become Unreliable

When you lie, people will take you the way you present yourself – as a liar. Even your partner and other people close to you will not believe in you and will not trust you at all.

Chapter 18: Speed Reading

Speed reading is one of the most popular and powerful methods used to identify differences in people. It is used to gain an in-depth understanding of people types and how this affects their behavior.

Speed reading utilizes several proven techniques to help you understand other people's motivations and emotions so that you can customize your approach to them for a more effective impact. In simple terms, speed-reading refers to the ability to read other people quickly and using this to influence their decisions and abilities. Speed-reading involves reading a person's body language signals. The difference between this and other types of people reading is that speed-reading does not involve the study of hundreds of nonverbal signals. Instead, the reader uses some form of intuition to gain information about others.

To be effective in speed-reading, it is advised that you focus on big signals, not the small ones. This technique involves concentrating on the other person and knowing when to trigger a conversation with them. These conversations will sometimes go well but flop at other times. As you converse with people, you must be quick enough to grasp some of your mind's evident signals to process.

The essence of speed-reading is to eliminate the struggle people go through to capture every signal sent by others. When you spend a lot of time trying to process these signals, the conversation may end as soon as it begins. It is not easy to be talking to someone while your mind is busy processing every kind of movement that the person makes. Doing this eliminates the possibility of identifying exactly what the person is thinking or feeling. To keep it simple, try applying the technique of speed-reading. Focus on the big movements and ignore the small ones.

For instance, a person who is bored with the conversation will always withdraw eye contact or turn to face the opposite direction. Smiling or nodding of the head automatically shows you that the person is happy. When it comes to speed reading, you should not waste your time trying to unlock the meaning of things you do not understand. When you do this, you may end up with the wrong interpretation of the person, resulting in the wrong judgment.

Speed Reading and the Law of Reverse Effect

Speed-reading is something that is done by the subconscious mind. Forcing your conscious mind to perform this duty results in what is known as the law of reverse effect. When looking for information to read from the other person, you may once in a while overthink some signals and start processing them beyond the subconscious mind. This can make you appear too distant from the conversation. The best way to avoid this is by allowing your unconscious mind to do all the processing. Trust your intuitions and gut instincts. This will help you to understand some signals without having to think deeply about their meaning.

Instincts are derived from real science. It is believed that some of the hollow organs of the body, like intestines, contain nerves that act as a secondary brain that transmits signals to the main brain. This is why a person's intuition is often referred to as his 'gut instincts.' Intuition is a way of the mind indicating that it already has received some information about the situation at hand.

Another most important aspect of speed-reading is the ability to remain calm during times of discomfort. This is one of the easiest ways that boost your ability to speed read other people. When you are at peace, it is easier to relax during weird circumstances, and this means that you will be able to handle any tension that arises when things get tough. One way to achieve this is through mindful breathing. You can do this by concentrating on certain simple exercises that help you slowly breathe in via your nose and breathe out through the mouth. This helps you to relax your panic muscles as you continue to read others.

Speed Reading and Receptiveness

Some people often try as much as possible not to send any non-verbal signals to others. Most salespeople and those whose roles involve negotiation often do this. You can get these people to reveal their true thoughts and feeling by doing something they least expect from you. This will cause them to be distracted, and as a result, they will display some genuine reactions. For instance, you can tease them in a friendly manner, or ask rhetorical questions that will stir their emotions at once.

You may also decide to use what is known as provocative therapy. This involves an act of trying to convince them otherwise or by bluffing them. This will confuse the person who will then reveal his true identity. Practicing these strategies while remaining focused can help you grow faster to become an expert in speed-reading.

Several guidelines apply when it comes to speed-reading; these are:

- Adopting the best approach – just like we said earlier, do not get distracted trying to read every signal sent your way. Also, you should avoid thinking ahead of what is happening at the moment. The process of speed-reading involves specifying exactly what you want to know from a person and concentrating on it.

- Monitor your Eye Movement – control the way you move your eyes. This is because the other person may also be skilled in seed reading and therefore, they might get the wrong signal just by observing your eye movement

- Maintain a certain pattern – speed-reading needs a sense of pattern or rhythm. Assess the person one trait or signal at a time. You may make a pre-list of the things you wish to find out and use this list to analyze the person. Avoid revisiting old signals and concentrate on learning something new, unless if it is necessary

- Process ideas, not words – when interacting with others, do not focus more on the words but the words' signals. The faster you read someone, the better for you since some people tend to hide their real emotions as the conversation continues. Seek knowledge about some of the signals that other people send. This will speed up the process of visualizing meaning from other people's reactions. As a result, reading sessions will be made shorter and more effective.

- Suppress your bad habits – human behavior is made of a collection of habits. It is ideal that when speed reading, you identify some of the bad habits you have and slowly work on minimizing them.

Speed-reading other people have a good number of benefits. One of them is that the technique trains your mind to become more focused, thus improving its processing capacity and capability. It also gives you a better understanding of others, and this influences how you treat them in the future. Speed-reading always flexes the brain and exercises brain muscles. This translates to better memory retention, and as a result, you will be able to become more alert during speed-reading sessions.

As you speed-read others, you may identify some information and traits that will improve your personality. Once you master the art of speed-reading, you will always appear more confident when with your peers, who will also see you as an emotionally intelligent person. You may also identify several new opportunities as you speed-read people. This is because most of them will trust your abilities and may recommend some good opportunities. Your ability to grasp things quickly will always act as a plus, and you will easily assimilate data, which you can use to innovate new strategies and ideas. Once you master the art of speed-reading, your confidence may pave the way for leadership positions, and this will result in better earnings in terms of salaries and allowances.

In conclusion, learning how to speed read requires a lot of patience. You must be a person that grasps processes and information easily. Even without a real speed reading session, you must be able to practice this technique frequently to become better at it.

Chapter 19: Cold Reading

Cold reading is known to be a con artist's best friend. It provides the illusion of mind reading and magical abilities without the use of actual supernatural power. It is often used by those who make a living through fortune-telling and psychic acts. Many people have been completely sold on the act. It is usually performed by someone who excels in reading others, has acquired enough general knowledge, and has practiced enough to deliver a very believable performance. However, such an act is only a form of psychology, and you could create this act yourself if you choose to. You would do this by creating the illusion of knowing more than you do through the power of observation. There are different names for the different techniques. How many people are present decides how you should approach it. Shot gunning, for instance, is done in a large room packed with people. This is often the choice of mediums who are creating the illusion of connecting to a passed loved one, because whatever they say, there is likely to be someone who can relate to the statement. When the medium speaks a few, usually vague, phrases, such as "I am connecting to an elderly man... the name John or Jack comes to mind. Does that speak to anyone?" he or she watches for anyone who expresses recognition. Jack and John's names are very common, and many people have lost a grandfather in their time. The medium will then choose one person and watch their face carefully. This is where the true psychology steps in.

Reading body language is essential to keeping up the ruse, as the medium will need to narrow down the descriptions of the audience members loved one. If, for example, the medium says something about a white picket fence, yet no familiarity comes to this person's face, he or she will have to carefully change their tactic. He or she might explain that he never lived within a white picket fence, but wanted to, or that another relative was also present. If the audience member agrees or seems excited, this medium will know they are getting warmer. This act is continued, and even peppered by what are known as rainbow ruses. These are contradictory phrases such as "He was a gentle man; however, he would occasionally display a stern side". Most people have experienced these contradictory moments in their personality; however, the word choice feels so specific that it seems as if it only applies to the supposed spirit the man or woman is referring to.

Another cold reading method, which may be more suitable to a smaller population, is to use previous knowledge when observing someone's behavior. This method is often used in detective dramas, as the act is dramatic and exciting to watch, and the character appears intelligent and clever. It is, however, easier than it may appear, as it only takes keen observation skills. For example, if you meet a new person and notice there is graphite smudged along the side of their left hand, you will know that they are left-handed, as those who are left-hand dominant must drag their hand along the previously written words to continue writing. As a left-hander myself, I would know. This phenomenon, which has been jokingly called "The Silver Surfer Syndrome", is an unquestionable indication that this person is left-handed. You may say so with confidence as you shake their hand. The confident statement will shock this person, and they won't think to look for physical indicators. This can be used as a fun trick to amuse others, or as a shocking factor to carry into a persuasive technique, as those who have recently been surprised don't always think every factor of a decision through.

Cold reading, as any other manipulation tactic, can be used on anyone. And it is. Many people studied in the ways of cold reading have used it as a career, such as psychics, fortune-tellers, and any kind of con artist. Such a complicated set-up is unnecessary to add this skill to your toolbox, as you only need your observation and shock factor. Another example is if you see someone you may already know is a student, you could confidently exclaim that they were studying late and fell asleep on their work as you note the imprint of math work on their left ear. These subtle observations build up over time, and you may gain a reputation with that person. The more you get to know someone, the more background information you will have stored away. For example, say you have a friend named Kyle. Kyle is a single father of an adorable six-year-old girl he spends every moment he can with. To support her, he works at a grueling desk job where he files paperwork all day long and takes rude phone calls. You know that he likes light coffee with a lot of sweetener, and that he is right-handed.

Today, Kyle arrives with a large coffee in his left hand. You two always meet up every Tuesday around ten in the morning. Today, it's almost eleven. In the back of his car is a pink hairbrush. When he gets close enough to greet you, you smell the strong aroma of black coffee rising from his cup, and you can see his clothes are wrinkled. Without asking him, what can you deduce from his situation?

I believe that his boss kept him very late and piled on the work the night prior. He's gotten papercuts before; however, even the light touch of his coffee seems too much pain this time, so he was working as quickly as possible. Even so, he got home late that night and overslept the next morning. Rushing to get her to school, Kyle likely tossed his daughter's hairbrush back to do her best with her hair on their way to school. Due to his exhaustion, he stopped to buy a coffee much stronger than he likes it before meeting with you. What situations you come to find yourselves observing will vary, as will the indicators that you notice.

You can also use cold reading to gather information you don't have, by acting as if you do. For example, if you are a business salesman in a clothing shop who encounters a shy, young girl that is close to the age of high school, you may focus on this observation to begin with. You could state or ask with confidence if she has an event coming up. It doesn't hurt to be aware of large school events nearby, as there may be a dance she wants to prepare for. She may nod or shrug. Either response isn't a no. After, you could press on and ask if she wants to wear something that will catch a certain someone's attention. Because she's shy, she may have difficulty speaking about her feelings to that cute boy from her math class.

Or, she may even want to look nice to feel superior to that girl who bullies her about her looks. Either way, this vague statement will technically be correct. With this much information, you can gather that she'll want to look elegant. Taking a look at her clothes that she currently has on will give you a clue as to her preference with style. If she's wearing long sleeves and baggy pants, she won't feel inclined to reveal something. You can work with this in two ways. You could persuade her to buy the dress with a low back and no sleeves by explaining how confident she'll appear while that yellow brings out the color in her eyes, or you could take the safer approach and find her a nice dress with long sleeves and a high neckline. This whole time, the girl never told you what she wanted or why she needed a dress, but you learned enough to make the sale anyway.

Cold reading isn't only useful in sales clerk settings and parlor tricks. You can also use it to gain a favor, shock someone into doing as you wish, and learning enough about another person to use to your advantage.

Chapter 20: How to Spot Insecurity

When someone is behaving irrationally, you have to remind yourself that this could be because they are acting out of a certain emotion. It could also be because their insecurity is behind this false sense of bravado. When you notice this, you will more likely procure a sense of empathy for these people who act arrogantly or rudely because what they are trying to do is covering their insecurity.

Their insecurity can be about anything—looks, power, money, smartness, getting better grades, and so on—and most of these insecurities creep out from a sense of material value. Sometimes, insecurity can be justified—but most of the time, it is not. Insecurity manifests differently, and it can range from the inability to accept that they've done a great job or accept a compliment to as far as not wanting to wear a swimsuit to the beach.

Factors Determining Good and Bad

None of these traits helps us to behave virtuously. There is a fine line between being insecure and being a brat. Here are some identifying factors that can help you separate the good and the bad:

1. Self-kindness is not self-judgment.

Compassion towards someone insecure is understanding and being warm to them when they fail, when they suffer or when they feel inadequate. We should not be ignoring these emotions or criticizing. People who have compassion understand that being human comes with imperfections and failing is part of the human experience. There will inevitably be no failure when we attempt something because failure is part of learning and progress. Having compassion is also being kind with yourself when challenged with painful experiences rather than getting angry at everything and anything that falls short of your goals and ideals.

Things cannot be exactly how it should be or supposed to be or how we dream it to be. There will be changes and when we accept this with kindness and sympathy and understanding, we experience greater emotional equanimity.

2. Common humanity and not isolation

It is a common human emotion to feel frustrated especially when things do not go the way we envision them to be. When this happens, frustration is usually accompanied by irrational isolation, making us feel that we are the only person on earth going through this or making dumb mistakes like this. News flash—all humans suffer, all of us go through different kinds of suffering. Compassion involves recognizing that we all suffer and all of us have personal inadequacies. It does not happen to 'me' or 'I' alone.

3. Mindfulness is not over-identification.

Compassion needs us to be balanced with our approach so that our negative emotions are neither exaggerated nor suppressed. This balancing act comes out from the process of relating our personal experiences with that of the suffering of others. This puts the situation we are going through into a larger perspective.

We need to keep mindful awareness to observe our negative thoughts and emotions with clarity and openness. Having a mindful approach is non-judgmental and it is a state of mindful reception that enables us to observe our feelings and thoughts without denying them or suppressing them. There is no way that we can ignore our pain and feel compassion at the same time. By having mindfulness, we also prevent over-identification of our thoughts and feelings.

Discovering Compassion

You're so dumb! You don't belong here loser! Those jeans make you look like a fat cow! You can't sit with us! It's safe to say we've all heard some kind rude, unwanted comments either directly or indirectly aimed at us. Would you talk like this to a friend? Again, the answer is a big no.

Believe it or not, it is a lot easier and natural for us to be kind and nice to people than to be mean and rude to them whether it is a stranger or someone we care about. When someone we care is hurt or is going through a rough time, we console them and say it is ok to fail. We support them when they feel bad about themselves and we comfort them to make them feel better or just to give a shoulder to cry on.

We are all good at being understanding and compassionate and kind to others. How often do we offer this same kindness and compassion to ourselves? Research on self-compassion shows that those who are compassionate are less likely to be anxious, depressed or stressed and more resilient, happy and optimistic. In other words, they have better mental health.

Identifying Someone with Insecurity

When we can identify when a person is acting out of insecurity can enable us to protect ourselves from engaging in a mindless power play and feel insecure ourselves. Insecure people tend to spread their negativity and self-doubt to others as well and here is how you can identify them and decide whether to show compassion or show them the exit:

#1 people who are insecure try to make you feel insecure yourself.

You start questioning your ability and self-worth and this happens when you are around a specific person. This individual can manipulate you and talk about their strengths and how they are good in this and that and in a way try to put you down. They project their insecurities on you.

#2 insecure people need to showcase his or her accomplishments.

Inferiority is at the very core of their behavior and for people like this, compassion to tell them that they are not what they think in their heads is just a waste of your time. They feel insecure and hide it, talk about their accomplishments, not in a good way but constantly brag about their amazing lifestyle, wonderful shoes, huge cars, and elite education. All of this is done to convince themselves that they do have it all and you have none.

#3 people who are insecure drops the "humble brag" far too much.

The humblebrag is essentially a brag that is disguised as a self-derogatory statement. In this social media age, you can see plenty of humblebrags who complain about their first-world problems such as all the travel they need to do or the amount of time they spend watching their kids play and win games or even the person who complains about having a tiny pimple when the rest of their face looks flawless. Social media is ripe with people who are narcissistic and this is not worth your time. Do not feel any less just because someone shows off how much of traveling, they need to do.

#4 people who are insecure frequently complain that things aren't good enough.

They like showing off the high standards that they have and while you may label them as snobs, it might be a harder feeling to shake off because you might be thinking that they are better than you although you know that it is all an act. They proclaim their high standards to assert that they are doing better than everyone else and make you feel less of yourself and miserable. Pay no attention to people like this.

It does make sense that people who have better self-esteem and compassion as if you are happier and optimistic about your future without having to worry about what insecure people have to say. When we continuously criticize ourselves and berate ourselves because we think other people are winning at life, we feel incompetent, worthless, and insecure ourselves, which these people want us to feel. This negativity cycle is vicious and will continue to self-sabotage us, and sometimes, we end up self-harming ourselves.

But when our positive inner voice triumphs and plays the supportive friend's role, we create a sense of safety and accept ourselves enough to see a better and clear vision. We then work towards making the required changes for us to be healthier and happier. But if we do not do this, we are working ourselves towards a downward spiral or chaos, unhappiness, and stress.

Chapter 21: How to Spot Romantic Interest?

 If we had the definite guide to spot a romantic interest, Tinder would go broke. That said, it is not hard to identify the telltale signs if someone is interested in you. Granted that some people are oblivious to it—but if you do focus, you'd come to the realization if that person is indeed romantically interested in you or if they are just being flirtatious.

Usually, that special someone starts with a casual acquaintance, which leads to friendship—and before you know it, you look at this friend in a different light and keep thinking about them. Do they feel the same way you feel? Identifying if someone is interested in you romantically requires the careful and skillful interpretation of signals and actions.

Ways to Figure Out If Someone Is Romantically Interested

Here are 15 ways to figure out if someone is romantically interested in you or if they are just flirting for the thrill of it

#1 Their conversations with you

Conversations, meaningful ones are ways a person shows a deeper interest in you and what you do. Do they keep asking you questions in an attempt to keep the conversation going? Pay attention to the questions they ask because it can tell you if they are genuinely showing interest in the things you do and like. A good and long conversation about your likes, dislikes, favorite music and so on is a classic sign of someone genuinely liking you and your company. If you are enjoying the conversation and the other person is engaging in it without looking bored or yawning, this is a sign that both parties are equally interested in each other.

#2 They keep bumping into you.

Call it fate but this can also be a sign that they like you and engineering any possible opportunities to meet you. This is sweet but also can be creepy if it becomes too much like stalking. If you feel that this person is following you or you suddenly feel uncomfortable, listen to your gut feeling and make a report. Stalking is serious and dangerous. If the person keeps bumping into you happens to be at places like the cafeteria or the lunchroom or neighborhood coffee place and not specific places like your gym that you've been going to for years, your house or anyway specific and private – make a complaint.

#3 They discuss plans.

Another sign that someone could be romantically interested in you is to plan for more dates or start talking about the near future because they see you in it. It isn't about plans to get married or buy a house but merely simple things like a concert in your area that they'd like to take you or even a friend's party in a week that they'd like you to come with. They have these upcoming events and they'd like you to be part of it.

#4 Five more minutes

If someone is interested in you, chances are they would like to spend a few more minutes longer with you. They don't mind adjusting their schedule just so they can spend an extra 5 more minutes to talk to you or even spend that extra 5 minutes on the phone just so they can continue talking to you. The fact that they do this is also an indication that they have romantic feelings for you.

#5 Reasons to spend time together

'I'm in the area—want to grab a bite?' or 'Oh you're having a cold? I can make a mean chicken soup—I'll bring it over' or even 'What are you doing right now? Want to go have dinner together?' Make no mistake that these could just be that the person likes spending time with you simply because you are a cool person to hang out with but if these reasons keep piling up and it only involves just the two of you, it is probably a big sign that this person likes you.

#6 Observe their body language.

If someone likes you, they mirror your body language and your movements. They sit in closer, they lean in, they smile when you smile, they find ways to touch you (not in a creepy way) like brushing against your shoulder, putting a strand of your hair behind your ear – all these are classic flirtation signs and if you are uncomfortable, say so. Still, if you are enjoying it, this person is clearly into you.

#7 The compliments are mountainous.

Complimenting someone excessively can be a sign of ass-kissing or just trying to be nice. But if this person compliments you sincerely, it could be that they are interested in you. Look out for verbal cues such as complimenting your fashion choice or the way you style your hair. It could be that they are just being friendly, but them dropping compliments every time you meet is a big sign of them being interested in you.

#8 They remember the little things.

The closer you get to know someone—the more information you divulge to them. Your romantic interest will pick up many interesting things about you and save it in their long-term memory. These things can be your favorite color, your favorite ice cream flavor, the first movie you watched together, where you first met – all of this is an indication that this person is genuinely interested in you.

#9 Conversation starters

Some people are shy and are not big talkers so while this is something to take note of, you cannot be the only one initiating contact all the time. If someone is willing to connect despite being shy, that means they want to talk to you. Having one-way initiations for everything is a definite NO that the other person doesn't like you and do not see the need to spend the time to talk or even meet you but if they initiate contact as much as you do, that is a sure sign that they are into you.

#10 Other people are off-limits.

Take note of when a person talks about someone else—do they talk a lot about other girls or guys when they are with you? Or is the conversation focused on just you and your person? What a person says in a conversation and how they refer to other people in their social circle can give you real clues into whether they are romantically interested in you. Talking about going on a date with a girl or guy is not a good indication that this person likes you.

Trusting your feelings and your intuitions in all these possible scenarios above is the best bet. Remember that different people do different things to show someone they care or are interested in them and cultural values, upbringing, and societal norms also play a big part in identifying these signs so nothing is set in stone. All the signs described above are a good telling sign that a person is interested in you especially if they like spending more time with you. Even if you are not sure, you can exhibit signs that you are interested in them so that they will also have an idea but to be on the safest side, telling someone that you like them. You'd like to get to know them better and even start dating is the best way forward to prevent any miscommunication or misunderstanding between two people.

Of course, the game of love is not as straightforward and as simple as it is. It takes a little bit of dating experience to figure out if someone is into you or not or you can just do the good old fashion trial and error, get your heart broken, kiss all the toads till you meet your prince or princess charming.

Chapter 22: How to Spot Dangerous Person?

There are always people at the extremes of each trait and, sometimes, these people can be dangerous. While most people exhibit a fair few 'good' personality traits, and perhaps a couple of 'bad' ones, some people exhibit a singular bad trait so strongly or even several bad traits at a low level. Such people can be anything from mildly annoying, lacking in social skills, downright manipulative or abusive. Most concerning is the fact that some people can mask these negative traits quite well. How many times have you met someone you thought was friendly enough to realize later that they are not someone you want to know at all? What about friends you have who act one way in one situation but can be completely different at other times? Everyone would do well to remember that no matter how good we get at analyzing and speed-reading others, there is always a chance that something important will escape our notice, or that the other person will be able to mask their intentions too well.

Despite this, there are some red flags for which we can learn to look out. These apply to all of our relationships – not just romantic ones. Identifying personality types that may harm us involves understanding what healthy relationships look like, whether they are with family members, friends, colleagues, superiors, and yes, romantic or sexual partners. Here is a list of some telltale signs that something's wrong in your interaction with another person. Their behavior points to their personality – and if their personality is harming you, you are always within your rights to step back, get out, and look for support to ensure your safety, physically, emotionally, and mentally. Identifying one of these red flags in your relationship with someone doesn't mean you have to cut ties with them immediately, but it should give you pause about how you'd like things to change in the future.

Red Flags

- Give and take: All relationships should be two-sided; there has to be give and take on both sides. Of course, the give and take will naturally wax and wane in all relationships, and in some cases, an uneven weighting is more appropriate (e.g. boss and subordinate). However, if someone is always relying on you for help, emotional support, money, time, etc. and doesn't show appreciation or gives little of the same in return, you may want to consider if they are taking advantage of you. Sometimes some inequity in these areas can be acceptable, even normal, and relationships shouldn't be like transactions, but if you feel that someone in your life is using you in some way, this may be a red flag.

- Emotional Awareness: Everyone's different, and everyone has a different capacity when it comes to expressing and understanding emotions. However, everyone can improve in this area and show that they are trying to understand your needs and feelings. If someone consistently claims that they "aren't good with emotions" and show no willingness to develop in this area, this may be a red flag.

- Ultimatums: Does this person often use ultimatums to get what they want from you? Do you often feel pressured to say certain things, act a certain way, or give up in an argument because you are concerned about the consequences? For example, does your boss or co-worker hold your employment and the threat of firing over your head unreasonably, for minor, resolvable workplace issues? If this happens to be the case, or if someone else you know uses ultimatums repeatedly even after you've pointed out the problem, this may be a red flag.

- Apologies: Someone's ability to give a good, meaningful apology is a strong indicator of their emotional maturity. People who cannot apologize properly or make amends in other ways demonstrate an inability to self-reflect, empathize with others, and take responsibility. If someone consistently struggles to give a thoughtful apology that shows they understand their wrongdoing and will change in the future, that can be a red flag. This is true even if they are someone 'higher' in the hierarchy than you, including bosses, parents, and older friends.

- Isolation: Manipulative people will often try to isolate others from the people in their life. It makes quite a lot of sense: if you don't have your friends and family to tell you how terrible they are, there's a greater chance you won't realize it! Be wary of people who try to monopolize your time, draw you away from your support systems, or tell you that everyone in your life doesn't 'get' you like they do. Especially in romantic or sexual relationships, this last one can be alluring. However, it can be a red flag that they want to assert control over you.

- Intuition: When it comes to red flags, the most important tool in your arsenal is intuition, or your gut feelings. In modern times, most humans have lost the ability to listen to our instincts. We are often too quick to dismiss them as irrational or paranoid. But how many times have you had a 'funny' feeling about a person or situation that turns out to be well-founded? It's quite common. Becoming more in tune with your body's physical responses to others (hair raising on your arm, an instinct to run away, a weight in your stomach or compression in your chest) will help you become more aware of potentially dangerous people – even those disguised as friends. Remember, if someone makes you feel bad constantly, you worry about seeing them, or you feel a little unnerved by what they say or do, this is a good indication that something's a bit 'off.' Trust your intuition.

- Negativity: People who bring negativity to your interactions set it off on the wrong foot every time. A tendency to focus on the negative side of things indicates a mindset that may negatively impact you. Of course, everyone has bad days where everything seems gloomy. Still, if someone is always nit-picking everything around them, bringing others down with negative feedback, or unreasonably conveying a sense that the world is against them, that may be a red flag.

- Physical Boundaries: All good relationships have well-drawn and respected physical boundaries. These boundaries will vary according to the relationship and the personalities of those involved. However, there is one golden rule: if someone feels uncomfortable about someone's physical behavior, they are within their rights to draw the line – strongly if necessary. It doesn't matter if the other person 'intended' just to be 'friendly' or just sees themselves as overly 'affectionate'; if you can't trust them to respect your boundaries, you can't trust them at all. And that's a red flag.

- Respect for You: Your coworkers and acquaintances (and even your family) don't necessarily have to like you, but they do have to respect you. People who subtly ridicule you, put you or your work down, or seem intent on changing you, don't have respect for you and your right to live your life autonomously. If someone you know is determined to see you a certain way that you don't agree with or wants to force you to do or say things, it's a sign that they don't respect you – a definite red flag.

- That Feel-Good Feeling: Do you know that feeling you get when you're on your way to visit a friend, loved one, or romantic partner, and you just can't get the smile off your face? That feeling when your body seems to glow, and you feel a pleasant sense of anticipation? That should be the goal or at least the general direction of all your relationships. Of course, you can't have this all the time in all relationships, but you can train yourself to be more aware and proactive about the ones that don't feel this way. This can help you to set up healthy boundaries, avoid traps of manipulation, and even physical, emotional, or financial abuse. To the best of your abilities, surround yourself with people who value who you are, show interest in your life, and have appropriately deep emotional connections.

Chapter 23: Becoming a Better Listener

Becoming a better listener is the best thing that you can do when you want to read people. People are not always great at communication. Meaning, they often miscommunicate their needs or wants. But if you are very careful and astute listener, you can find out all the clues that people leave around and create a more complete picture of what people are trying to say to you. By becoming a better listener, you also make people want to open up to you. They will want to talk to you more and tell you things. You will become the person that everyone wants to confide in, and then you will bear a lot of pertinent information about people.

Create an Aura of Caring

If you project that you care, people will trust you and feel at ease around you. They will be more inclined to talk to you and confess intimate things to you. Creating this image that you are a caring person involves making yourself look trustworthy and interested.

Body language is important in this endeavor. You should also lean toward the person who is talking. Hold eye contact. Nod now and then. You can cross your legs to indicate that you feel comfortable, but avoid crossing your arms as this makes you appear closed off. Try having a more open stance instead, with your chest facing the person speaking to you. Of course, always look at the speaker with a normal eye contact level to show your deference in listening.

You also want to show genuine interest. Nodding is one way to do this. Frequently murmur in an assenting or sympathetic way. You can input enough of your own words to keep the conversation going, but it is important to not talk too much. The focus needs to be on the other person.

Stop talking about yourself. As a human being, you will want to talk about yourself. It is natural. But to be a good listener, you should keep the entire conversation focused on the other person, at least while he or she is talking. Not talking about yourself or constantly trying to turn the conversation onto yourself will make you appear better listeners.

Mirroring is another way that you can make someone feel at ease around you.

Mirroring

You can set people at ease by mirroring their physical movements. You just want to copy whatever someone does during conversation. If someone leans forward, lean forward about four seconds later. If someone leans back in his seat, lean back in your seat.

Matching your breath to the same rhythm as someone else's is a subliminal form of mirroring that often will set a person at ease. The person won't even know why he feels so comfortable around you. But he will and he will open up.

It may be hard to do this if you are not close to someone. Just notice when his chest fills with air and inhale at the same time. When his nostrils inflate with exhalation, exhale as well.

Ask Questions

Get a person to talk about himself. Since people love to talk about themselves, asking lots of questions will make people happy in conversation. Keep the conversation focused on the other person and ask him plenty of questions to keep him going. For instance, if he is telling you about work, be sure to ask lots of questions about his job. Keep your questions calm and insert them at natural moments or lulls in the conversation to avoid looking like you are interrogating him.

If someone is passionate about something, definitely start asking him questions about his passion. This is a great way to get someone to open up to you. It also makes people want to talk to you. You can get to know people just by finding out what they like and then asking a few questions about it to get them talking.

Asking also is better than mind reading. If you want to understand someone, ask him what he is thinking. Ask him what he means when he says something that you don't quite understand. Don't attempt to play the mind reading game because this is how miscommunication can arise. Clear all miscommunication by asking questions instead.

Reduce Distractions

Nothing makes you look like you don't care as much as you are distracted. Put your phone away. Don't stare at the TV. Don't stare out the window or try to eavesdrop on other people. Give your full attention to the person that you are currently speaking to. Everyone that you speak to will feel valued and appreciated as a result. You will become more liked.

You will also free yourself of distractions to devote all of your energy to the conversation. This makes you a better conversationalist. You are better able to listen and retain information. You are better able to remember what is said. You can think of appropriate responses to keep the conversation from going flat or awkward.

Summarize What Was Said

After a person tells you something, it can help offer a recap to show that you were listening and make sure that you got everything understood correctly. Your summary can be brief; you don't have to regurgitate the entire conversation. But a brief recap can help both you and the other party assure that you listened well and the conversation was properly understood. It also assures the other party that you cared enough to reiterate.

Recognize What Is Unsaid

A large part of human communication is silent. What someone does not say in person is often said in other subtle ways, such as through sighs, long pauses, tear-glistening eyes, raised or lowered tone and pitch of voice, and tense body language. Notice when someone is not saying and ask if everything is OK. If the person doesn't want to talk about what he is not saying, don't press the issue. But watch his body language and eye contact to gauge what he is not telling you.

Don't Think Ahead

You may race to think ahead about what to say next. You think that you know how the conversation will go and what the person will say next, so you think that you can decide what to say ahead of time. Unfortunately, you are not a mind reader. Your predictions will often prove inaccurate. Prevent confusion or embarrassment by holding your tongue. Only decide what to say when it is your turn to speak. Then you know what was fully said and you can make an informed and suitable response.

Be Careful about Interrupting

Typically, it is wise to never interrupt. When you interrupt someone, you invalidate what he is saying. You can insult and even anger people by interrupting them. It is best to just wait your turn to speak.

However, there are times when you must speak out of turn. One good time is when the person you are speaking to begins to get overly emotional. You should interrupt politely to reassure him and tell him that he should not be so upset. Another time is when someone is talking about making a very foolish mistake. You can interrupt to offer cautionary advice. But be sure to only pick times when it is necessary to interrupt. Otherwise, avoid doing so, no matter how excited you are to jump in with what you have to say.

Determine If You Should Add Input

Sometimes, it is OK to just sit there and listen. Few people ever do this, so you will stand out as a good listener should you do this. By being silent, you allow the person you are speaking to the opportunity to unabashedly open up. He can vent and tell you all and you will absorb it all.

Other times, your input is required. People rely on for advice, for instance, or they need you to offer some words to show your interest. Wait for certain pauses in conversation when the person seems expectant. This is when you should add input.

A friendly conversation or a conversation where you are trying to get to know someone is usually a back and forth. This is when your input is required. You seem like a stick in the mud if you don't contribute to such conversations. A conversation where someone is explaining something to you or venting about his life is when your silence is required.

As a human being, you have certain social instincts. You should follow these instincts. You also know the person that you are speaking to and the nature of your conversation the best. Listen to your gut about when to speak and what to say.

Remember Things

 Remembering what people say to you is a crucial part of listening. If you can reiterate what someone says to you later on, you can prove that you were listening. You can continue the conversation where it was left off if you get cut off. You can also retain important information that someone imparts to you about him- or herself.

It is easier to remember everything when you genuinely care about it. But what if you don't care? Or what if you have a lot on your mind so you have trouble retaining information in the short term? The human mind chooses to dump any information that it does not find relevant and important to your overall life. Let's face it, a lot of the conversations you have are not that relevant or important. Therefore, it is hard to remember what you hear in conversation all of the time. Shocking or really important things might stick with you, but other details quickly fade away. You can certainly improve your ability to remember conversations by using some of the following tricks.

One trick to remembering what is said to you can be to think that you will narrate this whole conversation to someone else later. While this may not be true, it tricks your mind into remembering what someone says to you better.

Another trick is to memorize important images that stand out to you in the conversation. If someone talks about what she expects from a lover, assign images to the things she says. You can assign flowers to romance, for instance. Then, you will remember a series of images better than a long string of words.

The mind is often good at remembering emotions above all else. Therefore, you should try to remember the emotional textures of the conversation. What made the speaker very sad? What made you sad? Adding emotional charges to the conversation can help you remember its main themes better.

Chapter 24: First Impressions

First impressions are typically accurate. You should listen to your

gut. Your subconscious mind is adept at picking out clues about people that your rational mind cannot pick up on. Your gut will tell you the most accurate information about someone right off of the bat.

After you make a first impression, you may try to rationalize it. You may try to explain away negative feelings as poor judgment or jealousy. You may think that you read a person wrong. While these are vaguely possible, you will usually find out that your first impression was right in the end.

A good example is when you first meet a woman that you would like to be friends with. But your gut reaction to her is that she is not very nice. You decide to give her a chance since everyone else likes her and you get along after a while. However, after a while, you realize that all she does is say mean things about other people. Or she may betray you after years of friendship.

Your first impression is often all you have in business and situations like speed dating. So, trust it. Your first impression is most likely correct, so act on it if you do not have time to get to know the person further.

Red Flags

Some major red flags automatically tell you that someone is toxic. When you observe these traits or habits in someone, you know that someone is not good to be around. Run away when you spot these red flags. Do not somehow rationalize or justify these traits, as they are serious signs of underlying emotional issues or sociopath.

Easy to Anger

A person who is easily ignited has anger problems. One day you will probably be the victim of his anger if you are not careful. Therefore, you should avoid people who are angered easily.

A history of violence is one sign that a person is easy to anger. Another sign is if he seems to demonstrate an angry posture. He will talk about fighting people or getting angry. He will immediately appear angry over the tiniest setbacks, such as his food being late at a restaurant.

Blaming Others

Right off the bat, you will notice if someone frequently blames others for what is wrong in his life. He will tell you all about how he is a victim. He will complain about how his ex-spouse cheated on him and brought about the divorce, he will blame getting fired recently on the fact that his former boss is just a huge jerk, and he will blame his recent car accident on the other stupid driver. Nothing will ever be his fault. He will claim that everyone else is responsible for his problems. And he will have plenty of problems to talk about. He will always be a victim.

Someone who plays the victim will probably one day accuse you of doing something wrong to him. He will never see how he is at fault. He will certainly never own up to his bad actions or offer you any kind of apology.

Constant Complaining

A very negative person will just ooze that negativity through his speech. He will constantly complain about everything. It will appear as if the world is against him and nothing in life is good or worth doing. Just being around this person too long will make you feel depressed.

Sadly, many people are like this. They only see the bad in life. You can assume that a person like this will only bring you down. You will never be able to lighten someone like this up because he chooses to stay depressed.

Gossiping and Two-Facing

Some gossip is just human nature. Once you know someone well, a little bit of gossip now and then is normal. It is not a warning sign.

But when you first meet someone, the first thing you hear should not be a bunch of gossip about other people. A person who sits there talking about everyone else has a gossiping problem. He is two-faced. Don't be fooled and think that you are the only one that he gossips to. Once you leave the room, he will start gossiping about you.

If someone gossips a lot, you want to watch what you say around him. You do not want to reveal too much, or it will become public information in two seconds. You also do not want to let his negativity sour you against other people. He will try to make you hate everyone else with the juicy, horrible details that he shares, but remember that gossip is rarely true. Even if it is, you do not have to be a part of this gossip's drama.

Women have the worst reputations as gossips. But men can be just as bad. Anyone who talks about other people a lot is a gossip. Be careful around such people.

Lacking Compassion

Have you ever met someone who laughs when other people fall? He seems to get some sick satisfaction from the suffering of others. Even if he doesn't snicker at other people, he never demonstrates any remorse or compassion. When he speaks about other people, he uses very callous and cold language. When you point out someone's bad luck, for instance, he will snort and say that it is the person's fault. This is the sign of a sociopath or psychopath. This person is very dangerous and certainly not the type of person that you want in your life.

The average person is capable of at least some compassion in conversation. He will feel bad when you mention that you are going through tough times or when someone falls. Someone who does not show any compassion and just ignores you or offers a callous remark when you say something that calls for compassion is not someone that you should associate with. If you associate with this person, never expect him to show you compassion when you need it.

Things to Read

What He is Driven By?

Various things drive people. They will usually show what drives them by talking about it. For example, someone might say that he wants to go out to pick up chicks. Sex drives him. Someone who frequently talks about money and making money is driven by financial security and wealth. Someone who talks about socializing a lot is an extrovert who is driven by having social interaction.

What drives a person can indicate what he wants from you. Read a person's language to gather clues about what he wants in life. His drive can indicate why he is seeking any relationship with you, either professionally or personally. It also indicates what is important to him. If your goals align with his, then a relationship is a great idea. Otherwise, you may want to steer clear of this person.

What Feeds His Ego

Watch a person's ego to find out what feeds it. A lot of people are fed by accomplishments, such as making money or finishing a tough marathon. Some people are fed by flattery and being the object of desire. Some people are fed by sex and interactions with the opposite sex. What feeds someone's ego is apparent by what he talks about the most and what makes him smile.

Also, watch his responses to life situations. If a member of the opposite sex flirts with someone and his or her ego blossoms, you can assume that they have low self-esteem and require lots of sexual attention to feel good. If he brags about his boat and other material possessions, you can tell that material success makes him feel complete.

If someone has a fragile ego fed by superficial things like material possessions and sexual attention, you can be sure that he has little confidence. The issues that come with insecurity are thus probably prevalent in this person. He will also do things to satisfy his ego and chase after things and make stupid decisions to keep his ego buoyed. Expect vices in someone like this.

But if someone's ego is fed by more solid things, such as his accomplishments or the love of his family, then he is probably a secure and reliable person with healthy confidence and wholesome interests. You can trust someone like this to be a more solid companion in business or your personal life.

What Stresses Him Out

Watch out for someone's stressors. Everyone has a source of stress. What a person complains about the most usually indicates what causes him the most emotional stress. If he complains about family, communication, commitment, and not always getting his way or not feeling loved, he may stress. If he complains about work, his work line and the tasks that he must do are probably not well-suited to his personality. If he seems to get quiet or upset in large crowds, you can assume that large crowds are not his forte.

Knowing what stresses someone out is very useful information. You can learn what to avoid doing around someone. You can become more sensitive to what someone does not like and situations that a person does not function well in. This is great information to know if you hire someone to work for you or begin dating someone.

What Pleases Him

People will go on and on about what makes them happy. You will most likely find out what makes someone happy relatively early in conversation. But you can also look for clues in what makes someone smile or what someone fixates on with dilated pupils.

This is also useful to know. You learn what you can do to please someone. This can make you a better lover, friend, or even employer and co-worker.

How Does He Behave Under Stress?

How someone handles stress says a lot about how he will treat you when things get hard. Life can throw a lot of challenges your way, so you usually want people around to handle stress well. If a stressful situation arises and someone falls apart or gets fiercely angry, just know that he is probably not a reliable friend during times of stress. He is also not a good prospect in a stressful line of business. On the other hand, if he can remain calm and collected under stress, he is someone that you can rely on in the future.

Chapter 25: Personality and Birth Order

An individual's birth order can also reveal a lot of his or her personality. This isn't just restricted to pop psychology talk or mindless party chatter but based on a psychological analysis of how the person relates to their family members and how they are treated within the family based on their position or birth order. A person's family dynamics play a considerable role in shaping their personality. The role they fulfilled as children or during their adolescent years influences their behavior as adults. Our status quo as children establishes the foundation for our actions as adults. Notice how several times children born in the same family or raised in the same environment have dramatically diverse personalities.

Of course, other factors can determine their personality type in combination with a person's birth order. These factors such as the family's overall socio-economic status, education, number of children in the family, parents' professional achievements and more also impact an individual's personality.

Alfred Adler first came up with the theory of studying an individual's personality through their birth rank. He used it as a method for reading the behavior, personality and actions of his clients. However, it was Frank Sulloway who elaborated on the theory in his publication Born to Rebel. Sulloway's book identified five primary traits like extraversion, agreeableness, neuroticism, consciousness and openness.

The psychologist said that an individual's birth order impacts their personality even more than their environment. This means that the chances of two first-borns having the same personality type are higher than two children belonging to one family.

Here are some ways to read a person through their birth order.

First-Borns

Firstborn children are known to be responsible and ambitious leaders, who pave the way for others. They are original, creative and independent thinking by nature. Since they get more undivided attention and time with their parents, they have a clear edge over their siblings. Again, they are more proactive and take the lead when it comes to caring for the siblings, which makes them more disciplined, inspiring, responsible and accountable as adults. They are protective towards those weaker than them, and often lead others.

If parents place many expectations on the first in a household, the person may grow up feeling inadequate. This may not just lead to low self-esteem but also a weak personality that is marked by a constant need for validation, acceptance and approval. The person may end up feeling that they can never be good enough for anything.

Firstborn individuals are more goal-oriented and ambitious. They give plenty of importance to accomplishments and success. They thrive in or perform well in positions of authority, responsibility and maintaining discipline. There is an inherent tendency to be a control freak, while also being autocratic, dictatorial and bossy.

Because come first in the sibling hierarchy, these people are physically stronger than other children in the household, which gives them a marked dominant personality. They may have a high sense of entitlement.

First-borns are often high on determination, rule enforcement and attention to details.

Middle-born

Since they are caught between two siblings, middle-born develop a more complicated personality. They are neither given the rights and responsibilities of the older sibling nor the youngest sibling's special privileges. This makes them look outside the home for friendships and connections.

Middle-born often have very big social circles and are known to be excellent diplomats and negotiators. They are social creatures who function with a profound sense of peace and fairness. Middle-born are fiercely loyal to their loved ones and seldom betray people's trust. Typical personality traits of middle born children are flexibility, generosity and adaptability. They are known for their diplomatic nature and can play peacemakers in any situation.

Middle born children are primarily understanding, co-operative and adjusting. They also turn out to be competitive adults. Middle-born have a close-knit social circle who award them the affection they haven't received within their family. Middle-born are late raisers and discover their calling after plenty of experimentation, contemplation and deliberation. They are at the center of authoritative careers that allow them to utilize their power-packed negotiation skills.

Middle-born are generally social and operate with a deep sense of justice and fairness. They are good at teamwork and relate well with people belonging to multiple personality types since they have learned to deal with older and younger siblings. Middle-born display a more approachable nature, and they know how to wriggle themselves out of confrontations and conflicts. They are known to be resourceful and quickly master multiple skills.

Last Born

By the time the youngest child of the family is born, parents are well-versed in their parenting skills and more economically settled. This makes them less paranoid and more secure. They aren't excessively monitored, which makes them more independent and gives them more freedom. Last born persons are excellent decision-makers and operate with a high sense of entitlement.

The last born is known to be charming and risk-taking. They are independent thinking, original and adventurous. There is a greater tendency to rewrite the rules rather than following set norms.

Parents are less careful when it comes to their last born because they've already experienced being a parent, which helps them give more leeway and flexibility to the youngest child. Also, there are higher chances of pampering and indulging the child owing to a better financial status. Since parents are more relaxed and lenient with last-born, they don't turn out to be conformists. They are used to plenty of attention, and they don't worship authority.

Rather than walking on set paths, they will create their path. Since they've learned to compete with their siblings for their parents' time and attention, they are good at handling competition and aren't easily bothered by feelings of envy and insecurity.

Since they are more creative and independent, they thrive in careers such as standup comedians, painters, dancers, and authors. Typical personality characteristics include empathy, obstinacy, extroversion, manipulativeness, penchant for drama and more. These are your salespeople since they are glib and can talk themselves of almost any situation.

Sole Child

The only child doesn't have to compete with anyone for their parents' time and attention, making them self-centered. There is a tendency to think that everything revolves around them. They tend to spend a lot of time alone, which turns them into more original, resourceful, inventive and creative people. Sole or only children find new and innovative ways to keep themselves busy. By nature, they are more confident, self-assured, meticulous, expressive and firm. They express their opinions more assertively and confidently.

Since they do not have to deal with sibling rivalry of any kind, they are always used to having things their way. They become edgy and unsettled when they have to compete with others or things don't go their way. Sole-born find it tough to share the limelight with others. They almost always want to be the center of attention since they've never had to compete for attention at home through their childhood and adolescent years. Only-born are constantly seeking attention, respect and attention. In the absence of siblings as role models, their only role models are elders of the house. Since grown-ups become their role models, they grow up to be perfectionists.

Multiple factors impact a person's behavioral characteristics and personality. To make a more accurate reading of an individual's personality through birth order, psychologists offer some effective tips. They recommend analyzing a person's siblings while reading their personality since no two children in the same household ever share the same role. If one assumes the role of a caretaker, the other will invariably be the care recipient.

Other factors that are considered while analyzing an individual's personality through birth order are genetics, gender, social status and other factors (apart from their birth order). Together, these factors will help you make more accurate readings about an individual's personality than simply relying on birth order.

Chapter 26: Handwriting

Every person's handwriting is known to be as unique as their personality. You can make an in-depth analysis of everything from their behavior to personality to the thought process. Graphology is the science of studying an individual's personality through how they write. Handwriting goes beyond putting a few characters on paper. It is about glimpsing into an individual's mind to decipher what they are thinking and how they feel based on their handwriting.

Here are some little-known secrets about speed reading a person through their handwriting.

Reading Letters of the Alphabet

How a person writes his or her letters offers a lot of information about their personality, subconscious thoughts, and behavioral characteristics. There are several ways of writing a single letter and every person has their distinct way of constructing it.

For example, putting a dot on the lower case "I" indicates an independent-spirited personality, originality, and creative thinking. These folks are organized, meticulous, and focused on details. If an entire circle represents the dot, there are pretty good chances of being more childlike and thinking outside the box. How a person constructs their upper case "I" reveals a lot about how they perceive themselves. Does their "I" feature the same size as the other letters or is it bigger/smaller than other letters?

A person who constructs a large "I" is often selfish, self-centered, overconfident, and even slightly cocky. If the "I" is the size of other letters or even smaller than other letters, the person is more self-assured, positive, and happy by disposition.

Similarly, how people write their lower case "t" offers important clues into their personality. If the "t" is crossed with a long line, it can indicate determination, energy, passion, zest, and enthusiasm. On the other hand, a brief line across the "t" reveals a lack of empathy, low interest, and determination. The person doesn't have very strong views about anything and is generally apathetic. If a person crosses their "t" really high, they possess an increased sense of self-worth and generally have ambitious objectives.

Similarly, people who cross their "t" low may suffer from low self-esteem, low confidence, and ambition. A person who narrows the loop in lower case "e" is likelier to be uncertain, suspicious, and doubtful of people. There is an amount of skepticism involved that prevents them from being trustful of people. These people tend to have a guarded, stoic, withdrawn, and reticent personality. A wider loop demonstrates a more inclusive and accepting personality. They are open to different experiences, ideas, and perspectives.

Next, if individuals write their "o" to form a wide circle, they are most likely people who are very articulate, expressive, and won't hesitate to share secrets with everyone. Their life is like an open book. On the contrary, a closed "o" reveals that the person has a more private personality and is reticent by nature.

Cursive Writing

Cursive writing gives us clues about people that we may otherwise miss through regular writing. It may offer us a more comprehensive and in-depth analysis of an individual's personality.

How does a person construct their lower-case cursive "I?" If it has a narrow loop, the person is mostly feeling stressed, nervous, and anxiety. Again, a wider loop can signify that the individual doesn't believe in going by the rule book. There is a tendency to rewrite the rules. They are laidback, low on ambition, and easy-going.

Again, consider the way a person writes cursive "y" to gain more information about their personality. The length and breadth of the letter "y" can be extremely telling. A thinner and slimmer "y" can indicate a person who is more selective about their friend circle. On the other hand, a thicker "y" reveals a tendency to get along with different people. These are social beings who like surrounding themselves with plenty of friends.

A long "y" is an indication for travel, adventure, thrills, and adventures. On the other hand, a brief cursive "y" reflects a need to seek comfort in the familiar. They are most comfortable in their homes and other known territories. A more rounded "s" is a signal of wanting to keep their near and dear ones happy. They'll always want their loved ones to be positive and cheerful.

They will seldom get into confrontations and strive to maintain a more balanced personality. A more tapering "s" indicates a hard-working, curious, and hard-working personality. Ideas and concepts drive them. Notice how cursive "s" broadens at the lower tip. This can be a strong indication of the person being dissatisfied with their job, interpersonal relationships, and or life in general. They may not pursue their heart's true desires.

Letter Size

This is a primary observation that is used for analyzing a person through their handwriting. Big letters reveal that the person is outgoing, friendly, gregarious, and extrovert. They are more social by nature and operate with a mistaken sense of pride. There is a tendency to pretend to be something they aren't. On the contrary, tiny letters can indicate a timid, reticent, introvert, and shy personality. It can indicate deep concentration and diligence. Midsized letters mean that an individual is flexible, adjusting, adaptable, and self-assured.

Gaps Between Text

People who leave a little gap between letters and words demonstrate a fear of leading a solitary life. These people always like to be surrounded by other folks and often fail to respect other people's privacy and personal space. People who space out their words/letters are original thinkers and fiercely independent. For them, they place a high premium on freedom and independence. There is little tendency for being overwhelmed by other people's ideas, opinions, and values.

Letter Shapes

Look at the shape of an individual's letters while decoding their personality. If the writing is more rounded and looped, the person tends to be high on inventiveness and imagination! Pointed letters demonstrate that a person is more aggressive and intelligent. The person is analytical, rational, and a profound thinker. Similarly, if the letters of an alphabet are woven together, they are methodical, systematic, and orderly. They will rarely work or live in chaos.

Page Margin

If you thought it's only about writing, think again. Even the amount of space people leave near the edge of the margin determines their personality. Someone who leaves a big gap on the right side of the margin is nervous and apprehensive about the future. People who write all over the page are known to have a mind full of ideas, concepts, and thoughts. They are itching to do several things at once and are constantly buzzing with ideas.

Slant Writing

Some people show a marked tendency for writing with a clear right or left slant while other people write impeccably straight letters. When a person's letters slant towards the right, they may be friendly, easy-going, good-natured, and generally positive. These people are flexible, open to change, and always keen on building new social connections.

Similarly, people who write slanting letters that lean towards the left are mostly introverts who enjoy their time alone. They aren't very comfortable being in the spotlight and are happy to let others hog the limelight. Straight handwriting indicates rational, level-headed, and balanced thinking. The person is more even-tempered, grounded, and ambivalent.

There is a tiny pointer here to avoid reading people accurately. For left-handed people, the analysis is the opposite. When left-handed people have their letters slanting to the right, they are shy, introverted, and reserved. However, if their letters slant to the left, they may be outgoing, gregarious and social extroverts.

Writing Pressure

The intensity with which an individual write is also an indicator of their personality. If the handwriting is too intense and full of pressure (indentation), the individual may be fiery, aggressive, obstinate, and volatile. They aren't very open to other people's ideas, beliefs, and opinions. There is a tendency to be rigid about their views.

On the contrary, if a person writes with little pressure or intensity, they are likely to be empathetic, sensitive, and considerate towards other people's needs. These people tend to be kind, enthusiastic, passionate, lively, and intense.

Signature

A person's signature reveals plenty about an individual's personality. If it isn't comprehensible, it is a sign that they don't share too many details about themselves. They fiercely guard their private space and are reticent by nature. On the contrary, a more conspicuous and legible signature indicates a self-assured, flexible, transparent, assured, confident, and satisfying personality. They are generally content with what they've accomplished and display a more positive outlook on life.

Some people scribble their signature quickly, which can indicate them being impatient, restless, perpetually in a hurry, and desiring to do multiple things at one time. A carefully written and neatly-organized signature indicates the person being diligent, well-organized, and precision-oriented.

Signatures that finish in an upward stroke demonstrate a more confident, fun-loving, ambitious, and goal-oriented personality. These people thrive on challenges and aren't afraid of chasing these dreams. Similarly, signatures that finish with a downward stroke are an indication of a personality that is marked by low self-esteem, lack of self-confidence, low ambition, and a more inhibited personality. These folks are likelier to be bogged down by challenges and may not be too goal-oriented.

Stand Out Writing

If a particular piece of writing stands out from the other text, look at it carefully to understand its personality.

For example, if the text is generally written in a more spread out and huge writing, with only some parts of the text stuck together, the person may most likely to be an uncertain, dishonest, or mistrustful individual, who is trying to conceal some important information.

Concluding

Though studying an individual's handwriting can offer you accurate insights about his or her personality, it isn't completely fool-proof. Several other factors are to be taken into consideration to analyze a person accurately. It has its shortcomings and flaws. At times, people may write in a hurried manner, which can impact their writing. Similarly, the way people construct their resume or application letter may dramatically vary from writing a to-do list or love letter.

If you want an accurate reading of someone's personality, consider different personality analysis methods like reading verbal and non-verbal communication techniques. Various techniques may offer you a highly in-depth, insightful, precise, and comprehensive understanding of a person's inherent personality.

Chapter 27: How to Avoid Mistakes

Mistakes. You think about them, talk about them, and lastly obsess  regards to them. These mistakes help a human being to grow but, side by side they are very much embarrassing, shameful, and put companies to a great loss.

Everyone has the same old habit which they want to change by doing some mistake or the other. It is a part of human psychology to repeat the same behavior again and again. Therefore, changing the old behavior can be difficult but not impossible. It can only be eradicated by proper planning and staying positive while doing any work.

In human life, mistakes are very common things by which he/she learns a lot.

Sometimes when we work too much, some careless and silly mistakes will happen, especially when doing your best. There is a number of examples of mistakes like sending an e-mail to the wrong person, overlooking a balance sheet, not ready for a presentation, and innumerable others.

Indeed, the person who is good at analyzing people easily judges whether they have done some mistake or not by non-verbal communication channels.

Here you will come to know "How to avoid mistakes at work"?

First of All, Acknowledge a Mistake

Until and unless you fully appreciate what exactly has happened, till then it is impossible to avoid it. Some of the individuals are very hard at failure but forgot to re-examine what is to be done to avoid the mistake next time. So, keep these things in mind before doing any work: -

Don't be overconfident while doing any work as it leads to missing any information and you will tend to make a mistake

There are many bad habits which can be the reason of mistake so avoid any bad habit

Doing mistake means you are trying your best but do overdo it

Concentrate on What You Are Doing

Just focus on your tasks and projects firsts. At the office, make work your priority and avoid any kind of activity while doing office work. On the other hand, don't be a multitasked as it kills the overall productivity.

Moreover, start the work from the smallest and easy task and then take up a tough one.

Furthermore, at the start of the day give importance to those tasks which are significant.

Don't Fear Mistakes

This is one of the essential points to keep away from doing mistakes. The reality is in the fear of making a mistake, you try to be perfect but forget that only you learn a lot by mistakes.

As an individual, if you have given your best in doing work then also cross-check the work again and again so that there are no chances of mistakes.

Try to analyze your work by taking the help of your manager, supervisor, or any experienced colleague.

Notwithstanding, getting a second eye on the work is a good method of improvising your work. And also, they make you understand overlooked errors which you are not able to understand.

Be Clear with Regards to Your Role in the Organization

Do you know- what is the role your company has given you?

It is essential to know this otherwise you will mess up all the things to complete every task.

On the other hand, surety of work offered to you makes you comfortable and will be mistake-free.

However, if you have any doubt about your duties and responsibilities then ask your boss to define it, and after that things will work much easier. In this case, there are no chances of errors.

Learn from Every Mistake Which You Will Do

In case any mistake is done by you, don't blame it on others rather take the responsibility of that mistake for what you have done.

As an employee of any organization, learn from every error done by you and from others. Always note all the mistakes done by you and by your colleagues and do the best effort not to repeat it.

Moreover, when you show a positive attitude towards the mistakes, it will become a stepping stone to your success.

Indeed, this process makes you analyze yourself and others which are best for making strong relationships.

Always Find the Root of the Mistake

Every human being makes mistakes but once it is done, taking precautionary measures to not repeat is mandatory.

If you want that this mistake will not happen again, try to determine the root cause of the mistake.

After that think deeply about that issue and what are the steps you can take to prevent it further in the future. This will also help you to analyze your capability to get successful in life while observing others.

Try to Have a Healthy Conflict

A single human being does mistakes; but, in some cases, it might be due to conflicts between colleagues because of clashes in ego and opinions.

Make sure that you build a healthy relationship with each other so that every solution can be sought with colleagues' help. Make yourself friendly and make a good rapport within the organization.

We all are human and mistakes are our part of life. The person who learns from the mistakes and tries not to repeat it is the best human being. So, with your own mistakes, you can analyze other individuals also the way they react and act to the mistakes and judge their personality.

Chapter 28: How to Detect Trickery, Con, And Deceits?

Detecting trickery, con, and deceits is not an easy project because many police detectives usually apply some precarious strategies to analyze suspects' statements and reports. This strategy is called statement analysis, and it can help them to detect lies in the report. The detectives will examine the words and comments made by the suspects in writing independently while checking for any facts.

This process will help them discern the truths in the statement, and if there is any omitted information, such omission will be queried. Some intentional additions made to the report aimed to conceal the truth, but a careful investigation will reveal such lies and deal with it subsequently.

Detectives usually follow some processes while analyzing reports, especially if they are discerning a classic truthful statement based on the norms. They will be able to analyze these norms and even detect any deviation from the typical, resulting in fabricated statements. FBI detectives apply some steps in making a concrete analysis of every information supplied by suspects to detect deceits in disguise.

According to the FBI Law Enforcement Journal of 1996 entitled, "What Do Suspects Words Reveal?" Detectives endeavor to identify any aberration from the standard and even analyze what is distinctive of an ingenious report.

Let us analyze some concrete signs of deceit and falsehood that criminally-minded persons use to wiggle their way out of a case.

Making Uncertain Remarks and Expressions

A suspect will try to dodge the criminal intelligent officer's interrogations by making uncertain and vague statements. Such expressions are meaningless and full of ambiguities and doubts. However, when criminals make this type of reports, they tend to seek for ways to make additions or amendments later on.

Some of the expressions and words that could deceive an interviewer are supposed, almost, thought of, about, maybe, could have, guess, perhaps, approximately, and sort of.

Talking About Past Events with Present Tense

Liars and Cheats speak of past events using the present tense. This attitude connotes that such persons have taken time to practice and meditate on such incidences in their minds to use present 'action' tenses. The ultimate intention of using these types of tenses and statements is to deceive and con the listeners and judge alike in a court of law. An example of this type of statement could be seen in the following lines, "When I got to the office this morning, I met nobody at the reception room, but I find out that the window is open. As I approach director's office, I notice his door open, and his laptop is nowhere to be found".

The beginning of this statement contains correct tenses, but towards the end, the speaker intentionally diverted to wrong tenses to pull the wool over the detectives' eyes. However, their ability to identify this anomaly in the suspect's speech will help them know that his statement is flawed.

Responding to Questions with Their Questions

Responding to questions with questions is another smart way employed by tricksters to dodge giving investigators the right answers. They know that blatant lies could be detected after investigations; therefore, they try to camouflage the truth by masking it with carefully crafted questions. Some of these questions include "How can I take money out of my drawer and claim that it was stolen?" "Do I look like a thief?"

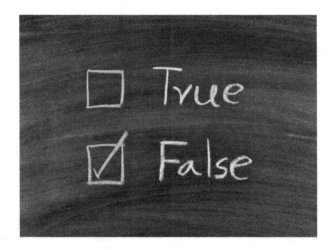

No Reference to Themselves in Their Statement

If you want to detect trickery, con, and deceits from a suspect's statements, you will notice that he will not be referring to himself in his speeches rather he will prefer to use neutral comments. For example, "The office was not locked" or "The money was taken away" However, the statement should have been, "I did not lock the office" or "I took the money away" if he wants to be truthful and refer to himself.

In the statements above, the suspect commented in the passive voice instead of in the active voice.

Convincing Interviewers with Oaths

The use of swear words, oaths, and pledges are the deceptive ways liars and fraudsters employ to manipulate or deceive investigators. They use these tactics to convince everybody that whatever they are saying is nothing but the truth. Some of the anomalous expressions that they use are "Let God be my witness," "I can swear," "on my honor," and "I cross my heart."

On the contrary, truthful persons don't have to use any cuss word to prove themselves, but they believe that their words' authenticity will prove their innocence.

The Average Number of Words per Sentence

The average number of words per sentence is determined by the total number of words in a report divided by the total number of sentences. This is also regarded as "mean length of utterance."

Most persons tend to use longer sentences to analyze issues in a statement. However, some sentences contain about fifteen to twenty words making them longer than a standard phrase.

A Truthful Sentence Should Contain the Narrative Balance

A truthful statement made by a suspect describing an event should have the 'narrative balance.' In a narrative statement, you should expect to see the prologue, main action, and epilogue. The 'prologue is the beginning part of the narrative describing how the event began or explaining the causes of the issue at hand while the 'main action' expresses the incident that occurred as it happened.

Then, the epilogue is that part of the statement that expresses how the incident ended.

Experts have argued that the percentage indications of the whole narrative should be as follows: prologue should be up to thirty percent long, the main action should be forty percent long, while the epilogue should be thirty percent long. Moreover, they further argued that any part of the statement that does not meet up to the percentage mark is indented and should be further analyzed as important facts could have falsified the whole report.

Simple and Brief Statements Indicate Falsehood

One of the ways to detect a false report is by the brevity of the statement. In most cases, truthful occurrences are narrated in detail, but false reports are usually modeling with no analysis. It is also a known fact that accurate statements do not answer the question at hand but go into other aspects of the story's causes and effects to project nothing but the truth in the event.

However, liars and deceivers tend to evade the truth about the statement and tell just what they know can help them to escape judgment and penalty

Deception Entails Talking About Intended Actions

When suspects talk about proposed actions without saying that they did such things it becomes an allusion or merely a suggestion. For instance, a student answering a question concerning a missing book in the school library but does not want to state that he or she stole it, said, "I decided to go to the library and borrow some books whenever I had assignments to do. Yesterday, I got to the library, but the librarian was away, I tried to wait due to my project's urgency, but he was nowhere to be found. After checking the books in his absence, I left the library to complete my project.

Now, from the preceding, did the student meet the librarian? Did he wait for him to come back? Did he take any book from the library in the absence of the bookkeeper? The student narrated all these incidences without stating that he stole any book from the library. This is called 'allusion of actions' whereby the suspect talked about all he did without saying that he was culpable in the case.

Making Euphemistic or Vague Statements

Euphemistic remarks are made to present the suspect in a favorable and auspicious position in the case, to prevent hurting the personality of the person involved in the case. Examples of vague statements a subject can make to deceive the detectives are "the item was missing," rather than "the item was stolen," "I borrowed the book from the library," rather than "I took the book from the library,"

These are most ways an FBI agent or a detective can analyze statements made by a suspect to determine the veracity of such claims before conviction or acquittal.

Chapter 29: What is Personality Development?

All individuals possess certain traits of personality that set us apart from the rest of the world. The mix of good and bad traits tells us how you respond to the situation. According to some studies, it is stated that these traits are genetic and remain fixed throughout life.

But according to some psychologists, they suggest that if you want, you can change these traits for the benefit of self or you can say for people.

So, personality is what makes a person unique and admirable. The personality of an individual consists of several components like temperament, environment, and character. With all these components' help, you can determine how that person will become or right now is.

Talking about temperament, it is a genetic determine factor that shows a person's approach towards the world and how they learn about the world. Indeed, there are no specifically meant genes for personality, but genes control the nervous system, which, as a result, has some effect on human behavior.

Another component called the environment is an adaptive pattern related to the surrounding of the person they live in. Some psychologists have researched that the first two components that are temperament and environment influence human personality the most.

Lastly, the third factor called character, which includes emotional, cognitive, and behavioral patterns, which are learned through experience, determines how a person can think, behave, and feel throughout his life.

Other than this, the character also depends on our moral values inherited in us through our ancestors.

Importance of Personality Development

To achieve success in both personal and professional life, a great overall personality is crucial in an individual's life. An attractive and renowned personality automatically influences every person. Whether it is a job, interview, while interacting with other human beings, and many more sectors, you must have certain traits and features that compel other human beings to say yes! What a great personality!

Nowadays, in every field, the personality of a person matters a lot. For instance- in the interview to impress the interviewer in business to influence the client and make them believe in you.

Therefore, the demand of personality has surged drastically over time. These days with the advent of personality, every school is careful about it, and they make their students a perfect example where they can excel in every field.

Some years ago, the overall concept of personality was very common, and no one approached it. Parents also rarely gave importance to it. It was just looking good while wearing good clothes, which is more emphasized in a work-related environment. Indeed, the interviewer just wanted good working skills of the person and not interpersonal skills.

But now the scenario has changed a lot in this age of competition and economic revolution. Let's put some light on the various points of personality which are considered very crucial in personality development: -

Personality Development Inculcates Numerous Good Qualities

Good qualities can be in any form like punctuality, flexibility, friendly nature, curiosity about things, patience, eagerness to help others, etc. However, if you have a good personality, you will never hesitate to share any kind of information with others, which benefits them.

According to the rules, you will follow everything like reaching on time at the office. All these personality traits not only benefit you but also to the organization directly or indirectly.

Gives Confidence

Great personality tends to boost your overall confidence. If you know that you are properly groomed and attired, it makes you more anxious towards interacting with people. Other than this- in any of the situations, if you know how to behave, what to say, and how to show yourself, your confidence is automatically on the peak.

Overall, a confident person is liked and praised by everyone both in personal and professional life.

Reduces Stress and Conflicts

A good personality with a smile on his face encourages human beings to tackle any hurdle of life. Trust me, flashing a smile on the face will melt half of the problems, evaporating stress, and conflicts.

Moreover, with a trillion million smiles on your face, there is no point in cribbing over minor issues and problems which come in the way of success.

Develops a Positive Attitude

A positive attitude is that aspect of life, which is a must to face any hard situation and one to one progress in life. An individual who thinks positively always looks on the brighter side of life and moves towards the developmental path. He/she rather than criticizing or cribbing the problem always tries to find the best possible solution with a positive attitude.

So always remember, if any problem occurs, then take a deep breath-in, stay cool, keeping in mind the positivity anyhow. This is because developing a positive attitude in hopeless situations is also part of personality development.

Improves Communication Skills

Nowadays, a lot of emphasis is given on communication skills as a part of personality development. A good communicator always lives an excellent personal and professional life. Indeed, after your outer personality, the first impression tends to fall on another person is what you say and how you say it.

Verbal communication of the person makes a high impact on another person. Individuals with good communication skills ought to master the art of expressing thoughts and feelings in the most desired way.

Helps You to Be Credible

It is a good saying that you cannot judge a book by its cover, which also applies to a person. Means people judge a person from their clothing and how it is worn. Therefore, dressing plays an essential role in the personality of an individual.

So, be careful while picking up clothes for yourself. It doesn't mean you will buy expensive clothes, but they should be perfect and suit your personality.

How to Develop a Personality

So, there are multiple characteristics on which an individual has to work while developing his personality. Here you will know some tips on developing personality: -

Be a Good Listener

If a person has good listening skills, they can make another person feel important in front of them, so be a good listener.

Take an interest in reading and expanding your horizons

The more you learn about various aspects, the more you become famous in your personal and professional life. So, read more and cultivate those interests in yourself, which make you stand in front of others with confidence.

On the other hand, when you meet people, you can share things with the individuals by making them flat.

Dress Up Well

While going to the office, party, or on any other occasion, wear a dress according to that which suits you. Good looks no doubt add to your personality, but what matters is how you dressed up for any occasion. Thus, dressing sense plays a very crucial role in personality development and building confidence.

Observe the Body Language

While interacting with people, try to use positive gestures, which make another person comfortable and relaxed. Some studies stated that 75% of the work is done by verbal communication in which another person judges a person's personality.

So, keep an eye on body language.

Remain Happy and Light-Hearted

Try to see the joy in the world and every work that you do. Spend precious and laughing with others so that you feel happy. Always appreciate people in one way or the other. So, smiling and laughing plays a significant role in making your personality awesome.

Stay Calm in Tensions

Some people have a good personality until and unless they come across some tense situations. Don't be that kind of person who becomes angry in tensed issues and shouts on everybody. Therefore, be relaxed and stay cool while finding out the best possible solution for a problem.

Develop Leadership Qualities

It is believed that good leaders have an excellent personality that can impress another person easily and effectively. However, leadership skills don't mean giving orders to subordinates. Rather, it means how well you can as a leader manage your subordinates to accomplish any task. Indeed, work hard to set an example for them who work with you so that if in the future they will get a chance to work with you, they will feel very excited.

Work On Your Inner Beauty

Most people only work on external appearance, but when you behave or speak outside, everything gets reflected. So, it is true that the outer look is essential, but inner beauty is also very crucial to be a full-proof personality.

Indeed, it takes only a few days to change your outer appearance, but, sometimes it takes years to change the inner world. So, work on that, and you can see the difference.

Learn From Your Mistakes

As a human, mistakes are part of life which makes an actual individual. If you are learning any new thing, you are bound to make mistakes. Always get ready to learn from your mistakes while saying or feeling sorry. Saying sorry will make a significant place to make a respectful corner among your friends or colleagues.

Indeed, if you have made a mistake, forgive yourself and move on.

Always Make Compliments to Others

If you see that someone is looking great or gorgeous, don't hesitate to say something positive. This will make your image or standard up.

Be Original

The next essential step in making your personality awesome shows what you are. It is a very eminent saying that original is worth than copied things. So, follow this and be how it is; rather, pretending what you are not.

Other than this, one should not copy someone's personality. But, you can adopt some habits of other individuals who are good and help you in developing your personality.

Meet New People with a Smile

Try to meet new people who will make you aware of a new environment and culture by which you, as an individual, can learn new things. Moreover, it also broadens your horizons.

Make Your Own Opinion

The opinion is something that cannot be changed or stolen from another person. For example, while sitting in a group when someone asks your opinion, give them your opinion, which is unique and is for everyone's betterment. This attitude will make you more interested and stimulating to be sociable.

Get Out Of Your Comfort Zone

Be ready, and always get prepared to challenge yourself to learn new skills. Like for most people- learning new things is quite challenging work. But with a positive attitude and confidence in yourself, you can tackle anything.

Don't Give Up At Any Point

Whenever you try to do anything and fail, give yourself a second chance to improve it. So, don't give up at any cost and try, try, try until you succeed.

Don't Make Yourself Aggressive

Well, in everyday situations, there are numerous assertive situations that make you angry. But, be careful because it is a big turn off to people, both in social and professional life.

If your nature is like pushy, then be honest to yourself and change it as soon as possible.

Don't Strive Hard For Perfection

Keep in mind that you don't have to attain perfection in any field because no one is perfect in this world. When a person is willing to show imperfection, then he/she is putting people at ease.

Evaluate Yourself

Evaluation is the best technique to change yourself towards positivity, so keep evaluating yourself regularly. In this case, take the feedback from your friends, colleagues, and other near and dear ones seriously, which will help you to improve gradually.

Conclusion

I would like to end this book with a very important technique that you should learn and master so that your ability to read and analyze people will continue to grow and expand and you can leverage the advantages of this skill. This technique is the art of listening and honoring your intuition.

While body language cues, psychological theories, and personality types are great factors to help you tune into the underlying things that people are trying to say and do, your intuition or your gut feeling is the element that helps you interpret the data suitably. A powerful intuition can help you catch hidden signals that can take your analysis level to a much greater height than if you did not use your intuition. Here are some intuition tips that you can use:

Always listen to and honor your gut feeling

Listen to your gut feeling when you are meeting people, especially for the first time. A first impression is a visceral feeling that lasts just an instant. Hence, if you are not keenly hooked on to your intuition, you likely miss this reaction. This initial gut feeling lets you know whether you are at ease or not with the person. It is your inner truth meter telling you whether you can trust this person or not.

Pay attention to goosebumps

Feeling your skin's tingling through goosebumps is a very powerful intuitive element that cannot be missed. These goosebumps are signs telling you that something is resonating with the person sitting in front of you. Goosebumps are also indicators of a déjà vu feeling when you recognize something you feel deeply for. Pay attention to these.

Watch out for insightful flashes

During a conversation, a small almost indiscernible remark or gesture could give you a flash of insight and if you are not keenly observant of your inner self, you will miss it. You must pay a lot of attention to make sure that you catch these insightful flashes that are important keys to unlock people's minds.

Keep a lookout for emotional energy

Emotions are powerful tools that light up your intuition. We can easily gauge whether what you feel towards the person sitting in front of you is a positive or a negative vibe. You will notice that some people can make you feel good simply by their presence and some people can make you feel horrible. This is true even when you do not know anything about this person and have met them for the first time. This 'vibe' is the emotional energy around the person that could be negative or positive. Watch out for this emotional energy when trying to read and analyze people.

Lastly, when you decide to read and analyze people, the first thing you must do is to drop all biases and inhibitions. Do not carry any negative or positive legacies of the person in your mind. Even if you do, attempt to see those legacies in a new light or a new perspective. If you carry unnecessary baggage, your judgment is bound to be clouded and you will make more mistakes than if you remove the excessive baggage.

Reading and analyzing people is a lot of fun and you will find the joy of being correct as you get better each day. However, I would like to say that using this skill to hurt or cause harm should not happen. Use this wonderful skill judiciously and watch your popularity among your family and friends grow exponentially.

The next step is to transition from the book-practice to real-life practicum. The experiences are what make us into what we are today. After reading about human personality analysis and people-reading with speed and quality methods, you are better equipped with the tools and techniques necessary to effectively understand people and interact with them. This is your chance to go out there and start proving your worth by not only differentiating your friends from your foes but also by turning the threat of failure into an opportunity for success. No longer should you fumble around with words to say in front of a stranger, or let misunderstandings ruin your relationships. Don't let people or environmental factors get the best of your efforts and well-intendedness or let your misguided observation or judgmental views get the best of people's good wishes around you. Look into their personality, try to understand their behavior, explore the possibilities, and analyze their intentions. This will help you sustain the old relationships and build the new ones and let you get successful by remaining one step ahead of your opponents.

Although we admit that the subject of human behavioral psychology is very vast, no way can it be summed up on a limited range of pages. However, we did try our best to accumulate the most sought after and relevant techniques that are easy to understand and focus more on action than mere wordiness to be learned and implemented right away.

BODY LANGUAGE OF PEOPLE

Introduction

Analyzing people can be a hard nut to crack. It requires a lot of mental work, from studying the body language to understanding facial expressions and how to manage the emotions expressed by people and their egos. It takes a huge amount of effort to analyze people. However, the mental work and activities required can only be possible if you can read people, and not just read, you have to be excellent at it.

The ability and capacity to be able to read people is something that you have to develop with constant practice. Quite naturally, the people who have acquired knowledge, combined with real-world practice, are essentially the best at reading and analyzing people. Reading people is a natural act. Human beings and social creatures are wired to read and study people every time they interact with each other.

People are involved in the proceedings of this world, and in studying them, they could either cooperate or not want to. However, even when people think they are not giving you the chance to study them to analyze them better, they still are. Sitting by yourself in the corner of the room away from everyone also requires cooperation on some level with the society.

For instance, some nations are not attempting to war each other because of the interconnected network of human behavior designed to instill peace and harmony functions as it should. Therefore, it is essentially the cooperation and behavior of several people cooperating on some level by essentially, keeping away from participating in acts that might lead to harm in another person,

People Are Not As Good As They Think They Are

When you contact a stranger, how long does it take you to evaluate the individual before you arrive at your first impression?

Several people believe it took them less than a minute to do this; however, science has found that it takes a lot less time than people believe it to be. Psychologists at Princeton University have established through several studies that it takes an individual only about one-tenth of a second to make the first judgment of someone, and it is primarily based on the body language of the other person.

Dr. Albert Mehrabian discussed a fact in one of his books that only about 7% of communication is made through the use of words. The remaining 93% is a result of vocal clues and nonverbal messages such as posture gestures and facial expressions, among others.

Meaning, you need to be aware of how people come across to you and how you come across to them, as they form the vast majority of human interaction. Being able to identify these cues could either make or break the career of a budding professional.

If you are seeing to move up the ladder in a social situation, be it at work, in your community, etc., you have to be able to harness body language and nonverbal cues, as they provide you with a huge advantage in both professional and non-professional circumstances. The ability to speed-read, and analyze people accurately could be what makes you impress the people you look up to and embarrass the people around you.

All of these, however, brings to mind an important question: how can you improve your ability to read people?

What Are You Doing Wrong?

Before we go on to answer the query "how to improve your ability to read people?" We first need to establish what you are doing wrong, so that these discrepancies will cease to come up, and you will be able to read people better.

There are some common errors that people make in a bid to understand people and read them better. These errors may include:

Ignoring Context. This is an important fact people tend to overlook. The context in which the nonverbal clue being expressed does matter a lot. The fact that you have your arms crossed does not necessarily indicate that the room is cold or the chair you are sitting on does not have armrests. A good number of times, things have to go beyond the common sense situations attached to the environment. It is therefore essential to ask yourself the question: "Should someone in this situation act in this manner?" You should remember that the arms might be crossed in a bid to fend off danger or simply hide or protect the torso, it might be crossed for the individual to self-reassure his/herself, or because the individual is angry. Always make sure to include the context in which the individual is exhibiting these cues.

I am not looking for clusters. This happens to be one of the biggest mistakes you can make. Looking for a distinct voice might be great in movies, but it is different in real life. In real life, it is more about a consistent grouping of actions. An example of such is the case of poker players, rather than the distinct voice described in movies. A consistent grouping of actions that include sweating, touching the face, and stuttering together describe what you might find to be meaningful. It is therefore vital to ask the question: Are most of the behaviors exhibited by this person associated with "X"? For instance, an angry person will not cross his arms alone; he would probably frown and fume and exhibit a group of behaviors that will indicate anger.

You are not establishing a baseline. Baselines are essential if you know for certain the nonverbal and verbal behaviors exhibited by an individual. The fact that the individual is jumpy does not indicate anything. However, if the individual is always jumpy and then suddenly stops moving, you should ask yourself the question: "Is this the normal way they act?" When you do not establish a baseline with which new behaviors can be compared, it will be difficult to understand and ascertain if the exhibited behavior is normal to the individual.

You are not conscious of Biases. The first impression you make of an individual is bound to affect your judgment of the person. If you already dislike or like the individual, then you are bound to judge based on it. If the people who come close to you and often compliment you are the same people you like and approve of, it might sway you unconsciously. It will also be a long while before you can become impressed by people you do not approve of. (Saying these tricks do not apply to you is also a bias. The biggest bias of all occurs when you think you are unbiased).

Why Is It Important To Know How To Read People?

Being able to read people comes with its benefits, and it is so much more than playing Sherlock Holmes. It is about observing the people you communicate with and adjusting how you communicate with them.

In every area of life, there are myriad personality types to deal with, and it is essential to recognize them if we are going to tap into their strengths. For instance, if you have an employee or a friend you observe to lack self-confidence or have low self-esteem or, you should be able to adjust your tone to put up their insecurities in a way that motivates them. It would be wrong and inefficient if you were loud and boisterous in your manner of dealing with them. However, if the individual you are dealing with is an extrovert, being solemn and serious is inefficient to get through to them.

The world of today disconnects us from one another and even nature than ever before. Today, we hardly make eye-contact with the barista who hands us our coffee over the counter. The power of observation and the need to read people accurately is, therefore, not necessary for communicating effectively. It is only a tool that helps to promote the connection between us as human beings.

Reading People

The ability to read people has more to do with nonverbal communication and body language alone. The essential things to look at before you can successfully read people include posture, gestures, physical movements, the person's appearance, facial expressions, tone of voice and willingness to make eye contact during conversations, etc. There is a study that finds that you can read someone only 7% from the words they say, 38% from their vocal clue, such as tone, pitch and volume, and finally, 55% from their body language. The study was, however, focused on reading someone on a first impression basis.

You also have to think through the context in which the behaviors are exhibited, personality, and the possibility that anybody might try to deceive you by manipulating the communication.

These clues, however, do not make you privy to the innermost thoughts and feelings of other people; however, if you are observant, then you will be able to read their body language.

Chapter 1:   What Is Body Language?

Body language, or non-verbal language, can be an external reflection of a person's emotional condition. This reflection is manifested through non-verbal messages that can be universal or specific to a specific geographical area or culture. Still, in any case, they have a specific meaning that serves to express a feeling, a thought, or a state of mind. Every movement and gesture are an indicator of emotion that an individual feel at a certain moment.

When is the non-verbal language used?

We can safely answer "always!"

Nonverbal expressions and gestures go hand in hand with the words spoken and sometimes when we do not speak, for example, when we have to be silent in a library, we use our hands to communicate with other people. Therefore, we express ourselves by gestures or while we are in a place where there is particularly noise and we gesticulate to make ourselves understood.

Non-verbal language is used when speaking with a person, with a group of people or while using a telephone even if you are fully aware that they cannot see us on the other side of the telephone. Non-verbal communication is something independent, body language starts automatically, with or without words and communicates the real feelings and sensations of who is speaking to you.

The key to reading body language well is to understand a person's emotional conditions by paying attention both to their verbal communication and to everything they transmit with non-verbal language, knowingly or unknowingly, and identifying the situation in which they are expressing themselves. This allows you to distinguish truth from imagination and reality from fantasy.

We assume that the key to reading body language is not simple. Still, it can become easy, strangely many people believe that doing this is a very difficult thing. This is because many know nothing about body language. Knowing little or nothing about something we need to do, and if we don't put in even a minimum effort to find a solution, then it is logical that we will never succeed in what we are doing. This applies to any concept, even to body language.

The struggle of all this lies in the fact that these movements are many and very fast and can have different meanings. To facilitate their understanding, scholars have divided them into various groups and subgroups, according to which part of the body is affected by the movement.

Since many times what a person says when he speaks to us does not coincide with his body's gestures, it becomes indispensable to be able to decipher these movements, because this discrepancy is an indication of lies. To do this, one must first be able to recognize these gestures and then attribute the right meaning to them.

When we humans say that a person is intuitive or perceptive to others, we refer to the ability to read the various body languages of others and compare the signals with the words they pronounce. Being able to do this puts us in a position to understand the true intentions of those around us and to anticipate their actions, both for better and worse. Some people manage to do it automatically and unaware; others need to work on it a bit.

This is also what is called public awareness or relationships with a group. A person can quickly understand if the person or audience he is addressing is interested and attentive to what he says. For example, suppose a certain audience is comfortably relaxing with their arms crossed and their chin lowered. In that case, the speaker who is giving the speech will realize that perhaps he is not expressing himself in the best way, but above all, he is not using the body language in the best way. He will, therefore, have to take a different approach to be able to get the audience involved.

If, on the other hand, the speaker continues to speak in the same way without doing anything to attract the audience's attention, it means that he does not have great speaking skills and will not be able to convey his message and, therefore, his ideas and opinions.

If during a speech this happens and that is that the attention of the public is lacking, it means that the speaker certainly has gaps in the knowledge and management of body language; otherwise, he would not have reached that point. Good knowledge and mastery of body language often lead you to have excellent results in the field of communication and to be more intuitive. This knowledge can be applied to others who interact with you.

In general, women are much more intuitive than men, which led to the term "intuition of women" that people commonly use in stories about women. In most cases, women are fortunate to have, n in most cases, an innate ability to decipher non-verbal cues and have an impeccable eye for small details. This is one reason why very few husbands can lie to their wives and get away with it. It is also why women can, on the contrary, pull the wool over a man's eyes without the man noticing.

Research conducted by Harvard University psychologists has established that women are much more attentive to body language than men. They showed short films while the sounds were turned off. The films consisted of a woman and a man in a conversation. Participants were then asked to decode what was happening by reading the couples' expressions. According to the research, women have been able to accurately read the situation 87% of the time, while men have just achieved a 42% accuracy score. Men, who are cultivating professions such as breastfeeding, acting and artistic, have done almost as much as women. Gays, on the other hand, also scored quite well. The ability of women to be more intuitive than men has been studied and is connected to the fact that it is precisely the woman who has to take care of her offspring from the first day of life, from breastfeeding to weaning in particular, to develop skills that will be useful for deciphering and understanding everything that happens in her immediate neighbor just to be able to protect her children. These innate abilities then adapted to what is daily, social and professional life in the course of evolution, which is why females are often more intuitive negotiators than males because they tend to practice reading signals in advance. Body language is an instrument that is used practically throughout the day, every day and three hundred sixty-five days a year; it is used with animals, regardless of your mood, whether you are alone or in the company, at home or work, with your partner or with your employer, with children or with the elderly.

Body language can be defined as open, if it involves opening gestures that tend to be expansive, such as the gesture that involves bringing the palms up or showing them and keeping them well in sight. This is a clear sign of openness, and that is usually done automatically when you want to convey a sense of honesty, truth, and clarity.

Errors in the interpretation of gestures represent the greatest difficulty when talking about body language. This is because you may happen to see very similar movements, such as shrugs, and make the mistake of attributing the same meaning to everyone. Nothing more wrong! For example, if today you ask John if he knows where his friend Mark has parked the car, and he says no, and in the meantime, he shrugs both shoulders at the same time and prolongs the movement for a few seconds, then it means that he doesn't know. If instead, you ask Paul what happened between

Mark and Sam, and he replies that he does not know he wants information about it, but while he says this he only raises a shoulder for a fraction of a second and then lower it immediately then he is lying because his movement shows disinterest.

Another gesture that we can find several times, even on the same day, is the smile on a person's face. The smile indicates a positive emotion, expresses a positive feeling. So are all the people we meet who smile happily? And here the donkey falls! Oh yes, because it has been shown by several studies that individuals not only manage to smile in a piloted way, but they also manage to do it in a very convincing way, especially when they want to hide a disappointment or something they don't like. This is the case of the classic fake smile or also called "Duchenne smile," from the name of the scholar who discovered and analyzed it. The difference between a true and a false smile is that the first one involves almost all the facial muscles and causes the so-called "crow's feet" wrinkles around the eyes, an irrefutable sign "while the second does not.

Have you noticed that just introducing the topic of body language, starting only to define it, a range of options and facets applicable to daily life has opened up? And we have not yet started talking specifically about the various types of body language and the movements of each of them!

You have already noticed, making only a few examples, as it is evident that some things we already know, some small gestures that we have seen thousands of times done or that we have even done thousands and thousands of times but without considering them much, can have important meanings and can they give us the

592

solution to understanding many things that we didn't even notice before? In the following pages, we will analyze most of the gestures that are part of body language. For convenience, I will divide them into categories and sub-categories to simplify and speed up their learning as much as possible.

We can, therefore, divide body language into three main major groups:

- The language of the head, which includes facial expressions and movements of the whole face;
- The language of the trunk, which includes the gestures of hands and arms and the movements or positions that the trunk assumes;
- The lower body's language includes the movements of the legs and feet and how they can be positioned.
- Besides, three very important factors affect each of the body languages and are:
- Posture, which indicates the position that an individual assumes with his body;
- Proxemics ie, the social distance between individuals;
- Physical contact during a conversation. Posture is the fundamental component that most influences body language because it is like a person's business card.

It is the initial thing you notice when you meet someone before you notice the color of the eyes, the shape of the lips, or any other body movement. Do you think this material is enough to start taking your first steps in the world of body language? I think so! Now let's start analyzing one topic at a time.

Chapter 2:   Universal Non-verbal Signals

Non-verbal communication will be different for everyone, and it is in different cultures. A person's cultural background will define their non-verbal communication because some types of communication, such as signals and signs, have to be learned.

There are various meanings in non-verbal communication, there can be miscommunication when people of different cultures communicate. People might offend another person without actually meaning it because of the cultural differences. Facial expressions are very comparable around the world.

There are seven universal micro-expressions, and they are content/hate, surprise, anger, fear, disgust, sadness, and happiness. It could also be different to the extent of how people show these feelings because, in certain cultures, people might openly show them where others don't.

You are an American, and you take a trip to Italy. You don't speak Italian. You don't take a translator with you, and you forgot your translation dictionary. You have to rely on non-verbal communication to communicate with others.

You found a nice quiet restaurant you want to try, so you point at your selection on the menu. You pay your bill and leave. The workers nod at you as you go being a satisfied customer.

There could be other times when things won't go as well due to non-verbal communication, such as people not making eye contact or they get offended when you do make eye contact.

Nods could also have various meanings, and this causes problems. Some cultures their people might not say "yes," but people from a different culture will interpret as "no."

If you nod in Japan, they will interpret it as you are listening to them.

Here are different non-verbal communications and how they differ in various cultures:

· Physical Space

People in diverse cultures will have different tolerances for the space between people. People from the Middle East like to be close together when they talk to others. Other people could be afraid to be close to others while talking.

Americans and Europeans don't have as much acceptance about people entering what they consider their physical space. This is even less when talking about Asians. Everyone will have their personal space that they don't want others to enter. There are many cultures where close contact between strangers is very acceptable.

· Paralanguage

The way we speak constitutes what we talk about. Pitch, rhythm, volume, vocal tones, can speak more than what the words are expressing. Asian people can keep themselves from shouting because they have been taught from childhood that this isn't acceptable.

This is what is known as vocal qualifiers. Yelling, whining, and crying are vocal characterizations that can change the message's meaning. In certain cultures, giggling is a terrible gesture. Several emotions can be expressed through vocal differences but are all a part of a person's paralanguage.

· Facial Expressions

Our faces can show emotions, attitudes, and feelings. Cultures can determine the degree of these expressions. Americans will show emotions more than people from Asia.

Most facial expressions are the same throughout the world, but certain cultures won't show them in public. These meanings are acknowledged everywhere. Showing too much emotion can be seen as shallow in certain places where others make it weak.

· Posture and Body Movement

People can get a message or information from the way your body moves. It can show how a person feels or thinks about you. If they don't face you when you are talking, it might mean that they are shy or nervous. It could also show that they don't want to be talking with you. Other movements, such as sitting far away or near someone, could indicate that they are trying to control the environment. They might be trying to show power or confidence.

A person's posture, such as sitting slouched or straight, can show their mental condition. Having their hands in their pockets could show disrespect in various cultures. If you are in Turkey or Ghana, don't sit with your legs crossed, as this is considered offensive.

· Appearance

This is another excellent form of non-verbal communication. People have always been judged for their appearance. Differences in clothing and racial differences can tell a lot about anyone.

Making yourself look good is an outstanding personality trait in many cultures. What is thought to be a good appearance will vary from culture to culture. How modest you get measured by your presence.

· Touch

Touch can be considered rude in many cultures. Most cultures view shaking hands as acceptable. Hugs and kissing, along with other contacts, are seen differently in various cultures. Asians are very conservative with these types of communications.

Patting a person's shoulder or head has various meanings in different cultures, too. Patting a child's head in Asia is very bad because their head is a sacred piece of their body. Middle Eastern countries consider people of opposite genders touching as being terrible character traits.

Where and how a person is touched can change the meaning of the touch. You have to be careful if you travel to different places.

· Gestures

You have to be careful with a thumbs up because different cultures view it differently. Some could see it as meaning "okay" in some cultures but being vulgar in Latin America. Japan looks at is as money.

Snapping your fingers might be fine in some cultures but taken as offensive and disrespectful in others. In certain Middle Eastern countries, showing your feet is offensive. Pointing your finger is an  insult in some cultures. People in Polynesia will stick out their tongue when they greet someone, but in most cultures, this is a sign of mockery.

· Eye Contact

Most Western cultures consider eye contact a kind gesture. This shows honesty, confidence, and attentiveness. Cultures like Native American, Hispanic, Middle Eastern and Asian don't make eye contact as a kind gesture. It is thought to be rude and offensive.

Unlike Western cultures that think it is respectful, others don't think this way. In Eastern countries, women absolutely can't make eye contact with men because it shows sexual interest or power. Most cultures accept gazes as just showing an expression, but staring is thought to be rude in many.

Chapter 3:   How the Body Reveals Emotions

Have you ever thought about how the body reveals emotions? Well, you are not alone. Lots of people do. But the great news is that a group of biomedical engineers provided a solution to this old question.

They drew the way the body reacts to emotions in 700 people and observed that the patterns were similar irrespective of where they lived.

The study, done by a team from Finland, depends on visual feedback offered by candidates from Taiwan, Sweden, and Finland. External Sensors or Brain Mapping could have been utilized to measure physiological outputs and neurological changes like body temperature and sweat. However, by offering the subjects to human body figures and requesting that they point out precisely where they felt activity decreasing or increasing, the team was able to gather private information that was usually impossible. It means the study depends on the self-assessment of candidates correctly without bias.

Although each emotion created a precise map of bodily sensation, researchers pointed out some regions of overlap. Basic emotions like fear and anger resulted in a rise in the excitement in the upper area the chest, likely corresponding to increases in the rate of respiration and pulse. The only emotion that was tested that caused a rise in the sensation all around the body was happiness.

The findings improved the understanding of researchers on the way we process emotions. Despite differences in language and culture, our substantial experience regarding feelings is amazingly steady across various populations. The researchers feel that the additional growth of these bodily sensation maps may lead to a new method of pointing out and treating emotional disorders.

How Body Language Reveals the Real You

Body language is a part of communication that is often overlooked. However, it is crucial to provide support for your spoken words and message. Although the majority of the time, it takes place automatically. You will be able to learn to manage your gestures, postures, and facial expression keenly. Once you discover your body language, you will undoubtedly get a more elaborate understanding of the individuals around you and significantly enhance your ability to persuade others.

The Connection to the Limbic System

What Is the Limbic System?

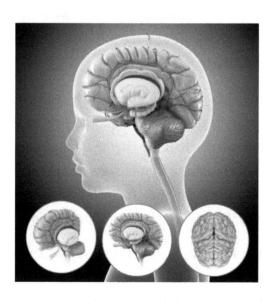

The limbic system is a complicated placement of structures that lies on both parts of the thalamus, underneath the cerebrum. It consists of the hippocampus, hypothalamus, amygdala, and numerous other areas close by. It

600

seems to be majorly responsible for our emotional life and has much to do with the creation of memories.

Parts of the Limbic System

Hypothalamus

The hypothalamus is a little area of the brain situated underneath the thalamus on both parts of the third ventricle. The ventricles are parts in the cerebrum filled with cerebrospinal fluid. They also link to the spine's liquid.

The hypothalamus lies above the pituitary gland and just within the two tracts of the optic nerves. The hypothalamus is one of the busiest aspects of the brain, and its primary concern has to do with homeostasis.

Homeostasis has to do with taking something back to a set point. It functions as a thermostat. When surroundings become too cold, the thermostat passes the information to the furnace, which then comes on. When your room heats up and the temperature surpasses a specific point, it sends another signal that informs the stove.

The hypothalamus regulates your response to pain, thirst, hunger, and sexual satisfaction, levels of pleasure, aggressive behavior, and anger, among others. It also controls how the autonomic nervous system functions, which also helps in regulating elements like breathing, blood pressure, arousal, and pulse in response to emotional situations.

The hypothalamus gets input from a range of sources. The vagus nerve offers information about the gut distention or how full your tummy is and information about your blood pressure.

In the reticular formation in the brainstem, it attains information regarding the temperature of the skin. From the optic nerve, it achieves information relating to darkness and light. The unusual nerves lining the ventricles provide information about the cerebrospinal fluid's contents like toxins resulting in vomiting.

From other areas of the limbic system alongside the olfactory nerves, it attains knowledge that aids in regulating sexuality and eating. The hypothalamus also possesses some receptors that offer it information regarding blood temperature and ion balance.

In a recent discovery, we have a protein known as leptin that is released by fat cells when we overeat. The hypothalamus seemingly senses the leptin levels in the bloodstream and responds by reducing appetite. It also seems that there are individuals who possess a gene mutation that creates leptin, and their bodies are unable to inform the hypothalamus that they have eaten enough. But many individuals who are overweight do not possess this mutation, so much research still requires it.

The hypothalamus passes the instruction to the remainder of the body in two methods. First is the autonomic nervous system. It lets the hypothalamus have complete control of things like sweating, breathing, blood pressure, and digestion alongside all the parasympathetic and sympathetic functions.

The other means by which the hypothalamus controls things is through the pituitary gland. It is chemically and neutrally linked to the pituitary, which then pushes hormones known as releasing factors to the bloodstream.

Hippocampus

The hippocampus is made up of two horns curving back from the amygdala. It seems to be crucial in transforming present thoughts in your mind into ideas you will not forget in the long run. If the hippocampus suffers damage, a person would be unable to create new memories and instead live in a world where all they experience fades off. In contrast, memories from before the damage remain untouched. Many individuals who experience this damage end up getting institutionalized.

Amygdala

The amygdala is two masses of neurons that are almond-shaped on either part of the thalamus at the end of the hippocampus. When it is electrically stimulated, the response animals give is aggression. When you take out the amygdala, animals no longer react to stimuli that would have previously caused a sexual response or fear. They also do not respond to things that may have resulted in rage already.

How Is Body Language Connected to the Limbic System?

When something has to do with nonverbal behavior, the limbic part of the brain is responsible because it naturally responds to our surroundings and the stimulus it consists of. The actions our limbic brain produces are a more honest response over those regulated by the neocortex.

In essence, the limbic brain regulates emotional body language making it our top means of indicating what the body feels. The limbic brain is responsible for controlling the torso, hands, feet, and head when an individual feels ashamed or embarrassed, happy or excited, fearful, or sad. The limbic system is wired into our nervous system and goes with us back in time through our evolution.

Although our neocortex can sometimes subdue the limbic brain, it is only possible when it is not preoccupied with other things. The neocortex has the responsibility of carrying out complicated conscious tasks like engineering and calculus, etc. So when it is turned off entirely or overwhelmed, the body accidentally lets out emotional body language that others can read. The neocortex is controlled consciously and is the least honest and least reliable aspect of the brain.

Research has shown that during deception, the neocortex is the most active region of the brain. This reason is why it has been termed the lying mind. Deceivers may have the ability to take charge of the words they utilize in describing their thoughts, but they are unable to control the way they react to these words. They are also unable to control the expressions that they let out. This inability is precisely how we can read stress and anger and also capture liars.

When thinking of the limbic system, consider the unplanned response when a loud bang startles us. Our bodies become tense instinctively, our hand is drawn inward, and our heads hide in our torso while the nervous system places our heart at high speed via a burst of adrenaline.

It is the same area of the brain that makes your hands shake or feet fidget when you are excited. It is also the one that results in sweaty palms when dealing with pressure. Our limbic system also heads into hyperdrive when a person wins a lottery or sees a loved one; we have not seen in a long time. Irrespective of what you do, you would not be able to prevent this reaction from occurring. The only possibility is to learn to reduce behaviors like clenching the hands together to minimize shaking when excited or inserting the legs behind a chair to keep them in place when you want to run off.

But by doing these actions, they reveal body language that tells others the neocortex is making efforts to subdue the instinctual brain, thus creating another leaked body language we can read. At an accident scene, it is fully expected that the limbic system takes over, creating discomfort, nervousness, and shaking. Thus, if the cops get there, they will consider something wrong if the caller is completely relaxed and calm while the victim is almost dead and bloodied.

Naturally, the calm individual will be pulled aside as the prime witness. Therefore, we always need to link them to the context, so we know when something is wrong. When limbic responses cease, we are aware that their production motivation has also stopped, so we must then locate the reason.

The limbic brain is the aspect of our mind that is in charge of our root processes. To understand this concept, think about the activities of a lizard. Because it is cold-blooded, it looks for the sun to hasten his metabolism, drinks when it is thirsty, eats when hungry, and fights, freezes, or flees when scared. It does not do calculus or construct huge buildings because it does not have the ability, but irrespective of that, it stays alive because the limbic system informs it on all the necessary things to do.

In terms of evolution, our limbic system is the same. It informs us when to be scared and what we should do—minimize movement so our assailants can't find us, freeze, run and point our feet to the appropriate direction, or let our hearts start pumping so we can run. It is also in charge of our root emotions. It informs our feet to jump in excitement and move. It also tells the feet to fidget with the readiness to leave when we are bored.

Basically, without the limbic system, there would be no body language to read in the first place.

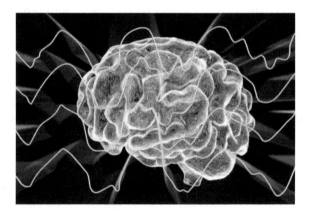

Chapter 4:   Body Language and Emotions

Body language is tricky because most body positions, postures, and movements can mean different things or not mean anything, depending on the environment. To discern what body language signals are significant and which ones are not, you should learn how several basic emotions are generally expressed through various simultaneous movements. In other words, you should try and discern patterns of movements that typically accompany certain emotional states, rather than dragging yourself through the tedious, often unreliable, practice of committing to memory hundreds of individual physical actions and the meaning of those actions might be.

Thoughtful or Focused

The states of either being thoughtful or focused are usually

characterized by a person being noticeably devoid of movement. A person's stillness in this instance reveals concentration on either some unspoken string of thought (if thoughtful) or what the other person is trying to say (if focused). Occasionally, a focused or thoughtful person may perform minor movements repetitively, such as tapping a pencil against a table top or twiddling their thumbs. A thoughtful or focused person will unconsciously display this body language, and this body language will be present and consistent for extended lengths of time.

Some of the other body language that is indicative of a person being thoughtful or focused includes:

- Holding the head in the hands

- Consistently staring at something

- Consistently maintaining strong eye-contact

- Furrowed brow

- Arms folded with vacant stare

- Looking up

- Laying the chin on fingers or hand

- General absence of movement

- Tilting the head

- Leaning back in the chair

- Scratching the head

Bored

People generally become bored when they do not want to be wherever they are and do not want to be doing whatever it is that they are doing. When a person is bored and wants

608

to go somewhere else, the body will show signs that it, too, wants to go somewhere else. The tension between wanting to leave and having to stay causes people discomfort. Therefore, bored people will generally engage in some physical activity to distract themselves from that discomfort.

Some of the common movements associated with boredom include:

- Eye rolls
- Leaning backwards and forwards in the chair
- Wandering eyes
- Furtive looks at objects such as a watch
- Heavy sighing
- Staring into the distance
- Yawning
- Shifting their weight
- Foot tapping
- Twiddling thumbs
- Finger tapping
- Uncrossing and crossing arms
- Uncrossing and crossing legs
- Scribbling or doodling

- Playing with small objects such as paper clips, pens, coins, etc.

- Pointing the body away from the speaker

- Side to side head movement

- Preening clothes or fingernails

- Stretching

- Trying to do something else

- Holding the chin in the hand and looking around the room

When people are bored, they engage in some kind of physical activity to stay attentive. If a bored person does not engage in these physical activities, they may fall asleep. Because of the necessary presence of physical activity, boredom is among the easiest emotional states to spot and among the most difficult to hide.

Some of the signs of boredom are the same or similar to those of someone attentive or thoughtful. The key distinction between the two is the absence or presence of movement. Remember that if a person is staring off into space and is completely still, they may be thinking something over. If that same person is staring off into space while fidgeting with something, odds are that person is bored out of their skull.

Angry

An angry person will express that anger by becoming withdrawn, aggressive, or defensive. Anger in the form of aggression is the easiest to spot, being characterized as a flushed face, puffed out chest, a set jaw, tight lips, and a loud and forceful voice. However, many people try not to express their anger so outwardly, or they at least try to control that expression, and will then tend to become withdrawn or defensive.

Some common signs of the three types of anger include:

- Flushed face

- Sarcastic or feigned laughter

- Irritated movement of the arms

- Crossed legs

- Crossed ankles

- Crossed arms

- Finger pointing

- Firm posture

- Phrase repetition

- Lips that are closed tight

- Quick speech

- Quick body movements

- Fixed facial expression or grimace

- Shaking

- Clenched fists

- Set jaw

- General tension

- Quick, shallow, or short breaths

- Hands placed on hips.

- Invasion of personal space

Frustrated

The two forms of frustration are surrender and confrontation. Confrontational frustration is characterized by the person who is under the impression that they can fix whatever is causing the frustration by directly approaching the problem. The signs of confrontational frustration can therefore mirror those that would otherwise indicate anger. The frustration of surrender happens when that irritated person realizes that they cannot fix whatever is irritating them. Surrender frustration is characterized, not by signs indicating anger, but by signs of passive irritation.

Some common signs of frustration of the confrontational variety are:

- Direct and consistent eye contact

- Repetition of certain phrases

- Invasion of personal space

- Should shrugs

- Finger pointing

- Hand gesturing

Signs exhibiting the onset or frustrational surrender include:

- Over-emphasized movement

- Hands to head

- Scowling

- Sighing

- Quick exhalation

- Hands resting on hips

Signs that the frustration of surrender has been reached include:

- Hands thrown in air

- Shoulder shrugging

- Turning away

- Walking away

- Closing the eyes

- Rolling the eyes

- Head shaking

Although confrontational frustration can easily turn into anger, it is important that you not confuse the two and thereby throw off your analysis. It is also important that you do not mistake boredom for surrender type of frustration. While several bored signals mirror those of surrendering out of frustration, bored people are not necessary frustrated, just as those who have surrendered to a situation out of frustration are probably not going to be bored.

Depressed

Clinical depression is an animal all its own. Someone suffering from clinical depression may be entirely unable to function, suffer from eating disorders, find concentrating on anything almost impossible, and disregard hygiene. Clinical depression requires medical treatment. We will not here be describing clinical depression. What we mean here by "depression" is the average type of day-to-day depression that we all have felt at some point in our lives.

Depression affects almost every one of your body's functions, including your body language and voice. Depressed people move and speak differently. Someone who is depressed will be sluggish and glum. They will be wholly unenthusiastic and tired. Thus, in addition to analyzing someone's body language when searching for signs of depression, remember to pay attention to that person's voice. That is another avenue by which depression is sure to manifest itself.

Specific signs of day-to-day depression include:

- Lack of concentration

- Poor memory

- Intentional and slow movement

- Relaxed posture

- Increased appetite

- Decreased appetite

- Slow and quite speech

- Lack of focus

- Eyes downcast

- Isolation

- Diminished capacity to plan in advance

- Lack of attention to personal hygiene

- Lack of attention to personal appearance

Nervous

Being nervous, just like being bored, causes discomfort. Again, like

 boredom, to distract themselves from that discomfort, a nervous individual will move their body. Being nervous creates a lot of energy, and a nervous person will need to find something to do with all that extra energy.

Signs that are typical of nervousness include:

- Body tension

- Eyes moving back and forth

- Curling up of the body

- Rocking

- Side to side shifting of weight

- Uncrossing and crossing arms

- Uncrossing and crossing legs

- Tapping hands

- Tapping fingers

- Tapping feet

- Throat clearing

- Lip biting

- Nervous coughing

- Adjustment of, or fidgeting with, hair, jewelry, hands, pens, coins, clothing, fingernails, or any other small object

- Hand squeezing

- Nervous smiling (frequently and rapidly alternating between smiling and not smiling)

- Nervous talking

- Eyes downcast

- Shaking

- Biting finger nails

- Preening cuticles

- Sudden silence

- Upper body rotation from side to side

- Sweating

As you can see, nervousness comes with a great deal of signs, many of which are shared with other emotional states. However, nervous people will generally exhibit more than just one of the signs listed above. Therefore, when analyzing whether someone is nervous or not, look for two or three signs to be sure you are not misreading the situation.

Embarrassed

People who are embarrassed typically conceal their embarrassment, making embarrassment a rather tricky feeling to track. Further, how someone acts when they are embarrassed varies from one person to the next. It is important, then, to understand and identify the behaviors that typify embarrassment so that you do not mistake one of those behaviors for nervousness, anger, fear, secretiveness, or defensiveness.

Common indications that a person is feeling embarrassed include:

- Averting their eyes

- Lack of eye contact

- Head shaking

- Laughing nervously

- Smiling nervously

- Flushed fact

- Leaving the situation

- Avoiding contact with others

Confused

Practically speaking, confusion rarely manifests itself independently of other emotions. A confused person will often also be showing signs of indecision, frustration, or fear. It will be useful to think of a confused person as someone who is lost in the woods and is searching for a reliable path.

Typical signs of confusion include:

- Indications of frustration

- Repetition of statements

- Fidgeting or shifting

- Picking something up then immediately setting it down

- Indications of being indecisive

- Behavior that conflicts with itself

- Inconsistent behavior

- Repetition of movements

Fear

Fear is one of the most fundamental emotions humans experience. Fear generally starts as surprise, and then quickly transforms into a nerve-wracking

combination of nervousness and defensiveness. In the modern age, fear does not occur as frequently as, say, anxiety, but it is healthy to have an idea of what mannerisms characterize fear in case you ever need to identify it. Keep in mind that everyone reacts to fear differently, so attention will need to be paid to determine the emotion you are looking at accurately.

Signs of fear include:

- All signs of surprise
- Eyes opened wide
- Shaking
- Breathing heavily
- Placing hands over face
- Flushed face
- Holding on to others
- Putting the hands in front of body
- Turning the body away
- Shallow and rapid breaths
- Screaming or yelling
- Paralysis
- Exaggerated swallowing
- Gulping
- Wringing the hands or holding on tightly to something

- Not breathing

- Glancing around (keeping the head on a swivel)

- Leaning backwards

- Rapid walking

- Lip licking

- Rigid posture

- Taking slow, hesitant steps

Surprise

The amygdala's sudden adrenaline production characterizes surprise in response to unexpected stimuli (i.e., the "fight-or-flight" response). Given its sudden and unexpected nature, surprise can result from several different emotional states, including pleasure, pain, fear, and excitement. Regardless of the cause, the physical response follows the same basic formula. That is, there is some kind of rapid movement of the body accompanied by a transitory inability to control the smaller types of muscle. Once these reactions take place, a surprised person will usually take up their pre-surprised position rather quickly. The surprise response is generally the same regardless of whether the catalyst is a good or bad thing.

Indications include:

- Going wide eyed

- Extension of the arms

- Jumping

- Screaming

- Yelling

- Gasping

- Mouth agape

- Taking backwards steps if the person is on their feet

- Leaning back if the person is sitting down

- Extension of the legs

Chapter 5:   Gestures of Man and Woman

Recognizing the Attraction Signals

The game of love is two things. It's not simple, and it's not straightforward. You might have to go through a lot of broken  hearts before you finally learn the ropes. Kiss a lot of toads before you finally find the one. You might misread a lot of signals that lead to misunderstanding, perhaps even miss the signals entirely and be so oblivious you can't tell when someone might see you as more than just a friend. Unless that is, you learn to read their body language accurately. From the voice to physical signals, the signs of a romantic interest could be right in front of you once you know what you're looking for.

There are some general body language cues that a person emits if they are romantically interested in someone. For example, they may find ways to touch you, like brushing against your shoulder, putting a strand of your hair behind your ear.

These are classic flirtation signs and if you are uncomfortable, say so but if you are enjoying it, this person is clearly into you. Identifying a romantic interest requires careful and skilled interpretation of signals and actions.

The last thing you want is to read the signals wrong and perhaps end up jeopardizing a perfectly good friendship (assuming you were friends at first) because you misread them. Now the situation has just become uncomfortable.

Oh, body language may have been around for a very, very long time, but little has changed since then when it comes to signaling romantic interest in the opposite sex. It makes sense that when we like someone, our body becomes a beacon bouncing signals all over the place. After all, we've got all the body language signals we need when we want to silently tell someone to back off or stay away from us.

Why wouldn't we have signals that tell a romantic interest hey, I like you? Once the heart and mind have decided you know what? I think I like him/her; our bodies immediately start subtly signaling our attraction in several ways. If our romantic interest is observant enough, they can tell.

General Body Language Indicators That Signal Romantic Interest

The question now is, how do we start recognizing these signs? Let's begin with some of the general indicators applicable to both men and women. If you happen to spot any of these signs on display, perk up your attention, there could be some flirtation going on:

· Like Looking in A Mirror - You subconsciously mirror the body language of the person you're interested in. Their gestures, movements, even facial expressions. When they smile, so do you. When they shift slightly in their seats, so do you.

· The Head Tilt - Tilting your head towards the person who speaks to you indicates that you're interested in what they have to say. In women, body language experts claim that tilting the head is a submissive gesture because it exposes your throat and neck, making you look smaller and a lot less threatening. The next time you're talking to someone you like (or if they're talking to you), take a quick peek at how they position their heads. Feeling shy around your love interest? Don't worry, that's perfectly normal, especially when it's still new. Even if you're feeling shy though, when someone is interested in you, they will try to maintain eye contact and their head will be tilted slightly to signal their interest.

· The Blush - Possibly the most obvious and telling indicator is blushing in the presence of your crush. It also happens to be one of our most primitive body language signals telling someone you're interested in them. Flushing or blushing is our body's way of mimicking the effects of orgasm. Blushing is a common occurrence in the early stages of courtship. Women mimic this same effect through make up each time you put on your blush or lipstick.

· The Lean In - In general, when we like anyone (romantically or not), we tend to lean forward to signal our interest. Leaning forward when they're talking signals our engagement in the conversation, and this signal is spotted often when we are around family, friends, and anyone that we like or care about. In a romantic situation, our bodies are only too eager to lean towards the object of our attraction.

· Pointed Knees, Pointed Feet - Your knees and feet will be pointed towards the direction of the person you've set your sights on. This

624

maneuver is done subconsciously, and most prominent when we're in the sitting position.

What's His Body Language Telling You?

Locking eyes across the room with that tall, handsome stranger. You feel a nervous flutter in your stomach as you nervously run your hair through your fingers. Does he think I'm attractive? Is he interested? How can I tell if he is interested? A hundred questions and more are probably swimming through your mind as you go back and forth, trying to decide if you think he likes you. The expectation has come to be that men should be the ones to make the first move, although many women these days have no qualms about being the one to approach the man first.

What about the less confident women, though? The ones who still worry about embarrassing themselves are why they never want to be the one who makes the first move. But it isn't easy for men to make the first move either. They have feelings too, and they are just as worried about humiliating themselves and getting rejected, the way women are. That's a lot of pressure on the man's shoulders to make something happen. Women can make it easier by meeting them halfway, like learning to recognize the signals that indicate he might be romantically interested in pursuing something more.

- Indicator #1: The "Open" Face - Warm, friendly and welcoming. He'll even greet you with a smile when he locks eyes with you. When a man is keen, it's written all over his face, and everything about him is inviting you to have a conversation.

- Indicator #2: The Eyebrow "Flash" - The "eyebrow flash" happens when a man raises his eyebrows and then drops them again in a quick motion, signaling that they're interested in what they see.

- Indicator #3: Parted Lips - A move often spotted during the first initial stages of the meeting, if you notice a man's lips may be parted when he's looking at you, it could be an indication of a romantic interest.

- Indicator #4: Subconscious Grooming - He grooms himself without realizing it. Some examples of what this might look like include stroking his beard if he has one, smoothing down his clothes to look presentable, even running his hands through his hair to groom it.

- Indicator #5: Standing Tall - When a man is romantically interested, he will attempt to make himself appear taller by straightening his posture when he's around you, even more so when he's standing next to you. His feet might even be positioned slightly apart to widen his stance, making him appear tall and strong. He may stand with his hands on his hips, which helps accentuate his physique and size.

- Indicator #6: Holding Your Gaze - Some men may be a lot shyer than others or struggle with eye contact in general, but if he is interested, most of the time he's going to hold your gaze for as long as possible until one of you look away. When he has caught your eye, he will smile during eye contact, maybe even touch his face (called the preening move) when you're looking at each other.

- Indicator #7: Leaning Forward - If he's sitting down, he will subconsciously try to be as close to you as possible by sitting on the edge of his seat.

- Indicator #8: Guiding You - He attempts to guide you when you're out walking together. This is often done by placing his hand on the small of your back.

What's Her Body Language Telling You?

What a different world it is that we live in today. There was a time when men were the only ones expected to make the first move if they were interested. They had to woo you, wine and dine until they finally made a significant enough impact that led to romance. Today, though, both party can make the first move, and the ball doesn't always have to be in the man's court.

There's nothing wrong with a woman making the first move if they think a man may be interested. Men have feelings too, and if you're self-conscious about getting embarrassed, so are they. No one likes to get their heartbroken, squashed or stomped on, so if you're interested in a man, there's no harm in letting him know.

- Indicator #1: Pouting Lips - A woman may pout her lips (or lick them), to signal her romantic interest in a man. This is often accompanied by another body language move, where she lowers her lashes while looking upwards at you.

- Indicator #2: Flick of Her Wrists - She shows off the most vulnerable part of her body, her wrists when she's talking to signal her romantic interest. This move is easier to spot when both are sitting down.

- Indicator #3: The Hand on Chin - Referred to as the "head pedestal moves", a woman will place her hand under her chin to subconsciously signal her interest. This move is symbolic of "placing her head in a pedestal", and her body language is doing this hoping to get your attention.

- Indicator #4: The Hip Jut - When both are standing and talking to each other, a woman's interest may be apparent if she's standing slightly outwards with one hip thrust.

- Indicator #5: The Ankle Cross - A romantically interested woman will have her ankles cross and knees pointing towards you when she's sitting down.

- Indicator #6: The Hip Sway- Women naturally sway their hips when they walk, but if she's romantically interested in a man, this move might be even more prominent.

The Vocal Change

There are distinct differences biologically between the way men and women sound. Women's pitches are much higher than the deep, low pitch that men have, and the differences in the way we sound are attributed to evolutionary pressures (choice of mates included). Observing the animal kingdom, pitches are linked to larger animals, which means they are a bigger threat. In the human world, a man's low pitch is a display of dominance against his competitors and appears more sexually desirable to women.

There's even a study that confirms women are attracted to men with a lower pitch sound to their voices. On the other hand, men find women with higher-pitched voices more attractive, as one study confirms. In women, the higher your pitch, the greater the femininity.

Chapter 6:   Body Language at Work

To Avoid When Having an Interview or Conversation at Work:

Exaggerated Gestures

When talking to people, avoid exaggerated gestures because using such gestures may imply, you're overstretching the truth or trying to hide dishonesty. To show honesty and confidence, use small and controlled gestures.

Don't Look at Your Wristwatch

Looking at your wristwatch, especially when you do it consistently is a sign of complete disrespect interpreted to mean you aren't interested in the conversation or you find the current conversation boring. It could also make you seem an impatient person.

Don't Look at the Door

Don't constantly glance at the door and completely avoid looking at the door except of course when the conversation is over and you'd like to take your leave.

Don't Turn Away from Others

People interpret turning away from them as rudeness or as a sign of discomfort. Turning away could also make it seem like you're uninterested in the conversation or don't trust the person speaking.

Don't Cross Your Arms or Legs

Crossing your arms and legs is a closed body language. Crossed body language isn't good for business. When you display closed body language, business associates may interpret it to mean you're being dishonest, hiding something, or are deliberately shutting the other person out. Crossing your arms and legs could also signify stubbornness or defiance.

Being Too Pedantic

Body language needs to be used naturally or others will think you are hiding something or are just irritatingly happy or good-willed. If you are trying to sell something or intimidate people with your body language don't be surprised if they notice what you are doing. Hand gestures should be used sparingly and should not risk be hitting other people in the face. Your posture doesn't always have to be perfect so that you look like a soldier on parade.

Lacking Assertiveness

Assertive might not be the correct word here, but it lets you know how you need to behave more than the vague idea of 'not being confident'. What you need to avoid is defaulting to being too submissive when you are questioned or when speaking to someone that you need to connect with. This can mean making sure you maintain eye contact and only breaking it by looking to the side and not glancing down. It can mean being willing to question others when you think something isn't right and directing the topic of a conversation.

World Dominance

If you are dealing with someone more reserved, quiet, nervous, or perhaps not very confident in themselves, you should adapt to that. These people will generally want space and lower-energy body language from you. This means not getting too close, not putting pressure on them to speak up, and not being open with your body to putting them on edge.

Reading this can be difficult at first, and you will need to learn how

to match energy levels with other people. Mirroring and matching and reading other people through baselines will help you a lot in this regard.

Knowing your place in a social hierarchy is important as well. If you try to be too assertive towards someone who is your superior or even just an elder, this can lead them to think you are disrespectful and arrogant. This might not always be as obvious as it first appears either. You might technically outrank the office secretary, but if they have been with the business a long time you will want to show them respect as they may have more power than you in certain matters despite the fact you 'outrank' them in the office hierarchy.

Insensitivity

Following the last mistake, being insensitive to the feelings and norms of the place you are in is often a big mistake when it comes to body language. In most cases if you're being insensitive with your body language, it's because you aren't being sensitive with your thoughts and communication. However, sometimes you might have your arms crossed across your chest because you are cold or comfortable. So, make sure you pay attention to what you are doing when it matters most. There is a learning curve in certain situations, and it can be steep. If you've never had to care for an injured person before it is difficult to make sure you are using the right kind of comforting body language.

Inconsistent Facial Expression Is Bad

Your words and tone of voice should match your facial expressions. You cannot be speaking strongly and passionately, expressing displeasure and at the same time, smiling. This sort of inconsistency will send the wrong message and may end up confusing your addressee.

Avoid Heavy Nods

Heavy nodes make you appear as if you're inventing an understanding the topic in discussion. Although nodding is a sign of agreement of concentration on the discussion, avoid heavy nods and whenever you don't understand something, rather than nod, ask directly related questions because questions. Questions make you appear attentive and interested. If you don't understand something, ask the other party for clarification.

Avoid Clenching Your Fists

Clenched fist is a form of closed body language that makes you seem defensive and argumentative.

Don't Get Too Close

Respect people's personal spaces and avoid getting too close to them except if you already have a personal relationship with the person you're engaging in conversation or discussion.

Body Language Techniques When in a Job Interview

To ensure you're the one who scores that job after an interview, you should:

Sit Properly

Sit firmly and straight with your back resting on the chair. This shows your interviewers that you're very confident person. If you're so accustomed to slouching that you find it difficult to sit straight, you can adopt this helpful trick – sit straight and assume an imaginary string hanging on the roof and pulling you up from the crown of your head. This will help you avoid unconscious slouching.

Use Hand Gestures

During interviews, you should also use hand gestures to your advantage. When you fail to use your hands, interviewers can misinterpret this to mean you're hiding your hands, which means you're either anxious or not confident. These're not the things you want to project during an interview.

Put Your Palms Up

Keeping your palms open signifies honesty and having nothing to hide. During interviews, adopt an open body language that includes putting your palms up to build trust and project yourself as a confident and straightforward person.

Plant Your Feet on the Ground

Sit straight, face the interviewer, and plant your feet on the ground. At no point during the interview should you turn away from the interviewer or even look at the door.

Breathe

Telling you not to be anxious before, during, and shortly after an interview would be asking too much of us because everybody, even the most confident person, feels a bit of anxiety and apprehension before an important interview such as a job interview.

Even when your inside is a nervous wreck, learn how to control your anxiety so that it doesn't appear so obvious. One way to control anxiety is to breathe: inhale and exhale when you speak so that your anxiety doesn't seem obvious and slow down your heart rate.

Walk Confidently

Your walk is part of your body language; walk confidently with your shoulders pulled back and your neck elongated. Walk with your feet pointing towards the interviewer, initiate eye contact with the occasional side-glances until you get to where the interviewer is, and then initiate a handshake before you sit confidently.

Nod When Listening

Don't just sit there looking when the interviewer is speaking, nod your head as he or she speaks to show understanding, concentration, and intelligence. You can even smile warmly if the situation calls for it. Lastly, lean in. You can also lean in to couple your speech with body language.

It Starts Even Before the Interview

The use of proper body language starts with the receptionist. Many interviewers ask the receptionist for feedback on your attitude and behavior. Assume that the person walking with you to the elevator might be your interviewer or future boss, never take anything or anyone for granted.

Be Open

Avoid making barriers between you and the interviewer. Sit up straight, showing your neck, chest and stomach area. You may not feel confident enough to do this but try it. Remember, do the actions and your brain will follow suit. Do not cross your arms over your chest, keep your hands lightly clenched on your lap or the desk. Keep your lap free and put your bag on the floor, if necessary. Do not slouch or look too relaxed. You might give the impression that you are lazy or arrogant.

Give a Good Handshake

In this case, you want to acknowledge the interviewer's authority, so feel free to offer your hand with the palm slightly up if you feel it's necessary. Allow the interviewer to take a slightly dominant position in the handshake if they try. This will make the interviewer see you as a person who will not be difficult to work with. Take your cue from the interviewer and follow the strength of his or her grip. Mimicry will also give a good impression. Follow the interviewer's pace and stride as you're led to your seat.

Respect Personal Space

If you're not sure, wait for the interviewer to indicate where you should sit. I necessary, ask where you may sit. Sitting in the interviewer's space is a big no-no. Leaning slightly forward can indicate interest but leaning too far forward may cause you to invade the interviewer's personal space.

Make Eye Contact

The base of this imaginary triangle should be above the lips. Focus on this triangle to show interest. Blink occasionally in order not to stare awkwardly. This will demonstrate that you are interested and trustworthy. Be careful not to gaze below the imaginary triangle as this could give a different meaning.

Make Open Palm Gestures

While speaking, use your hands to articulate your ideas. Use open palm gestures and keep your hands below your face and above your waist (make sure your hands can be seen). The open palms indicate that you are knowledgeable and willing to use what you know to help the company.

Show Interest with Your Legs

Keep both feet on the floor, pointing towards the interviewer. Avoid unnecessary and repetitive leg movements like shaking and jiggling as this could signal boredom and disinterest. Women wearing skirts can appear more businesslike if they simply keep their knees together and avoid crossing their legs. Crossed legs can be acceptable as it signals submissiveness. It is especially important not to pair crossed legs with crossed arms as this would indicate an overall negative viewpoint or unwillingness to communicate.

Chapter 7: Body Language in a Relationship

 Knowing whether someone loves you or not from the conversations you have is not rocket science. All you need to do is relax a bit and don't put all your focus on the conversation. Instead, try to pick out some of the nonverbal cues that they unconsciously leave.

As you already know, communication involves tone, spoken words, and body language. You don't have to stay stuck on observing only one of those.

There are some cues that people leave to show that they are in love based on the main groups of body language.

1. Facial expressions

-Pupil dilation or brow-raising

When someone is in love, their facial features become soft. They might show it by dilating their pupils or raising their brows.

You should know the look if you've been with people who love you. Their faces will seem filled and swollen with emotions even when they do not change their expression. Although when someone loves you, they can choose to tell you or not, they can control that.

639

But then they will not be able to control the way they respond subconsciously.

-Smiling

This is one very obvious sign and you may think it should not be included because it's something we all know. However, people can give off fake smiles that you can mistake for a love interest. You should look out for a true smile. A true smile is the kind of smile that creases at the corner of the eyes. That sign is how our brain detects a true and genuine smile from the ordinary smiles that we flash to show politeness. When the person you're on a date with is flashing you lots of real smiles, it means they enjoy your company. This could also indicate that they like you.

-Blushing

Whenever you are with someone you like or crush on, there will be a little reddish tint on your cheek as the conversation goes on. When you're with a person and they blush at intervals, it means they are very comfortable and enjoying your presence. This is a good sign you should look out for.

2. Gestures

When the person you're communicating with physically opens up to you or makes an effort to care for you then it's a sign they are into you.

Whenever they are with you, they like to stay face to face with you and acknowledge your presence. When they meet you, they will try as much as possible to keep the center of their heart close to you as much as they can. Some of the gestures they can display include picking up your coat for you or pushing a stray hair away from your shoulder. These things they do without you asking show that they want to take care of you.

3. Paralinguistics

Take note of the way the loudness, pitch or inflection of their voice fluctuates.

When they are with you, they can raise their voice tone to feel secure with them or reduce it so you can feel loved and calm. However they change it, any shift they make in paralinguistics will show that they are trying to win you over or sway you. When a person changes their paralinguistics it means that they are trying to convince you of something and in this case, it could mean that they want you to become attracted to them because they already are smitten by you.

4. Posture

This is all about the way they carry their bodies or place their feet towards you.

Of course, we know that body language includes posture and this is the way our body shows what it feels or thinks. When a person is in love with you, you will see them trying to carry themselves in a particular manner whenever you are around and most times they do it so they can become more attractive to you or show that they are interested in you. What you should look out for is their sitting position and how they cross their legs and arms.

They are opening up their bodies for you. When they try to broaden their shoulders, it should indicate that they have confidence and are willing to connect with you.

5. Proxemics

One amazing way you can find out a person's love interest towards you is how they enter your personal space.

Usually, culture and some circumstances may determine the kind of space between two people. But apart from any regulations, it is normal for people to engage in casual conversations within 18 inches and four feet apart from each other. If you are with someone and they are frequently coming into your space or doing things like sitting closely, constantly trying to whisper little info to you or holding your arms whenever you both are walking, then it means they are into you.

This does not mean that everybody who comes close to you is in love with you but when the action is backed by love, they do it unconsciously. They just find themselves wanting to be around you.

6. Mirroring

Here, your date tries to copy the things you do. It is more like an empathetic response. Whenever you do something, your crush will do the same. When you add them to your plans, they will do the same. If you call, they also call back.

If you notice that the person you like is following your lead more often, they are mirroring you. This is one way that shows that they are interested in you.

7. Eye Contact

Every time, people say the eyes are the doorway that leads to the soul and other things that show how much information we can read from our eyes. If you are on a date and keep trying to make eye contact, then it means that they desire to build a connection with you.

A lot of the emotional expressions people make involves using the eye strongly. The eyes can share more information about how a person truly feels than every other part of the body. So, even when they maintain eye contact, of they are attracted to you, there will still be signs of pupil dilation and they will put all their concentration on you.

Although we may fake some gestures with our body, our eyes are not easily manipulated and you can't fake a connection. When you walk into wherever they are, you will notice that they are focused on you even when you are with others. They try to seek out for little details about you and cast several glances at your chest, arms, hands, and lips.

7. Haptics

When someone is into you, they'll touch you a lot.

Touch is one very powerful way of communicating. We can deduce many things about someone's feelings for us from the way they touch us. When we touch, we try to show attraction, comfort, affection and many other feelings. People who love you will find an excuse to touch you. Even when you hug, they will want more and that shows that they feel something for you.

-Touching or Playing With Hair

We see in movies where a guy touches a girl's hair and we regard them as mushy couples showing affection. The truth is that this is not only about movie scenes. When the person you like plays with your hair, it means they are flirting with you subtly. It could be that they want to play or are very nervous and excited and can't contain it, so they find something to express.

-Light Touching

If you're having a date in a secluded and calm setting, you will notice them making light touches on your arm or leg. This is a way that they want to show their connection and to tell you that they like you.

-"Accidental" Bumping

When you go out on an action date that involves constantly moving around and being on the move, many things happen. An action date will help you to create memories and experiences that will last. When you're taking such action dates and romantic walks through the city, you will notice that they accidentally bump into you. Don't fret, just smile because this is another method similar to playful touching and they are just trying to make connections.

8. Appearance

You know one very not so obvious way to that a person likes you or feel comfortable with you?

Normally people would wear basic colors, or dress casually

But when you notice that they are putting in more effort and going out of their way to groom themselves before they show up to see you. If they like you, they will want you to see them in the best possible way.

Chapter 8:   Recognize the Lies

Non-verbal Signals

By now, you might be wondering how you can tell if a person is lying. This could get complicated. Many people have instincts for detecting a lie, and these are quite strong, but our instincts could fail us at times.

There are some signs you could look for when trying to spot a lie. The author of The Body Language of Liars, Dr. Lillian Glass, stated that when trying to see if someone is lying to you, you first have to know how this person normally acts. Certain habits, like pointing while talking or oversharing, might be just part of that person's character.

Remember that these signs are only indicators of being dishonest and nowhere near positive proof. Some people are such perfect liars that they could get away with not showing any signs at all.

Keep all that in mind while looking at some signs that someone might be lying to you:

- **Sweating or Dryness**

Changes to a person's autonomic nervous system could trigger a person telling a lie to begin sweating in the T-zone on the face. This is the forehead, chin, mouth, and upper lip. They could also turn dry around their mouth and eyes. They might even start to swallow hard, lick or bite their lips, blink excessively, or squint.

- **Changing Their Head Position**

If you see someone quickly moving their head while you ask them questions, they might be lying to you. Their head might also jerk backward, tilt to one side, or bow down. This happens right before they are expected to respond to your question.

- **Complexion**

Have you ever been talking to somebody and they turn ghostly white? This is another sign that they aren't telling you the truth. This show the blood has rushed out of their face.

- **Breathing Changes**

If a person is lying, they might begin to breathe heavily. This is normal. If their breathing begins to change, their shoulders will rise, and their voice will get shallow. They will run out of breath since their blood flow and heart rate has changed. Your body goes through these changes if you begin to feel nervous or tense when you lie.

- **Mouth**

If a person's lips begin to roll into the point that they begin to disappear, it might mean that they are leaving out important pieces of information. When someone does this, they are holding back emotions or facts.

People that lie will purse their lips if they are asked very sensitive questions. Pursing of the lips might mean that someone doesn't want to be a part of your conversation. This is an automatic reflex. This shows that they are not interested in talking.

- **Standing Extremely Still**

People will normally fidget if they get nervous, but you should look for people who aren't moving at all.

This might be a sign of the body's fight mode rather than the flight response, as it gets ready for a confrontation. When you engage in conversations, it is normal to move around in subtle, relaxed, and unconscious movements. If you notice somebody in a rigid, catatonic stance where they aren't moving at all, this is a big warning that something is very wrong.

- **Eyes**

A person who is lying might either look away or stare during crucial moments. If they move their eyes a lot, it could be a sign that they are trying to figure out what they would like to say next.

Geiselman from UCLA found that liars will look away very fast when they are lying. In a 2015 study performed at the University of Michigan, it was discovered that liars would stare at others more often than people who were telling the truth. Around 70 percent of the people who lied would stare directly at the person whom they are lying to.

There have been debates about this, but an article published in Plos One in 2012 said this concept. They concluded that people would look in a certain direction if they are lying. While it is very easy to read too much into how a person is acting, you can gain a lot from their eyes.

- **Touching Their Mouth**

A sure sign that a person isn't telling the truth is they will place either their hands on their mouth if they aren't interested in answering a question or facing a problem.

When adults cover their mouths with their hands, they show you that they aren't truthful in what they are saying, and they aren't interested in telling you the truth. They are showing you that they are closing down all lines of communication.

- **Being Fidgety**

Some other signs of deception might include a person who is shuffling their feet, moving their head from side to side, or rocking back and forth on their feet or in their seat. This is created by fluctuations in our autonomic nervous system that regulates functions throughout our bodies and could also create an effect. If someone is shy, these fluctuations could cause a person to feel itchy or tingly, and this might cause them to fidget even more.

R. Edward Geiselman, a professor at UCLA, conducted some research and found a very similar conclusion. He found that people will display certain grooming behaviors like playing with their hair if they aren't truthful.

- **Covering Vulnerable Body Parts**

649

This could include parts such as the chest, head, throat, or abdomen. Go to any courtroom and just watch people. You will be able to spot when a witness is lying or if a testimony hits a nerve with the defendant if their hand goes to their throat.

- **Hands**

Liars like using gestures after they have spoken instead of before or during the conversation state Traci Brown, an FBI consultant. Their minds are busy doing many different things like making up their story, trying to see if people believe them, and adding in more details. Common gestures that regularly happen just before speaking usually happen after they talk.

The University of Michigan performed a study in 2015 that studied 120 video clips of relevant court cases to help them understand the way people act when they are lying versus when they are telling the truth. This study showed that people who lie would gesture using both hands. People who are telling the truth usually use just one hand. People used both hands around 40 percent of the time compared to 25 percent of the people who are telling the truth.

If a person is lying, they will normally turn their palms away from their speaking person. This is an unconscious signal to you that they are withholding emotions or information. They might even put them under a table or in their pockets.

- **Shuffling Their Feet**

This is their body taking over. When people start to shuffle their feet, this shows you that they are nervous and uncomfortable. It shows you that they want to walk away from the conversation. This is a great way to spot liars. What their feet and they will tell you a lot.

- **The Point**

If a person gets hostile or defensive, they are trying to turn things around on you. If they get confronted about a lie, they might begin using aggressive gestures like pointing.

- **Staring But Not Blinking**

If a person is lying, it is common for them to break eye contact, but some liars will go the extra mile to keep eye contact to manipulate and control you. If someone is telling you the truth, they might occasionally shift their eye and might look away now, and then, Liars will use a steady gaze to control and intimidate. Watch out for rapid blinking, too.

Verbal Signals

Here are some changes to a person's voice when they are lying:

- **Hard Time Speaking**

If you have watched a suspect get interrogated and know they are guilty, you will see it hard for them to talk. This will happen because their nervous system lowers the flow of saliva in stressful times, and this causes the mucous membranes of the mouth to become dry. If they purse or bite their lips, these are also signs that they are lying.

- **Voice if High-pitched**

If someone is nervous, their vocal cords might tighten up, causing their voice to sound high-pitched. Their voice might also creak. They might clear their throat, meaning they are trying to cope with how uncomfortable their throat feels. It could also signal a lie.

- **Giving Lots of Information**

If someone is constantly talking and giving you all sorts of information and this information isn't anything that you haven't even asked for, and they seem to be providing a lot of little details, this is a good indicator lying. Liars will talk more because they hope that talking a lot and being open will make people believe them.

- **Changes in Volume**

If a person is telling a lie, they might raise their voice. Their voice might get louder because they are feeling defensive.

- **Repeating Specific Words or Phrases**

This happens because they are trying to convince themselves and you of something. They are trying to prove the lie to themselves. They might repeat, "I didn't... I didn't..." constantly.

This repetition is a way to buy them some time while they try to gather their thoughts.

- **They Use Certain Phrases**

If someone likes using phrases like: "let me tell you the truth," "honestly," or "I would like to be honest with you." These are all signs that they might be trying extremely hard or little to convince you that they are honest.

- **Slip-Ups**

Many people aren't born liars. Most of the time, we will let the truth slip out. Take notice if someone says things like: "I got fired – no, I meant I quit" or "I had dinner with Frank – no, I meant I had to work late." You might just have a liar in your presence.

- **They Use Certain Words**

If a person frequently uses words such as: "um," "like," or "uh," they are using what is called vocal fill, and these are all deception indicators. People will use these fillers to figure out what they need to say next.

Chapter 9:   Principles of Body Language Intelligence

Principles of Body Language Intelligence

The following are few principles of body language intelligence:

Body Language Precedes Words

Individuals say and do things in response to what others say and do. These external happenings act as triggers or cues that inspire innate responses.

Cues could equally be internal. For example, where concerns and thoughts result in a change in the position of the body. You may also ask, "Considering their body language, what could they be feeling or thinking?"

Cues are a crucial aspect of conditioning where actions and emotions are paired with a signal. When the cue shows up, it triggers a range of feelings and likely associated actions that the individual may try suppressing. This cue response could also be natural, like the way some creatures cause a fear response.

Context Is Everything

Context may impact how a person acts, feels, and thinks. What is happening in the immediate surroundings could have an obvious effect. For example, when men are around appealing young ladies, they indulge in posturing and preening.

The broader context of an individual's life may have an impact on their body language. It typically indicates excitement, anxieties, and anticipation. If you are not aware of such modifiers, your efforts to read their body language could have a severe effect on your efforts.

Search for Clusters

While changes in body language can show up as single happenings, like the folding of arms, they often show up as a group of diverse movements that occur at the same time or one after the other. For example, individuals may cross their arms, change their posture, lean back slightly, frown, and purse their lips as simultaneous evidence of disagreement.

Clusters of body movement send obvious signs when they all specify the same thing. This awareness may occur when each has a related meaning, or where the entire group of movement merges to create one definition.

At times, cluster movements oppose one another. For example, when an individual rubs his nose, which shows a possible deception, and smiles. The subsequently mixed signals will likely result in you feeling uncomfortable, and it would be smart to be vigilant for these gut feelings while searching for why you may be feeling this way.

Character

The general character of the other individual is a factor that can compound and explain a lot. An individual who is an extrovert, for example, may show regular and large body movements, while a more introverted individual may utilize more precise gestures.

Confusing these personality qualities for others like timidity is easy. In a bid to categorize others, we frequently misread limited body signs and filter things we see using these inaccurate mental models.

Mood, temperament, and short-term emotions can also function as modifiers that impact body language, making it much harder to interpret. Suppose you can determine the present emotional state of a person. In that case, you will be able to apply this insight in your interpretation and attain a better understanding of the actual meanings of their motions.

Sudden Changes Are Relevant

A crucial thing to look out for are changes. For example, when an individual scratch their nose suddenly, it could be a sign of discomfort.

When you observe changes in body language, search for cues that may have caused the transition. For example, when an individual suspected of telling lies is asked a question and he looks away.

Individuals in sales are always on the lookout for body language changes like subtle cues, positive responses, and leaning forward as signs that a client is becoming persuaded. The salesperson then utilizes this knowledge as a sign to head to the next phase in closing the deal.

Chapter 10: Understanding People through Body Language

You may be wondering what is the importance of learning other people's body language. It may be a challenge but is it important that you are aware.

Identifying People's Hidden Thoughts through Body Language

Gaining the art of understanding people's nonverbal communication is a hard thing. You may be wondering how can you focus on learning other people's cues while you do not know yourself fully. Well, the book must help you demystify the art of understanding the body language for different people.

All of us are subconscious experts in interpreting the thoughts of other individuals towards us. In the Woolly Mammoth Age (25,000 years ago), we developed these abilities since our life depended on them, and the unconscious mind would work more efficiently than the conscious mind. But when we make this unconscious understanding conscious, it does not have a good result. We can respond with lightning speed to dodge a fist that some whiny brat throws in our way or jump out from the way of an approaching car, practically before we can think about it explicitly.

Allied and Opposed

How would you tell whether somebody is your ally or not? The fundamental nonverbal communication to search for to decide if individuals are united to you or restricted is generally speaking physical position and their direction. This makes for engaging people viewing. When you're on to this part of conduct, you'll see that it is easy to get.

Simply, individuals who are in understanding will general mirror each other's conduct. One will lead, and the other will pursue. This is particularly simple to tell when there are three individuals present, and you need to make sense of who's your ally and who isn't. Search for the person who has a similar essential body direction as you. For a test, move and check whether the other individual sticks to this same pattern in the following thirty seconds.

Strong and Subservient

In space and height, the story of power in a room is written. Scan the alpha. If possible, he or she would be the greatest person in the room. That's why kings and queens have had daises thrones since they started ruling others.

Powerful individuals are also taking up so much space: splaying out their legs or arms, or hogging more space in the room. That's why influential people get larger apartments than fewer men, and that's why taller people in their careers are significantly more likely to rise faster than short people.

Powerful individuals use a host of bolder indicators of their dominance to indulge in shorter breaks, from upsetting smaller individuals to talking more. We make more or less eye contact based on their choice. They monitor the communication of the second speaker's ballet with the eye and the outside contact.

Committed and Uncommitted

Commitment is when you close the offer, the contract ink, get the job, and get the' go forward.' It's a key moment, and it's important to be able to see it so that you aren't doing the wrong thing at the pivotal moment. People learn to you when they are serious. They are transparent, submissive at times, always genuine, and generally well connected.

It starts with your eyes: they're completely open and you're focused. Likewise, the face is open. It will be very close to yours more than anything. It's all about completing the sale to close the distance. That's why car sales representatives regularly shake your hand. The torso, if not engaged, is accessible and nearer to you. From the arms and hands, feet and legs, there is no oppositional chatter. If appropriate in the situations, the person or persons may well mimic you. The act of communication is often indicated by a change of nonverbal communication, which suggests a decision has been made.

Open and Closed

The very first way to determine the motives of others is the most important one their level of transparency. It is the most important since interaction will start if people are honest with one another. Nothing good can happen if they aren't. You ought to be prepared to scale individuals more along the lines quite easily in an almost automated way with just a little training. But don't ask for an immediate reading what people these days call thin-slicing. In reality, it takes a little time for each new individual you meet to measure the performance of conduct. The idea isn't capable of carrying out this role immediately but to size up somebody with high efficiency in terms of whether this person is open to you within a few minutes.

Arms and Legs Crossed Suggest Opposition to Your Ideas

Legs and arms crossed are obstructions that indicate that the other individual is not receptive to what you tell. You find that, even if they tend to engage in the good conversation and smile, most of the time the real truth is revealed through body language. A case is studied by authors who were doing negotiations for their new book on reading body language. They held many meetings and later revealed that among all the meetings, not one resulted in an agreement whenever one of the parties crossed their legs and feet when negotiating. Mentally, legs crossed and arms mean an individual is being mentally, emotionally, or physically stopped from what's before them. It's not deliberate so it's so surprising.

Copying Your Body Language

Have any of you ever met somebody and found that they do the same if you cross or uncross your legs and feet? Or maybe when you're thinking, they lean their heads the very same position as yours? In reality, that's a good indication. If we experience a bond with another person, mirroring body language comes in unintentionally. It's an indication that the discussion moves well enough and another group is receiving your message. Such information can be particularly helpful when bargaining, as it tells you what the other party feels about the contract.

The Story Is Told By Posture

Have you ever seen someone come into a room and immediately know that they are in control? This influence is primarily about the body's language, and often involves an upright stance, movements with the palms facing forward, and  generally open and expressive gestures. The brain is programmed to balance energy with the number of people taking up space. It's a position of authority to stand straight with your shoulders back; it seems to maximize the amount of storage you fill. On the other hand, slouching is the product of the collapse of your shape; it seems to take up less space and less energy for activities. Maintaining good posture commands respect and fosters commitment, regardless of being in a leadership position or not.

The Eyes Are Crinkled By Genuine Smiles

The mouth can deceive whenever it applies to laugh, however, the eyes can never lie. Genuine smiles touch the ears and wrinkle the skin in front of them to build the crow's feet. Individuals sometimes smile to conceal what they might feel and think, so watch for crinkles at the edges of their eyes the next time you want to know if somebody's smile is real. If they're not there, something covers the smile.

Discomfort In Raised Eyebrows

Three fundamental feelings cause your eyebrows to go up shock, stress, and the feeling of fear. Have a go at causing a stir when you're having a casual calm discussion with a companion. It's hard to do, would it say it isn't? If someone conversing with you happens to have raised eyebrows, yet the subject of the discussion isn't one that would consistently cause shock, stress, or dread, there is something different going on.

Misrepresented Nodes Signal Nervousness about Acceptance

When you're telling somebody something and they keep nodding too much, this implies they are stressed over what you consider them or question their capacity to adhere to your guidelines.

A Held Jaw Signals Pressure

A gripped jaw, a fixed neck, or wrinkled temples are altogether indications of stress. Despite what the individual is stating, these are indications of significant inconvenience. The discussion may be diving into something they're on edge about or their psyche maybe somewhere else, concentrating on what's worrying them. The key is to look for that befuddle between what the individual says and what their strained nonverbal communication is letting you know.

Chapter 11:   Handshake

Handshaking is certainly one of the oldest gestures known to man: not that from the beginning of time we have shaken hands exactly as the Westerners do today, yet in principle it is a gesture shared and recognized throughout the world, ancient and modern. On the other hand, behind a handshake there is culture, sociality and history. For this reason, it is a gesture that deserves to be carefully analyzed: shaking hands with an acquaintance, a boss, and a potential customer is like offer your business card to the interlocutor, which is no small thing, don't you think?

A Bit of History

Since the beginning of time, the handshake has been one of the most commonly used gestures to get in touch with another person: today with the handshake we break the ice, introduce ourselves to a  stranger, start or conclude a meeting, we congratulate a friend or perhaps end an argument; all thanks to body contact, but also thanks to the story that lives behind the handshake.

We already shook hands five thousand years ago: the Egyptian hieroglyphics that depict the establishment of pacts between men and gods thanks to significant handshakes tell us this. Even in Babylon the monarch used to shake hands with the divinity: it was a symbol of respect and the handshake also meant, not least, the transfer of powers from God to the King. The gestures did not take long to spread throughout the East, but it seems that even the ancient West knew its power well. In Greece and Rome, they shook hands slightly differently than we do today: We preferred to grasp the forearm or maybe the wrist and the carpal tunnel (the narrow portion of the wrist) to emphasize the peaceful encounter.

In Medieval Europe, even local gentlemen hugged their forearms: it was a way of confirming that they did not hide weapons in their sleeves and to guarantee the peaceful character that the meeting would have had.

Not Just Something Manly or For Men Only

In the past, the handshake was a gesture mainly referred to male members: especially in societies that knew a strict separation between the sexes, the handshake between men and women was frowned upon. Muhammad's followers would never shake a woman's hand, no matter how usual and encouraged among men. Even in Western Europe it was unusual to see a handshake between a man and a woman; the costume was also mainly male: shaking hands made it possible to keep the distances between men (particularly sensitive to respect for one's proxemic space since always) and clearly showed the intentions of the other.

Of course, things have changed profoundly today and gestures equally involve women and men, especially in working contexts: the formal act has become indispensable to facilitate the approach between individuals. That to shake hands is a man or a woman. Today's meaning is always the same: we authorize interaction and show ourselves open in comparison with others, implicitly confirming that our intentions are peaceful.

A Personal Gesture

It will also be a social gesture, the value of which has been learned since childhood, but this does not mean that shaking hands is an impersonal act; everyone does it in their way and for this reason it is a way through which you have the opportunity to know a few more details about the person in front of you. Shaking hands is a serious matter!

There is a lot to unpack behind a handshake, especially in the workplace, this gesture sounds like a business card: it helps to give oneself a good or bad impression. It tells something more about the personality of the person making the gesture. These are not conclusions that have been reached by mere experience; studies conducted on this confirm what our grandparents have always suspected: behind the handshake there is much more than a mechanical and courteous gesture. Physical reasons dictate everything: when you shake hands, some areas of the brain become activated or show greater sensitivity. Amygdala and superior temporal sulcus are activated by increasing the unconscious positive evaluation of the individual in front of you.

Therefore it is not only a useful gesture to show friendliness, but also a winning card to be used in society to give oneself, at first glance, a positive impression. All very true, provided that the hand is squeezed in the right way.

So, as we see, a handshake says much more than a hundred words about us, so it is good to find out which ones to avoid, capable of giving a bad initial impression, which will make it difficult to erase or make people forget. Especially when we are in front of a recruiter, during a job interview, or when we find ourselves face to face with a customer, to give confidence in our person does not only think about our way of doing, our clothing, our perfume or our smile: even if unconsciously the handshake can turn into a winning card capable of giving a positive turn to the meeting.

Handshakes You Should ALWAYS Avoid

The following is a list explaining in details what handshakes you should avoid and why!

· Handshake dead fish

In the first position among the handshakes to avoid is the dead fish handshake: it is weak, it is elusive and most of the time it is cold and damp; nothing more unpleasant. This handshake conveys coldness and mistrust and is typical of those who are distant and uninvolved.

· The Dutch handshake

It is a handshake related to that of a dead fish although the hand, in the case in question, is slightly more rigid and less wet. Not even this kind of handshake gives a big impression of itself.

· The handshake in vice

It is a dominant handshake: normally the wrist is slightly rotated enough to push the other with the palm facing down. Normally it is a vigorous handshake accompanied by a few pats on the shoulder. Those who grant it have the more or less explicit intention of immediately assuming a control position.

· The handshake breaks bones

Perhaps it is one of the least appreciated, which leaves a very unpleasant memory of itself: it is aggressive and painful, often accompanied by a wide smile, clearly not sincere. Remember that an account is an energetic hold and an account is a hold capable of ovalizing the interlocutor's rings.

· The match-maker's handshake

Who is the matchmaker? He was the one who once dealt with mediating business and contracts in many traditional and agricultural societies, especially in the world breeding. I do believe every one of us has been a victim of it at least once: the hand is grabbed vigorously, pulled by the interlocutor and moved rhythmically up and down several times. As soon as you understand that you are the victim of such a handshake, the first thought is to get rid of it. Urban legends tell of endless sensual handshakes.

· The remote handshake

It is characterized by an unusual rigidity of the arm and is typical of aggressive people who want to keep the interlocutor at a safe distance. It is an unusual and friendly handshake, but less annoying than others.

· The partial handshake

In this case the feeling is not pleasant: the interlocutor only gives us the fingertips and the goal is to keep a certain distance with the person in front of us.

· The magnetic handshake

To characterize this handshake is the attempt to drag the arm and the interlocutor towards him, bringing him to his own "space" where one feels more secure. At times, foreigners who know less personal distances also use this kind of handshake: in any case, with this kind of grip one tries to impose one's own behavioral rules.

How to Have a Proper Handshake and Further Considerations

It is good to remember that the right handshake exists. Offering it is simpler than you might think: it is a firm and rapid grip, which denotes security, sociability and curiosity. However, this mustn't become too strong and long: it would be a symptom of aggression or worse of exhibitionism.

The handshake is an indispensable gesture to show friendship towards our interlocutor. Still, it can also prove a winning card to give oneself, from the first moment, an excellent impression, which becomes of fundamental importance during a job interview or professional meeting.

All this is because the handshake is not only a social convention but also a real business card that talks about us. Suppose the hands, during the meeting, are squeezed unusually. In that case, this immediately jumps to the eye of the interlocutor: for example, soft or too strong handshakes do not go unnoticed, it is impossible not to notice that the interlocutor lends us a close of a partial hand, holding out only the fingers, or that during the grasp you rotate the wrist excessively.

Even an inattentive observer notices these peculiarities, but an excellent observer can better know who is in front of him, observing his handshake's peculiarities.

Handshakes: How to Read Them

Shaking hands is a serious and meaningful thing: studies conducted on the matter affirm that the interlocutor who shakes the hand by slightly twisting the wrist and forcing the other to turn the palm upwards is an individual with a dominant character, who wants to impose a relationship of subjection immediately. The same applies to those who, shaking hands, give a pat on the back.

If, on the other hand, the handshake is too weak and the interlocutor offers only the fingertips, you are likely in front of a person who does not like physical contact, who is an arrogant, shy and in the worst case opportunistic individual. On the other hand, a too weak handshake has never convinced anyone, right?

Even the sweating level of the hand can tell us a lot about the person in front of us: unlike the rest of the body, the hand sweats not because of an increase in temperature, but rather due to a sudden emotional stress. A wet handshake is not only sensory unpleasant, but it also tells us that the interlocutor probably has a bad stress management ability or is not comfortable in that situation. The unusually cold hand is an indication of low sociability, a tendency towards introverted temperament and neurotic and depressive behaviors: this is especially true when a woman holds out her hand, although it is essential to remember that women are characterized by less efficient peripheral circulation and this often causes, for physical reasons only, a cold hand. In the knowledge phase, a cold handshake is therefore a factor to consider but with caution.

Let's move on to a too strong handshake: this normally characterizes an individual with a strong and dominant personality, particularly rational and self-confident. However, when the tightening becomes excessively strong, this can signify an exhibitionist character and in the worst case aggressive.

If the pressure in the grip is not very penetrating, almost non-existent, the person in front of you is likely to be shy, shy and in some cases suspicious. According to some studies, a too weak handshake could indicate depression and melancholy.

Chapter 12:   Facial Expressions

Wrinkles convey the intensity of emotions and the degree of originality of the emotion. In most cases, wrinkles convey hardship and suffering, as well as extreme anger. Wrinkles can also indicate one is always smiling, senile, or nasty.

Facial expressions and emotions are related. Facial expressions can create an emotional experience. Smiling tends to induce more pleasant moods while frowning induces negative moods. In this manner, facial expressions may cause emotion by generating physiological changes in the body. Through the self-perception process, people assume that they must be sad or happy because they are smiling or frowning, and these cause emotions.

Other factors beyond facial expressions cause emotions. For instance, emotions are largely a function of the human system of beliefs and stored information. In other terms, you feel angry when you score less than average marks because the current system equates that to not being smart enough. And the stored information reminds you that you risk repeating the test or not securing a plum employment position, and this entire matter makes you feel hopeless, upset, and stressed.

There is a possibility that if the belief system did not deem less than average as a failure and the stored information shows a positive outlook for such a score, you will feel happy or excited.

Additionally, twitching your mouth randomly; either way indicates that one is deliberately not listening or degrading the importance of the message. The facial gesture is realized by closing the lips and randomly twitching the mouth to either the right or left akin to swirling the mouth with mouthwash. The facial expression is also to indicate outright disdain to the speaker or the message. The facial expression is considered rude to express disgust with the speaker or the message and should be avoided at all costs.

Where one shuts their lips tightly, it indicates that the individual is feeling angry but does not wish to show the anger. Shutting the lips tightly may also indicate that the person feels uneasy but struggles to concentrate at all costs. The source of the discomfort could be the immediate neighbors, the message, or the speaker. Through this gesture, the individual indicates he or she simply wants the speaker to conclude the speech because not all people are enjoying the message.

When one is angry or strongly disapproves of what the speaker says, the person will grimace. A grimace indicates that the person is feeling disgusted by what is being said. In movies or during live interviews, you probably so the interviewee grimaces when an issue or a person that the person feels is disgusting is stated.

Showing a grimace indicates one harbors a strong dislike for the message or the speaker. A person that is feeling uncomfortable due to sitting on a hard chair, a poorly ventilated room, or sitting next to a hostile neighbor may also show a grimace, which is not necessarily related to the message.

If one is happy, then one is likely to have a less tense face and a smile. Positive news and positive emotions are manifested as a smile or a less tense facial look. On the other hand, if one is processing negative emotions, then the person's face is likely to be tensed up due to exerting pressure on the body muscles. A genuine smile like when one is happy is wider than an average curve and is temporary. A prolonged smile that is very wide suggests the individual is smirking at the message or the speaker. A prolonged smile may also suggest the individual is faking the emotion.

By the same measure, a frozen face may indicate intense fear. For instance, you have seen terrified faces when attending a health awareness forum on sexually transmitted diseases or some medical condition that terrified the audience. In this setting, the face of the audience will appear as if it has been paused. The eyes and the mouth may remain stationary as the speaker presents the scary aspects of the medical condition. It appears negative emotions may slow down the normal conscious and unconscious movement of the muscles of the face.

The appropriateness of facial expressions varies among subcultures of the same cultural group. Compared to the Japanese, Americans readily manifest anger, and this shows that individuals express emotion differentially across cultures.

If you are a teacher or trainer, then you encounter facial expressions from your students frequently. Assuming that you are a teacher, then you have noticed facial expressions indicating shock, uneasiness, and disapproval when you announce tests or indicate that the scores are out.

From these facial expressions, you will concur that the students feel uncomfortable, uncertain, and worried. The students will show lines of wrinkles, look down, eyes wide open and mouths agape when sudden and uncomfortable news is announced. Even though the students may indicate 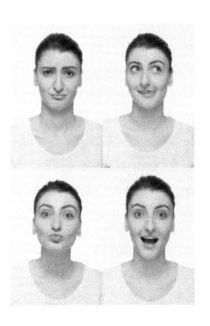 they are prepared for the test, their facial expressions suggest otherwise.

Like all forms of communication, effective reading of facial expressions will happen where the target person is unaware that you are reading even though they understand that their facial expressions are integral to the overall communication. In other words, when one becomes aware he or she is being studied, the person will act expectedly or simply freeze the expected reaction. It is akin to realizing that someone is feeling you.

Since the underlying emotion affects the facial expression that one shows. As indicated, the body language overrides verbal communication, which helps reveal the true status of an individual. One possible argument of the body language triumphing over verbal communication is that the body prioritizes its physiological needs over other needs. The physiological needs are critical to the survivability of an individual.

Over centuries the human body could have been programmed to increase survivability rate by prioritizing physiological needs. Body language largely indicates the physiological state of an individual, which is meant to help the individual and others respect the person's true physiological status.

Imagine what could happen where one is sickly, and it is worsening, but the person manages to manifest a convincing body language of happiness and enthusiasm. The outcome would be prioritizing the emotional needs of the individual over the physiological needs. Apart from laboratory tests and physical examination, it would be difficult for other people to realize that something is amiss and ask the individual to take rest.

Without illness, when one feels anxious about the audience, he or she manifests disharmony of the physiological status. There is a necessity to make the person and the audience aware that the individual is suffering and that they should be understanding of the individual.

Chapter 13:   How to Tell If Someone Is Faking a Facial Expression

There are several reasons why people choose to hide their facial expressions. For some, it is a way suppressing their emotions towards a given matter. As much as their words portray a particular image in your brain, it is their wish that you do not get to see their actual emotions on the same subject. For example, you may be holding a conversation with a potential partner who likes you but they are afraid to let you know that – maybe because they are too shy or unwilling to be the first ones to reveal that. Because of their unwillingncss to express their emotions, they could try to fake their facial expressions. In such a case, it is up to you to discover that on your own. You have to look closely at their faces as they speak to you to get their actual feelings.

Some people have just too much ego that they wouldn't allow their facial expressions to be shown. When a particular matter has hurt them and that they are undergoing immense pain inside, their big egos would not let them reveal such details. These are the kinds of people who suffer in silence which could lead to a harmful situation – suicide, for example.

There is also this category of people who hide their facial expressions, not because they want to do so, but because they just do not know how to solve negative emotions. As negativity builds up from the inside and starts to show in the face, they soon device ways to hide any form of negative expressions to lock you out from analyzing them. They want to look happy when in real sense they are sad. They want you to see that they are having a good time but in reality, there is a sickness or school fees issue that has been stressing them for months. We all know that negative emotions can lead to frowning on one's face, which essentially makes them not so approachable or appealing. Thus, in an attempt to retain their attractiveness, they conceal any form of negative facial expression which would have otherwise confronted them.

In other cases, some people may hide their facial expressions just to please. These are the people who believe in the philosophy that what you do not know cannot hurt you. Their idea is that when they keep some information from you, you may still have a happy life. Thus, when they speak to you, they will struggle to build a certain kind of facial expression which conveys the message that all is well while in real sense that is further from the truth. Let's say one of your best friends gets bad news from the doctor that they have cancer and that they have only a few years with you. They love you so much and know how much such news could be devastating to you. To save you all the pain, they may choose to struggle with the pain on their own, believing that you will have a happy life if provided you do not know about it. Whenever they tell stories with you, they will do their best not to let you go inside.

677

From their facial expressions, they will be smiling for you whereas only they know the agony they are experiencing. You have the responsibility of decoding this so that you get the message they are trying to lock inside.

5 Signs Someone Is Being Fake: How To Tell They Are Faking Facial Expressions

1. Taking deep breath

This is a technique that seems to be universal amongst all people who express untrue facial expressions. You will often see them appear unrelated and continuously breathe in and out heavily in their explanations over a matter you just asked. Because they know that for you to believe the facial expression they just wore to impress you, they have to appear calm. That is what the deep breathes are meant to do – take in more oxygen so that they can recollect their composure and be cool. If you are not keen enough on the breathing pattern, their faces may appear calm to you and succeed in the deception.

2. Putting up a fake smile

A smile never says that someone is happy at all times. Someone who smiles and has a bubbly look on their face can win hearts and affection. As a result, many assume that with just the right smile, they will hide their feelings like anger or sadness. But a fake smile will always be fake. It may convince some people at the first glance but a keen individual will soon realize this smile is fake. How well you know the individual could help you distinguish between the smile they just put up and their real happy smile. But even if you do not know them that well, their inability to sustain the smile will eventually prove it fake.

3. Trying not to supporting the head

There is something about 'cooked' facial expressions that makes the head heavy. People who understand the technique of hiding facial expressions know this. Thus, they always try to make sure that their head is held up high to deceive you better. When you are keen on them, there will be these occasions when they can no longer hold the head up and end up burying the face in their palms for some seconds before realizing that they may show you that they are lying. Careful analysis of the struggles not to support the head could reveal that they are faking their facial expression.

4. Struggling to relax the face

A relaxed face can easily build up a deceiving facial expression. For example, your son may have committed an offense in school and they come to report the matter to you, hoping to come out as victims. If your first glance on their faces shows them as being relaxed, you could be deceived and even get on the wrong side with the teachers. However, if you saw their faces were not relaxed even before they started the explanation, you can tell right away that there must be a problem somewhere. When you speak to someone and their face is relaxed at one time and at the other one it is not, that is a sign of a problem. Within a few minutes their face could be straight while at another it is steel and acting like a tough guy. This shows that they may have tried to relax it up to a certain point when they could do it no more. There is something here; take a deep look at their faces and you shall see it.

5. Silent lip movements

To be calm, some people speak to themselves. They may say something like "Calm down, you can do this. Just stay cool." If you are not careful, they may succeed in being calm and creating a falsified facial expression. Through a keen look at the lip movements, you may tell that they have more things that they are hiding under their facial expressions.

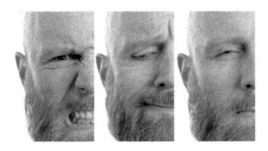

Chapter 14: Posture and Body Orientation

Posture and body orientation should be interpreted in the context of the entire body language to develop the full meaning and being communicated. Starting with an open posture, it is used to denote amicability and costiveness.

In this open position, the feet are placed openly, and the palms of the hands are facing outward. Individuals with open posture are deemed more persuasive compared to those with other stances.

To realize an open stance, one should stand upright or sit straight with the head upright and maintain the abdomen and chest bared. When the open posture is combined with an easy facial expression and good visual contact, it makes one look approachable and composed. Maintain the body facing forward toward the other person during a conversation.

There is also the closed posture where one crosses the arms across the chest or crosses the legs or sits in a facing a forward position as well as displaying the backs of the hands and closing the fists are indicative of a closed stance.

The closed posture gives the impression that one is bored, hostile, or detached. In this posture, one is acting cautious and appears ready to defend themselves against any accusation or threat.

The confident posture helps communicate that one is not feeling anxious, nervous, or stressed. The confident posture is attained by pulling oneself to full height, holding the head high, and keeping the gaze at eye level. Then bring your shoulders backward and keep the arms as well as legs to relax by the sides. The posture is likely to be used by speakers in a formal context such as when making a presentation, during cross-examination and project presentation.

Equally important, there is postural echoing and is used as a flirting technique by attracting someone in the Guardian. It is attained by observing and mimicking the style of the person and the pace of movement. When the individual leans against the wall, replicate the same.

By adjusting your postures against the others to attain a match, you are communicating that you are trying to flirt with the individual. The postural echoing can also be used as a prank game to someone you are familiar with and often engage in casual talk.

Maintaining a straight posture communicates confidence and formality. Part of the confidence of this posture is that it maximizes blood flow and exerts less pressure on the muscle and joints, enhancing the composure of an individual. The straight posture helps evoke desirable mood and emotion, which makes an individual feel energized and alert. A straight posture is a highly preferred informal conversation such as during meetings, presentations, or speech.

Correspondingly being in a slumped position and hunched back is a poor posture and makes one lazy, sad, or poor. A slumped position implies a strain to the body, making the individual feel less alert and casual about the ongoing conversation.

On the other hand, leaning forward and maintaining eye contact suggests that one is listening keenly. During a speech, if the audience leans forward in an upright position, it indicates that they are eager and receptive to the message.

Furthermore, if one slants one of the shoulders when participating in a conversation, it suggests that the individual is tired or unwell. Leaning on one side acutely while standing or sitting indicates that you are feeling exhausted or fed up with the conversation and are eagerly waiting for the end or a break.

Think of how you or others reacted when a class dragged on to almost break time. There is a high likelihood that the audience slanted one of their shoulders to left or right direction. In this state, the mind of the individual deviates to things that one will do next. In case of a tea break, the students' minds will deviate to what one will do during or after the tea break.

By the same measure standing on one foot indicates that one is feeling unease or tired. When one stands on one foot, it suggests

683

that the person is trying to cope with discomfort. The source of uneasiness could be emotional or physiological.

For instance, you probably juggled your body from one foot to ease the need to go for a short call or pass wind. It is a way to disrupt the sustained concentration that may enhance the disturbing feeling.

If one cups their head or face with their hands and rests the head on the thighs, the individual feels ashamed or exhausted.

When the speaker mentions something that makes you feel embarrassed, you are likely to cup their face or head and rest the face on the thighs. It is a literal way of hiding from shame.

Children are likely to manifest this posture though while standing. When standing this posture may make one look like he or she is praying.

Additionally, if one holds their arms akimbo while standing, the individual shows a negative attitude or disapproval of the message. The posture is created by holding the waist with both hands while standing up straight and facing the target person. The hands should simultaneously grip on the flanks, the part near the kidneys. In most cases, the arms-akimbo posture is accompanied by disapproval or sarcastic face to denote attitude, disdain, or disapproval.

When one stretches both of their shoulders and arms and rests them on chairs on either side, then the individual is feeling tired and casual. The posture is akin to a static flap of wings where one stretches their shoulder and arms like wings and rests them on chairs on either side. It is one of the postures that loudly communicates that you are bored, feeling casual, and that you are not about the consequences of your action.

The posture is also invasive of the privacy and space of other individuals and may disrupt their concentration.

If one bends while touching both of their knees, the individual feels exhausted and less formal with the audience. The posture may also indicate extreme exhaustion and need to rest.

For instance, most soccer players bend without kneeling while holding both of their knees, indicating exhaustion. Since in this posture, one is facing down, it may be highly inappropriate in formal contexts and may make one appear queer.

When one leans their head and supports it with an open palm on the cheeks, it indicates that one is thinking deeply and probably feeling sad, sorrowful, or depressed.

The posture is also used when watching something with a high probability of negative outcomes such as a movie or a game. The posture helps one focus deep on the issue akin to meditating.

Through this posture, an individual tries to avoid distractions and think deeper on what is being presented.

If you watch European soccer, you will realize that coaches use this posture when trying to study the match, especially where their team is down. However, this posture should not be used in formal contexts as it suggests rudeness. The posture should be used among peers only.

Then there is the crossing of the legs from the thigh through the knee while seated on a chair, especially on a reclining chair. In this posture, one is communicating that he or she is feeling relaxed and less formal.

In most cases, this posture is exhibited when one is at home watching a movie or in the office alone past working hours. If this posture is replicated in a formal context, then it suggests boredom or lack of concentration.

For the posture where one crosses the legs from the ankle to the soles of the feet while seated, it communicates that one is trying to focus in an informal context such as at home. For instance, if a wife or a child asks the father about something that he has to think through, then the individual is likely to exhibit this posture. If this posture is replicated in a formal context, then it suggests boredom or lack of concentration.

Chapter 15: Arms

A great deal of our emotions is expressed through our arms. Much of our productivity depends on the accuracy of our arms when completing tasks. The movements of the arms are quite obvious as they are used as a complement to verbal expression. The arms are able to extend towards an individual, either in a threat or in a very friendly manner when they moved either quickly or directly.

However, they may give much comfort when they are curved and moving more slowly. The arms can also extend laterally. The arms can also be used to show aggression and some sort of confidence. The arms can also be used in shaping, as they are waved out to the world to pass out certain information. These parts of the body can also be used as certain adjuncts to the words that we speak, as they are used to show how something is either big or small. When we are either confident or excited, the arms can be used to pass the message. We may wave them out to show our displeasure or excitement. Each time we lose our confidence, our shaping will be next to our bodies and a bit smaller. The waving of the arms requires control, and an individual who claps or beats their hands-on certain things may be considered to be showing some sort of clumsiness.

Raising the arms is also a way of saying something. When the arms are raised immediately, it shows that the speaker is dismissing certain things. When it is done with both arms, it even exaggerates the whole matter. A typical two arms that are raised shows a sign of giving up and frustration. It can also be used as a sign of showing surrender, like in the case of someone who is cornered in a fixed situation. When the arms are raised and coupled with a shrug, it can show some confusion.

It is also very important to note that the arms can be used as weapon. The arms can symbolize the spears and clubs as they

 strike out some foes in the imaginary spaces. The arms can also be very defensive, at times, sweeping and blocking away attacks from enemies. This is most common in the martial arts spaces.

The arms that are crossed can also be used to show some communication. Arms can be used as the main entrant to the body of a human being. When the arms are crossed, they tend to create a closed and defensive shield, and barring the outside world. The shields are used to playing two major roles; one is to stop all the incoming attacks, while the other role is to show that a person is hiding and does not want to be seen. The crossed arms may also show some sort of anxiety that can be fueled either in the absence of trust in the other person or even an internal discomfort. It can also be used to show a vulnerability that can be deeply anchored in childhood traumas.

The extent to which an arm is closed how a person might also be firmly closed. In most cases, this could vary from just a light cross of hands to folded arms or the ones that are wrapped around someone. A tightly closed arm with the hands formed as fits is one extreme version that can show someone is in a new hostility status. If the legs are also crossed, then much is added to the signal. The hands in the crossed arms may also be used to hold the individual in a kind of self-hug, for instance, grabbing the upper arms in a folded arms position or even wrapped around the torso, while holding the sides. If by any chance, the thumbs are up, then this could be a full indication that the person is in full agreement or approval of what is being said.

Arms that are crossed, particularly when holding each other can indicate that the person is trying as much as possible to remain calm and still. It can also be a way of suppressing any other signals that could have been passed out. In other instances, it can also be used to show a repressed kind of anger. There are certain cultures where this kind of arm signal is used to show that the person is holding themselves still so that they can pay much attention to the person they are talking with, and therefore, comes out as a great compliment. Crossed arms, particularly those in a folded position can just be used that the person is feeling very comfortable, particularly if there is very little tension somewhere in the body. When a person is comfortable, it becomes evident that they are fearless, and that mostly happen when someone is with friends. Arms that are folded with just a little more tension may show that the person is in a judgmental kind of situation.

When the arms are not closed, they tend to expose the torso and other parts of the body, making them appear so vulnerable. Apart from signifies comfort, it also shows some signs of trust. It can also be the position of power that dares the other person to go ahead and attack while knowing that the other person might not dare. Crossed arms are one of the most obvious arm signals. When it is done in front of a huge number of people, there are higher chances for them to feel rejected and later on respond. It is also very important to note that all crossed arms are defensive, like in the case of a person who is just relaxed.

The crossed arms signals are also used when the person feels some cold and want to get warmth by tucking the arms to keep them warm. There is a very common method that salespeople do to their customers. They ask them to hold something for them or give them their hand. This is a way of breaking the closed arm position of the customers in a polite manner.

Reaching forward to the other individual can be scary as it poses some dangers such as an attack. A sudden forward thrust can also be a very aggressive signal, particularly is the hand is shaped or pointing out just like a fist. The arms can also be pulled back to pass a message. When these body parts have been pulled back or in a thrust forward kind of position, they become in great danger or attack. When one feels defensive, they may opt to pull back their arms out of any impending danger.

When the arms are held behind, they are hidden from a place where people can easily see them. When this happens, it may be because it has a hidden intention or is trying to conceal something. All in all, it can be a very threatening signal. Arms in the backside expose the torso, which, in return, creates some sort of vulnerability. It can either signal comfort or submission. The main reason for comfort could be that the person is in the company of friends or feels so powerful and confident that others can't attack them.

Chapter 16:   Hand and Leg

How to Read Hand Gestures

Hand gesturing is a natural part of us. We use it without even thinking twice about it, sometimes a bit too much when excited or extremely emotional. Hand gestures are just as much a part of our communication process as our words.

When used correctly, gesturing makes people notice what you are trying to say, especially when you accompany those gestures correctly with the words you are trying to emphasize. Hand gestures reveal hidden clues about what a person may be thinking or feeling.

Here is how to decipher some of the most commonly used hand gestures:

- Brow Rubbing: This gesture indicates that a person could be worried or doubtful.

- Scratching the Head: Scratching the head could indicate a person who is in deep thought or trying to solve a problem; depending on the context, it could also indicate confusion.

- Running Fingers through Hair: Closely related to head scratching, this is often an indication that a person feels uncertain or unsure or trying to think of something.

- Eye Rubbing: An indication that a person is feeling fatigued.

- Index Finger on Temple: This gesture indicates that a person could be thinking of something. Sometimes, it is also an indication of a person in critical thoughts.

- Nose Touching: Generally associated with being an indication that a person is lying. If casually done, it could be an indication that the person feels pressured about something.

- Covering of the Mouth: If this gesture appears when a person is listening to someone else, it is an indication that the listener does not necessarily believe the speaker. If someone does this while talking, it could be an indication of dishonesty. Sometimes, it is also an indication that a person is thinking hard about something

- Lip Holding: This is often an indication that a person is feeling greedy.

- Putting Fingers in the Mouth: This gesture indicate that a person may need further reassurance before making a decision.

- Stroking of the Chin: This gesture normally indicates that a person is thinking.

- Ear Rubbing: Rubbing behind the ear is an indication that a person is afraid of being misunderstood or afraid of not understanding.

- Earlobe Touching: Touching the earlobe is an indication that a person is looking for comfort.

- Open Palms or Outstretched Arms: An indication of openness, trustworthiness, and acceptance.

- Palms Down: Palms down normally indicates confidence and is sometimes a sign of rigidity and a sense of authority.

- Hands behind the Back: Hand behind the back is an indication of confidence—most commonly used by men.

- Finger Pointing: This gesture is an indication that a person is feeling authoritative. At other time, it serves as an indication of aggressive or angry emotions.

How to Read Leg Movements

Who would have thought the position of a person's legs could reveal so much about what a person is thinking and feeling. Most of the time, we focus so much on what the upper body language of a person communicates that we forget about the legs and the story they tell.

Here are some hidden messages that a person could reveal with his or her leg movements:

- Sitting Down, Legs Slightly Apart: This indicates that the person is feeling both relaxed and comfortable.

- Legs Crossed While Standing: This indicates that the person could be feeling shy. We can consider it a submissive stance or indicate that a person does not feel entirely comfortable in specific surroundings or the company.

- Legs Crossed and Relaxed While Sitting: A very common gesture in many Asian and European cultures—70% of people generally cross their left leg over their right. However, when accompanied with arms crossed over the chest, this gesture can indicate an emotionally withdrawn or closed off person.

- Sitting Down, Ankles Crossed: An indication that the person is feeling fairly relaxed. If accompanied by clenched hands, this could indicate that the person is feeling rigid or tense, or a signal of self-restraint.

- Sitting Down, Ankles Crossed, and Tucked under Chair: This gesture could indicate a person trying to hide his or her feelings of anxiety.

- Sitting Down, Knees Pointed: If the person's knees are pointing towards you, it is an indication that the person finds you interesting or that he or she likes you. If the knees point away from you, it is an indication of disinterest.

- Standing, Leg Bouncing/Foot Tapping: This gesture indicates that that the person could be feeling impatient.

- Sitting, Leg Bouncing: If a person is moving his or her legs up and down while sitting, it is an indication of impatience. Sometimes, depending on the context, the person could be bouncing his or her leg or tapping the foot when either relaxed or enjoying the environment (for example, if music is playing in the background).

- Standing Parallel, Feet Close Together: This is an indication that a person is displaying a neutral attitude—often considered a more formal standing position.

- Standing, Legs Apart: This is predominantly common among men. It indicates a person is firm and standing his ground. Often seen when a person is trying to display a sense of dominance.

- Sitting, Figure Four Crossed Leg - If accompanied by both hands clamped down on the crossed leg, it is an indication that the person could be someone who has a competitive, stubborn, or tough nature.

Chapter 17:   Touch and Eye Contact

Touch

We engage in touching regularly, and it includes patting someone

on the back or granting someone a hug to indicate we care. We commonly shake hands as greetings or assign to signal shared understanding. Touch, as a form of communication, is called haptics. For children, touch is a crucial aspect of their development. Children who do not get adequate touch have developmental issues. Touch helps babies cope with stress. At infancy, touch is the first sense that an infant respond to.

Functional Touch

In the workplace, touch is among the most effective means of communication, but it is necessary to adhere to etiquette's common rules. For instance, a handshake is a form of touch used in the professional environment and can convey the relationship between two people. Pay attention to the nonverbal cues you are sending next time you shake someone's hand.

Overall, one should always convey confidence when shaking another person's hand, but you should avoid being overly-confident. Praise and encouragement are communicated by a pat on the back or a hand on the shoulder. One should remember that all people do not share the same comfort levels when using touch as nonverbal communication. For instance, an innocent touch can make another person feel uneasy, and for this reason, applying touch requires reading the body language and responding accordingly.

Additionally, touch can become complicated at the workplace when touch is between a boss and a subordinate. Standard practice is that those in power are not allowed to touch subordinates rather than the other way around. For this reason, you should examine your motives for even the most trivial touches and resolve to enhance your communication techniques with your juniors. A standard measure is that it is better to fail on the side of caution. Functional touch includes being physically examined by a doctor and being touched as a form of professional massage.

Social Touch

Most forms of communication require some kind of touch. A handshake is a primary touch in social touches. Handshakes vary from culture to culture. It is socially polite and one is allowed to shake another person's hand during an introduction in the United States. In some countries, kissing on the cheek is the norm. In the same interactions, men will allow a male stranger to touch them on their shoulders and arms, whereas women feel comfortable being touched by a female stranger only on the arms. Men are likely to enjoy touch from a female stranger while women tend to feel uncomfortable with a male stranger.

Equally important, men and women process touch differently, which can create confusing and awkward situations. In most contexts, it might help unnecessary physical contact in social settings, especially those of the opposite sex. One should try to follow societal norms and to take cues from those around you. For instance, while you stand close to a stranger on an elevator, it is not acceptable to engage in any unnecessary physical contact.

Friendship Touch

The types of touches allowed between friends vary depending on contexts. For instance, women are more receptive, touching female friends compared to their male counterparts. The touches between female friends are more affectionate and often in the form of a hug, whereas men prefer to shake hands and pat each other on the back. Within family members, women touch each more other compared to men.

Additionally, same-sex family members are more likely to touch than family members of the opposite sex. Displays of affection between friends are critical in expressing support and encouragement, even if you are not a touchy-feely person. One should be willing to get out of their comfort zone and offer their friend a hug when they are going through a difficult time. Helping others enliven their mood is likely to uplift your mood as well.

Eye Contact

Reading eye contact is important in understanding an individual's true status, even where verbal communication seeks to hide it. As advised, body language should be read as a group. We will focus

698

on individual aspects of body language and make the reader understand how to read that particular type of body language.

Starting with pupils, the pupil dilates when one is interested in the person they are talking to or the object we are looking at. The pupils will contract when one is transiting from one topic to another. We have no control over the working of pupils. When one is speaking about a less interesting topic, the pupils will contract.

Effective eye contact is critical when communicating with a person. Eye contact implies that one looks, but does not stare. Persistent eye contact will make the recipient feel intimidated or judged. In Western cultures, regular eye contact is desired, but it should not be overly persistent. If one offers constant eye contact, then it is seen as an attempt to intimidate or judge, which makes the recipient of the eye contact uncomfortable.

Some studies suggest most children fall victim to attacks by pet dogs if their eye contact is constantly regular as that causes the dog to feel threatened and defensive. Initiating an overly persistent eye contact is a sign of an individual's over-awareness of the emitting messages. Lying can be detected by the individual avoiding eye contact.

Evasive Eye Contact

Having evasive eye contact is a mark of discomfort. We avoid looking at a person if we feel ashamed to be communicating with them. When we feel dishonest about trying to deceive people, we avoid looking at them. While it is okay to blink or drop eye contact temporarily, people who consistently shun making eye contact are likely to be feeling uneasy with the message or the person they are communicating with. For emphasis, staring at someone will make them drop eye contact due to feeling intimidated. Evasive eye contact happens where one deliberately avoids making eye contact.

Crying

Human beings cry due to feeling uncontrollable pain or in an attempt to attract sympathy from others. Crying is considered as an intense emotion associated with grief or sadness though it can also denote extreme happiness known as tears of joy. When an individual forces tears to deceive others, it is known as crocodile tears, which imply faking tears to deceive others. If one cries, then the individual is likely experiencing intense negative emotion.

Blinking

In most cases, blinking is automatic, and our emotions and feelings directed towards the person we are speaking to can cause us to alter our rate of blinking subconsciously. If the average rate of blinking is six to 10 times per minute, then it is a strong indicator that an individual is drawn to the person they are speaking to, and it is indicative of flirting. In normal contexts, men and women blink at the same rate as each other.

Winking

In Western culture, winking is considered a form of flirting that should be done to people we are in good terms with. There are cross-cultural variations on the issue of winking with Asian cultures frowning on winking as a form of facial expression.

Eye Direction

The direction of the eyes tells us about how an individual is feeling. When someone is thinking, they tend to look to their left when they are recalling or reminiscing. An individual who is thinking tends to look to their right when eliciting creative thoughts. It can be interpreted as an indicative sign of someone trying to be deceitful in some situations such as creating a version of events. For left-handed people, the eye directions will be reversed.

Additionally, when one is interested in what you are saying, he or she will often make eye contact. Some studies found that when people are engaged in an interesting conversation, their eyes focus on the face of their partner, about 80% of the time but not wholly on the eyes. Rather, the eye contact on the other person's eyes is for the duration of two to three minutes, then move down to the lips or nose then back up to the eyes. For a brief moment, the person initiating eye contact will look down then back up to the eyes. Looking up and to the right demonstrates dismissal and boredom. Dilation of the pupil may indicate someone is interested or that the room is brighter.

In some instances, sustained eye contact may signal you want to speak to the person or are interested in the person sexually. At one point, you have noticed a hard stare from a man towards a particular woman to the point the woman notices and asks the man what is that all about. In this case, eye contact is not being used to intimidate, but to single out the targeted person. You probably have seen a woman ask why that man is staring at me, then she proceeds to mind her own business, but on taking another look in the direction of the man, the stare is still there. In this manner, eye contact is used to single out an individual and make them aware that one is having sexual feelings towards the person.

However, people are aware of the impact of body language and will seek to portray the expected body language. For instance, an individual who is lying is likely to make deliberate eye contact frequently to sound believable. At one point, you knew you were lying but went ahead to make eye contact. You probably have watched movies where one of the spouses is lying but makes believable eye contact with others. The reason for this faked body language is because the person is aware of the link between making eye contact and speaking the truth.

Like verbal language, body language, and in particular, eye contact can be highly contextual. For instance, an individual may wink to indicate he or she agrees with the quality of the product being presented or that he or she agrees with the plan. Eye contact in these settings can be used as a coded language for a group of people. One of your classmates may have used a wink to indicate that the teacher is coming or to indicate that the secret you have been guarding is now out.

Chapter 18:   Use of Space

Beyond just considering how someone holds themselves in general, you must also look at how the individual wants to interact with the space around them. You can typically break down space around someone into several different categories. You can look at it in terms of horizontal and vertical space, and we will be considering both. Ultimately, people will naturally place themselves within different areas within the space around them, and you can usually figure out a lot about what is going on in their brains. You  may realize that they seem quite confident in what they are doing— they know that they are making a decision to stand in the way that is going to help them, for example, or keeping the right distance to create the right impression.

There are two ways to look at this—horizontal proxemics will refer to how far away someone is willing to hold themselves from you. This can vary greatly from person to person and can shift depending upon what someone is comfortable with. On the other hand, there is the use of vertical proxemics. This refers to how high or low someone places themselves concerning those around them. Some people will naturally be higher than others just due to their natural heights, but even someone that is naturally quite short can make great use of vertical proxemics quite simply.

Vertical Proxemics

Vertical proxemics refers to the difference in height between two people and how the individuals will interact with height in general to show body language or to convey something. Generally speaking, people, like most other animals, tend to relate bigger or taller, with better and more dominant. While we as a species do not only follow the biggest men around, we still make great use of this use of space around us. Some people will naturally carry themselves highly—they will look at the world around them in a way that reflects this. Others will naturally try to shrink inwards and make themselves smaller.

In general, however, you can make use of this regardless of the height. Even if you are short and wanting to display dominance, all you have to do is create the illusion that you are taller and, therefore, more dominant. You can do this with very simple tricks—you could, for example, try standing in a way that tilts your chin up and back so you are looking down your nose at the other person. Instead of being seen as submissive because you are smaller, you have turned things around and you can position yourself in just the right way that they have no choice but to accept that dominance that you are asserting. All you had to do was tilt your head a little bit.

Of course, this can work the other way, too. When people are not very confident, they tend to tuck their chin inwards. This forces them to look in an upward direction to make eye contact. When you do this with someone else, you are naturally submitting to them in a sense—you are telling them that they get to dominate and control that setting in some way, shape, or form, and you are granting that control to them.

You see this a lot in flirting as well—women will usually look up through their eyelashes at the men that they are attracted to, while men will typically hold their heads up high when they are interacting with other women that they find attractive. This is a natural way that you can see this sort of dynamic play out. You have the man who is showing dominance and the woman who is naturally submitting to the man to some degree, showing that she is willing and ready to accept the man's dominance because she is interested in him.

You can see this in other contexts as well. Suppose you were to interact with a child, for example. In that case, you may find that you naturally get down on one knee when you want to have a heart to heart conversation with them—you do this because it allows you to place yourself not above, nor below the child—rather, you are facing the child directly. You are putting yourself on equal footing with the child to get your point across and this will help the child then understand the message better. This is commonly used in schools to help the students learn what they are learning from teachers—when teachers get down to their students' levels, the children tend to be more receptive to the information at hand in general, and that is quite powerful and compelling.

Horizontal Proxemics

However, when you want to look at horizontal proxemics, you are going to be considering just how far away you position yourself from other people. Generally speaking, this indicates the intimacy between people—when two people have a closer relationship with each other, they will usually find that they gravitate closer to each other. They will naturally attempt to position themselves so they can get closer just due to being in that particular relationship status.

For example, think about the last time you saw a married couple walking around together—you may notice that they do not seem to have any physical boundaries. They are entirely comfortable working incredibly closely with each other because they trust each other. They may even end up standing while touching each other closely because they do not mind—they are totally happy being within each other's bubbles.

When you compare that to the way that strangers will keep themselves naturally spaced out, you will see a huge difference. Strangers will usually attempt to resist having to get that close to other people—they do not want to feel like they have to sort of infringe upon each other's bubbles. If they do have to do so for any reason, they will usually do so without acknowledgment.

Ultimately, the horizontal distance that you keep from other people can primarily be broken down into four distinct distances: The intimate distance, the personal distance, the social distance, and the public distance. These become those bubbles that you want to protect and defend from being infringed upon when interacting with other people. Let's look at each one of these distances:

Intimate Distance

This particular distance is reserved for those that you are the closest to, as you would probably assume. This is getting very close and personal to someone else—you are generally within a foot or two of their general person, or you could even be touching them actively. This particular distance is only for those that are allowed to infringe so much upon you—you may allow for people such as your young children or your spouse to enter this space around you. These are people that are naturally going to be more intimate with you in general. You and your intimate partners will most likely be touching each other to some degree or another, and when you have young children, you know that they are all about being touched, held, and cuddled. Young infants need to be cuddled close to be able to nurse or to be bottle-fed, and even as they do get older, they want that sort of natural interaction between themselves and those around them. They crave that intimacy and it is a need for them, so babies typically get a pass to this entire system.

Personal Distance

This next distance is reserved for family and friends. Generally speaking, the closer that you get to the other person, the closer your relationship is with that person. Those that are the closest to you, such as parents, older children, and best friends may be allowed to get closer to you within this zone—they are allowed to approach more or less to that intimate zone level.

However, those that are not as close to you, such as those that you do not know very well or that family member you have only met at family reunions but never even spoken to otherwise, will typically be held further away. This distance is generally anywhere from about 1.5 to 4 feet around your general person.

Within this distance, you are close enough that you can interact closely with someone else—you could potentially hug or shake hands. You are close enough that you do not have to talk very loudly, nor do you have to do very much to interact further. You are generally deemed, at the very least, some sort of friend at this stage, or perhaps an acquaintance for those on the outermost rings of this radius.

Social Distance

This distance is for people that you are actively interacting with but may not know very well, or at all. Generally speaking, those within your social distance are those you can interact with to some degree. It may be that person who just said hi to you to be polite, or it could be the person you are asking for help from at the grocery store. When you see this sort of interaction with other people, you can generally assume that the other person is not feeling very close to the other person and they do not care to stand that close to each other. They may not know each other, not like each other, or not trust each other, and ultimately, that will be up to some degree of interpretation.

Most often, this distance ranges between 4 and 12 feet—you may find that you are comfortable allowing some people closer when there is some barrier between you.

Public Distance

Finally, the public distance is a distance that is typically considered used for public speaking. When you are using this distance in any context, you are trying to ensure that you interact with other people in a crowd without singling anyone out or leaving anyone else out. This is the distance that you would take to be able to do just that—it is what changes a casual conversation into a more intimate interaction between yourself and someone else.

This distance is generally considered to be anything beyond roughly 12 feet and it is no longer held hostage by the fact that people used not to be able to yell very far. You now have access to speakers, microphones, and even large screens that can stream you acting or talking in real-time—this can be used so you can expand upon that public distance quite greatly, which is something that many people do these days. Just look at modern concerts—stadiums are huge to accommodate everything and everyone who wants to go and see the concert. This is accommodated through the use of a screen that will broadcast the feed for everyone else to see. Then, everyone can see, even if they are sitting too far away, to hear someone if they did not have that microphone or that camera in the first place.

Chapter 19:   Breathing

There are different ways you can read someone's body language. It can be read by their leg and arm movements, facial expressions, eye contact, or smiles. Do you realize that how a person breathes has meaning, too?

Emotions and how you breathe are connected. You could read a person's feelings by watching the way they breathe. If emotions change, how they breathe might be affected. See if you can notice breathing patterns in your family, friends, coworkers, or significant other. They may not tell you exactly how they are feeling and it might depend on certain situations.

·   Deep breathing might indicate excitement, attraction, anger, fear, or love

Deep breathing is the easiest pattern to notice. If somebody suddenly starts to hold their breath, they might be feeling a little scared. If someone takes a deep breath and then shouts, they could be angry. Excited people, are experiencing shock, or are surprised might suck in a deep breath. They might also take in a deep breath and hold it for a few seconds. If their eyes start to glow this might indicate that they are surprised or excited. A person might start to breathe deeply if they feel an attraction toward another person. You may notice someone take a deep breath in, suck in their stomach and push their chest out to impress somebody they are attracted to.

· Sighing might signal hopelessness, sadness, or relief

When you sigh, you are letting out a deep, long breath that you can hear. Somebody might sigh if they are feeling relieved after a struggle has passed. They are thankful that their struggle is over. A sign might show sadness or hopelessness like somebody who is waiting for a date to show up. It could also show tiredness and disappointment.

· Rapid, heavy breathing might show fear and tiredness

You may have just seen a person rob a place and the police are chasing them. You notice they are breathing very rapidly. This is because their lungs need more oxygen since they exert a lot of energy. After all, they are running. Their bodies feel tired and their lungs are trying their best to keep up. We feel the same effects when we feel scared. This will happen when we experience fear; our lungs need more oxygen, so we begin to breathe faster. You will easily see when somebody has been scared or running by noticing the way they are breathing.

Another interesting fact about breath is that smells can influence breath. Any odors that are tied to emotions can change a person's respiration rate. Several studies have shown that the body will respond to bad and good smells by breathing differently. If you were to smell something rotten, you would end up breathing in a shallow and rapid manner. But, if, instead, you smelled baking bread and roses, your breath would be slow and long. The really exciting part of this is that the breathing rate will change before the brain has ever been able to conscious register if the smell is good or bad.

According to Scientific American, the emotions that we have with smells and scents are extremely associative. We started learning about these different smells in the womb, and then during our lives, our brains learn to refine our views of emotional rewards, pleasures, and threats that are contained within a certain odor. If a person breathes deeply, they feel that something is safe, and it creates a pleasurable emotional state. This means if you notice a person's breathing rate suddenly change, let your sense of smell catch up first. It could be that they have gotten a whiff of something they either like or dislike.

The interesting thing is that while we can learn how people feel based on how they are breathing, the way a person breathes can also affect their emotions. In a 2006 study, published in Behavior Response & Therapy, they discovered that undergraduates who practiced slow-breathing exercises for 15 minutes had a more positive and balanced emotional response afterward than the group who were faced with 15 minutes of unfocused worrying and attention.

And it doesn't even have to do with just being calm. In a study by the French scientist Pierre Phillipot, he asked some participants to identify the pattern of breath connected with certain emotions such as sadness and joy. They then asked a separate group of people to breathe in a certain manner and probed their feelings.

712

The results they got were excellent. If the subjects were told to live in a particular way, even if they were unaware of it, they said that they felt the feeling associated emotion, apparently, out of nowhere.

This is something that you can't readily do, but it is still impressive.

A new idea that is being studied about emotions and breath is that what you exhale also plays a role in emotional response. The chemically analyzed exhales were able to figure out how the person felts. In an article from Science News, the chemical makeup of the air within a soccer stadium varies when people begin cheering and  the same is true in movie theaters. They studied 9500 people as they watched 16 different films that ranged from rom-coms to horrors, and then they checked the air composition of the room to see if it changed during certain scenes that were rather emotional in one way or the other.

The crazy thing is that it did. In suspenseful moments, more CO_2 and isoprenes are in the air, which are chemicals associated with the tensing of muscles. Every type of emotion came with its chemical makeup.

Chapter 20: Laughter

The laughter is a response biologically produced by the body in response to certain stimuli. The smile is considered a soft and silent form of laughter. There are currently various interpretations about its nature.

It is popularly considered a response to moments or situations of humor, as an external expression of fun, and related to joy and happiness. However, according to numerous studies, such as Robert Provine, laughter is motivated by a comic stimulus in a minority of everyday cases. It usually appears, more or less simulated, as an emotional complement to verbal messages, and in situations of stress or playful behaviors such as tickling.

Some medical theories attribute beneficial effects on health and well-being to laughter, since it releases endorphins.

Forms of Laughter

Depending on the force with which it occurs, laughter can vary in its duration and tone and characteristics. Thus, we use different words to describe what we consider different types of laughter: click, laugh, laugh, giggle, contemptuous, desperate, nervous, equivocal laughter. Other types: caquino, jingle, evil laugh, hypoid.

Among the emotional cues, the smile is the most contagious of all, and smiling encourages positive feelings. Like the laugh itself, the smile is innate, and deaf and blind children smile. It usually appears at six weeks of life and is the first language of the human being. Initially it is a physical behavior, and gradually evolves into an emotional action. Self-induction of the gesture of smiling can improve our mood. Another property is to induce an increase in NK cells' activity and thus improve our immune status.

Some studies show that laughter varies by gender: women tend to laugh in a more singing way, while men tend to laugh snorting or growling.

Physiology of Laughter

It occurs when a stimulus - internal or external - is processed in primary, secondary and multimodal association areas of the central nervous system. The processing of emotions is carried out in the limbic system, which is probably responsible for the potential motors that characterize laughter, including facial expression and the muscles' movements that control ventilation and phonation. Once the stimulus has been processed and the aforementioned automatic motor acts, a generalized autonomous activation is carried out, which has an exit through several routes, among which are the Hypothalamus-pituitary axis and the autonomic nervous system. All these components make up the emotion. This process involves, when it comes to joy, the motor act called laughter.

There are two structures of the limbic system involved in the production of laughter: the amygdala and the hippocampus.

Some Studies

Laughter can be induced by stimulating the subthalamic nucleus, and it has been proven in patients with Parkinson's disease. A recent work by Itzhak Fried et al., Of the University of California, has allowed us to locate an area of the brain called a supplementary motor area. When stimulated using electrodes, it produces the smile and, with a more intense stimulation, laughing out loud. The supplementary motor area is an area very close to the language area. This mechanism was discovered accidentally while treating a young woman with epilepsy.

Experiments have been conducted to determine exactly in which area the sense of humor resides. In a study, presented in 2000 by scientists at the University of Rochester, volunteers underwent functional magnetic resonance while asking them various questions. They concluded that this characteristic resided in a small region of the frontal lobe. However, another London team performed the same test on individuals who were told jokes. The results were that the brain area that was activated was the ventral prefrontal cortex and other regions involved in the language process when the joke's grace resided in a pun.

Robert Provine: Laughter as Communication

Popularly, laughter and smile are associated with happiness and good humor; however they are not reliable measures of mood. According to recent studies, laughter is a communication mechanism. It follows that the triggering factor of laughter is not happiness or joy in themselves, but the fact that there is at least one other person who can receive the message, in the form of playful nonsense. It has been proven that the relationship between

716

laughter in society and laughter in solitude is 30 to 1. We need more people, and that they can laugh, to laugh.

Field Study

Provine sought to adopt a "naturalistic and descriptive tactic" to reveal the subconscious triggers and instinctive roots of laughter. He initially observed subjects in his laboratory, but found that laughter was too fragile, illusory and variable under direct scrutiny. Therefore, he decided to keep the appearance of natural and spontaneous laughter in daily life. He began to listen and secretly record the conversational laugh (the one that typically follows the conversation speech a second later), documenting 1200 episodes. He later studied the patterns of who laughed and when, to analyze their qualities. He concluded that for laughter to occur, more than one person is necessary, the minimum element being a dyad, a speaker and a listener (except in the case of a spectator laughing aloud watching television, for example). Laughter tended to follow a natural conversational rhythm, splashing the speech after complete statements, and especially after changes in volume or intonation. The most interesting thing was that less than a quarter of the previous comments were humorous. Provine suggests that laughter synchronizes the speaker and the listener's brains, in such a way that it serves as a signal for the receptive areas of language, perhaps switching the activation between competitive brain structures of cognition and emotion.

The observations of interpretation students laughing at the right time led him to conclude that laughter is under a relatively weak conscious control, and that the most natural-looking laughter is

717

caused by subconscious mechanisms, which explains why method acting can lead to the reproduction of emotions more effectively.

Tickle and Laugh

Probably, tickling is the oldest and safest way to stimulate laughter. Tickling and laughter are one of the first forms of communication between mother and baby. Laughter appears between three and a half to four months of life, long before he speaks. Thus, the mother uses the tickles to stimulate the baby's laughter and thus establish communication. Laughter in turn encourages the mother to continue to tickle, until there comes a time when the baby begins to complain, at which time the mother stops.

For the same fact that it is more difficult to laugh alone, it is also difficult for a person to tickle themselves. Tickling is an integral part of the game, so when you pet a person, you try to escape and laugh, but try to return them. In the process of giving and receiving tickles, there is a kind of neurological programming that causes people to establish links, and the same thing happens with sex. The armpits, the palms of hands and soles of the feet are areas whose stimulation by tickling laughter produces more easily.

Laughter Is Contagious

Like yawning, laughter is a neurologically programmed social behavior, whose origin lies in synchronizing the state of group behavior. Is, for example, why there is a hint of laughter in sitcoms on television? When we hear another person laugh at something, we immediately look at it and consider it more fun than if that person does not laugh, and then we smile or even laugh.

Laughter and Sex

Both men and women laugh to the same extent. However, the situation that produces the most laughter is when a man talks to a woman, or vice versa, and in this situation the woman is the one who leads the laughter and the man the leader of laughter production. As with speech, the laughter of women generally presents a more acute tone than that of men. One of the characteristics of the most attractive men for women is the sense of humor,  although not precisely the ability to laugh. That is, the woman looks for a man who makes her laugh and does not laugh too much.

Laughter as a Mechanism for Controlling Others

The relationship between laughter and world events is modulated by culture and society. Currently, we relate laughter to the idea of "being happy and feeling good." However, Plato and Aristotle, among other authors who wrote about laughter, had a darker view of her. For example, they found public executions fun, something that is currently politically incorrect, just as they also laughed, in addition to the people in their group, people from other groups, such as other ethnicities or races. At present, our language nuances such a difference: laughing at someone is not the same as laughing at someone. For Robert Province, ridiculous laughter is an ancestral instinctive mechanism different from group laughter that served to modulate the behavior of individuals who did not belong to the group itself, for them to adapt and integrate into it.

The anthropologist Verena Alberti uses the terms «laughter of welcome» and laughter of exclusion.

According to the scientist, that is the reason why people laugh in embarrassing or unpleasant circumstances. He affirms that laughter is an instrument to change the behavior of others. In an uncomfortable situation, such as a dispute, laughter represents a gesture of appeasement to lessen anger and tension. If the other person is infested, the risk of confrontation is dissipated.

Provine's observations suggested that social rank determines patterns of laughter, especially in the workplace; bosses easily provoke laughter from their subordinates and make jokes at their expense, telling that the phenomenon is generally a response to submission to the domain.

Laughter as the Origin of Language

According to Robert Provine, linguists and language scholars do not pay due attention to laughter. In contrast, physiology of the larynx and various parts of the vocal pathways does play a role in the production of sound. In his own words:

Laughter is a portion of the universal human vocabulary, and if we want to understand how the brain produces sound we should analyze behaviors that everyone has in the same way; that is, studying laughter - if we're going to understand human behavior - will be like using E. coli, or the fruit fly, to understand the mechanism of genetics. Instead of facing the immense complexity of nature, we try to concentrate on a small molecule, which is a part, which can be better accessed.-Robert Provine

Chapter 21:   Mixed Signals

Understanding one another is a communication challenge that many people experience from time to time. One of the causes behind this is that everyone seems to see the world through their perspective. It is, after all, the only way that makes sense. Your experiences, your story, and your interactions form the guideline

for your life and how you assume everyone else should live their lives.

Because of this block perception, miscommunication happens more often than most people can admit. This explains why we jump to conclusions or make assumptions where we should not. The problem with mixed signals is that everyone ends up dealing with the aftermath of consuming false information. In most cases, people don't respond. They react, and it never ends well until they both realize it was all miscommunication from reading mixed signals.

Many relationships have suffered the curse of mixed signals, and since many people are afraid of being vulnerable, things can get murky very fast. Mixed signals are about inconsistency. They happen a lot in personal relationships, especially when someone's actions and words do not align, and the only thing consistent about them is the misalignment.

In some cases, mixed signals might be intentional and some accidental. Intended mixed signals include a situation where someone you like is not ready to commit to you because perhaps they are hoping that they can find someone better. An accidental scenario is when someone sends you a message, trying to express their feelings toward you, but the news does not come off the way they intended it.

Whichever reason behind mixed signals, they generate unnecessary stress and frustration. You might even start doubting yourself, wondering whether you are in the right place with the right person or whether you deserve to be there in the first place. When you are continually feeling unsure of your position, unaware of your role, you can start feeling insecure.

This is one of the challenges behind misreading people. When you meet someone and misread their body language and other communication cues, you can assume something about them when they don't feel the same way. Mixed signals are widespread in young relationships because you are unsure what you are getting into. You are not sure whether this is the right thing to do or whether they are the right person for you and so forth. There are many uncharted territories in new relationships, and as you are trying to learn more about each other, the risk of vulnerability is always high.

Why Mixed Signals Happen

Unless you were a target for specific reasons, very few people get into a relationship to mislead you. People tend to be genuine, or at least they try to be. One of the challenges they experience is poor communication. If you like each other, there is a fear of saying or doing the wrong thing. You want to be perfect in the eyes of this new person you like, and as a result, you create an environment where you are always walking on eggshells to impress them. Your intentions might be clear and genuine, but miscommunication breeds mixed signals.

So how does this happen? Well, first of all, many people don't know how to express their feelings. Relationships today are so complicated. One person might be in several relationships simultaneously, each of which is serving a different purpose in their lives. It gets worse when you are in a relationship without being fully aware that you are. This hinders your ability to express your true feelings to someone. Besides, what exactly are your true feelings? If you can't understand what you want, it is difficult for someone else to. Enter technology, and the swamp gets muddier.

We can hide so much behind our screens. You can exchange thousands of text messages with someone, throw in some emojis and memes to make it even juicier. Still, in reality, this only keeps you from opening up about your feelings and letting someone else know how vulnerable you are in their presence.

You don't get to experience body language in a text message. All you have is the text, which can be misunderstood and taken out of context. Without any other clues, it is not easy to decide over text messaging.

Instant messaging and communication today is something everyone enjoys. When you keep messaging someone all the time, it feels weird when they don't respond to you instantly. One of the worst and standard mixed signals today is "delayed response." People can read so much into silence. Perhaps you are intentionally ignoring them. Maybe you are no longer interested, perhaps you are with someone else, or perhaps you don't have your phone. Many thoughts occur when someone takes a radio silence approach, even when the situation was not in their control. Well, how else would you have known that, right? By the time you get back to them, all the thoughts that had crossed the sender's mind have them in a mood, which affects the nature of your communication.

Interpreting Popular Mixed Signals

The thing about mixed signals is that you have been a perpetrator or victim at one point in time. If you have been at either end of the spectrum, you can easily understand how frustrating it can be. How do you interpret the mixed signals? What do they mean for you or the person you are trying to communicate with? The following are some examples that might help:

When the Effort Fizzles Away. You might know this too well. You meet someone, and you can't seem to get enough time to spend together. However, a few days or weeks later, the effort to impress you is not there. It feels like they are not even trying. What happened? What changed? Are you not worth chasing after?

724

There are many possibilities behind this. One explanation is that the other person is struggling to keep up appearances. This happens when they set themselves up to fail. How does this happen? On the first meeting, someone portrays themselves as something else, someone else than who they truly are. Everything about the persona they introduce you to is fake.

However, soon after you have known each other for a while, they may feel they can now get back to being their true selves and live the life they are used to. The challenge here is that they leave you at a crossroads because, while you are worried, they might have changed because of something you did or lack, it is all about them.

Lukewarm Reactions and Responses. One moment, you are all having the time of your life, then suddenly, someone is distant and withdraws like you did something wrong. Sounds familiar? Well, Katy Perry says it better in "Hot n Cold."

It is challenging to deal with someone who operates like this. How can they sustain a very healthy and deep conversation that is so fulfilling and satisfying, then the next minute they are so empty you can fill them up with a gallon of water? Why can't someone make up their mind at once and let you in?

In this case, most people have their options open. You might think you are in the right place, but they are not. They are hoping something better comes along, and they will move on as soon as it does. Apart from those who keep their options open, you also might be dealing with someone who has an avoidant attachment method, which means they will pull away as soon as they feel something stable and reliable is about to happen in their lives.

Whichever the case, interacting with such a person is not easy. It is frustrating because you will never be good enough for them. They cannot communicate what they want or how, and they would instead go about their lives oblivious to your suffering.

Communicating Without Mixed Signals

Mixed signals are frustrating for everyone—recipient and sender alike. The misunderstanding and misinterpretation can turn you into a villain when you meant well. Effective communication depends on the kind of response you get. To get the best and appropriate response, you must also ensure you don't send mixed signals.

Try to ensure your body language aligns with your words. Body language can throw someone off your vibe and distort the intended message completely. Pick your words wisely. Some words carry more weight than others in different situations. If you need to be assertive in a conversation, use emphatic words. Aggressive words will distort your communication.

If you are meeting someone, be keen on your posture. An assertive stance makes you more approachable. Relax and keep your head up. Speak in a warm, assuring tone, and try to vary your style through the sentences to make them assertive.

If you have to highlight a point, use the right gestures to help you. It would be best to encourage participation from other people around you too so that they feel they are part of the conversation and not just a passive audience.

Written communication can easily be confusing, especially since the recipient has no idea what was going through your mind. Try to eliminate any source of ambiguity in your writing. If you have to convey emotions, make them clear and precise. You can explain further where you feel you need to so that there is no doubt in the recipient's mind about what you mean.

Punctuation is another area where mixed signals are standard. Use the right punctuation marks. A comma in the wrong place can change the perceived meaning of a sentence to something else. Avoid using capital letters where they are not needed. Capital letters usually read like you are shouting at the reader (Rabern, 2015).

When communicating with someone over the phone, you must think your conversation through before you call them. Plan what you want to discuss with them ahead of time. This allows you sufficient time to get in the right frame of mind and not miss the point. Since you have had enough time to prepare for the call, listen to the recipient, and allow them enough time to convey their response.

In the same manner that you would convey your message to an audience, use tonal variation to stress the critical messages. Ensure the listener acknowledges the important parts of the message.

Always present yourself in your true form. This is one of the best ways you can avoid mixed signals. Authenticity is very difficult to fake. Do not change your mannerisms because you want to impress someone. Be who you are. Be genuine so that if someone reads and interacts with you, they are not conflicted in the person they are dealing with. It also helps because you will be interacting with their genuine reactions and responses.

It is important to hold everyone accountable for inappropriate communication skills, including yourself. Try to encourage everyone around you to be clear in the way they address issues. If you don't do this and instead allow the communication to prevail, you create an environment where people's mixed signals are okay.

Chapter 22: Can I Learn How to Fake My Body Language?

The next thing that we need to take a look at is how to fake your body language. Some people feel that manufacturing this kind of thing is impossible. They know that it is hard to hide many of the body signs that you are trying to show to others. This doesn't mean that the process is impossible to work with, but it takes a lot of time and effort.

Many people are not aware of the different body language and nonverbal language cues they send to the world. But this doesn't mean that you are not able to fake some of it, and get others to think that you feel and act in a certain way. Keep in mind here that doing this is going to be difficult sometimes. It is not always as easy as it seems, and you have to be constantly aware of what you are doing. If you forget to do this and aren't paying attention to the different parts of your body language and how they are working together, you will find that some part of you will betray you, and you will lose the trust in the person you are trying to work with.

The good news here is that with a little bit of practice and some hard thinking at the same time, you can control the various aspects of your personality and figure out how to make people see different things with your body language. Some of the things that you should focus on include:

The Eye Contact

The first thing that we are going to focus on when we need to fake our body language is eye contact. You need to make sure that your eye contact is on point. This is one of the easiest things to fake, and if you are messing up with this still in your personal and professional life, then it means that you are going to have to work on that before you get a chance to work with some of the others.

Think about the last time you talked with someone who was not able to maintain eye contact. Whether it was them focusing down all of the time, looking at their phone or their watch, or even glancing towards the door all of the time, it felt like they wanted to look anywhere but at you. Eventually, it made you feel like you were not necessary, and you tried to stop the conversation and move on, no matter how important the information was.

Don't be a person like this. You don't want to make the other person feel like they are not necessary. You want them to know that you are interested in them, that what they have to say is worth your attention. And the best way to do this is to make sure that your eye contact is good.

There is a nice balance here. You do not want your gaze to be so intense that you make the other person feel uncomfortable. We all know this kind of look. It includes no blinking and may feel like you are trying to stare down with the other person. Focus on a gaze that shows that you are interested, but include some blinking and some emotion in them.

Your Arm Movements

Pay attention to the arm movements that you are doing. If you want to show another person that you are excited and happy about something, it probably is not a good idea to stand with the arms crossed. Happiness and excitement are going to include a lot of arm movements going all of the time. The bigger the movements (within reason, don't try to hit the other person with the flailing arms), the more animated you will appear to others.

However, if you want to appear like you are calm and collected, or like you are more withdrawn (there may be times when you want someone to leave you alone for example), then crossing your arms, or at least keeping the arms and hands close to the body, maybe the right option for your needs.

So, when you are trying to fake your arm movements as a part of the body language, the best way to do this is to figure out what mood you want to portray to the other person. If you're going to show that you are animated and excited, then the arm movements need to be away from the body and nice and big. If you're going to show that you are more withdrawn, then the arms and hands need to be close to the body.

The Smile

It is essential to spend some time focusing on the smile that you give off. Many of us have been trained on how to give a fake smile in any situation, but there is a big difference between the phony smile and a genuine smile. You may be able to fake it with some people, but you often need to try and get a real and genuine smile on your face to impress those around you.

Remember that with a genuine smile, you need to use more than the sides of the mouth. This one includes the whole face and even some crinkles around the eyes. This can be done even when faking it, but you need to do some practice. An excellent way to do this is to spend some time in a mirror, work on the smile, and try to get the whole face into it.

Doing a smile in front of the mirror is going to make a big difference. You can look at how the smile will appear to others, and get a general feel of how it will feel to do this. Then, when you are in front of someone else using this smile, you will know how to make this smile appear for you without the mirror present.

Your Stance

The last thing that we are going to look at is your stance. You need to make sure that you are picking out the right kind of view to impress another person and let them know that you are interested. Of course, the posture is going to be an essential part of all of this.

You want to stand upright, rather than to slouch, and you want to make sure that you show off the confidence inside you.

There is more to this one than just the posture that you use, though. If you can add a few more things into this, you will find out that it will help you get some results with how comfortable others are around you. The first thing to look at is your feet. If you want the other person to think that you are interested in them and that your whole attention is on them, make sure the feet are pointed in the right direction. They need to be pointed at the person you are talking to, rather than to the side or even worse, towards the door.

The way that you lean is important as well. If your posture has you leaning towards the door, or at all away from the other person, then this is going to give them the thought that you are not interested in them at all. But, leaning slightly towards them, with your body leaning in, shows that you are interested in what they are saying to them.

It is hard to fake the body language that you are doing with another person. While we often wish to show off a certain kind of appearance to others, it will be tough to do this. You have to be careful about how you do this. But with some practice and tips, you will become more aware of the different cues that our bodies are giving off to others, and it is a lot easier for you to give off the appearance that you would like.

Chapter 23:   How to Have a Positive Effect on Others

 Part of coming across as respectable to other people and getting along with them is projecting confidence and positivity. Someone who is seen as a positive person will have a much easier time connecting to a wider range of people and enjoying better opportunities in life, due to their approachable nature. This makes it highly important to learn how to come across this way.

How to Have a Positive Effect on Others

It's not as hard as it seems to become a positive influence for those people around you, and you can start right now. Here are some simple actions that can have a positive effect on others:

- Approachable Facial Expressions: A genuine smile tells the other person you are warm, confident and approachable. This build trusts.

- Subtle Mirroring: Match the other person's movements subtly. This helps build rapport through establishing a common ground. It also shows your similarities as you mimic others. People will naturally observe this even if they aren't aware of it on the surface, and will instantly like you more.

- Nodding: Nodding while someone is talking shows you are engaged and listening. Many people are used to people being distracted while they are talking, so this is a simple way to show you care and are truly hearing the other person and listening. Also, you can nod while you are talking to help influence the person to agree with you. It is no guarantee, but when you nod while asking a question, people often unknowingly nod as well, signifying that they agree with what you are saying.

- Don't Sit Down: Standing up helps you feel powerful and confident. This is useful when giving presentations. Just make sure not to stand over anyone, as that is a sign of a threat to most people.

- Be Mindful of your Head Position: Tilting your head or body toward someone shows you are interested. If you make others feel important then you have the opportunity to influence them positively.

- Pointing your Feet: The way your feet point says a lot about whether you want to be where you are. Much like head positioning, the position of your feet can also have a subconscious effect on someone. Pointing your feet towards someone shows you are interested. It is a positive signal that builds trust. On the other hand, pointing your feet away shows that you subconsciously are waiting for a chance to escape as soon as possible.

What Can Mastering Body Language Do for You?

It's possible to improve your life and interpersonal interactions greatly by becoming mindful of your nonverbal cues. Research shows that having correct nonverbal language will aid you in the following ways:

- Less Misunderstandings: This can help connect with others, meaning that you are less likely to be misunderstood. Since misunderstandings are at the base of most negative interactions and resentment, this is a must.

- Better Performance: The right posture will help you with your performance, since it directly impacts how you come across and your mood. Utilizing "power postures" will help you feel more confident. You can also embody the idea of determination in your posture to make yourself feel stronger and more confident.

- Small shifts in your nonverbal cues can have a great effect on your existence, overall. Here are some specific ways that this can happen for you.

- A Posture of Power: Our body language has a direct role in the people we are, whether we're aware of it. This simple factor directly shapes our personalities, abilities, power, and confidence levels. Not only does the way you carry yourself send others a clear message about you, but it sends your brain a clear message, as well, and impacts the way you act and feel.

Our animal relatives show their dominance and power by making themselves larger, expanding, taking up more room, and stretching their bodies out. In other words, establishing power is all about opening your body up, and people do this as well. If you are feeling nervous, small, or incapable, simply open your body up and pay attention to your mood shifts. You should feel suddenly much more capable and self-assured.

736

For example, you might wish you feel more confident or powerful in situations where you are interviewing for a job and wish to showcase your abilities and assertiveness. You might also wish to show that you're confident in a classroom situation or a leadership position. As you walk into a negotiation, you would want to send a message that you know what you want and are well-aware of your abilities.

For situations like this, or any others you need a confidence boost in, you can stand erect, with your shoulders pushed back, your stance wide, and your head upward. Raise your arms to make a "Y" as in the YMCA dance, and you will instantly feel more powerful and energetic. What is it about this posture that helps us feel better and more confident? It affects our hormones, resulting in a couple of key ingredients in the feeling of dominance. These are cortisol (the hormone of stress) and testosterone (the hormone of dominance).

Males in high, alpha positions of power in groups of primates have low levels of cortisol and high levels of testosterone, but this isn't just primates. Effective and powerful people in leadership positions have the same pattern, meaning that they are assertive and powerful, but don't react strongly to stress. Even in tough situations, they can stay calm and handle business effectively. Research shows that adopting the power position we just told you about for a minimum of a couple minutes will lower your cortisol levels while boosting testosterone. In other words, you will be priming your brain to deal with whatever situations might pop up during the day.

More Postures for Improving Your Levels of Performance:

The posture of our body directly influences our mind, which results in our specific behaviors and actions. This means that if we can convince our physical bodies to lead our minds to more positive places, our performance will skyrocket. Here are some postures that are recommended by professionals for positive results.

• Tensing up for Willpower: If you're in a situation that calls for more willpower, you should tense your muscles. This posture shows your body that you're tensed and ready for anything, no matter what. This will send the message to your brain that resilience is needed on a mental level.

• Hand Gestures for Persuasion: If you're in a position where you need to persuade other people in conversation, make sure you utilize gestures of the hands. This shows that you believe in what you're saying and also helps you come across as more convincing. Others will feel more positive about you if you do this.

• Cross your Arms for Persistence: Having crossed arms can mean that you're closed off, which is bad in certain circumstances. In others, however, this is a useful frame of mind. For example, you might be in a situation where stubbornness is a good quality and you need it to stay persistent. This is a good time to cross your arms.

How to Gain the Advantage in Body Language:

Body language is a whole new world that can change your life. When it comes to any situation that handles interactions with others, it's a must for being successful. Here are some tips for getting ahead in this area.

- Raising the Eyebrows: When someone is out in public and sees someone they know, their eyebrows will move up automatically, just a tiny bit. No matter what culture, this response is present. The good news here is that you can start using this to your benefit anytime you meet a new person. Try to do it in the first few seconds that you're talking to them. Raising your eyebrows just a bit will make you appear more approachable and friendly, creating a positive connection between you and the other person.

- Remember Times you were Enthusiastic: Having charisma just means that you have enthusiasm and that it shows clearly to other people. This means that wanting to look charismatic to others requires simply appearing enthusiastic. To do this at will, simply call to your mind another time that made you feel enthusiastic. Once you re recalling this past event that made you very excited and enthusiastic, this will come across in your nonverbal cues, showing that you're charismatic and confident. This is a contagious effect and others will feel more positive from noticing your enthusiasm and charisma.

- Smile for more Resilience: If you're faced with a hard task, you can make it feel easier to yourself by smiling. The body's natural reaction to reaching exhaustion is making a pained grimace. However, experiments have shown that smiling increases your ability to press on and keep going through that feeling. Athletes were shown to be able to do a few more reps if they started smiling during their performance.

Grimacing sends your brain the message that you aren't able to continue doing what you're doing. Your brain then reacts to that by pumping you feel of stress chemicals, adding to your exhaustion and difficulty. Smiling, on the other hand, shows your brain that you can keep going, resulting in a better performance and more resilience.

Using these cues will help you a lot with your general positivity and how others perceive it. Shifting your nonverbal cues and body language will influence how those around you perceive you and how you see yourself. On top of this, your facial expressions and postures are always sending your brain messages which then influence the hormones your body is releasing. This is a great power to have if you're aware of it and use it in the right way, but not being aware of it can have negative results and effects, not only on yourself but also on others. Take the power into your own hands and become more positive by using this connection.

Chapter 24:   Confidence and How It Is Displayed

Confidence is a very powerful emotion in today's society. An individual who appears very confident can go to a very far places. By appearing confident, a person can attract suitable mates and be given promotions based on their perceived leadership skills. Because of this, confidence is very commonly displayed in different ways. However, confidence is also faked a lot of times to get ahead in life. We will go through the common ways that confidence is displayed through body language. Besides, we will also go through how you can spot a lack of confidence in an individual.

Displaying Confidence

· Posture

Posture is very important in the appearance of confidence. An individual's posture can say a lot about their perceived level of confidence. Confident posture is defined by legs lined with the individual's shoulders and feet approximately four to six inches apart. Weight is typically distributed equally on both legs, and shoulders are pushed back slightly. A straight back is also very typical of someone with extreme confidence. Individuals with this sort of posture are considered assertive and tend to project confidence. This is because an individual with this posture is seen as being able to "stand tall" regardless of their height and are also perceived as being very open to those talking to them, as they are unafraid of any attacks or criticism.

· Hands

Hands are very important in trying to appear confident. It is important to remember when trying to display confidence through your hands to keep them calm and still. Rapidly moving one's hands is a sign of nervousness or anxiety.

· Eye Contact

Having the ability to maintain long and strong eye contact with another is a good sign that an individual feels confident. This is because showing eye contact with another person is a very vulnerable feeling and position. This is because our eyes can show a lot about how we feel in a situation. By maintaining good eye contact, we show the other person that we are unafraid of what they may see within our eyes. This is a sign of extreme confidence, as it shows that you are self-assured in your feelings and believes that you are unafraid of how a person will interpret what they see in your eyes.

· Mirroring Body Language

Mirroring the body language of those around us elicits a sort of understanding and seeks acceptance from those around us. This raises our confidence level as we humans  strive to be liked by those around us. Because those around us will subconsciously begin to like us more by mirroring their body language, they will also be confident because of their positive view.

· Fidgeting

It is very important to remember not to fidget when you are trying to display levels of confidence. Fidgeting in any form—no matter what part of your body is doing the movement—shows signs of nervousness and anxiety. In addition to this, it can simply annoy those around us. People are often irritated by constant rhythmic tapping or brushing noises. This is something to keep in mind if you are an individual who likes to bounce their leg or tap their foot at simple moments.

Ways to Spot a Lack of Confidence in a Person

· A very common sign of lack of confidence in an individual is if they are constantly touching their phone while in social situations or while alone. If an individual finds themselves unable to sit still during a social situation where they don't know very many people, this may be a sign that they lack confidence. Checking their phone is a sign that they feel uncomfortable in a social situation and cannot connect with those around them.

· Another sign of a lack of confidence in an individual is a quick backing down during a disagreement to avoid arguing with another person. An individual with an extreme lack of confidence will not want to cause problems with a person that they disagree with. Because of this, they often negotiate their views to avoid conflict. This shows that people lack confidence because they are not assured in their own opinions and would rather back down than express themselves honestly.

· Another common sign of a lack of confidence in an individual is their inability to leave their homes without makeup or hairstyling.

743

This is a very obvious sign of a lack of confidence because it shows that individuals don't feel that they are worth being looked at unless they have something on their bodies or face to make them look more beautiful. Putting makeup on or doing their hair gives a false sense of self-esteem to an individual, which people with low self-esteem or confidence rely on very heavily?

· An individual with low confidence will also tend to take constructive criticism far too personally. If a person gives this individual constructive criticism about something, they will take it way too seriously and end up feeling very strong negative emotions. This is a huge sign of low confidence and low self-esteem because this individual is not emotionally balanced enough to handle constructive criticism from those around them.

· Individuals who have low confidence or self-esteem will also find themselves afraid to contribute their opinion in a conversation. They will often second-guess themselves before they say anything instead of diving into an interesting conversation. They may find themselves stuttering or putting themselves down. This is because these individuals don't know how well their opinions will be received and are afraid of others taking their opinions negatively. This is a sign of low confidence or self-esteem because they care very deeply about how the people they make contact with view them.

· An individual who has difficulty with confidence also find themselves extremely indecisive with very simple and basic decisions. They may change their minds very often after coming to a decision. This is a sign of low self-confidence because this individual cannot trust their own opinions or decisions. This is

744

especially a sign of low self-confidence when this applies to very simple tasks or simple decisions.

· Individuals with low self-confidence will also have extreme difficulty handling genuine compliments from those around them. They tend not to think that they are worthy of such good compliment, and they usually put them down or not accept them.

· Individuals struggling with low self-confidence will also tend to give up very soon with things that they are trying to do or achieve. They may have goals and dreams that they want to accomplish but will give up before they begin. This is a sign of low self-confidence because they do not believe that they can accomplish these goals and dreams before they even start.

· Individuals that struggle with low self-confidence will also tend to compare themselves with those around them. They tend to have very strong attention to the people who are doing better than them and will point out all of the ways they are not doing and those around them. This is a strong sign of low self-confidence because it says that the person in question does not view themselves as very successful or doing very well.

· Slouching is a very common display of low self-confidence in an individual. Why so? It is because lowering the center of a person's body is a sign that a person is unwilling to hold up the weight of their upper body themselves. It sends off a signal that that individual is not proud of himself/herself. Because of these things, this is a big sign of low self-confidence.

To detect low self-confidence in an individual, all you have to do is look out for some of these common signs of low self-esteem and self-confidence. You can also detect low self-confidence or low self-esteem within yourself by looking out for these common signs. If you find that you or someone you know has low self-esteem or confidence, you can begin to work on them by saying very positive statements about yourself regularly.

Chapter 25:   Mirroring

Have you ever sat in a restaurant and people watched? It can be quite amusing to sit back and watch all of the people out and around you, attempting to identify how their relationships must be going through body language alone. Yes, it is quite possible to understand how people get along at their briefest glance. You can tell how much or how little people get along simply by watching them together and seeing how they naturally orient their bodies around each other. This simple skill is referred to as mirroring, and it is crucial if you want to be successful at influencing or persuading others. When you understand mirroring, you essentially have a built-in system where you can judge just how well people are likely to listen to you. You can tell if you are successful in developing rapport, and if you have not, you will be able to push the act of earning a connection a little quicker. You can utilize mirroring in a wide range of ways that can be beneficial to you, and you can use it in ways that can be useful to others.

What Is Mirroring?

First things first, you must learn what mirroring is. At the simplest, it is the human tendency to mirror what is happening around them when they feel a relationship

747

to whatever it is that is around them. For example, if you look at an old married couple, they are likely to mirror each other's behaviors constantly. It is essentially the ultimate culmination of empathy—the individuals are so bonded, so aware of each other and their behaviors, that they unconsciously mimic any behaviors that their partner does first. The two married people at the diner may both sip at their coffees simultaneously, or if one drinks, the other will follow shortly after. If one shifts in his seat, she will do so as well, always leaning to mirror her husband's position. If she brushes off something on her shoulder, he will unconsciously touch his shoulder as well. This act is known as mirroring, and it occurs in a wide range of circumstances.

You do not necessarily have to be a married couple that has been together for decades for mirroring to be relevant, either—you can see it everywhere. The person interviewing you for a job may begin to mirror you when the interview is going well, or the person who thinks that you are attractive may mimic some of your behaviors as well. You can see these behaviors mimicked started quite early on in terms of how long people have been interacting as well—sometimes people will even hit it off right off the bat and begin mirroring each other, emphasizing the fact that they seemed to have clicked.

Mirroring is essentially the ultimate form of flattery—it involves copying the other person because you like or love them so much. Children mirror their parents when learning how to behave in the world. Good friends often mirror each other. Salespeople wanting to win rapport, mirror people. No matter what the relationship is,

748

if it is positive, there are likely mirroring behaviors, whether unconscious or not.

Uses of Mirroring

You may be wondering why something as simple as mimicry can be important to others, but it is one of the most fundamental parts of influence, persuasion, and manipulation. When you mirror someone, you can develop rapport. Rapport is essentially the measurement of your relationship with someone—if you have a good rapport with someone, you have developed some level of trust with them. The other person is likely to believe what you are saying if you develop rapport. However, if you have not developed rapport yet and you need the other person to listen to you, you can artificially create that rapport through one simple task— mirroring. If you mirror the other person, you can essentially convince him to develop a rapport with you, whether it was something he wanted to develop on his own or whether you forced the point.

By constantly mirroring the other person, you essentially send the signs to their brain that they need to like this person because this person is just like them. Remember the three key factors for likability? The first one was able to relate or identify with the other person. In this case, you are presenting yourself as easily related to because you want the other person to like you simply. With liking you comes rapport. With rapport comes trust, which you can use to convince the other person to buy cars, or do certain things that will benefit you. Building rapport even builds up the ability to manipulate the other person—you need to be trustworthy for the other person to let you close enough to manipulate in the first place.

How to Mirror

Luckily, mirroring is quite easy to learn. While it may seem awkward and unnatural at first, the more you practice it, the more natural it will become to you, and the more effective you can get at it. Remember, if you want to mirror someone, you will need to toe the line between too much and not enough. If you are too overt, the other person will catch on and will likely be more put off than convinced to like you. Take a look at these four steps so you can learn to mirror for yourself.

Build Up a Connection

The first step when you are attempting to mirror someone is to start building a connection somehow. If you do not feel connected with the other person, they are not likely to be feeling a connection either. Keeping that in mind, you should begin to foster some sort of connection and rapport. This can be done with four simple steps on its own.

- Fronting: This is the act of facing the other person entirely. You start with your body oriented toward them, directly facing the other person to give them your complete attention.

- Eye contact: This is the tricky part—when you are making eye contact, you need to make sure that you get the right amount. See the steps provided in the earlier section on eye contact to make sure you get this part right.

- The triple nod: This does two things—it encourages the other person to keep speaking because the other person feels valued and listened to, and it makes the other person feel like you agree with them. It develops what is known as a yes set. The more you say yes, the more likely you are to develop a connection with another person.

- Fake it till you make it: At this point, you have spent a lot of time setting up the connection, and it is time for the moment of truth. You should imagine that the person is the most interesting in the world at that particular moment. You want to believe that they are interesting to you. Then stop pretending—you should feel that they are interesting to you at this point. This is the birth of the connection you had been trying to establish.

Pace and Volume

Now, before you start mimicking their body language, start by paying attention to the other person's vocal cues. You want to make sure you are speaking at the same speed as the other person. If they are a quick speaker, you should also speak quickly, and if they are a slower speaker, you should slow your own speaking pace down to match. From there, make sure you are also mimicking the volume. If they are louder, you should raise your voice. If they are keeping their voice down, you should follow suit. These vocal cues are far easier to mimic undetected than the rest of the physical cues.

The Punctuator

Everyone has a punctuator they use for emphasis. It could be like a hand gesture that is used every time they want to emphasize something, or it could be the way they raise their brows as they say the word they want to stress. No matter what the punctuator is, you should identify what it is and seek to mimic it at the moment. Now, frequently, this cue is entirely unconscious on the other person's part, and as you begin to mimic it, the other person is likely to believe that you are on the same wavelength. This should do it for you without making what you are doing obviously.

The Moment Of Truth

Now, you are ready to test whether you have successfully built up the rapport you need. When you want to know if the other person has officially been connected to you, you should make some small action that is unrelated to what you are doing at that moment and see if the other person does it back. For example, if you have a conversation about computers, you may reach up and rub your forehead for a split second. Watch and see if the other person also rubs at their forehead right after you. If they do, they have connected to you, and you can begin to move forward with your persuasive techniques.

Chapter 26: How to Influence Anyone with Body Language

People are an open book. If you pay a keen attention to what they do and look at their facial expressions as they speak, you will likely get a better picture of their attitudes and personalities. It is important to analyze people as this gives you an upper hand in different situations. This will demonstrate the different reasons as to why you should analyze people.

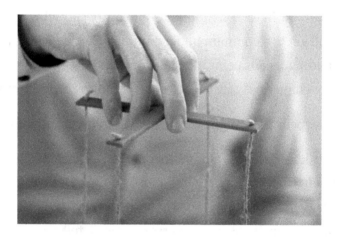

1.   Helps strike healthy friendship

A common misconception about the analysis of people is that it may lead to trust issues. That is entirely untrue. When you analyze people before becoming friends, you get to know them better and form healthy friendships. You know their likes and dislikes, and can even tell if they are genuine or not. With these facts, individuals who know how to analyze people will always get into helpful and healthy friendships and relationships. You do not want to get into relationships and friendships that will lead you to being taken advantage of. The only way to guarantee that is not just to take in the words said by the other person but also to tell whether the two agree.

2. Helps find a common ground

If you know how to analyze people, you can put that skill into arriving at a common ground. This is a skill that you will not just use with a few people. It can also be used while delivering vital speeches to various audiences. As you say something, you gauge what their reactions are through people analysis skill. When you realize that you have gone too far, you can backtrack slightly so that you all get to a common understanding. Getting to a common understanding means being at a position that is neutral for both of you, hence chances of getting into confrontations are minimized.

3. Helps speak in a language understandable to your audience

When you know how to analyze people, you can tell when they understand what you are saying and when they don't. You can easily see when whatever you have been saying hasn't been understood, even if the other person doesn't tell you that. For example, as a teacher, you could see from your student's faces that they are lost and require proper clarification. Similarly, as a parent, you may give your children instructions, but that doesn't mean they will understand whatever you said right away. Through the people analysis skills, you can gauge whether another person is understanding your communication style or whether you need to change your mode of message delivery.

4. Makes you dependable for advices

Your friends are bound to get into trouble from time and again with their boyfriends or girlfriends. Because you know how to analyze people, you can listen to their side of the story while analyzing them too and also get to interact with their partners before giving an advice. People tend to reveal more with their facial expressions. You can analyze these to get the hidden message behind their words. The advices you give are more likely to be genuine and helpful. They are based on facts rather than assumptions, hence helpful to the person asking for your advice. Even if your advice would not be followed to completion as you would have wanted, time will prove that you were right. That goes a long way in solidifying your position as a dependable person for advices.

5.   You are always prepared

If you know how to analyze people, you will always be prepared for outcomes that would have otherwise been surprising. Whether you are getting ready for a meeting with the board of directors, or your juniors at work made a catastrophic mistake that they are trying to hide, you can analyze them and know it. We live in a world where however possess information has the upper hand. When you analyze members of your team, you can collect the information without them even knowing it. In case they were planning anything that isn't favorable to you, you can undo it before its occurrence. Let's say your boyfriend or girlfriend has been acting weirdly in recent days but they still tell you everything is fine. You could use your analysis skills to find out that they are actually cheating and even have plans to break up with you! They may think that their plans are well hidden but in real sense you already have the facts and just decided to play along. When they eventually decide to come out of the hiding and drop the bombshell, it won't be much of a bombshell.

6.   It makes you more considerate

The fact that you analyze people gets you to understand why they may act in certain ways. You develop some sense of protection towards others, a protectionist behavior that the average person may not have. If you are the boss at your workplace or in any other organization and conflicts are brought to you, you will want to first analyze the conflicting persons before decide. The ability to listen to all the people will not be motivated by you having too much time but by the desire to analyze everything so that you do not make the wrong decision. During the analysis, important information is revealed to you like what would have made people to act in such and such a manner. Thus, as you start making the final decision, you will put all these facts into consideration. This is in contradiction to individuals who make decisions based on what they hear. The decisions of such individuals could even be biased and may end up punishing the wrong person. As a person with people analysis skills, punishment is not within your scope because you know sometimes people act not out of their will but out of a background force. This force is only revealed to you when you analyze them.

7.   You get really smart

Not to brag but knowing how to analyze people makes you smart. From the many years of doing this, you wire your brains to think in a certain manner that other people's brains do not. The process

756

has also led you to know the many different types of people on our planet and can form topics that anchor well with these. You form well formulated opinions on topics and can't wait to speak them out. You are the kind of a person who can deliver an electrifying speech on different occasions with various audiences. All you have to do is analyze the audience and choose the direction in which your topic should move.

Furthermore, the people analysis skills empower you to stimulate anyone's brain. Thinking, talking, discussing and conversing are your erogenous zones and anyone can tap into those in a stimulating way. Having understood the other person, you know what you can say to get them stimulated and what to avoid as it could lag them behind.

Chapter 27: How to Use the Knowledge of Non-Verbal Language in Practice?

Pay attention to the gestures you use in everyday life - they are your main traitor; they give out your thoughts and feelings. Practically anyone will figure out your deception if you keep your hands at your mouth and hide your eyes. These bright lies are known even to a child. Therefore, be careful - do not do what can betray your deception. In order not to impersonate, you must very strictly monitor your hands, body, facial expressions. Follow the rule: no unnecessary movements. At first, it will be very difficult to do without hands, because we are so used to helping ourselves non-verbally in the process of speech, that it will be very difficult to get rid of this habit. But you have to force yourself; otherwise they will know your deception.

Unlearning to gesticulate and change facial expressions is difficult, but in reality, it will be even harder to learn to hide the involuntary reactions of your body. These include holding your breath, increasing heart rate, and trembling of the body. Some techniques allow you to hide these signs of deception.

You must train your body so that it does not betray your deception. Ask someone from relatives or friends to test you on a lie detector at home. Your partner should be at a very close distance from you and fix your pulse while holding your hand on your wrist. Let him control you in everything, watch your breath and changes of your facial expressions.

Then he asks you some questions. The first two or three questions should be the most elementary, for example, "What is your favorite dish?", "Skylark you or an owl?" that you will answer without difficulty. But the next question is provocative, for example: "Have you ever lied to your friends?" You can hardly answer this question without changing your face. The list of questions should be unknown to you; otherwise the experiment will lose its meaning. Continue the experiment until your interlocutor stops noticing changes in your condition. You can train long enough until you learn to control your body. You may not be able to fool a real lie detector, but you will hide your deception from a living person.

To repel an attack of a manipulator or an aggressive-minded person, you must first keep a distance, not let a dangerous person into your personal space. You will be able to maintain your independence and avoid its influence, if you leave in time or manage to keep it far from yourself. Suppose a person expects to greet you, when meeting you, and thus invade your space. You are sure that he has unkind intentions, for example, he decided to deceive or outwit you, and you should find any possible way to avoid of dodging hugs or kisses of foe to your intimate zone.

Do not allow a person, who has unkind intentions, to use nonverbal familiarities like tapping your shoulder or beating your cheek. Try to avoid such kind of contacts. You can take signs of attention from his side, but do it very carefully to avoid falling under his influence.

If you feel that a threat is emanating from a person, you should look away, look at another object. The fact is that prolonged eye contact with such a person is very dangerous; because an experienced manipulator can hypnotize you; convince you of something against your will. Therefore, try to look away; do not look intently at your interlocutor.

You can make a person understand that you do not intend to obey him; you do not want to engage in a long frank conversation with him. To do this, you can use closed gestures: cross your arms over your chest or put them in your pockets. You can make it clear to your interlocutor that you do not want with the desire to continue the conversation by constantly looking at your watch.

To impress, remember a few rules. The first rule is appearance: you must be careful, restrained in details, not too pedantic. If you doubt which style to give preference - then stop your choice on the classic version: it is always a winning option. Pay special attention to the accessories, they make your style unique; they talk about your personality.

You can rehearse your appearance in front of the mirror - practice your walk and salutation. Do you want to make an impression? There is nothing easier. Learn to walk properly. Previously, to make their gait and posture beautiful, the girls wore jugs of water on their heads. In our time, this tradition is outdated. But you can use a similar technique, not only for girls and women, but also for the stronger sex. Put a few books on your head and walk around so that these books do not fall. You should achieve the following effect: when you move quickly, no book will fall off your head. Gradually you can increase the load.

The gait of a woman is her personality. She can tell a lot about her owner. For example, the hips' active wagging indicates that the girl is too frivolous, trying to attract the attention of men. If a girl paces like a durable tin soldier, she is most likely unfriendly, unkind. The gait of a woman should be soft, smooth, with a "plastics of a panther before jumping." If your gait is not good enough, you should correct it.

There is a method of Marilyn Monroe, and from her walk, many men lost their heads. Remember that heels make a woman a woman. If you do not wear shoes with heels, then it's time to start. Legend has it that Marilyn Monroe had a heel on one of her shoes a little lower than the other, so she had to walk very slowly because of this inconvenience, she gently shook her hips.

A man should have a confident gait, with a wide step, but without waving his arms. It is advisable to stand firmly to give the impression of a self-confident person who knows his worth on whom to rely.

Greeting ritual is also very important when creating a first impression. When meeting you should follow the rules and norms of etiquette, for example, if you go to a business meeting, you should not hug your companion at the meeting or kiss on the cheek. For such cases, calm handshake is suitable. A handshake is a standard greeting ritual that can be used even by women in a business meeting. A handshake should not be too short, but it should not have a goal to seize the leadership position, for which some people deliberately hold their partner's hand for too long - this is considered a bad form.

A kiss on the cheek is a greeting that can be used when meeting two girlfriends or on a first date with a man. Make this kiss just a light touch. Some girls kiss the air not to spoil the makeup and do not stain your companion. But this is considered a sign of disrespect and a bad form. If you have bright red lipstick on your lips, you can warn about it or suggest a disposable tissue to wipe the print.

If you fulfill these conditions, consider that the victory is in your pocket. You will immediately be taken more seriously, and they will consider you a pleasant person in all respects.

Public Speaking Rules

For your speech, you choose a convenient place. Of course, if this is an organized event, then the organizers will do it for you. But if a crowd of people is an improvised rally or gathering, you should take care of where to get up. Find a place so that you can be seen from any position. You can climb a chair, or a table, or any elevation. You have to be head and shoulders above everyone for the public to feel that you have some advantage. You should be visible from all sides so that you can use the whole arsenal of non-verbal means of influence on the audience.

You must master the science to attract attention. How to do it? It is best to use non-verbal means. Your gestures should resemble the gestures of an actor on a large stage. For performances at public events usually use the following gestures.

You can spread your arms to open your arms. This gesture has a symbolic meaning: "I am your patron. If you have any problems, I will solve them. "To attract the attention of the audience, raise your hand and hold it until silence prevails. This gesture means: "Quiet! I will speak". This is a very bright, eloquent gesture that can be used not only at the beginning of a speech, but also in the middle, if, for example, you feel that attention is being dispelled.

Any gesture you use should be bright, big, and noticeable. Small gestures for performance in public will look like a curse, no one will see them. If you, for example, are going to use an enumerating gesture, then you should raise your hand to the level of your face, spread your fingers wide and bend them, making a big swing with your other hand.

Learn to use your voice properly. There is an opinion that for a large audience you should always speak loudly. You should not always resort to a loud voice — you will get tired quickly. Just speak clearly and pause so that your words are clear. In exceptional cases, you can whisper. The audience will think that you are communicating something important, uncovering a secret, and will listen to you.

To attract the group's attention, you must use special, chamber, gestures aimed at attracting the attention of a large audience. When talking to a small group, do not shout, do not swing your arms to gain confidence. We compared the behavior of a person, who performs in public, with the behavior of an actor: speaking in a group is akin to performing in a small stage, close to real life.

If you plan to say something important to the group members, you need to organize the group so that everyone can hear and see you.

If you are communicating with a large audience, of course, you will not be able to review all those gathered, but if you have a small group, you should take turns paying attention to each participant. Look at one member of the group, then at another, so that no one feels deprived of your attention. Visual contact will help you to feel each person, to notice the reaction to your words. If you look from one person to another, the whole group will be under your control. Also, each member of the group will feel that you are speaking specifically for him.

Chapter 28: Body Language and Persuasion

Persuasion is a technique that authors use to present their thoughts via logic and reason, to influence their readers. Persuasion may convince a particular action to be performed by readers or use an argument to convince the readers. It is an art of writing and speaking; writers earn their opinions plausible via logic to the audience, by demonstrating their credibility, and by invoking emotions.

Kinds of Persuasion

Persuasion has three Fundamental kinds:

1. Ethos

It's connected with integrity and morality. The viewer should know his comprehension of the subject and ascertain if or not a writer is not.

2. Logos

Logos includes logic writers utilize logic, reasoning, and rationality to convince viewers of the viewpoints.

3. Pathos

The method is pathos, which allure and communicates to the feelings of the crowd. That is contrary to logos since it poses arguments without using justification or logic. Many authors believe love, anxiety, empathy, and anger because variables that are powerful to affect the audiences' emotions.

Role of Persuasion

Persuasion is a literary technique. We do not discover it. Authors express opinions and their feelings by appealing to the viewers emotionally and logically. It is a method to acquire over the audience or readers. It provides them with an opportunity to research facts and helps pupils to unearth reasons. Students may comprehend the character of work while creating a comprehension of how their ideas and activities can alter and affect.

How to Persuade With Body Language

Your body language may help to get across your message, or it may send the incorrect message. Understand what to do with your palms, your voice, and your own eyes to optimize persuasion and influence. I've covered to make messages that are strong in episodes the delivery is required by effective persuasion. Your body language can help you to get across your message, hinder even worse or even your sway, send the message. I will discuss how to convince and influence body language now.

Request in Individual

Do not send an email in case you've got an important request. It is far better to inquire. Your petition will be persuasive if it manufactured in person. Coincidentally, it is easier to say "no" into an email petition than somebody's face. Because you talk, but by seeing the body language of your conversation collaborate you'll be able to tailor your message. For instance, let us say when describing the advantage of your proposition, you see a slight "no more" nod. This is a hint your spouse and you may not agree, also you may utilize that information. Anyway, emotions and passion are infectious in individuals. Do not feel that? Has a laughing fit because somebody laughed? The purpose is that however many different points, smiley faces, or hearts you put in writing, they are no substitute for actual emotions experienced in person via facial expressions, voice, and expressions. Think about it's to listen versus studying it to the podcast. It is an entirely different experience. Persuading on the telephone presents challenges; you won't have the chance to see facial expressions or expressions of the individual on the line and you might not have their whole attention. So, if you are asking something of somebody, ask to fulfill in-person. Proceed to them. Invite them or to get java. Call a meeting if you are attempting to convince a group. When meeting in person isn't feasible, try out the next thing: video conferencing.

Assess Your Body Language

Remember that when you are meeting, the first thing that will be seen by dialogue partner is the position, and that is going to send an immediate message. Make certain that you comply with your grandmother's recommendation and stand up tall! It will make a difference. You have made the impression before you open your mouth. Eye contact is an important instrument in perception of trustworthiness. Use hand gestures to highlight and to encourage your messages and possess them. When you're certain, your audience is receptive, much more relaxed, and prepared to listen. Envision I'm standing tall in front of you, as it is logical, grinning using my arms to create gestures, and making eye contact with you. How would I perceive it by you if I stated the next? Imagine me saying the identical thing, but this time Arms folded, my mind down, poor eye contact, no expression in my head, and a voice that was none. What would your response be? What could you be thinking about me?

Be Consistent With Body Words and Language

The isue with this case is communicating that is inconsistent involving also my own words and my body language. The often-cited research on nonverbal and verbal communication of Albert Mehrabian shows the value of consistency in your speech. The listener must choose which to think if your body language and words conflict. Mehrabian's work indicates that if our messages battle, the listener almost always relies on to create their choice. If you are attempting to convince an audience of your body language, the company must support you. Shady gestures such as fidgeting, changing eyes, or smirking will excite suspicion. Open little gestures, arms, and facial expressions that reveal your audience will be engaged by emotion that is favorable and make you believable. Political debates are a fantastic spot between phrases and body language. You may observe a candidate grinning climbing gas rates or while talking unemployment. 1 candidate may say he respects another; however, the camera captures him scowling smirking, or rolling his eyes. With messages, we pay attention and quit listening to the words. That something as little as a smirk can cost the candidate votes and trust

See Yourself

A word of warning when we are anxious, we grin. If you describe a significant injustice or create a request for service or assistance, a  grin will communicate the wrong message. Always ensure by assessing what your face looks like, the remainder of your body language and that your facial expressions communicate the emotions. Your body language is the most persuasive you're genuine. Body language is more difficult to control than simple words. Your body language will be persuasive if you're truly on your beliefs.

Chapter 29: Non-Verbal Signals of Aggression

The main gesture of aggression is a clenched hand. This gesture may have different degrees of aggression. If your interlocutor's hands are stretched out fully, while both are clenched into fists, then this is a sign of an increase in the negative in a person, he adjusts to fight. If the fists gradually rise, reaching the chest's level, then this is an alarming factor. The man accepted the fighting stance, prepared for the strike, and only seconds remained before the open manifestation of aggression. If your interlocutor begins

to scratch his fists - he rubs his fingers with one hand on the other hand, which is clenched into a fist, and has a negative attitude towards you.

If your interlocutor puts his hands on his shoulders - this is a sign of restrained aggression. This means that a person is ready to rush into battle, but is trying to restrain himself. If you do not intend to engage in a duel with him, then, having seen such a gesture, you must change the negotiating tactics: change the subject, change the tone.

A gesture characteristic of a person, who is aggressive towards you, is his hands behind his back with a wrist grip. This gesture is dangerous, since it is invisible to the interlocutor, if a person puts his hands behind his back, it seems that he is hiding something from you; perhaps this is a weapon for the upcoming fight. But even without a weapon, this gesture, in itself, is very dangerous and means that the person has unkind intentions.

To smooth the aggressive mood of your interlocutor, you can use the following non-verbal means. First, try to reduce the distance between you, use the tactile impact - touch the person. Remember, all your actions, movements must be extremely slow, so that your interlocutor does not take them for an offensive on your part. Remember also that if he is set up "unconditionally" aggressively, that is, he plans to fight in advance, regardless of your behavior, and then no means will help you. You should think about interrupting your conversation and going to a safe place, allowing him to throw out aggression on someone else.

A warrior's posture can indicate an aggressive attitude of a person: a person spreads his legs wide to feel confident that there is support under his feet. Its body is slightly tilted forward. As a rule, he tries to cover certain parts of his body in case you start attacking first. These areas are the most vulnerable places of a person. For men - this is the groin area, nose, and jaw. In women (although such a bright manifestation of aggression among women is not so popular, but still possible) is the chest area and face.

An aggressive gait is very bright - a person walks very widely, sometimes even jumps to get to his goal faster, while actively waving his arms, sometimes he can go running - this is a sign of a high degree of tension.

If you suspect your interlocutor in bad intentions, you should pay attention to his posture. If your suspicions are correct, then your interlocutor does not stand up straight, stretched to his full height. He sat up a little, pressed his head into the shoulders - he had grown into the ground, had become compact, now it is convenient for him to strike. If you are sitting, then your interlocutor can stretch the neck forward and shoulders back. Moreover, his head will be slightly tilted so that your forehead will be fixed in your direction, the hardest part of your head, ready to take your blow.

Aggression is a kind of protective reaction of the body. A person begins to show aggression as soon as he realizes that he is inferior to you in some things. It can be a result of anger, hatred, and envy. Perhaps your interlocutor is weaker than you in oratory, does not possess the talent of persuasion, and understands his intellectual inferiority; therefore, in the absence of other arguments, he desires to defeat you in an accessible way force.

The mimics of aggression is very active - these are eyebrows shifted to the bridge of the nose, swollen nostrils, staggering cheekbones, sometimes with creaking of teeth, very tightly compressed lips. These are mimic signs that your partner is very aggressive. Not always these mimic signals are reflected on the face all together, most often there are one or two signs. If you notice at least one of the above-cited signals on your interlocutor's face, be on your guard - he is not very happy about you.

Pay special attention to the look. In an aggressive person, the gaze eloquently tells that its owner is ready to tear to pieces his opponent. This is a very heavy, piercing gaze, so the predator looks at his prey in preparation for the attack.

If a person is aggressive, he usually raises the volume of the voice. And he does it unconsciously either to provoke you into actions beneficial to him, or to intimidate him. Perhaps your opponent does not have a competent verbal argument, so he tries to explain his point of view in other ways, that is, he does not resort to the power of the word, but the volume of his voice.

He is trying to "intelligibly", at a slow pace to explain his point of view. As a rule, he fails. He provokes you, tries to, as they say, "drive in": "Do I explain incomprehensibly?" All this is done to arouse fear in his interlocutor, to gain an advantage over the fight. He will try to provoke, putting into motion disparaging and caustic intonations, chuckles, grins.

For an aggressive-minded person is characterized by a decrease in voice tone, the use of lower tonalities, intonations, sometimes with hoarseness. Such voice changes are also intended to scare the interlocutor.

Sometimes the aggression does not have time to develop into a fight, and the person breaks into a scream. A person holding back aggression is in a state of intense tension. If you did not give him a reason for the use of force, this will not reduce his tension. And he still needs detente. Very often such a discharge occurs in the form of a cry. This is also a kind of non-verbal form of exit aggression. If he fells to a cry, then he is unlikely to use force against you. He just did not have the power to fight. In such a situation, you'd better wait until his anger subsides and he calms down.

You can try to relieve the stress of your interlocutor with non-verbal signals. Use the power of your voice to calm and defuse it. You must speak slowly, gently, as if to lull, put to sleep his vigilance. You can say anything, for example, to insist on your opinion, which put him off balance, but with all your non-verbal signals, he should read the following: "Do not be afraid of me. I am your friend. Take it easy. Do not worry. Better be friends with me - this is more profitable. " If you can correctly use your voice capabilities, then your aggressively-minded interlocutor will submit to you, moderate his ardor, and his aggression will go away or be turned to a different direction.

Chapter 30:   Using Body Language to Negotiate

Whether it's a new car or a new job, knowing how to use your skills at reading body language to improve any negotiations you find yourself in can make a significant difference when it comes to the amount of money you either receive or pay in many diverse scenarios. Studies have shown that over 30 minutes, a pair of negotiators can trade over 700 different & distinct nonverbal cues. Here are some tips to guarantee that your body language will help things eventually work out in your favor.

Start poised for success: When it comes to making the best first impression, studies show that those entering into a negotiation with multiple items in their own hands or on their person are statistically likely to begin the negotiation from a negative position. Ensuring you enter the room the negotiation takes place in as streamlined & ready for business as possible will make your overall odds of success much higher in the long run. It's important to take this momentum & keep it going by choosing a seat that indicates you hope this will be a collaborative process, not an adversarial one this means aiming for a chair that's at a 45-degree angle from that of the opposite party.

Take stock of the other party: Blinking, sweating, shaking, murmuring & erratic looks or gestures are all strong indicators that the other party isn't ready for the negotiation. While few negotiators are so obvious, it's important to take stock of the other party to see if you can quickly determine a baseline that you can use when moving forward. Be aware of negotiators who're too ill prepared, they may be putting on a show to lure you into a state of false security.

Keep eye contact as much as possible: During any negotiation, maintaining eye contact indicates trust, sincerity & openness both for you & the other party. What's more, failing to do so can make it difficult for you & the other party to build the sort of rapport that's more likely to lead to a mutually beneficial position. This doesn't mean you should hold the other party's eye contact indefinitely, only when you're speaking directly to them. Too much eye contact will instead make you seem overly aggressive & will make the other party less likely to give into your demands.

Lock down your facial expressions: Common emotions are tied to similar facial expressions the world over. This means that if you allow your face to give away your positon during the negotiation it'll be unlikely that you'll be able to prevent the other party from seeing your true intentions. Take the time to quickly practice how you hope the negotiation will go beforehand & consider what types of facial expressions would drive your specific points home. On the other hand, it's equally important to keep an eye on any expressions the other party might accidentally let slip, they could

776

just give away key information that you otherwise might not be aware of.

Consider the personal space in the room: Studies suggest that the ideal amount of space between negotiating parties is roughly 4 feet. This essentially gives each party enough space to feel comfortable without providing either party an advantage that they can use over one another. Remember, if it's possible to gain any extra height compared to the other party it's in your best interest to take it. Likewise, if you're negotiating with a superior anything you can do to make the interaction less personal will ultimately work in your favor.

Act relaxed & confident: Even if, internally, you're extremely nervous about the way the negotiation is going either for you or against you, it's important to maintain an outward composure that's calm, collected & always in control. Ensure that your feet are firmly planted & that your arms & hands are loose & relaxed. Whatever you do, it's important not to twitch or fidget as doing either will betray your lack of confidence & cause the negotiation to turn back in the other party's favor. It's also important to avoid any outward nonverbal cues which signal discomfort in the other party. Depending on what it's in regards to, this can either be the sign that you just need to push your advantage or pull back to avoid losing the other party entirely.

Avoid smiling: In these situations, smiling is akin to giving in & saying that you're the weaker party in this exchange. Negotiating is serious business, show that you treat the current discussion as such & keep a calm face until the final details have been ironed out to your satisfaction.

Mitigating negative body language: If, despite your best efforts, the other party remains unwilling to accept your best nonverbal cues & continues to display negative body language, there're some things you can try to get them back to the comfort zone. One of the most effective strategies in this scenario is to hand the other party something relevant to the negotiation that they can hold & hopefully interact with. This will also get them in the mindset of changing their body language which will help to get their mind changing as well. Use this as a chance to take control of the negotiation & get the results you know you deserve.

Chapter 31:   Effects of Misreading People

The ability to read people and analyze them can help you become aware of your relationships and interactions. It becomes a useful tool that will help you build quality relationships. However, this is only a good thing if you get it right. Many times, people try to read others, and they fail. You get the wrong impression and make the wrong decision. Human nature is indeed complex. It takes a lot to analyze someone correctly. You must find the link between spoken words, facial expressions, body language, and so forth. Not everyone can get this combination right, at least not at the first attempt.

Misreading people is common, especially when you make assumptions or approach them with presumptions. You look at someone and form an opinion without giving them a fair chance to present their case. Body language is essential to communication, but it is also one of the easiest things to misread (Spaulding, 2016).

It is very confusing when you try to read someone but can only get mixed signals. Some people are so good at this. They throw you off their tracks. Others are just edgy, and in some cases, your inability to understand your inhibitions affects your ability to read people correctly.

Observers always look for consistency in behavioral clusters and clues regarding your behavior based on what they believe are normal or true for you or someone in your position. Perhaps you are used to seeing someone who is always happy, social, and outgoing, but one day, you meet them and notice something is off.

They don't have their usual charm. The foremost thing that comes to your mind is that something is wrong. However, this might not be true. Perhaps they are just exhausted.

This is the problem with making assumptions of people. In most cases, you don't know half the things you think you know about someone, and if anything, most of the information you have on them is inaccurate or untrue.

The Problem of Assumptions

It is very quick to assume something about someone and misread them or analyze them wrongly. Assumptions form when your information is incomplete. With incomplete information, it is sensible to seek clarification from the subject. However, since you might be unwilling to do this, you draw your conclusions, filling in the blanks with distorted information that suits a certain persona you might have created.

The information you use to complete the assessment is often your biased interpretation of what you feel, think, see, or have heard about someone. It might be from an earlier interaction with them or similar experiences you might have had with someone in the same situation.

With this information, you are ready to complete the puzzle. No one loves to be left hanging, so you complete the story and give it your perfect ending. The problem here is that the perfect ending is only credible to you and your mind because that is how you want it to be. It is not the reality. You make connections between the past and something that's happening in the present, yet these connections are unreal.

Assumptions are not the best way to read someone. Making assumptions over a rational concern can be disastrous. Imagine what happens if you make assumptions over emotional issues. Emotions and sensitivity go hand in hand. When you assume something about someone and the assumption triggers an emotional memory, the result will be disastrous, especially if it was painful.

Assumptions form because of your unwillingness to question or seek clarification when you should. They are dangerous for everyone involved, and this is why you should strive to analyze the situation better and get clarification to avoid misreading someone.

Laziness. Making assumptions is one of the laziest things you can do to read someone. You feel that asking for more information or waiting for the subject to deliver is too much work, so you choose the easiest way out.

You might get away with one or two assumptions. However, as you get used to it, you become careless in your assessments, and before you know it, you barely allow anyone to represent themselves fully. You jump to conclusions at your earliest convenience, and this becomes your plague.

Wrong Readings. You are making decisions based on the information you don't have evidence to support. This can only lead to more errors.

Responsibility. Another reason why you should stop making assumptions is that you stop taking responsibility for your actions. Each time you assume someone or a situation, you conveniently choose to hide your actions behind the most convenient explanation. This way, you don't have to own up to your mistakes. Instead, you can blame it on someone else for not going according to the script you assumed.

Holding on to the Past. Most assumptions are formed from things that happened in the past. Each time you have incomplete information, you take a trip down memory lane to fill the gaps. This is unhealthy behavior. Other than the fact that you end up with the wrong readings all the time, you also struggle to leave the past in the past. If you conclude from a painful event, you will struggle to heal. You must let the past go and move on.

Foster Negativity. It is quite unfortunate, but most assumptions we make about people are usually about negative sentiments. Since they hurt you in the past, you believe they will hurt you again. You cannot expect something positive from someone even if they try to change because you are holding on to a painful history.

The problem with this is that over time, the negativity grows beyond your mistrust and takes over your life. Your mind associates any actions from anyone else similar to what you experienced with negative sentiments. As a result, your view of the world is an unhealthy place where everyone is out to hurt you.

Create a Bad Habit. Assumptions are very easy. They are the easiest way out; they are comforting because they help you make a situation that didn't concern you, about you. You take center stage, and it feels good, especially in the short run. Instant gratification might work, but it never lasts. Since it is easier to feel good so fast, you get used to it, and assumptions become your go-to move whenever you cannot explain something about someone. This is how you end up creating a bad habit that ruins your friendships and relationships.

Empower Your Pain. The fact that you keep referring to painful moments when making assumptions only empowers the pain and makes it a part of you. You deny yourself the opportunity to heal and move on to greater and better things in life.

How do you overcome assumptions? To read someone correctly, you must understand them. Do not be afraid to ask questions. It is better to ask and be correct than ignore and be wrong about everything. Besides, when you assume something about someone, you do something with that information, and they realize what you think of them. Perhaps they held you in high regard, but your action challenges that perception. They see a different version of you that they might not like.

Asking for the truth is not easy. It can be painful at times, but it is better than not knowing at all. Your conversations with people are better and more productive because you allow them to express themselves. Everything is not about you anymore, but everyone else gets their moment.

Conclusion

It is not realistic to expect that most of us will develop the kind of extra-sensory perception that will make us mind readers. However, all people can learn to identify the non-verbal clues that others demonstrate every day.

Most of the time, we do not stop thinking about our body's language, what we transmit in non-verbal communication. It is even more important than the words we use, gestures, posture and facial expression reveal more than we can suppose or intend to demonstrate. To have control of these movements is to be able to pass the message of the emotions and thoughts in a balanced way, reinforcing the words with the gestures. Research indicates that only 7% of our communication is word-based. The body language is responsible for another 55% and the tone of voice for 38%.

A negative body language can convey weakness, insecurity. And we do not want our interlocutor to have that impression. Having the knowledge and mastery of our body makes a lot of difference in personal and professional relationships from the moment we recognize their power. A correct and upright posture requires training and corrections until you reach perfection. Sitting in the right way according to the environment, without overexposing yourself, demonstrates education. Standing without arms crossed or hands in pockets conveys confidence and security. Walking elegantly, even with very high heels, without much movement in the hips and without looking at the ground, projects positivity. The body should always be moved smoothly without sudden changes or drama.

Accelerated or aggressive rhythm generates a sense of stress and a lack of confidence. Carrying your hand over your mouth while talking or looking away from the caller gives the impression of lying. The look, then, is extremely revealing. No matter how hard we try to hide our emotions, it shows the truth of our feelings. How many times do we say one thing believing another? Those who pay attention to their eyes will realize how much truthfulness there is in words. An unfocused look can be confusing as if you are looking for a mental image for support. The famous twist of eyes denotes irritation and contempt. To contact the forehead means tension, doubt, or nervousness, a very negative point. Crossing one's arms away from the others represents the imposition of a physical barrier, that is, no opening as to what is being said. On the plus side, a firm handshake demonstrates confidence. Speaking calmly, articulating the words well, and maintaining tranquility, conveys credibility. Who believes in someone who does not express himself correctly, speaks in a fiddly way, without coherence of thoughts?

Knowledge and mastery of body language techniques add value to our relationships in any environment. Analyzing and learning how to deal with our gestural is a differential in social relations, there is no denying.

Reading people is a critical skill for anybody to have. This is because it will allow you to understand the complete message somebody is passing across when you are conversing with said person. This will put you ahead in your dealings with people and help establish you as a force to reckon with. Humans, for a fact, say more nonverbally than they do verbally. If you are to grasp what someone is communicating honestly, you should be able to read and understand their nonverbal communication.

Listening to nonverbal communication is an art that requires training to develop. This particular means of communication, as you now know, says, and hints at much more than you are liable to hear and get from having an oral or written conversation with somebody. For instance, body movement can be used to communicate a message in four different ways.

Being adept at the art of nonverbal communication requires that you master some five principles. These principles will allow you to identify nonverbal cues, but it will also help interpret them correctly. Without mastery of these principles, you will be prone to make mistakes where reading people are concerned.

Being a master nonverbal communicator also requires that you continuously work on yourself. For instance, emotional awareness, attentiveness, and constant practice, among others, are areas that you need to work on and strengthen if you are to become adept at reading what people are saying nonverbally.

Nonverbal communication has a host of benefits some of which are;

•to complement what is being communicated verbally,

•to deceive others into thinking something other than what you feel,

•to regulate what you are communicating verbally,

•to express your feelings and emotions on a particular subject and a specific person, and so on.

Another important thing you need to do when developing your nonverbal communication skills understands personality types. This will enable you to identify the motives behind people's actions, which will allow you to know what they are saying.

While being good at reading people is a great skill set, combining this with charisma is even better. This will enable you to resonate with people, empathize, and build great rapport with them. All of these are essential, especially if you are passionate about helping people become the best versions of themselves.

Speed reading people is especially important if you are a leader, a politician, or somebody who has a job that involves dealing with people. As such, you must learn and develop the skills necessary to become a good reader of people and nonverbal communication. This will put you in an excellent position to handle people and negotiate with them.

Body language can fill you in on the hidden bits of information that people don't want you to know about. It can let you know if a person is interested in what you have to say or if you are simply wasting your breath. You may discover a person that you thought didn't like you, actually does. You never know what you will learn through body language, and that's what makes it such a powerful tool. Use the ability to read people wisely, though. Some people are simply fidgety, so you can't assume that everybody who picks their nails is lying. Look at the big picture as well and make sure you know the person before you jumped to any conclusions based solely on their body language.

CPSIA information can be obtained
at www.ICGtesting.com
Printed in the USA
BVHW050205090223
658191BV00031B/1043